OBSERVING YOUNG READERS

OBSERVING
YOUNG READERS

SELECTED PAPERS

MARIE M. CLAY

EXETER, NEW HAMPSHIRE
HEINEMANN EDUCATIONAL BOOKS
LONDON and AUCKLAND

Heinemann Educational Books Inc.
4 Front Street, Exeter, New Hampshire 03833

LONDON   EDINBURGH   MELBOURNE   AUCKLAND
HONG KONG   SINGAPORE   KUALA   LUMPUR
NEW DELHI   IBADAN   NAIROBI   JOHANNESBURG

Library of Congress Cataloging in Publication Data

Clay, Marie M.
    Observing young readers.

    Bibliography: p.
    1. Reading (Primary)—New Zealand.   I. Title.
LB1525.C59   1982   372.4'09931   82-12047
ISBN 0-435-08200-0 (US)
      0-435-80232-1 (UK)
      0-86863-266-X (NZ)

Printed in the United States of America

Contents

IV   *Tangled Tots and Reading Knots*

V   *Observing Writing Behavior*

NOTES TO RESEARCH STUDENTS

Acknowledgments

The author and publishers are grateful to the following for permission to reproduce copyright material. References to volume numbers, date of publication etc., will be found in the bibliography.

Chapter 1, English Journal
Chapters 3,13,14,22, New Zealand Journal of Educational Studies
Chapters 4,7, Journal of Verbal Learning and Verbal Behavior
Chapter 5, British Journal of Educational Psychology
Chapters 6,23, Education
Chapter 8, Journal of Experimental Child Psychology
Chapter 9, Visible Language
Chapters 11,12, The Reading Teacher
Chapter 11, The Rotarian
Chapter 15, Monographs of the Society for Research in Child Development
Chapter 16, New Zealand Educational Institute and Price Milburn
Chapter 17, Remedial Teachers' Association of Queensland, P. Gunn, M. Toohey, and S. Miller
Chapter 18, Language and Speech
Chapter 19, International Journal of Psychology
Chapter 20, Issues in New Zealand Special Education and Hodder and Stoughton
Chapter 21, Journal of Special Education
Chapter 24, Theory into Practice, College of Education, The Ohio State University
Chapter 25, Educational Review
Chapter 26, Language Arts

Marie Clay's comments and reflections on her research will be found at the beginning of sections and chapters. This new material has been set in italic type to distinguish it from the research that follows.

Introduction

I would be the first to argue that cultures are different and that what is found in one culture will not be directly helpful for solving the instructional problems in another. However, as most research on learning to read English comes from Great Britain and U.S.A. it may be useful to add this report of a program of research work from a different country, New Zealand.

The research program began in 1962 and the aim at that time was to record exactly what children were learning in their first year at school using the methods of studying child behavior from the discipline of developmental psychology. After the final report was presented in 1966 new questions emerged and further research was undertaken. We have not arrived at definitive answers but in addition to some changes that have been made to instructional programs as the result of this work three procedures have emerged as stimulating for the professional development of teachers. We have learned that effective teachers need:

- to schedule time to observe exactly what their pupils are learning.
- to learn to put into words accounts of the behaviors they observe and what these might indicate.
- to share these tentative hypotheses with colleagues who may or may not agree with them and to think through their own rationale for proceeding to make their own decisions about instruction.

It is easy to arrive at false assumptions about a process as complex as learning to read. Firstly, we are likely to average a vast amount of evidence in order to arrive at a program decision. Secondly, we may do this on the basis of superficial or highly selected observations. Thirdly, our assumption may be the result of an oversimplified, logical analysis of the task which bears little relationship to the ways in which individual children learn. Teachers are less likely to make such gross averaging judgments about children's needs when they work alongside individual children, observing their responses and using techniques which increase the sensitivity of their observation. Under these circumstances teachers will arrive at more insightful assumptions and make fewer naive or superficial ones. So the link between the research reports brought together in this volume and the work of the classroom teacher lies in discovering what behaviors it is important to observe in early reading and how it is possible to carry out the observations. The essence of the research method is to control many factors so that it is possible to observe in a more controlled way what actually occurs. If some of the techniques for observing used in research could also be used by the teacher this might lead to field hypotheses of better quality. The values of observation for the teacher are obvious but I should make some of my arguments explicit. The formal aspects of direct instruction differ markedly from program to program. Any theorizing we do about learning to read has to take into account that well-trained teachers teach more than 80% of children to read under a variety of theories, programs or sequences of instruction. From this I draw two conclusions. Children supplement the program with their own efforts, and teachers adapt to individuality more than any program description implies. Teachers who are sensitive observers of children's progress are in a position to notice more and more of the behaviors that confirm a valid theory and they are able to reject notions that do not fit with the careful observations they have made. At the same time their questions and their creative solutions will be subjected to feedback from their own careful monitoring. Taking observation records may act like self-correction in early reading; it may provide teachers with a basis for improving their own theories of instruction.

Techniques used for monitoring children's reading behaviors can also allow the teacher to enrich her program. Taking a record of behavior as a child reads enables the teacher to observe progress on any selection of materials so that a shift from a reading series to texts with more literary qualities could be taken with minimum risk because monitoring techniques were used. If self-correction behavior is observed it becomes a key indicator that progress is satisfactory and that the text is providing a learning experience.

Every teacher must be qualified as a decision-maker to answer instructional questions and to make decisions between equally effective and attractive practical alternatives, taking into account the present characteristics of the particular children she is trying to teach, and what other teachers have done with them (or should it be 'to them'?) in the past.

I acknowledge that the roles of researcher and teacher are not the same and that a continuing dialog between professionals with diverse roles should lead to a rolling revision of both theory and practice, providing a system of checks and balances on the excesses of each specialist. At times it is important that the theorist steps beyond the evidence and asks 'But what if . . . ?' Teachers should recognize when this is occurring. It is when there are no observations to back the discussion or when a researcher gives an interpretation which goes far beyond the data he provided.

In my research program I was trying to find out what children were doing, how they read, what the strengths and weaknesses of their reading behaviors were, given the program under which they were being taught. I wrote a text for teachers in which I tried to present alternatives to some traditional ideas about the reading process in the first year of learning to read, as a result of what I saw New Zealand children doing. For example, I wrote:

Reading behavior concerns all the things teachers have always thought it did — word knowledge, meaning, story sense, word study skills. It also includes directional behavior, letter identities, pronounceable clusters, grammatical sense, fluent processing of cues, and error correction. Reading involves the use of items of knowledge

- to anticipate what can occur in meaning and in language
- to search for cues
- to self-correct
- to form intuitive rules that take the child beyond what he already knows.

The good reader manipulates a network of language, spatial and visual perception cues, and categorizes these efficiently, searching for dissonant relations and best-fit solutions. Familiar responses which become habitual, require less and less processing and allow attention to reach out towards new information that was not previously noticed.

(Clay, 1979a p. 244)

This text, *Reading: The Patterning of Complex Behavior* was not the result of posing new hypotheses and asking 'But what if . . . ' questions. It provided accounts of what experienced, sensitive teachers already knew, in their own way, but it explicity documented this information for new and inexperienced teachers.

In a separate but linked publication, *The Early Detection of Reading Difficulties,* I described the techniques that had been devised for observing reading behavior (Clay, 1979b). Weighing the time demands on teachers, the adjustments children must make to school, and the evidence of early failure, I recommended that each child's progress should be checked after one year at school. With continuous entry to school in New Zealand this was a feasible proposition. The diagnostic survey was written for teachers who were not psychometricians. It gave some guidance as to which children the teacher should select for assessment and described how to measure the accuracy with which they read their texts, noting self-correction, directional movement, error types, letter identification confusions, concepts about print, and writing vocabulary skills.

What has not been readily available, particularly to readers outside New Zealand, has been an overview of the research upon which those earlier publications were based. This volume provides just that. I have not repeated the descriptions of observation procedures or the analysis of what this information means to the teacher of reading in the early years. These are available in recent editions. What this publication does is to bring together the research reports which show the development of my ideas between 1962 and 1980, and to show the broad base in developmental psychology that I believe should underpin pronouncements about reading instruction. I hope it will also be obvious that I value highly an approach to research which attempts to capture the ways in which children change over time in a reading program, an approach too rarely taken in reading research. It is not enough to administer achievement tests before and after a program or to probe deeply into the reading process. An important additional source of research information lies in accounts of what changes occur in what children in what sequences as they learn in their classroom programs. As a researcher this has interested me; it is, of course, what concerns the teacher.

Over the period of 18 years the program of research has taken us into issues related to continuous entry to school, teaching reading to five-year-olds, cross-cultural comparisons, multilingual subgroups, the prevention of reading difficulties, an early intervention program, and the inservice training of teachers.

I Observation for Teachers

1 Looking and Seeing in the Classroom

The following article was an invited comment. The editor suggested that the emphasis I place on careful observation was useful for all teachers of language subjects, not merely for teachers with interests in Early Childhood.

It may seem strange to suggest that teachers should look more closely at language behaviors. Surely one can only look at the answers to comprehension questions or at essays and exercises in written expression. A recent emphasis in research has been to go beyond these products and to observe the process of producing them.

My own research began with a dissatisfaction with theories of reading acquisition. I had a background in normal child development research and in the study of atypical children, and I became particularly interested in the prevention of problem behaviors, social and academic. How early could one see the process of learning to read moving off-course? I asked. The obvious way to approach this problem was to use the strategy of biological science in studying unplotted territory, and that was to observe and record exactly what occurred in the natural setting. I found ways of observing the first steps into reading, became fascinated with early progressions in writing, and began to attend with new interest to changes in oral language acquisition in children of school age. As a developmental psychologist I already had some methodologies for child study and I was particularly concerned with the changes that occurred. How could yesterday's behaviors evolve into tomorrow's?

Over the years the procedures I designed for my own use have been adapted for classroom teachers who want to ask questions about particular children. What processes is this reader or writer using? Knowing what the pupil does leads to a more significant teaching interaction because the teacher poses a question designed to bring a new aspect of the process into salience for a particular pupil.

Achievement levels, grades and competency scores may be used to equalize groups of students but how they get their scores can still be vastly different. These differences are important for how we teach the next steps of a more advanced process.

To become observers we have to decide on the language units to be studied and we need to define the conditions to be used for capturing and recording the behavior. There will be a task, a process of working towards a solution, and a product. The task and the product may be open in nature or closely specified or constrained.

A piece of creative writing would be an open task with an open product. The writing vocabulary task which I have used with six-year-olds is a constrained task. They are asked to write down all the words they know. The word lists differ from child to child and so are open products. For a year or two this is a very discriminating indicator of who is becoming a writer; it is a good way of capturing the changes that are occurring at this stage.

Two examples of observations of oral language activities for young children would be a sentence repetition task and retelling a story. A carefully graded series of sentences of increasing syntactic complexity can reveal different levels of control over the structures of the mother tongue. The task is constrained in every detail. The child is told, 'Be sure to say exactly what I say.' The product is also constrained as any deviation from the sentence delivered to the child suggests that the child is not able to group the language delivered to him in the linguistic packages given, but rather, in dealing with the task, reassembles the message within more familiar and comfortable sets of linguistic usage. The required task with a required product still leaves room for the child to interact with the task and process the sentence through his own set of linguistic learning. The task reveals to the observer something that might never have been noticed without the setting up of those constraints.

A much more open task is the retelling of a story. Any appropriate story can be used. The task is required but it leaves the child free to reveal strengths and strategies, and any two children will proceed in different ways, and produce different results. It is easy to find examples of the child's language through which a traditional story is told: 'One day Cinderella was doing all the work when the ugly sisters said, "Do me up." So she did. . . . And the fairy said, "Yes, I'll change your dress." And it was a lovely yellow — a really, really nice dress.'

I have had surprised students who found children, apparently well-prepared for school, unable to retell a simple tale. How would they read their reading books? the students asked.

When one turns to reading behaviors many that I observed were also discovered about the same time by Ken and Yetta Goodman. We all set out to record what children said and did as they read aloud. The task is constrained by the author's text. An accurate rendering is a constrained product, but, as in sentence repetition, there is scope for work done by the child to reveal something of the processes by which he learns. One thing readers do is that they correct themselves without any prompting or sign from others that an error has occurred. Why should this be? To explain this 'error behavior' one has to begin to ask what the child could have been responding to. Was the sense destroyed? Was an unEnglish structure uttered? Was there something inconsistent in the letter-sound pattern of the word the reader uttered with the text word? Was the reading fine within the sense of the sentence but nonsense in terms of a previous page? Such questions begin a train of thought in the observer who wants to understand, which leads to ideas about complex cognitive and perceptual processes going on inside the head as the active reader reconstructs the author's message.

An interesting change occurs in teachers who observe closely. They begin to question educational assumptions. My students in a summer course assured me that local US children of five years would not be able to write anything. I insisted that they went out and checked on that, and they were delighted with the products they brought back — attempts on the part of pre-schoolers to make sense of the print world around them, recording logo-like forms, sprinklings of initials, and their own names written like confetti anywhere on the page. They also found the children very willing to 'read' what had been produced. Seeing how far the kindergarten children had moved into the world of print in terms of the concepts they understood, if not in extensive control over the medium, they asked, 'Why do schools seem to assume that children will not be able to write before they read?'

Observations like this can lead to other important questions like 'When is it appropriate to demand accuracy?' or 'Does one really learn one perfect performance followed by another perfect performance?' It is a little shattering to one's theory of learning correct responses to record the conversational speech of competent adults and to find that many of the sentences are ungrammatical. The place of error or miscue or estimate or approximation in language learning becomes an interesting topic for observers to discuss.

Studies which record change over time in the same individuals will show in reading, and in writing, the same phenomena that have been recorded in language acquisition: children generate errors according to the rules which they are formulating to guide their creative or productive or generative behaviors, and those errors change as they are seen by the child to conflict with other evidence. In their place come a new set of errors occurring at the point where the new theories are not yet refined enough to cope with further evidence. And so the early theories or hypotheses of the child serve to sustain a level of productivity needed to continue a learning process and by means of these hypotheses language activities widen in scope to include more and more options, fitting more and more closely to the permissable usages of the language.

A kind of learning occurs in natural language tasks which is rarely thought about. Proceeding by rough and ready theories but operating self-correction processes the child practices old learning, giving it minimum attention, while new learning is laboriously worked over until it has found a place in the system. Every time a child reads a sentence or writes a story each letter sequence and language form in that sentence is, by its use, moving from somewhere on the novel language dimension towards being used with minimum attention. The hard-to-spell new word seems to be the one which requires processing but every other word in the sentence profits by being used, moving further towards fluency, 'automatic responding' and flexibility of use. High frequency words move most rapidly to this state. So when we record a series of 'correct' responses for the child reader we are not really noticing this continuing process of learning and overlearning.

Observations should occur under conditions which reduce the error of personal bias in the observer to its absolute minimum. If this is not so, and the observations are carried out to confirm our assumptions there would be nothing in the results to surprise us. The observer has to become objective in data collection, analysis and interpretation. An observer can easily influence the observations and must take all precautions not to. There are other things that can distort the value of the record. The child's behavior today may not be a good indicator of his behavior tomorrow so that the record we have may not be a reliable one. Then the program that the child has been exposed to will have acted like an experimental treatment. It will have trained some behaviors and will have overlooked others, or it may have attended to the parts of the activity and may have omitted to provide opportunities for the child to learn how to orchestrate the parts in a continuous, ongoing, productive activity. So, along with the influence of the program on what we may be able to observe we have the problem of the lack of opportunity to learn, or to change in certain ways, that is, the effects of the restrictions imposed by the program.

The noticing teacher not only discovers new behaviors, and changes in behaviors, but also begins to think about children's learning in new ways. For example, sometimes the reader, accurate by the teacher's standard, nevertheless goes back, repeating himself, rerunning the message. Is this immaturity, uncertainty, incompetence, or error? Or could it be that the child has been surprised by what he read, and has rerun to monitor his own behavior to ensure that it is correct? Monitoring one's own language activities and correcting error when it occurs has a great deal of relevance in formal and informal educational experience. It has to be important and needs to be encouraged. Teachers who are not good observers could well punish the very behavior that would make their pupils more accurate.

It is helpful to become detached observers of children at work, seeing *how* they go about the tasks we set them. If we keep today's record as a baseline, and over several occasions observe the child again we can over a short series of observations record change over time, capturing the progress. It is interesting to look back over the learning that has taken place.

II Observing the Young Reader

The procedures developed in my research for observing young readers have been used in different programs with beginning readers of different ages, and they have been tried successfully in several different countries. They have been used in classrooms with individual children and in well-designed studies of groups. Powerful statistical analyses have shown that these procedures which permit more detailed recording of individual responses than a normative test nevertheless have proved to be sound measurement devices.

The studies gathered together in this section report the first work I did on the behaviors recorded as the child read a text. The Reading Behavior of Five-Year-Old Children *provides an overview of the first research project, a longitudinal recording of weekly observations of children throughout their first year at school.* A Syntactic Analysis of Reading Errors *was part of that study and* Self-Correction Behavior *is from the same study.*

Then, skipping the second year at school, attention focuses on the third year of instruction. The Reading Behavior of Children in Standard One *(who would be seven to eight years of age) is another general overview of behaviors at this level, to be compared with the behavior of five-year-olds to note the changes that have occurred.* Juncture, Pitch and Stress as Reading Behavior Variables *explores further recordable behaviors which tell us something about how the child reads. Juncture can be thought of as pausing, and stress is self-explanatory. The last study in this group is, in my opinion, an important one. On the one hand the results are obvious. As good readers read more and more they find it harder and harder to read reversed or inverted print while poor readers have as much difficulty with normal print as with reversed and inverted print. Readers making good progress pay attention to quite different features of print from poor readers. On the other hand it is strange how little attention educational practice pays to the (revealed) differences in those groups making different progress.*

Most of the tasks used to observe the behaviors described in this section are detailed in The Early Detection of Reading Difficulties *(Clay, 1979b). Special tasks designed for particular studies are reported in those studies. Applications to bilingual populations are reported in a later section of this volume.*

The last two papers in this section are somewhat different. Spatial

Characteristics of the Open Book *is a paper which capitalizes on the unusual opportunity to study identical quadruplets and it asks 'what if . . .' questions about the neurological patterning of reading behaviors. The* Concepts About Print *review was written by Yetta Goodman and I have taken the opportunity to reply to some points which she raised.*

2   A Longitudinal Study: Research Design

To avoid repetition in several research reports I shall briefly describe how this first longitudinal study was carried out. I planned to start the study at school entry. (In New Zealand children enter school on their fifth birthday which may be any day of the school year.) I wanted to use an intensive longitudinal method, making weekly observations but also to administer a test battery within two weeks of the child's reaching 5:0, 5:6 and 6:0, providing an unusually tight control over age variability. I chose to record observable behaviors in an individual reading situation and attempted to obtain a total record. I deliberately adopted an atheoretical, no-hypothesis stance to data collection.

Such an approach had potential for several outcomes:

- I should obtain a detailed description of what happened to Auckland children in their first year of instruction and this might lead directly to ideas for improvements in instruction or administration practices.
- Within the year-long program I might be able to capture evidence of the child's adjusting to school, variability in children's performance, and adjustments within programs made by the teacher for particular children. There would be time for instruction to show effects and for trends to become apparent.
- The search would be directed towards behaviors that would detect early difficulties rather than toward methods of stimulating high progress readers. However, all children entering school would be used so that those having difficulty would be seen against the backdrop of the children who were succeeding.
- Despite the atheoretical initial stance an integration of findings with a review of theory and research might be possible.
- The results would have validity only for urban New Zealand children.

The Sample

The sample of 100 children (56 boys and 44 girls) was drawn from five schools in districts classed as middle class (2), working class (2) and decaying city center (1). Schools were selected to yield a typical urban spread of parent occupation but every child entering those schools in a particular time span (February to May 1963, 1964) was included in the study.

The children entered school between 5:0 and 5:2 (mean age of entry 5:1) and they were 5:11 to 6:1 at the end of the study. The group were shown to be not significantly different from expectation in intelligence (urban), parent occupation (urban), reading readiness (national norms), and sex distribution (national comparison). Ratings showed them to be average in adjustment and to be receiving above-average instruction (national comparison). A pre-study decision was made to exclude from the sample all children with language experience other than English. The urban bias gave the sample the advantage of higher than average intelligence and better than average instruction.

The Classroom Program

This study was a field investigation which sampled behavior responses under natural learning conditions. The investigator exercised no control over the instruction the children received.

Between the end of the pilot study and the beginning of the main study in 1963, a major curriculum revision occurred. With the free distribution of a new series of reading books, the centralized Department of Education ousted the word-learning method of the past 10 years and placed New Zealand reading outside the bounds of methods promulgated in the reading literature. In response to the requests of teachers' committees, the Department of Education had officially discarded letter-sound approaches as central to reading in 1950. Now, the teachers' recommendations were to reject a sight-vocabulary approach, and the new curriculum supported this change.

The classes were following a published reading scheme (Simpson, 1962) with a standard series of reading books (New Zealand Department of Education, 1963). However, the children read many other interesting short story books in addition to the basic series. The texts of the books were written for New Zealand children and use 'natural speech that makes for longer sentences' (Simpson, 1962). The reading scheme emphasized the use of grammatical and semantic cues in natural language texts and minimized instruction in letter-sound correspondence. A distinction was made between two vocabularies; content words of high interest to the children and the heavy-duty words of English. Pupils were expected to learn, that is, to accumulate, the latter vocabulary but not the former. Teachers would introduce the new concepts and the language and the plot of the short story to a reading group, and within 1 or 2 weeks, children would have completed the book. The approach has been called 'a book experience approach'. It is analogous to language experience methods, but the stories are introduced to the children rather than elicited from them. Comprehension would have the highest value from the beginning. Teaching points would arise as the child read, and prior teaching of sounds or of words in isolation would seldom occur. The reading behavior likely to be stressed was fluency, reading for meaning, learning as one reads, and flexible word-solving techniques, with only slight attention to letter-sound associations, vocabulary learning and word analysis (Simpson, 1962).

The teachers, who were rated slightly above average on a national comparison by five school inspectors, followed this published reading scheme and a standard series of reading books, but each had freedom in the prereading, supplementary reading, and creative writing programs, and in the detailed methodology of lessons. The slim Teachers' Manual written by Simpson provided only guidelines to implementing the program. It was not a day-to-day prescription for teaching.

The program was flexible in another sense. Children were grouped and regrouped by teachers according to their rates of progress at any time throughout the year.

The findings are reported in the full realization that they were the outcome of one approach to beginning reading. No attempt was made to decide whether this was better than any other approach in any quantitative sense.

The Weekly Records

Once every week of the school year each child read to the investigator those pages of his reading book for which his lessons had prepared him since the last record was taken. Behavior entered on the weekly records was analyzed in two stages, the preparation period prior to promotion to the basic series of reading books and the book-reading stage. For the preparatory stage before the child began reading the basic series the findings are mainly descriptive of the child's drawing, the story he had composed or dictated and his attempts to re-read this story. The records for the book-reading stage yield averaged tallies from longitudinal records of each child from the week he was promoted to the basic reading series until his sixth birthday. Therefore, children who were promoted to books early had more weekly records, and more satisfactory sampling of behavior than children who spent longer in the preparation or readiness period and less of their first year on book reading.

At one observation session it was usual for a child to read a little book of 12 pages or a story unit of four to six pages from a larger book. Every response was categorized as true report, error, repetition, or self-correction. Motor responses having to do with directional and spatial qualities of the text, such as finger pointing and stressed vocal juncture, were recorded. The investigator was particularly careful to act as a recorder of, not a stimulus to, behavior. Comments, teaching points, helpful replies, leading questions and pointing guides were avoided. Six observers trained for one hour on scoring taped recordings showed no significant differences from the investigator's original scoring for either errors, or self-corrections.

The Test Program

Within two weeks of school entry, again at 5 years 6 months, and within three weeks of his sixth birthday, each child was given a battery of seventeen tests. Tests of language skills included articulation, comprehension, and two tests of the grammatical aspects of language (morpheme completion and sentence repetition). Digit Span was included as a test of immediate auditory memory. Another set of tests probed activities correlated with visual perception and reading (but not pure tests of either). This group, referred to as tests of perceptual correlates, included spatial drawing, letter identification, a test of awareness of the conventions used to record written language, and two experimental procedures exploring the child's reactions to the orientation of words and to partial letter forms (reduced cues). Finally, a reading readiness battery (Metropolitan, 1943) was administered at *each* age level to explore the relationship between readiness score and reading progress. All test reliabilities were 0.77 or above.

The Test of Progress and Data Analysis

Records were analyzed one year after recording. A test of word recognition given at 6:0 was used as the criterion for selection of four quartile groups called High (H), High Middle (HM), Low Middle (LM), and Low (L) progress groups. The test combined a word test of items selected from the basic readers on the basis of frequency, with the Schonell R.1 test (1956). For this combined test the internal consistency reliability was 0.92, the item difficulty range was from a z-score of +1.65 to -1.65, and a validity coefficient of 0.93 was obtained with accuracy on book reading. The combined test discriminated well between readers at all levels of progress. The confidence that could be placed in this assessment of progress overcame one of the major obstacles to studying *early* reading progress, namely, the unavailability of good measuring instruments. The significance of differences between the four progress groups was determined by Mann-Whitney U-tests.

3 The Reading Behavior of Five-Year-Old Children: A Research Report

Introduction

The pedagogical dilemma behind the variety of methods of teaching reading is to decide what is the best way to 'cut the cake' represented by mature reading skills (Robinson, 1963). The young child cannot learn all the complexities of written language in a brief period of time, especially if he attempts this when his spoken language and visual perception skills are themselves at varying stages of immaturity. So, different methods have advocated different cuts. Decisions have been made as to which small parcels of linguistic elements should be placed before the child, and all too frequently there is an implication behind the advocacy of a method that a 'best' or 'true' cut exists. This seems unlikely if one bears in mind the variability of children, the variable ages of beginning reading, the varying qualities of instruction and the varying structural characteristics of languages. But it is important to note that different ways of simplifying the language will result in different aspects of the mature reading process being taught at different stages.

The usefulness of a 'method' is its value to the teacher, in that it provides a focus and a progression along which she can plan her class activities, with due allowance for individual differences. But the teacher who needs a central core to her program is faced with the problem of knowing which children are likely to be handicapped by her method so that *special or supplementary provisions* can be made for them.

One danger of a 'method' is that progress may be assessed only in terms of what the method stresses and what is happening in other areas of related behavior may not even be noticed. It should be borne in mind that a child does not learn only those things which a method claims to teach, and we cannot assume, as we tend to do, that children have learned by the method we have used.

For these reasons it seemed appropriate to look closely at the behavior of children who were beginning reading and to record precisely and objectively the manner of their responding. A longitudinal approach was adopted following the children from their fifth to sixth birthdays.

Results for the Preparation Period

1. Sequence and Timing of Promotion

Considerable uniformity of promotion procedure was noted in the five schools studied. The median child of the H group was given a caption book after five weeks at school but the median child of every other group arrived at the same point two weeks later (Table 1). In individual cases children waited much longer than this (sometimes as long as six months) but on the whole school entrants were judged ready for some direct contact with a very simple book after about five to seven weeks at school.

Table 1
Promotion to First Books: Total Weeks From School Entry

Median Child	Caption	Supplementary	Red 1	Red 2	Red 3
H	5	14	16	21	26
HM	7	18	21	24	27
LM	7	21	31	35	36
L	7	28	36	45	51

Most children spent a further nine to twenty-one weeks on classroom activities aimed at calling their attention to letters and words before they received their first reading book. In four schools this was a preprimer of an American basic reading series. In the fifth school children were promoted directly to the first book of the *Ready to Read* series, (Red 1). Table 1 lists the time in weeks from school entry to promotion to caption, supplementary and *Ready to Read* books 1-3, for the median child of each quartile group. Table 2 shows the number of weeks between promotions, bringing out more clearly the points at which children who were making slower progress were held.

Table 2
Promotion to First Books: Weeks Between Promotions

Median Child	Entry to Caption	Caption to Supplementary		Supplementary to Red 1	Red 1 to Red 2	Red 2 to Red 3
H	5	9	(11)	2	5	5
HM	7	11	(14)	3	3	3
LM	7	14	(24)	10	4	1
L	7	21	(29)	8	9	6

The findings suggest that teachers judge children's readiness for book reading not from behavior prior to contact with books but rather from children's attempts to respond to books. (Contrast the uniformity with which teachers introduce children to caption books with the differential timing of the transfer to supplementary and basic readers, especially if the latter are combined into one category.)

2. *Reading Behavior During the Preparation Period*

An attempt was made to record in a systematic manner the unstable, poorly differentiated, tentative beginnings of emerging reading responses.

New entrants drew pictures and attempted to write letters or words. They talked about their drawings and what they had written. They were asked to point to their work as they spoke about it. Most schools encouraged paper and pencil or crayon work and few children worked on blackboards during reading periods. Until a child was given a book to read a record was taken each week of his drawing, printing, talking, reading and pointing behavior.

The records suggested that the children had to learn new responses in three areas:

I   Visual sensitivity to letter and word forms (evident in the child's printing responses);
II   Directional constraints on movement (which appeared more complex and more critical than mere awareness of a 'left to right sweep');
III Constructing appropriate types of speech responses, composed into syntactical groups, word by word.

A fourth set of responses, termed 'matching behavior', seemed to be very important. The child who had gained some skill in the three sets of behavior noted above began to show some capacity to integrate informaton from two or more of these sources matching what he said to the print *in some respect*.

In the full research report (Clay, 1966) a range of behavior in each of these four areas was described. The research did not establish a developmental sequence on the basis of these signs. It is doubtful whether one sequence will be found through which all, or even many, children pass. Chance happenings may lead one child to new insights, by-passing many of the steps which another child may follow. Conversely, one must agree with Gates (1947) that children may stray off into poor procedures at many points of the process. It was felt that a clear statement of the range of behaviors recorded might help a teacher to become a more sensitive observer of pre-reading behavior and to notice when an individual child became stranded for a long period at one point and failed to progress to a response of better quality. Halting in some aspect of the complex process appeared to be a major reason for some children of above-average intelligence remaining in the non-starter group for long periods.

Space does not permit the detailing of these signs in this report but, since 28 percent of the research children were held in the preparation stage for nearly a year, it would appear that failure to graduate from the preparation period in the first year at school could be making a significant contribution to the schools' reading retardation problems. Only a few of these slow-progress children were there for reasons of general intellectual immaturity. (The median IQ of the lowest quartile was 106 and the range 87 to 121.) A few children had specific difficulties with one of the three sets of behavior (speech, visual perception and directional behavior). Some encountered a hurdle in learning to integrate these into matching behavior. Others *learned* inappropriate responses, such as a consistent right to left approach to print, or how to *invent* sentences and stories like those of the reading book.

3. *Self-correction Behavior in the Preparation Period*

When a child was trying to read he sometimes rejected an error response and tried again. Such spontaneous self-correction was an important variable in the records of book-reading behavior. When the observation records of the preparation period were examined it was found that self-correction behavior was recorded for 90 percent of the research children within a three-week period prior to their promotion to the first book of the *Ready to Read* series. This appeared to support the observational data on matching behavior since the child who was attempting to match visual and speech cues was more likely to detect an inconsistency in his reponse and to show self-correction behavior.

4. *Stressed Word Juncture in the Preparation Period*

The children responded to caption books with a fluency that was typical of their oral speech. As they developed skill in matching behavior, fingers were used to point to those parts of the text that were supposed to correspond to the vocal responses. Fluency gave way to word by word reading. At this point the child's reading became staccato as he over-emphasized the breaks between words. He could be thought of as 'reading the spaces' or 'voice pointing' at the words. Such behavior was seen as a high point of achievement in the preparation stage and not behavior to be frowned on as 'word reading' *or to be hurriedly trained out.* Over a period which ranged from days for the fast learners to months for the slow ones, a transition usually occurred from finger-pointing, to voice-pointing, to a lighter stressing of the breaks between words, and finally to increased dependence on phrasing. A slow learner took several weeks to establish the integration of vocal and motor skills (i.e., precise locating of what he was saying) and a further period was needed for this to retreat from the supporting stage of finger- or voice-pointing to a mere visuo-motor habit.

A search of observation records showed that three weeks *prior* to promotion to *Ready to Read* books 40 percent of the children had begun to use stressed word juncture, and a further 9 percent were children making fast progress who had once used the props of finger- and voice-pointing but had already discarded them and presumably had established the required visuo-motor habits. Thus, for 49 percent of the sample this was learning which took place in the preparation period. For the remainder this had to be learned on the *Ready to Read* books.

Results for the Book Reading Stage

1. Sex Differences

The proportion of boys and girls in the L, LM and HM groups did not show significant differences. However there was a significant sex difference in the H group with fewer boys than girls making very fast progress in their first year at school ($x^2 = 12.01$, df = 3, $.01 > p > .001$).

2. Distance in the Reading Series

Figure 1 shows the spread of attainment in terms of books of the *Ready to Read* series completed at 6 years to a level of accuracy of 90 percent or more. The first book of the reading series had not been completed by 11 percent of the children and 28 percent had not gone beyond the first book. The curve of attainment bore no resemblance to a normal curve at this stage and only a few children had reached the larger books of the reading series by their sixth birthdays.

3. Quantity of Reading

The total number of words read under observation conditions showed statistically significant differences between all groups (Table 3, Columns 1 and 2). The differences in quantity of reading might have been predicted, but their size and consistency were interesting. Probably they reflected the amount of teaching time spent with each group and it would not be surprising to find progress in the second year of school closely related to this quantity of reading accomplished in the first year. If reading to the investigator were taken roughly as one sixth of the child's reading experience the child making superior progress read something in excess of 20,000 words in his first year of instruction, the HM child 15,000, the LM child 10,000 and the L child less than 5,000 words.

Figure 1
Progress On The Ready To Read *Books At 6:0*

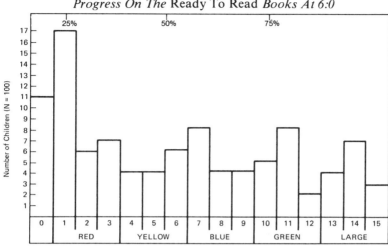

Last Book Read With 90% Accuracy

4. *Error Ratios*

When error ratios were calculated L children made one error in every three words and LM children made one in eight. HM made one in fifteen and H one in thirty-seven (Table 3, Column 3). The very best readers made less than one error in every hundred words. However, only the H group read at a level of 95 percent accuracy with any consistency (Table 3, Column 4). All sub-group differences on error ratio are statistically significant.

5. *Self-correction Ratios*

Errors which the children managed to correct spontaneously were listed as self-correction behavior. The observations showed that when children became aware that 'something was wrong' they revised their responses and corrected their errors 26 percent of the time. The H group corrected one in three errors and the HM group one in four. The LM group corrected one in eight and the L group only one in every twenty errors (Table 3, Column 5). The significant difference between the HM and LM groups seems to indicate two different ways of behaving, one characterized by the two top groups and the other by the two bottom groups. Half the self-correction behavior (52 percent) was achieved by a strategy of returning to the beginning of a line.

6. *Repetitions*

Records were kept of repetitions to confirm a correct response (or to gain time or regain equilibrium or fluency). Of all re-reading of this type 34 percent involved a return to the beginning of a line.

7. Information-processing

When error ratios and self-correction ratios were plotted graphically, as in Figure 2, the significant difference between the top two and bottom two groups was marked by a line indicating one correction in every five errors. A line representing 95 percent accuracy separates the H from the HM group. A rank correlation of –0.79 indicated an inverse relationship between error ratio and self-correction ratio. An interpretation of these differences was made as follows. The H group made few errors and related all incoming cues efficiently. The HM group made many errors but through active processing (i.e., by relating, checking and confirming visual, sound and meaning cues) they managed to correct many errors. The LM group attempted to relate cues but their many errors created a confusion which made it difficult for them to detect the errors. The L group made little effort to relate or cross-check cues.

One must not infer that children were processing these cues in any explicit manner but rather that by actively engaging in search and check at an implicit level the children seemed to become more aware of what they were doing. MacKinnon reports a similar observation from his research with five-year-old readers. 'By recognizing what had to be done the children, in turn, seemed more able to recognize when they had been successful in their reading.' (MacKinnon, 1960, p. 155)

8. Sources of Cues

Three sets of evidence throw some light on the sources of cues available to children of this age for decoding the printed text.

A *Language tests:* Correlations showed that scores on language tests maintained more or less constant relationships with reading progress, varying around $r = 0.40$, and did not differ much at 5½ and 6 years from what they were at 5 years. Articulation showed an expected trend which could lead to terminal status of articulation skill around eight years. The skills of the L group in comprehension of language increased consistently six months behind the H group. However, on two tests of the grammatical aspects of language the L group made very little gain during the year.

B *Perceptual correlates:* Tests of perceptual correlates showed highly significant increases with age. Letter identification, knowledge of the conventions for writing English and categorizing visual stimuli within the directional constraints of written English increased from correlations with reading progress of about 0.40 at 5 years to about 0.80 at 6 years. The Metropolitan Reading Readiness scores followed the same pattern and all four tests differed in this respect from the constant manner in which language tests related to reading progress. The increasing difference between H and L groups on letter identification was noteworthy and pro-

Table 3

Differences on Reading Behavior Variables Between Progress Groups
Figures reported are for the Median Child of each Quartile Group

Reading Progress Group	Words Read During Observations Ready to Read 1.	All Books 2.	Error Ratio 1 error in X running words 3.	Mean Accuracy Level 4.	Self-Correction Ratio 1 in X errors 5.	Speed Secs per word 6.
High	2599	3570	37.29	97.32%	2.75	1.02
High Middle	1605	2601	15.20	93.42%	3.81	1.51
Low Middle	861	1679	7.86	87.28%	8.35	1.25
Low	114	757	2.58	61.24%	19.72	1.57

Mann-Whitney U-tests show significant subgroup differences at .01 level for all comparisons in Columns 1-4. The H and HM groups are significantly different from the LM and L groups in Column 5, and the H group is significantly different from all others in Column 6.

duced the highest relationship with reading progress at 6 years (r = 0.83).

C   *A linguistic analysis of errors showed:*

    i) Five-year-old children anticipated the linguistic class of a word which should occur next in a sentence with 79 percent accuracy.

    ii) These children used an acceptable substitution for the linguistic structure of a sequence of words 58 percent of the time.

    iii) Taken together single word and word sequence substitutions were linguistically equivalent to the text in 72 percent of all substitution errors.

    iv) Letter-sound correspondence between text and response played a much slighter role in error response, occurring in only 41 percent of errors. (Differences between i and iv, and ii and iv were statistically significant.)

The data on the sources of cues used by the children and the changes that took place over this first year can be summarized:

    a) Oral language skills and syntactical expectancies provided a rich source of cues.

    b) Further increase in language skills did not increase the size of their correlation with reading progress, but failure to develop flexibility in handling some of the grammatical relationships of language could have been a retarding factor.

    c) The visual discrimination of letter forms, one from the other, developed *slowly* over the first year of reading as the mean score was only half the letters of the alphabet identified at six years. Progress in this learning was highly related to progress in reading.

Figure 2

Error And Self-correction Ratios:
Median case of each quartile group
Interpretation Of Reading Behavior

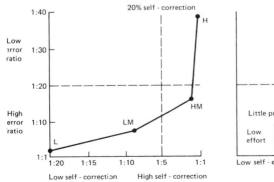

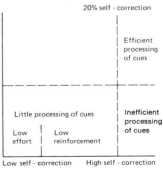

9. Speed of Reading

Rates recorded were self-pacing rates. HM, LM, and L groups took 1.44-1.57 seconds on the average to read a word and were not, as groups, significantly different on this variable. The H group read at a rate of almost a word per second and this was significantly different from all other quartile groups (Table 3, Column 6). These results could be explained as a contrast between the *decoding* behavior of the three lowest groups, which takes time, compared with *habituation* of response for the high progress group allowing a faster response. However, the investigator felt some dissatisfaction with the sampling of behavior in terms of speed and no firm interpretation of difference was thought to be warranted.

10. Effect of the Long Vacation

At the beginning of the new school year the children were asked to read the last book which, according to records, they had read successfully at a 95 percent level of accuracy. Only the lowest quartile of the sample showed a significant drop in accuracy. The remaining children read with little loss of skill (Table 4). However, it was unusual for the new teacher to *know* what book the child had last completed with success.

Table 4

*Sub-Group Differences in Accuracy
Before and After the Long Vacation*

(Percentages)

Median Child	December	February	Loss in Accuracy
H	100.00	98.77	1.23
HM	94.15	90.06	4.09
LM	90.00	88.33	1.67
L	85.45	76.36	9.09

11. Number of Teachers

Although only five new entrant classes in five schools were used in the study the 100 children were taught by thirty-two teachers before they were six years old. The staffing position could hardly be called unstable because, while three teachers left for maternity reasons and five probationary assistants left at the end of a year, no other teachers changed their jobs. It would appear that enrollment and promotion policies resulted in these children being confronted with several new teachers during their first year at school.

Application to the Classroom

1. A Predictable Environment

How important are frequent changes of teachers? It has been argued that one of the necessary conditions for learning for the young child is a predictable environment in which he can recognize consistency and regularity (Yarrow, 1961; Russell and Fea, 1963, p. 882). Part of this environment for the child of school age is the teacher, her personality and her teaching procedures. In this research, children who entered school at any time during the school year were moved according to their progress into new groups and classes. Such a policy of admissions and promotions can meet the individual needs of children but it may work against the provision of a predictable environment in two ways. Firstly, the steady flow of new admissions forces frequent promotion of groups from teacher to teacher within the infant department. Secondly, when the emphasis is on progress the time an individual child has spent at school is easily overlooked, so that fast learners in this study had as many as five teachers before their sixth birthday while slow starters remained in pre-reading groups for long periods, even up to one year.

Tests of the effects of the long vacation on reading behavior suggest that even after a break of seven weeks the top 75 percent of first year entrants have lost very little reading skill providing they are returned to material which they read successfully prior to the vacation. This implies that first reading responses are very specific to the materials studied and that records of the books children completed successfully in their previous class should always be available to new teachers.

This applies to times of promotion, all term vacations and *changes of school.* It would appear advisable, then, to begin the child on this material before introducing new books.

Records indicated that children came to school with very different behavior repertoires and individually different strengths and weaknesses. It seemed unlikely that any set sequence of learning tasks could be appropriate to many children. But in trying to create interesting activities for children of diverse experiences the teacher would need to be careful that her program presented some consistency and regularity to the individual child and was not so flexible, so varied and so wide in scope that the slower child would not be able to locate fragments of familiar knowledge in the variety.

2. Early Contact with Print

There is nothing in this research that suggests that contact with printed language forms should be withheld from any five-year-old child on the grounds that he is immature. (Intelligence quotients ranged from 85 to 156.) The descriptions of the four sets of learning observed during the preparation period suggest that these are fostered by contacts with written language. The visual perception of print, the directional constraints on movement, the special types of sentences used in books, and the synchronized matching of spoken word units with written word units will only be learned in contact with printed language. Group differences emerged as the fast learners mastered these tasks in a few weeks while the average and slow learners took much longer.

However, it should be noted that when a child takes six months to establish a consistent left-to-right approach to lines of print he will have had many opportunities to practice inappropriate behavior, while the fast learner is saved from such error practice by the early establishment of the habit. Slow learners cannot be pushed but there are dangers in leaving them practising poor procedures for prolonged periods. One might even suggest that six months of muddlement is more than enough to create poor readers out of children with average or superior intelligence. Certainly some planned action to speed up the learning of the preparation period could be initiated after the child has been at school six months.

To avoid making wrong decisions about children in the preparation period — for both undue haste or prolonged delay can be detrimental to the child's progress in reading — fuller descriptions of the tentative beginnings of reading behavior are needed and smaller classes will be required so that teachers may become more sensitive observers of this early behavior.

3. Active 'Search and Check'

The beginning reader may 'read' his first book by a low-level strategy of auditory memory for sentence, page and story. As long as this leads on to the behavior described below there seems to be nothing wrong with such a starting point.

When a child realizes that there is one and only one response equivalent to the text, he develops a need or willingness to decide between alternative responses. The child then has a vague awareness that he must employ self-instructions (M. D. Vernon), modes of processing (MacKinnon), strategies (Bruner), operations (Piaget), information processing (Gibson), or problem solving abilities (Moore, Downing), in order to discover a best-fitting response. Self-correction behavior was seen as overt evidence of such mental activity and was located in the records of 90 percent of the research sample *three weeks prior to promotion to book reading*. At the book reading stage high self-correction rates were associated with high reading progress and were inversely related to error rate.

Some active searching for differences, similarities or identity is implied. Awareness of only a few letter or word characteristics permits the child actively to relate what he says to what he sees. Differences are easier to detect because they need occur only in one detail whereas identity must be established as corresponding in every respect (MacKinnon, 1960; Birch and Lefford, 1963).

Re-reading a line is the versatile strategy frequently used by children to confirm responses or to search for better responses. This strategy may serve several purposes. It may clear away memories of previous error. It may assist in recollecting cues lost to immediate memory by a long delay at a difficulty. It may activate cell assemblies not activated on the first run. And, if the strategy succeeds, it places the response in its correct matrix of association which should make for better responding on subsequent occasions. Reinforcement flows from such successful decoding — which is not necessarily the same thing as correct rendering of the text.

There was little evidence in this research that beginning readers read ahead to complete a semantic context.

Re-reading in oral reading means re-hearing. Skinner (1957) believes the mature reader may read a difficult passage aloud to increase self-stimulation and McNeil and Keislar (1963) found that saying words and sentences aloud resulted in greater ability to recognize written words and sentences among beginning readers. When children apply a re-reading strategy they are also gaining from re-hearing the context.

Children appear to substitute words to keep the activity going. These errors are often looked upon as 'indiscriminate guessing', but for the child they have positive value. They lower the risk of 'senseless reading' or 'prolonged searching' or 'failure to respond'. The substitutions tend to be prompted by oral language habits and as such are useful first-stage expectancy responses that are related to fluent reading (Bruner, 1957; Solley and Murphy, 1960). If a child is to be encouraged to reduce the use of these he must be taught additional bases for making comparisons between words and relating cues. He must be given time to respond and must not be harassed because he searches at length, or because he fails to respond.

4. *Differential Treatments*

The spread of attainment described in this research has been interpreted by some people to mean that the reading books and the teaching method should be changed. Before any major changes are envisaged it would be appropriate to see what special or supplementary provisions could be made for groups of children within the general framework of the present scheme.

One could hardly wish for better progress than that shown by the top quartile group. They enjoyed reading, they were proud of their attainment, they made the transfer to the larger books of the series effortlessly, and they read fluently for meaning (if their efficient self-correction behavior can be used as a criterion of comprehension). However, despite their excellent progress, they knew too little about the letter-sound relationships of the language and could well have had more training in this respect. As soon as the H group could be defined as high progress readers, which was after six months at school, they could easily have added an awareness of letter-sound relationships to their skills.

The H M group contained highly intelligent children (Median I.Q. 118), but for these children the reading process did not go together smoothly. The timing of their promotion (Table 2) suggests that they were being hurried at a pace they could not sustain. The linguistic analysis of their errors (Clay, 1966) suggested that their responses were not guided by sentence structure or visual form and to correct this a temporary drop in fluency would have to be accepted.

The LM group made many errors and needed close supervision to reinforce their few correct responses and discourage their many inappropriate responses. This group, who were slow to graduate from the preparation period, contained some children with pronounced directional difficulties. There is reason to believe that responding within the directional constraints of written English is a prerequisite to self-reinforcing search and check activity, and that this behavior should be observed closely in the preparation period. The simple device of asking children to 'read it with your finger' applied to caption book reading provides a useful check on a child's directional behavior.

The L group did not produce enough correct responses. Rhythm, rhyme and auditory memory for the text would be legitimate props for these children with special attention to the predictability of their reading environment. Regular contact with familiar material rather than quasi-flexibility on varied texts seems to be indicated. Most of them needed to be helped out of the preparation period sooner by individual attention to their particular problems.

The lower 50 percent of first year entrants did not seem to do enough reading in their first year and perhaps two reading periods a day could be organized.

5. Poor Procedures

Studies of children who fail in learning to read have indicated that word-by-word reading and pointing with finger or voice are poor procedures to be avoided or trained out. In this research it was possible to locate records where children spoke so fluently that they could not locate the words they were saying, or who caught the meaning so well that they paraphrased the text.

Both pointing behavior and stressed word juncture appeared as useful props for the beginning reader who was taught by a method which stressed meaningful units and fluency. Part of the learner's task under these instruction conditions is to isolate word units both in his speech and on the page, and to match the two. (Later he must repeat this procedure with letter units.) At the point of transfer from prereading to reading books, and for some time thereafter, it is appropriate for the child to strengthen his locating behavior by pointing with his hand or voice. Once he has established accurate locating responses with his eyes alone there is reason to discard the finger pointing and to step up the demand for fluency. Word-by-word reading is not to be hurriedly trained out unless the teacher is certain that the child is visually locating the words he is saying. Some slower children were deprived of the very props they had spontaneously discovered when teachers forbade the use of the finger or insisted on the use of a card only, as a line guide.

6. *Visual Perception of Print*

The results reported above give strong support to the interpretation that for this sample of children, taught by this approach to reading, there was a heavy dependence on oral language skills, and especially on an awareness of what is possible and likely to occur in the language. Initially the child is producing speech responses, but is checking, first at the level of lines and sentences, and later at the level of phrases and words, to see if the text could have said what he had expected it to say.

If the child selects his reading responses on the basis of his oral language habits and limited visual cues (such as the initial letter, or a 'funny shape', or the pattern of letters, or the word's outline) by actively relating what he says to what he sees he may become more aware of other features in the words. His critical approach to his own responses would help him make new discriminations between similar words on those occasions when one word is a misfit for a certain slot. Thus he is likely to gain in noting new features at those very points in his reading when he experiences dissonance, that is when he makes an error that he notices.

When correct responses are made on the basis of limited cues the child *may* become aware of new features in the print. But not inevitably. In this research some children continued to produce linguistically adequate, fluent speech responses without gaining in awareness of the visual characteristics of print. It is the children who are making active efforts to compare words who are likely to gain in capacity to correct their own errors and also to increase their discrimination of the visual characteristics of print.

There is a critical distinction between claims that the most readily distinguished signals (a) differ in many respects, or (b) differ in only one attribute. Considering the immaturity of the five-year-old and the instability of responses in the early learning stage, a strong case can be argued for reading material that is *rich in cue sources* being more appropriate for the formation of self-reinforcing or self-correcting reading activity than material that has been controlled and regularized down to the just-noticeable-difference level. It follows that texts which aim to use the sentence forms and experience backgrounds of the children for whom they are intended would seem to be more psychologically appropriate than texts based on a logical ordering of linguistic elements.

The very high relationship found between letter identification and reading progress suggests that this is an important variable in the first year of learning to read (Durrell, 1958). Discrimination of letters one from another is only partially acquired by this sample at six years and further development must take place during the second year at school. Other methods of teaching might produce higher skill on this variable in the first year but slower progress is probably a price to be paid if it is important to stress fluent responses to interesting stories. The price does not seem too high providing the further discrimination of letters, one from another, can be fostered in creative writing and letter-sound association training during the second year.

7. Reading Vocabulary

A child will encounter some words over and over again. This would tend to build up fast recognition responses to the point where the child could recognize a word without having to check its fit in the matrix of meaning, syntax and visual form. If this were the case one would expect comparatively slow responding during the period when the child is decoding his reading word by word and actively searching for cues and checking relationships. In time more and more words would reach a stage of habituation and only an occasional word would need to be decoded. Speed records in this research tend to support such an interpretation. (The concept of 'sight vocabulary' and the success of word recognition tests could be accounted for in such a description.)

8. Reinforcement

The child's early tentative responses seem to require a very close check and prompt reinforcement by an interested teacher because he has limited control over cues and cannot cross-check his own responses. But once he learns to search for information from a variety of cue sources, even though his knowledge is limited and unstable, one basis of confirmation, and therefore the reinforcement of the activity, lies in the network of congruent signals from the code. The better reader, encountering new words at an appropriate rate, will be learning from making a few errors in a mass of correct responding. In the classroom there tends to be more time devoted to the advanced reading groups and less to the first reading groups. Perhaps some reversal of this trend is indicated.

Summary

Interpretation of the findings of this research suggested that the good reader manipulates a network of language, spatial and visual perception cues and sorts these implicitly but efficiently, searching for dissonant relations and best-fit solutions. Redundancy in cue sources allows for confirming checks and acts as a stimulus to error-correction. Habitual responses may be continuously emerging as the result of this successful slot-filling on successive occasions.

At some time during the first year at school visual perception begins to provide cues for encoding and verifying but cues from this source are, for a long period, piecemeal, unreliable and unstable. Slowly the early cue sources of situation and spoken language are supplemented by learning along new dimensions, such as letter knowledge, word knowledge, letter-sound associations and syllabic awareness. As differences within each of these dimensions gradually become differentiated the possibilities for dissonance and the chances of detection and correction of error are increased.

The oral language habits of the linguistically average child provide a source of relatively stable responses which can give some success in predicting what a text will say and when an error has occurred. However, it is not inevitable that under the support of oral language habits visual perception will proceed to more refined knowledge of letters-within-words. Some children maximize the importance of oral language and fail to attend to the visual cues. Seen in perspective the child's oral language skills make an excellent starting point since they provide a set of well-established stable responses. Adequate learning must proceed in the direction of more and more receptiveness to visual perception cues which must eventually dominate the process. They can hardly be said to do so in the first year of reading studied in this research where the average six-year-old could only discriminate half the letter symbols in his reading.

It would seem undesirable to prescribe a sequence of teaching to bring about the learning and integration of skills during the preparation period because progress must be dependent on the strengths and weaknesses of individual children who differ markedly in prior achievements and growth rates. If, on the other hand, school entrants are allowed to arrive at 'readiness' in their own time, and are placed in large 'holding' classes, some may choose to ignore the stimulating environment of the classroom with respect to written language, and others may get stranded somewhere along the developmental line and their difficulties may be overlooked. Only by sensitive, close observation of small classes can the teacher create learning conditions for new entrants that will facilitate this early integration of skills, and launch children successfully into their school careers.

An optimum level of error response of about 5 percent or less, prior to promotion from a book, was confirmed by results in this research. Repetition of a book at low levels of accuracy, or at high levels of accuracy achieved by the low-level strategy of auditory memory unaccompanied by active processing of cues, is of little value to the child. A new and easier book may stimulate him to greater attentiveness from which new insights may emerge. Therefore, the provision of 'little books' in the new reading series has distinct advantages. It seems probable that by making some errors and correcting them the young child gradually becomes aware, at the level of conscious reasoning, of what he is doing, and able to verbalize this.

There are other ways of learning to read with the primary emphasis on sounds, letters or sight words, but the description of reading behavior which emerged in this research seems to approximate closely what the mature reader does. If the child has begun to apply a range of skills to a limited universe of language in such a way that there is an almost inevitable accumulation of skill, through search and check procedures, then developmental goals can be set to achieve more precise categorization of stimuli and increasingly flexible approaches to more and more varied texts.

Note
This report is an abstract of sections of the author's thesis presented at the University of Auckland for the degree of Doctor of Philosophy, 1966. Grateful acknowledgement is due to Professor Ralph Winterbourn who supervised the study and to the teachers whose cooperation made the research possible.

4   A Syntactic Analysis of Reading Errors

The children's first guesses at points of uncertainty in their reading tend to be dominated by their control over the syntax of their language. In several parts of the world, researchers arrived at this insight about the same time in the late 1960s. The oral language habits of the linguistically average child provide a source of relatively stable responses that give the child some success in anticipating what kinds of words are likely to occur in a text and in detecting reading errors. At each point in constructing a sentence, in speaking or in reading, there are only a limited number of choices as to how one can proceed.

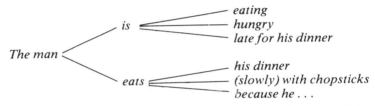

In that example the three structures which follow is *cannot follow* eats *and the opposite is also true. Following the selection of* is *the options are narrowed and the reader will search a limited range of possibilities. I do not think this aspect of the use of syntactic cues in reading has yet been fully explored.*

An analysis of 8,000 substitution errors made by the 100 children studied in the first longitudinal research showed a high incidence of syntactic equivalence between error substitutions and textual stimulus supporting the above argument.

When children who are beginning readers are asked to read a simple English text, some of their responses correspond to the stimulus words and some do not. A correct response gives no information about how the child arrived at the word chosen. An error may indicate some of the cues in the stimulus to which the child is reacting.

Linguists who write about learning to read have stressed phoneme-grapheme correspondence rather than other levels of linguistic organization (Bloomfield and Barnhart, 1961; Fries, 1963); and educators have been divided between advocacy of 'phonics' and 'reading for meaning' (Austin and Morrison, 1963). If it could be established that linguistic structure was a significant source of error substitution in beginning reading there would be a need to broaden these concepts to include a contribution to reading behavior from structural cues.

This research explored the influence of linguistic structure on children's word choices in reading. It was assumed that the children were guided by the semantic associations of what they read, but it was the aim of the analysis to examine the role of the syntactical rules of grammar in the reader's selection of a response. It is the contribution of syntax at a high level of generality that is explored; namely, position class, without regard to finer differences in structural relations.

Linguistic Analysis of Errors

When a child gave a reading response that was not an acceptable pronunciation of the stimulus word for the linguistic environment in which it occurred, an error was recorded. The errors corrected by a child without prompting were called self-corrections.

Errors were classified with respect to structural equivalence to the correct response on the basis of work by Harris (1946, 1951). The criterion of equivalence of two morphemes or two morpheme sequences was position. Two morphemes or morpheme sequences were equivalent if they could be substituted for each other in the sentence.

The morpheme classes used, P, N, I, T, A, and V, were similar to, but not identical with, traditional parts-of-speech classifications of preposition, noun, pronoun, article, adjective and verb. D, corresponding to adverb, occurred seldom in the reading books. Two other classes required were independent morphemes such as *Oh!* *Hello! too,* and questions, such as *where* and *who* when used with question intonation or question marks.

A series of errors was analyzed as a substituted sequence, running from the point of departure from the text to the point where correspondence recurred. This included three types of substitution: first, substitution of a sequence for a single morpheme or vice versa (*big bus* for *bus*); second, substitution of one sequence of morphemes for a second sequence of equivalent linguistic form (*his paint* for *the blue shed*); and third, substitution of one sequence of verbs for another sequence of verbs without regard to the substitutability of sub-groups of V (*looked* for *will like*).

Direct speech required special attention. It occurred in 73% of all lines in the texts but was not included in Harris' description. Sequences specifying who said something occurred in any of four linguistic environments:

> A: '————,!?' *said Mother.*   (83%)
> B: *She said,* '————.?!'   (8%)
> C: '————,!?' *he said.*   (4%)
> D: '————,!?' *said John,* '————'.?!   (4%)

These four sequences were treated as equivalent morpheme sequences.

To test the extent to which reading errors showed the influence of phoneme-grapheme learning, location points for correspondence between error and text were described, as shown in Table 1. Such categories result in a generous interpretation of the term 'correspondence.' This procedure could only be applied to single-word substitutions.

Table 1
Location Points for Phoneme-grapheme Correspondence

	Beginning	Ending	Both	Medial	Reversed Word	First-Last Letter
Letter	paint	said	head	—	let	paint
	picture	and	hand		tell	help
Cluster	Ann	How	—	skipped	—	—
	And	Now		hopping		
Syllable	today	painting	remembered	—	—	—
	tomorrow	hosing	recited			

Results

From all records for weekly observations of 100 children who were in their first year at school and between their 5th and 6th birthdays, 10,525 errors were obtained and 26% of these were self-corrected.

Of the 7674 errors that were substitutions, 72% occurred in equivalent morpheme-class or morpheme-sequence class structures (Table 2). When errors were single words in an otherwise correct response (5035 errors), the textual stimulus and the word substituted belonged to an equivalent morpheme class 79% of the time. Self-correction occurred more frequently in some linguistic classes than in others. Table 3A shows that noun and article classes had low rates of self-correction compared with rates for the pronoun class. When an error was from a nonequivalent morpheme class, the potential for self-correction was high.

Of all errors in sequence substitutions (2639 errors) 58% occurred in linguistically equivalent sequences (Table 2). The self-correction rates for errors in sequence substitutions tended to be lower than single-word rates except when both the main elements (NV) of the sentence were read incorrectly (Table 3B). The low self-correction rate for single nouns (21%) improved when the error sequence was a noun phrase (40%). Overall, it seems as though some of the constraints of the correct linguistic environment are lost in sequence substitution, and error is therefore less readily detected.

A second analysis was made of some single-word substitutions to estimate phoneme-grapheme correspondence. (The 5035 errors of the grammatical analysis were reduced to 2388 in the phoneme-grapheme analysis by a limitation in tabulation procedure. Noun-class responses were excluded.) Despite the very generous interpretation of correspondence, only 41% of the single-word substitutions showed that the child might be responding to some visual characteristics of the letters.

The results are relatively consistent across all levels of reading progress.

Table 2
Incidence and Linguistic Correspondence of Errors with the Textual Stimulus

	Total Group	Quartile Group			
		L	LM	HM	H
Self-correction rate	26%	11%	14%	28%	35%
Total errors	10,525	1208	2345	3551	3421
Grammatically equivalent single-word substitution	79%	86%	82%	72%	81%
N	5035	307	993	1771	1964
Grammatically equivalent sequence substitution	58%	50%	57%	62%	60%
N	2639	483	700	770	686
Total substitutions grammatically acceptable	72%	64%	72%	69%	76%
N	7674	790	1693	2541	2650
Phoneme-grapheme correspondence of single-word substitutions (excluding the noun class)	41%	43%	41%	32%	56%
N	2388	99	512	1173	604

Table 3

Self-correction Rates for Linguistic Classes

A: Percentage of error self-corrected in single-word substitutions

	I=I	I=T	I=N	P=P	V=V	A=A	T=T	N=N
Equivalent word substituted	60	60	54	46	35	33	27	21
	For N	For V	For indep. morph.	For P	For questions			
Nonequivalent word substituted	60	53	51	49	45			

B: Percentage of error self-corrected in sequence substitutions

	NV=NV	Whole sentence	Noun phrase	Source of direct speech	V	PTN		
Equivalent substitutions	56	56	40	23	23	20		
	N=V	?	For PTN	For source of dir. sp.	Whole sentce.	N!=NV	Indep. morph.	"Here" sentcs.
Nonequivalent substitutions	44	40	35	30	24	20	11	6

Discussion

This analysis indicated that the young child's guesses at points of uncertainty in his reading tend to be dominated by his control over the syntax of his language. Such a finding is consistent with research evidence. In word-association tests, young children give responses which have syntactic association with stimulus words while older children's responses have the same class characteristics as the stimulus (Ervin, 1961; Entwistle, Forsyth, and Muuss, 1964). Studies show that superior children have control over the grammatical aspects of English when they enter school (Menyuk, 1964; Loban, 1963). On the other hand, the learning of capital and lower-case letters plus two forms for *a* and *g* (54 symbols in all), is a large set of discrimination learning which might be expected to proceed slowly over a long period of time (Gibson, Osser and Pick, 1963). That a child should meantime depend on his oral control over language sequences is not surprising.

The spontaneous correction of errors in reading presumably stems from an awareness, however vague, that not all the relationships between words are a neat fit. Perhaps a wrong response produces some aural or visual cue which is incongruent in the matrix of word relationships. Dissonance may arise because of semantic, syntactic or phonemic cues in the language, or from visual perception. The child, feeling that 'something is wrong,' may search for a response which resolves the dissonance. Evidence that structural cues contribute to this matrix of relationships comes from three sources.

1. There is a high incidence of syntactic equivalence between error substitution and the textual stimulus.
2. Some morpheme classes are more readily corrected than others; for example, pronouns, which have relationships of concord with other parts of a sentence, have high rates of correction.
3. Since equivalent word substitutions (79%) occur more frequently than sequence substitutions (58%), it appears that some of the constraints of the correct linguistic environment are not available in sequence substitution.

The varying rates of self-correction for *linguistic classes* underline the fact that different expectancies or transitional probabilities apply to each linguistic class. If the linguistic characteristics of the beginning-reader texts had been described in terms of transitional probabilities, this might have provided a basis for arriving at tests of significance between linguistic classes. This was not attempted in an already extensive project. It must be emphasized, nevertheless, that the behavior recorded in this study is a product of interaction between psychological variables in the children and in the learning situation, with the linguistic characteristics of their texts and their oral language environments.

In some respects this analysis might have been more adequately effected by the use of a generative grammar. Substitutions which had to be treated as nonacceptable in this analysis might have been classified as acceptable in a transformational analysis.

Here is Grandma	This is a Friendship?
Grandma is here	Is this a Friendship?

This would have handled error behavior at sentence beginnings more meaningfully and would probably have increased the number of grammatically equivalent sequence substitutions.

5 Reading Errors and Self-Correction Behavior

It was possible to record the behavior of children who were establishing successful or failing patterns of reading progress in the first year of instruction. Rather more exciting, however, were the records of self-correction behaviors. These provided an unlooked-for explanatory variable by which one could argue that children could teach themselves many things about reading irrespective of the program they were in. Those children who used this strategy found it a powerful support for learning.

When I talked with teachers they recognized what self-correction was and reported that, without realizing it, they had been listening to children self-correcting and using this as a cue indicating progress, or difficulty with texts. Having seen the tutorial value of the child's willingness to struggle to find the error, to try alternatives and to make decisions about how to proceed, I encouraged teachers to give children time to discover their own errors and freedom to work on them, even if this results at times in an apparent messed-up rendering of the text.

The spontaneous corrections of errors presumably stems from an awareness, however vague, that there is always a neat fit between the spoken and printed word. Readers may become conscious of the difference between what they have said and one of the several messages of the text — semantic, syntactic, morphophonemic or graphic. The child, aware that 'something is wrong', may search for a response which resolves the dissonance.

Introduction

The redundancy of language codes enables us to understand messages when they are stripped of semantic or syntactic cues (Cherry, 1957), when they lose phonemic cues (Gimson, 1962), or when they contain errors and ambiguities. Because any work within a sentence fits a matrix of relationships—phonological, morphological, syntactic, semantic and graphic—a mature reader may use cues from one or more of these dimensions along which words differ. The beginning reader, by definition, has limited knowledge that these dimensions exist.

In the research reported below detailed records wre gathered of early reading behavior, at a time when the children were still establishing their movements across print, building their visual images of letter and word forms, and discriminating the units in their own speech that had significance for reading behavior. At this early stage of reading progress children noticed their errors and made efforts to correct them. Bruner's theory of perception as a decision process (1957) provides one framework for the discussion of such error-correction behavior which would pass through stages of cue search, preliminary categorizing, confirming check and final categorization. Bruner (1966) also describes ways of representing reality by action sequences, by ikonic representation in images, and by symbols, and he suggests that when there is conflict between two systems of representing reality the child may search further to resolve the conflict. One is reminded also of Piaget's description of assimilation and accommodation processes by which psychological schemata are differentiated (Lunzer, 1960). Bolinger (1954) presents a description, from a linguist's point of view, of the search for identity in language units occurring at the levels of figure, part-to-whole, and coded comparison among linguistic units ordered hierarchically. Neisser (1963), who made a distinction between multiple and sequential thought processes, showed that visual searching for several cues at the same time is not only possible with adult subjects, but is a highly effective procedure (1964). He states that 'multiple processing exhibits superior ability to deal with novel or irregular input' (1963, p. 1) and that 'mental processes of this kind seem to be common whenever there are situations too complex for ready logical analysis' (1963, p. 2). Linguistic categories are highly irregular, the graphic representation of language is novel for beginning readers and children of this age are, according to Piaget, at a prelogical level of thinking. Is the young child capable of dealing with multiple relationships? Educationists have tended to think that their task was to simplify method and text in order to reduce the dimensions of difference in stimuli.

Some very intricate self-correction behavior sequences occurred in this research. The observations showed that a child who was aware that 'something was wrong,' often went back over the line or tried several responses with the result that an error was frequently corrected. Signs of children's dissatisfaction with their own responses were frequently noted. They stopped, looked puzzled, complained, repeated the line, or ran a finger along a word. An unsuccessful attempt at self-correction can be quoted as an example.

A high progress reader aged 5:6 came to the text *Look after Timothy* and worked at the word *after* in this way:
(1) 'It wouldn't be *at*, it's too long.'
(2) 'It wouldn't be *hats*.'
   (This was semantically appropriate but linguistically awkward.)
(3) 'It wouldn't be *are*, look, it's too long.'
   (This child pointed to *are* elsewhere on the page.)
(4) The problem was not resolved and the child left it.
(5) Three pages further on the word was read correctly.

It is exceptional for the school entrant to be able to state what he is doing in this way, and the verbalised reasons for the decisions of difference may not be the significant ones. In the above example the reasons for dissatisfaction that are verbalised are size and meaning but it should be noted that two of the three trials correctly categorize the stimulus *as a word beginning with 'a' and all three have at least two letters in common*. The focus of this research was this overt self-correction behavior of five-year-old readers. In a perceptual activity, such as reading, search and check behavior may be assumed to occur:
(*a*) with a correct response, no error having occurred;
(*b*) with an error response, no solution having been found;
(*c*) with an error, subsequently corrected.

The error subsequently corrected can be recorded objectively but must represent the observable part of the iceberg. One might expect (*a*) and (*b*) to be related to (*c*) and the presence of self-correction behavior may be diagnostic of processing that is not overtly observable.

Research design

Samples of the reading behavior of 100 children were taken once *each week* during their first year at school (See pp. 8-11, A Longitudinal Study: Research Design)

Results

Error-correction at the Preparatory Stage

In the preparatory period locating behavior (i.e., the child's attempts to find some print to match to the response he was giving) passed through several stages:
(i) from *page matching,* in which the child repeated a memorized text for the page without locating any detail in the print;
(ii) to *line matching* in which the child repeated a memorized line of print, locating that line as a whole;
(iii) to *locating some words* within a memorized line;
(iv) to *'reading the spaces'* and thus coordinating visually located word patterns with speech impulses and the spaces between

words with vocal juncture.

(v) This led to a movement-speech mismatch when there were too few or too many spoken impulses for the number of patterns available, *or* a speech-vision mismatch when a spoken word failed to coincide with its known visual pattern during the coordinating process.

The movement-speech mismatch tended to precede the speech-vision mismatch developmentally. Some quantitative results support this description. (Note that each higher progress group spent less time in the preparatory period than each lower group, Table 1.)

Table 1
Reading Behavior of the Preparatory Stage, Reported for the Median Case of Each Quartile Group of 25 Children.

Quartile Progress Groups	% Self-correction in last 3 records	Weeks to L—R consistency	Weeks in preparatory stage
H	100	7	16
HM	96	12	21
LM	94	20	31
L	64	15	36

(1) Consistent left to right movement across print in three consecutive behavior records was established within seven weeks of school entry for the H group and 15-20 weeks for the LM and L groups. This action sequence was established many weeks prior to promotion to basic reading books (Table 1).

(2) In 90 percent of the behavior records self-correction behavior was recorded at least three weeks *before* the children were promoted to basic reading books (Table 1).

(3) Records showed that 49 percent of the children had passed from fluent inventing of the texts of caption books, to stressing the juncture between words at least three weeks prior to promotion to basic reading books, suggesting that these children had established a one-to-one correspondence between speech impulses separated by stressed vocal juncture and word patterns separated by spaces.

Before promotion to the basic reading books a high proportion of children (*a*) gave evidence of self-correction, (*b*) had established left to right sequencing of movement across print which could lead to a movement-speech mismatch, (*c*) and about half of the children read word by word and might therefore be able to respond to a speech-vision mismatch as a cue to error having occurred.

Table 2

*Reading Behavior at the Book Reading Stage Reported for the
Median Case of Each Quartile Group of 25 Children.*

Quartile Progress Groups	No. of words tallied	Error rate	Self-correction rate	Weeks in book-reading stage
H	2599]	37.29]	2.75	19
HM	1605]	15.20]	3.81]	14
LM	861]	7.86]	8.35]	9
L	114]	2.58]	19.72	3

] Linked quartile groups were significantly different from each other *and* all higher or lower groups at .01 level (Mann-Whitney U-tests).

Error-correction in the Book Reading Stage

(1) There were large differences between progress groups in the amount of reading during the first year at school, each higher progress group being significantly different from each lower group at the .01 level (Table 2).

(2) 10,525 errors were made on the basic reading books. The rates at which children made errors were significantly different for all progress groups at the .01 level. The median H group child made one error in every 37.39 words read, compared with the median child of the L group who made one error in every 2.58 words read.

(3) Spontaneous self-correction of 26 percent of these errors occurred. The H and HM groups corrected one in every three or four errors and were significantly different in this behavior from the LM and L groups where self-correction rates were one in eight and one in 20, respectively.

(4) In a linguistic analysis of substitution errors (7,683 errors) self-correction rates for groups were: L 11 percent, LM 14 percent, HM 28 percent and H 35 percent (Clay, 1968).

(5) The relationship between error rates and self-correction rates is represented diagrammatically in Figure 1, plotted for the median case of each progress group, and an interpretation of the reading behavior is made in the second half of that figure. The low error and high self-correction rate of the H group is thought to result from efficient processing of cues. The higher error and high self-correction of the HM group indicates that efforts are being made to relate cues and resolve inconsistencies but that this process does not operate in an efficient manner. The self-correction rates of the LM group indicate attempts to process cues but because there are so many error

responses correct processing presumably meets with little positive reinforcement. The L group have high error, little self-correction, and fewer responses than the next higher group. Their response pattern has been characterized as low in effort.

(6) One category of error substitution may prove sensitive for revealing reading strategies. The *said Mother* and *Mother said* sequence of words (and similar sequences of the same construction) occurred frequently in the reading books. Self-correction rates for this construction were very high for the two top groups (62 percent and 53 percent) and extremely low for the bottom groups (6 percent and 9 percent). An interpretation of this difference could be that the high groups predicted the occurrence of the construction and were checking at the word or letter level for cues that would confirm whether the words *said* and *Mother* occurred. and in which order. The low progress groups were using the construction as a whole, fitting it into a slot within the sentence without attending to word or letter units, or to word or letter order.

Error-correction and the Linguistic Analysis of Error

A linguistic analysis of the errors is reported elsewhere (Clay, 1968) but three points are particularly relevant in examining the nature of self-correction behavior.

(1) Beginning readers substituted words which were syntactically appropriate for the sentences they were reading in 72 percent of all substitution errors and gave responses that were similar in some aspect of letter-sound relationship in only 43 percent of the errors. It is clear from this that grammatical competence would be a significant source of cues for an error-correction strategy.

(2) Verbs which were substituted in error for other verbs agreed with the text in both number and tense in 55 percent of the occur-rences (which is very different from chance in a 2×2 table), implying some response to contextual constraints.

(3) Nouns had very low rates of self-correction (20 percent) com-pared with the higher rates for pronouns (60 percent) which have to agree with some referent close at hand.

These examples support a view that the child is able to respond to dissonance or consonance in the grammatical and semantic aspects of his language behavior.

Statistical Analysis of Error-correction Behavior

The scores of the Reading Progress Test were normalized but the error and self-correction variables were curvilinear in distribution. Rank correlations and Eta coefficients for the total group, and Eta coefficients for a reduced sample (82 children for whom there were behavior samples of more than 120 responses) were calculated and an attempt was made to construct a three dimensional model of

Figure 1
*Error and Self-correction Ratios: Median Case of Each
Quartile Group. Error ratio reads: 1 error in every X running words.
Self-correction ratio reads: 1 self-correction in every X errors.)*

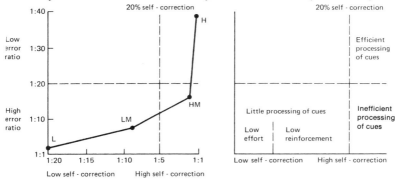

changes in error-rate, self-correction rate and reading progress. The interpretations of Figure 1 are not contradicted by any of these analyses although error rate always shows a higher relationship to reading progress than self-correction. After a certain level of correct responding has been reached self-correction may lose significance as an overt indicator of reading progress in high progress readers whose 'processing' may become covert and prior to responding, rather than overt and subsequent to the first response.

The Eta coefficients for the N = 82 group were 0.75 (error rate x reading score), 0.63 (self-correction rate x reading score) and 0.58 (error rate x self-correction rate).

Discussion

A reader may become conscious of a difference between what he has said and one of the several messages of the text, and experience feelings of dissonance (Festinger, 1958).

(a) The response may not make sense—in the sentence, in the story, or with the pictures. This creates cognitive dissonance.

(b) The response may make sense but something in the print may be incongruous with the response given. This creates perceptual dissonance.

In the first case a child may read, 'Dad, let me paint you,' and exclaim 'Hey! you can't paint YOU!' In the second case the child may read, 'Mother said' for 'Mother asked' and then protest, 'It hasn't got the same letters as "said"' (visual imagery), or 'But it starts with an "a"!' (letter-sound awareness). Berlyne (1960) suggests that a dissonant relation can exist between cognitive elements and an overt action that the subject has already executed or is contemplating. This type of dissonance might be expected in early reading behavior. The young child who learned in his pre-school world to recognize objects from a variety of angles, must learn to approach lines of print consistently from left to right. Movement across a line, and the finger pointing that supports it, are action sequences involved in the beginning reading process. Another action sequence consists of the speech impulses emitted as the child invents or reads a text. Somehow the word unit must be isolated from the flow of speech and matched to a word pattern located in the text, resulting in a sequential coordinating of visual locating and speech impulses.

Self-correction, appearing before children were promoted to their basic reading books, was first seen when the number of locating movements of hand and/or eyes did not match with the number of speech impulses emitted. This forced the child to consider alternative ways of expressing his ideas. Following this primitive need to choose between alternatives the child must develop an awareness that the precise identity of a word allows for no difference between *what makes sense* and *what is said*. This can be checked from grammatical and semantic cues which are available from oral language experience. After the child can coordinate his speech and locating behavior he may learn to visually check whether the word he is looking at really is the word he predicted would occur, but visual discrimination learning appears to take place slowly during the first year. In time, a smooth predict and check procedure may be established operating at the level of word groups but the competent reader would be able to descend to any level of detailed check, if the need arose, to resolve a conflict.

The child who coordinates cues from action, visual and language sources and who has an awareness that identity consists of agreement in all details, has developed a way of learning from his errors. As he searches and checks, more and more detail in the print attracts his attention, and he is possibly sensitized to more of the inter-relationships in language which provide cues and checks. Even H group readers made many errors which gave them plenty of opportunity to develop search and check procedures. But these errors were surrounded with large quantities of correct responding, and the long stretches of context with a full measure of syntactic, semantic, and story sequence cues provided a detailed background to the error when it occurred. The children therefore became progressively better at self-correction. It has been recognized that the proportion of error in reading is important and authorities recommend choosing books which allow the child to read with 95 percent accuracy. A higher error rate apparently blurs the matrix of cues to a greater or lesser extent so that instead of error behavior generating more insights with a progressive gain in skill the activity becomes non-progressive, and the child becomes more confused as the vocabulary load increases.

Will the L progress group arrive at some later point in time at the position of the HM or the H group? Are they merely slower to start? Because the data of this research were pooled observations over the period of one year, this question cannot be answered. Two other possibilities could be suggested. While the H progress children were building adequate images and vertical discrimination nets, the L group were not idle. They were responding with inadequate images and were possibly building erroneous discrimination nets. What research has yet to tell us is whether such initial confusion is a barrier to subsequent efficient processing of cues in reading, or whether, because of some transactional quality, the experiences are stored in such an unstructured form that they present no barrier to later vertical learning. Perhaps among the slow starters we might expect to find both the confused-and-blocked child and the unprogrammed-and-free-to-start-again type child.

The ability to relate information from different sources may favor children of high intelligence and strategies dependent on visual or auditory memory may prove better for children of average intelligence or below. There is no clear answer to this question in these data. The H and HM group are distinguished on progress but have almost identical distributions for intelligence (median IQ 122), while the same is true of the L and LM groups (median IQs 106 and 108). There is a significant difference between the two top groups and the two lower groups on self-correction behavior, however, which does coincide with a difference in median IQ. *Motor, perceptual and language differences would perhaps be of greater significance than general intelligence.* For example, if the coordination of motor and speech responses or of speech and visual behavior is blocked by immaturity of intrasensory pathways (Birch and Lefford, 1966), the advantage of the motor-speech mismatch orienting the beginning reader to choose between alternatives may be lost. If what the child says fails to coincide with what he sees most of the time, his responding must remain confused, approximate and non-progressive. Similarly, children with a poor command of the English language would have difficulty in predicting the constructions likely to occur, in remembering the sequences which do in fact occur, and in noticing the redundant cues which signal that errors have occurred. There is good reason to believe that the very complexity that provides rich cue sources for the child who is able to discover the regularities of the code may present confusion to the child of limited language skill.

Information processing would be given greatest scope if the method of teaching reading (*a*) allowed the child's spontaneous speech to be easily directed to the task, (*b*) stressed flexible and varied word-solving techniques, and (c) encouraged the children to work at their errors. The interpretations in Figure 1 would suggest that when there is little reading skill, teaching effort must be directed to stimulating interest which will produce a high level of responding. Then, until the child has discovered some regularities in print close observation and regular appropriate reinforcement of tentative responses would be necessary. As the information processing gained in strength the reinforcement would come from the task itself as dissonance was resolved. Behind the group making high progress was the HM group whose predictions were not sufficiently accurate and who needed specific instruction to raise the occurrence of correct categorizing of responses.

With regard to reading texts there is a critical distinction between claims that the most readily distinguished signals (a) differ in many respects, or (b) differ in only one attribute. Words in sentence structures which mirror the syntactic and semantic forms of the language which the child speaks fluently will increase the child's opportunities to detect errors and develop error-correcting strategies.

However simple the text, any learning process which is as complex as reading presents opportunities for missing links, weak links, devious routes where more facilitating ones could be taken, and contrasts between high skills which the child prefers to use and weak skills which he tries to avoid. There is scope in reading for much error-behavior and a good defense against this would be strong error-correcting strategies applied to texts rich in cue sources. That these strategies could be developed by the young child still in a stage of intuitive rather than logical thinking seems best explained in terms of Neisser's concept of multiple thought processes which he considers particularly appropriate for dealing with novel, irregular stimuli too complex for logical sequential thinking. It was one of the observations in the original research report that as children responded they gradually became aware of what they were doing. This would suggest that by responding intuitively to complex and irregular stimuli the children gradually become aware of some of the dimensions of those stimuli and perhaps become able to employ sequential analysis at a conscious level.

Acknowledgement. — This report arises from a Ph.D. investigation carried out under the supervision of Professor Winterbourn, University of Auckland, whose encouragement and guidance are gratefully acknowledged.

6 The Reading Behavior of Children in Standard One

Bryan Williams and Marie M. Clay

It was time to move to an older age group. Children in their third year of instruction were studied by one of my research students. The average age of the children was 7:10. A record was made of all observable behavior as the children read five graded passages: words correct and words incorrect, pausing, omitting or inserting or substituting words, ignoring punctuation, self-correction and repetition, attacking words, whispering, lip movement, finger pointing, and appeals for help and refusals. The techniques derived in the study of beginning readers proved equally appropriate for the older children. This, in itself, was interesting.

When learning to read is thought of as accumulating items of knowledge, a teacher aims to increase a child's sight vocabulary, his letter-sound knowledge, his skills in syllabic attack. There is an implied hope that better methods or smaller classes or a new set of reading books will increase the rate at which these skills accumulate and our reading problems will diminish. Perhaps if we thought about reading progress in a different way we might simplify our task and change our objectives.

In the past decade there has been an energetic search for more understanding of the reading process, with a new emphasis on observing exactly what children are doing rather than assuming that we know what they are doing. (We do not yet have many research accounts of what teachers are saying and doing, which is equally important.) New Zealand adopted a new approach to beginning reading a decade ago (Simpson, 1962). The changes stemmed in part from sensitive observation by classroom teachers who reported their criticisms of an earlier, imported program for beginning reading. From those discussions with teachers Simpson piloted and produced an interesting set of reading books and some novel suggestions about methods of teaching reading. Reports of what children actually do as they read have been published in Scotland, Canada and U.S.A, and New Zealand research studies have recorded the reading behavior of school entrants and of Standard 1 children taught under Simpson's reading scheme.

There is good research evidence to suggest that one hundred

school entrants taught by these methods and tested in Auckland in 1963-4 had, at the end of their first year of instruction, settled into a pattern of progress which shifted very little in follow-up studies, after two, three, four and five years of instruction. Such evidence has placed an important emphasis on the sensitive observation of first-year reading progress and on the additional need to cast a diagnostic net over children at their sixth birthday. Re-teaching programs devised at that stage for those whose progress is already observed to be off-course would help to reduce the incidence of reading failure.

But drastic things happen in individual lives, like sickness and tragedy, which may cause a slowing up of progress in older children. And New Zealand has a highly mobile population whose children change schools frequently. One does not have to suppose that a previous school was lax in its teaching standards to account for the drop in a child's performance when he changes school. The fact that programs differ, and that a new teacher takes getting used to before one understands her expectations, is enough to account for a drop in academic performance. Add to this a flow of newcomers to all classes of our school system from outside New Zealand and it is easy to see that, while a diagnostic survey at six years is essential, individual attention must still be paid to some children higher up in the school.

A new concept of learning to read is suggested by local and overseas research and is supported by research evidence of New Zealand children in their third year of school. If we could train the child to operate in such a way that every time he encountered a difficulty he learnt something new about reading, then he would tend to improve his own skill every time he read. The goal for reading instruction might then be thought of as creating a 'self-improving system'. A research study by Bryan Williams of Standard 1 children provides strong evidence to support this.

Who Were the Children?

The children studied attended six city schools in Auckland, two from each of high, middle and lower income areas. Every second child on the class roll was included (fifty-seven boys and sixty-three girls). The average age of the children at the end of the second term was 7 years 10 months and their general ability was average (mean IQ on the Peabody Picture Vocabulary Test was 102). Children were excluded if they were enrolled for speech therapy, if they had medical reports of hearing or eyesight problems, or if English was not the main language of their homes.

How Were They Studied?

The children's behavior was recorded as they read five graded passages. Human kindness and scientific needs were in conflict over whether all the children should be made to struggle with all five graded passages, and science lost out. When a child took more than five minutes to read a passage the task was discontinued. Therefore, some children read more than others, and they read more difficult material than others. However, the task did resemble the natural situation in which a child reads to a teacher who is paying particular attention to what he says and does. The behavior reported is close to what would be found under classroom conditions when materials have been matched to the different learning levels of the children.

A record was made of *all* observable behavior: words correct and words incorrect, pausing or omitting or inserting or substituting words, ignoring punctuation, self-correction and repetition, attacking words, whispering, lip-movement, finger-pointing, appeals for help and refusals. This behavior was recorded as the child read. (It can be done but it takes practice.) A check on the observer's recording was made using a tape-recording, and satisfactory reliability was achieved. This approach, first used with beginning readers, proved equally appropriate for seven-year-olds.

From the analysis of these records the children were divided into three groups. The High Accuracy group (H) made fewer than 5 errors in every 100 words. The Average Accuracy group (Av) made from 5-10 errors in every 100 words and the Low Accuracy group made more than 10 errors in every 100 words read.

These records of reading behavior were analyzed in several different ways.

The Importance of Language Structure

Almost all errors (90%) were single words that were omitted, inserted or substituted. Clay (1968) reported that 50% of error behavior of five- to six-year-olds occurred in sequences where whole stretches of text were substituted. Her children were taught by the same methods in the same city. Between the first and third year of instruction the children seemed to have shifted their focus from stretches of the language to the word as the significant reading unit.

More often than not the substituted word had the same grammatical function as the text word (a noun for a noun, or a verb for a verb). It was as if the child could predict the kind of word that was likely to come next in the English language. Such matching was easier for some parts of speech (like verbs) than it was for others (like adjectives), and one can guess that the predictability or unexpectedness of the text would affect this.

The possibility that cues from the structure of the language was explored further.

Suppose the sentence was:
The boy wrote the letter.
Was the error sentence acceptable English?
The boy read the letter.
Was it acceptable up to and including the error?
The boy goes . . .
Was it acceptable with the following text?
. . . wants the letter.
Or was it unacceptable English?
The boy writed the letter.
A high percentage of the substitutions made by seven-year-olds were of the first and second kind, wholly or partially fitting into the sentence up to that point, and the better the reader the more likely this was to be true (H 80%, Av 70%, L 62%). Similar results have been reported for younger children by Clay, and for older children by Goodman, who claims that good readers use a strong intuitive control over syntax when they read. Perhaps this is like looking up a dictionary of all possible words by first finding the part of speech needed. This would limit the range of words from which one had to make further selection. The more able readers were more responsive to this kind of cue.

Children whose control of oral language patterns is limited or whose experience with book language has been minimal will probably be less able to predict the language patterns of their reading books.

The Importance of Retaining Meaning

Substitutions may retain the *meaning* of the text wholly or in part. For the sentence:
The girl wrote to Santa Claus
the full meaning is retained in
The girl wrote to Father Christmas
but is only partially retained in
The girl writes to Santa Claus
because the idea of 'action in the past' has been lost. In this kind of analysis the better Standard 1 readers had retained meaning most often (H 80%, Av 65%, L 54%). Readers with low accuracy were more likely to produce an acceptable English sentence structure than to retain the meaning of the sentence.

Using Letter Cues

The analysis of words wrongly read showed that the readers kept some of the larger context of structure and meaning. What relation did the errors have to smaller elements of the word, like letter-sound relationships? There are many different ways in which an error may correspond visually to the text but it is possible to judge whether the errors and text have similar letters, letter clusters, or syllables, and similar beginnings, endings or other combinations of location points. Do the errors that Standard 1 children make reflect their attention to visual cues? Yes, they do, whatever their level of progress, as there was no marked difference between groups (H 83%, Av 91%, L 85%).

The correct order of letters was preserved in most single-word errors (86%). Reversal of letter order was rare. The beginning of a word was most likely to be correct (80%), the end of the word was correct in half of the substitutions (53%) and less accuracy was achieved with the middle of words. These findings suggest that attention went first to the left end of a word, with a quick visual sweep through the word to the ending, and attention was given to the middle only if more detail was still required. This was true for high accuracy readers as well as for low accuracy readers, and it is what has usually been reported in overseas research studies.

Word-solving

But what of word attack? This was called 'word-solving' and was defined as audible analysis of a word, or long delay followed by a correct response, or self-correction following an error, or repetition.

The audible analysis of words into sounds (sl-a-sh-ed) or syllables (sur-faced) was found for only 5½% of all instances of successful attack. A further 6% of responses involved a delay which might have been 'private solving', making 11½% of successful solving.

On the other hand almost half of the word-solving was achieved by self-correction. An error was made but the child solved the problem at a second or third attempt without prompting or help. If the error sentence was sensible and acceptable English, there was less likelihood of the error being corrected. The importance of this kind of word-solving is emphasized by the high rates at which it occurred. The High group corrected one error in three, the Average group one in four, and the Low group one in eight. From this error-detecting and correcting behavior the child learns how to search, how to use cues and how to check on his responses. Self-correction emerges in the beginning reading stage, has some continuing advantage in this third year of instruction, has been reported for fluent readers in their fifth year of instruction, and can be observed in adults who are asked to read aloud from a difficult text. (Try a science text full of new concepts, or a smudgy carbon copy).

The easy flow of reading is also interrupted when a child repeats a word which he has already read correctly. This kind of 'error' or non-fluency occurred almost as often as self-correction in nearly 40% of all successful attacks. Why? One can only guess. Perhaps the child was unsure of the word or its relation to other words. He may have expected something different. It may have sounded wrong. It may have looked wrong. Each assumption implies that the child who read correctly and repeated the same word was checking something and he was more likely to be checking back than ahead.

What Do These Analyses Imply?

Half the Standard 1 children in this study were very good oral readers of graded texts. They read accurately, solved new or difficult words, and corrected their errors. They used their knowledge of the English language as a guide to the choice of what types of words could occur, they used meaning cues and they used letter-sound relationships in association with other cues without audible analysis of words. Most errors had a high degree of agreement with the meaning and visual cues of the text word.

Have these good readers learnt a phonic repertoire? a sight vocabulary? a set of skills like 'word attack' or 'reading for meaning'? Or is it more likely that these children apply to the reading task operations and strategies which relate cues from different sources and ensure an ever-increasing control over more and more difficult texts? When a correct response is found it fits all the sources of cues like the last piece in a jig-saw puzzle. This is positively reinforcing. Successful decoding creates its own positive feedback. The capacity to convert a difficulty into an opportunity to master some new operation should make the system self-improving.

The poor readers in this study were reading easier material with lower accuracy. They used visual cues or letter-sound relationships as much as good readers but they frequently neglected cues given by structure or meaning. Imlach (1968) also found this focusing on detail in poor Standard 1 readers. At points of difficulty they depended too much on the letters of a word. One could guess that, not having several courses of cues to converge on the correct response, they do not have an adequate signal to tell them when they are right or wrong and so their reading behavior does not become self-improving. The surprising thing was the degree to which this unprofitable behavior persisted. In spite of its lack of success it did not disappear.

What adjustments are normally made for slow reading groups in school? One modification to a program is to give them easier reading books, which should reduce the error rate and so enable the child to have longer stretches of correct context to support his attempts at a few difficult words. That would be good practice in terms of the results reported above. But remedial programs also tend to focus the child on exercises which draw attention to the elements of words, word attack and sounding out. It is assumed that this is the means by which people do read, the way children learn to read, and the way failing children need to re-learn to read. None of those assumptions is necessarily true. Programs for slow readers are not known for their high success rates in any country, and remedial programs which have good results in treatment often have rapid loss of skill after treatment. Could we be directing the poor readers' attention away from the behaviors that would bring about the most rapid improvement of their reading? Identification of letters is important but not sufficient.

Conclusion

Illiterate five-year-olds become literate seven-year-olds despite a cognitive immaturity, a limited control over language and inefficient visual scanning and perception skills. Compared with adults, both five- and seven-year-olds have rather primitive strategies for learning. But some children learn in ways which lead cumulatively to control over reading and some do not. Good readers seem to teach themselves by search and check procedures using the main sweep of context as a primary source of cues. This is the very source of cues that the poor reader neglects. It seems that the strategies for discovering, sorting, selecting, and particularly checking on cues play a central role in the continuing improvement of reading.

It is important to observe, record and consider the actual reading behavior of poor readers in Standard 1. Correction should be directed initially to sentence structure ('Read the punctuation' and 'Listen: can you say it that way?'). Children with poor oral language patterns will find this a weak source of cues. A grasp of the syntactical patterns of oral English is vital and teachers need to develop oral language so that children will be able to develop this sense of incongruity, this feeling that something's awry. Attention must be paid to meaning, phrase by phrase ('Is that right?' 'Does that sound sensible?'), and then to the meaning of the whole sentence so far. (The comprehension of the completed sentence or the paragraph may receive less stress.) The child must be helped to use these two sources of cues from structure and from meaning along with his visual awareness of letters, bearing in mind that it is an agreement of cues that confirms a good response and the incongruity of cues which signals that more searching and checking is necessary. Repetition is an active and helpful strategy in attacking, checking and correcting, which teachers should recognize as valuable. 'How to make the cues agree' rather than 'How to sound out a word' would be an important goal for a Standard 1 child in improving his reading.

7 Juncture, Pitch and Stress as Reading Behavior Variables

Robert H. Imlach and Marie M. Clay

The initial study with five-year-olds had provided us with a set of behaviors which could be observed but there was no reason to assume that there might not be other behaviors which would reveal important aspects of the reading process, particularly in older children. One of my research students had studied descriptive linguistics and felt able to try to describe the ways in which readers used pausing, stressing and pitch variation in their reading. The next study represents this search for further observable behaviors and the outcomes may be represented by the comments of Gibson and Levin (1975). In the study it was concluded:

> *One is tempted to suggest that the best readers can work through a sequence of possibilities guided by the story, intersentence, and sentence cues, and can drop to the levels of phrase, word and letter possibilities if necessary, whereas the other groups work at best on the two- and three-word phrase and more usually at the word, syllable and letter level. (Imlach & Clay, 1971, 138-9).*

Gibson and Levin (1975) commented: 'This description of skilled reading fits well with our own conception'. (p. 107)
They went on to say:

> *... we took up the suprasegmental variables, juncture, pitch and stress because we believe that these provide guides to the analysis of oral reading skills and to the yet-to-be-researched stylistic differences between speech and oral reading. (p. 108)*

When reading is defined as the sequential decoding of print the activity involves complex perceptual and cognitive processing (Bruner, 1957a, b), constructive thinking (Neisser, 1967), and discrimination responses (Fellows, 1968). The educator's measures of progress (such as word recognition skill and accuracy in answering comprehension questions) have been of little value in clarifying either the organization of reading behavior between stimulus and response or the shifts in that organization that occur according to the length of exposure to instruction or the changing cognitive capacities of children aged 5-7 years (White, 1965). Currently there is an interest in better theoretical models of the reading process, whether in its figurative and perceptual aspects (Elkind, 1969), in its linguistic aspects (Goodman, 1969;

Ryan & Semmel, 1969), or in the relationship of success to failure (Wiener & Cromer, 1968).

Reports by the first author (Clay, 1966, 1968, 1969, 1970) on the variables of self-correction behavior, error behavior, and response to disoriented print have supported an information-processing model of reading behavior and differences found between quartile progress groups could be interpreted as differences in the sequential processing of cues rather than differences in the number of forms (words or letters) known. A further interpretation consistent with the data from these studies was that reading behavior becomes patterned close to the onset of instruction in ways that are determined by the visual and linguistic qualities of the texts, the emphases of the teacher and her method, and the developmental status of the pupil in visual, linguistic, and cognitive areas. This organization of behavior may change kaleidoscopically as new processing hierarchies of behavior are constructed, in which case lack of progress would be more serious than mere failure to accumulate items of sight vocabulary or phoneme-grapheme associations. Poor progress in reading could be interpreted as failure to structure a very complex set of response hierarchies.

The present study sought further evidence of such differential patterning of reading behavior by the analysis of three linguistic variables, juncture, pitch, and stress. One might expect these variables to carry significant signals of underlying processing (Lieberman, 1967; Lefevre, 1964), but the authors found no research relating them to reading behavior. The focus of this study was the vocal output (or read-out) phase of oral reading in children aged 7.5 years who had received instruction in reading for 2.5 years. Between stimulus and response, complex operations of visual scanning, perception, and cognitive processing of language cues would occur and if differences could be described in the output behavior they might point to some hypotheses about the organization of this sequential behavior.

Methods

Subjects

The sample of 103 children from one large urban school was representative of the Auckland urban area in parent occupation (N.Z. Census, 1961) and the ratio of 57 boys to 46 girls was not significantly different from the sex distribution in New Zealand schools. Four classes of the same level (Standard 1) were used and the method of instruction, which was prescribed by the Department of Education, was different for children who were at different levels of progress. The average chronological age at midyear (1 June 1966) was 7 years 7 months (*SD* 4.4 months), and the average time at school was 2 years 7 months. There were 14 boys and 7 girls over 8 years and 1 boy and 4 girls below 7 years. The mean reading age was 7.53 years (*SD* 1.5 years), close to that expected for the mean age of the group, and a little below the mean of another Auckland research sample from nine schools obtained by Williams (1968) of 7.98 (*SD* 1.4 years). Only 12 of the 103 children came from homes where English was not the mother tongue.

Test Material

Each child read from four standard selections taken from story books (Imlach, 1968). Text samples were taken from *Nobody Listens to Andrew* by E. Guilfoile, *Greg's Microscope* by M. Selsame, *A Lion in the Meadow* by M. Mahy, and *Building a New House* by G. R. Gilbert. An analysis of the texts was made because the authors believed that the characteristics of the stimulus must affect the sequential decoding activity, and that this variable is not given sufficient attention in reading research. The analysis showed that differences existed between passages, as shown in Table 1. Running words and number of different words increased from Story 1 to Story 4. Number of sentences was not a good indication of increasing difficulty but the sentence structure showed a gradient of increasing complexity from repetitions of the same question and answer form in Story 1, to short, simple sentences in Story 2, to a variety of sentence types in Story 3, to sentences with subordination, qualification, and apposite structures in Story 4. The average length of sentence increased from passage to passage. A change was noted in the direct speech constructions: Story 1 gave the dialog-carrier first; Story 2

Table 1
Textual Description of the Four Stories

	Story 1	Story 2	Story 3	Story 4	Total
Words					
Running words	176	160	352	219	997
Different words	64	80	115	122	282
Content words	48	65	82	88	225
Function words	16	15	33	34	57
Words pre punctuation point	3.8	4.4	6.0	5.7	5.0
Words per line	3.8	4.4	7.1	8.1	5.7
Sentences					
Average length in words	5.4	6.4	8.9	9.5	7.5
Number of sentences	29	25	42	23	119
Structural features	Repetitive	Simple	Variety	Complex	

reversed the order; Story 3 used both forms; and Story 4 had some speeches where the speakers were not identified. If a child has to anticipate what type of construction is likely to come next (Clay, 1968), such features could increase the difficulty of his task. The number of characters in the story and features of format (like sentences beginning on new lines and indentation of, new speeches) were other factors which were simplified in the first two stories and complicated in the last two stories. Illustrations were not used. Each of these variables could have effects on oral reading fluency.

The first story was easy and the last was sufficiently difficult for the best children to show the full range of their skills. These passages were graded for difficulty by five teachers, none of whom disagreed with the selected order of difficulty. The passages were all typewritten with the style and setting of the original books retained.

The Linguistic Variables

Descriptive linguistics describes the sound systems of languages, including the suprasegmental variables of juncture, pitch, and stress. The present study has a narrower frame of reference. It describes the occurrence of those features in the oral reading behavior of seven-year-old children. Although the study of reading behavior does not fit neatly into the field of speech behavior studies in descriptive linguistics, definitions and criteria from linguistics were thought to closely approximate the needs of this research.

Juncture

Closed juncture is that characteristic pause by which a sentence or segment of speech is finalized and is usually signified in written language by a full stop or question mark. Open juncture is much shorter and occurs between and within words (Hill, 1958, pp. 22-24; Gleason, 1961). In this research, juncture was used to describe a pause in the continuous flow of oral reading and the degree of analysis did not include juncture which is the break between sounds within a word. The categories of juncture were defined as follows: (1) A very brief pause, longer than that normal space between the sounds within a word, was labeled J1. (2) A slightly longer pause, labeled J2, was often represented in written language by a comma, or occurred at the end of a sentence if the reading was very soft and very fluent. It also occurred in reading at the end of direct speech which was followed by a dialog-carrier like 'said mother.' (3) The pause normally occurring in careful speech at the end of a sentence, where it signified the completion of the utterance, was labeled J3. Hesitations in reading which were over 2 sec in length were also included in the J3 category. (It is now seen as cause for regret that the J3 indicating 'end of utterance' was not categorized separately from J3 caused by uncertainty in reading.)

There were 178 pauses signaled by fullstops and commas in the four Story passages and this punctuation count was called the Standard Juncture Score. The pauses made by a child in his reading were his Raw Juncture Score which could be more or less than the Standard Juncture Score. Where he made more stops than punctuation indicated, he had not read with the fluency that the text demanded. Where he made fewer stops than he should have, he had not transmitted voice signals for some commas and fullstops. The Corrected Juncture Score (Raw Juncture minus Standard Juncture) was a positive number for those children who made more stops than they should have done, and a negative score for those who did not make the required number of stops. The Standard Juncture Score varied from child to child depending on how far he read in the time allowed. Corrected Juncture Scores yielded moderately high rank-order correlations with the Burt Word Reading Test scores (r = .74) and with reading accuracy on the Four Stories (r = .75).

Pitch

Pitch refers to the rising and falling tone of the speaker or reader. Linguistics has used several different notations for recording pitch but in this study a graphic system showed the pitch level as horizontal lines placed above the printed line at four heights. These graphic positions can be labeled, Low, Mid, High, and Extra High.

The criteria used for allocating pitch levels were those described by Gleason (1961, p. 46):

The normal pitch of the voice of the speaker is /2/ called *mid*. It varied, of course, from speaker to speaker. Moreover, most people raise the pitch somewhat when they are speaking more loudly, and at various other times. Pitch /2/ is relatively common and serves as a standard comparison for others. Pitch 1, called *low*, is somewhat lower, perhaps two or three notes below /2/, but the interval will vary from speaker to speaker and from time to time. Pitch /3/, called *high*, is about as much higher than /2/, as /2/ is above /1/. Pitch /4/, called *extra high*, is higher than /3/ by about the same amount; or maybe somewhat higher. Pitch /4/ is much less frequent than the other three.

Tape recordings could be replayed for children who were quick or quiet readers to enable the scorer to pick up the variations in pitch.

Stress

A simple definition of stress as loudness (Hill, 1958), although not a precise definition of stress, was considered adequate for this research. Primary, secondary, tertiary, and weak levels of stress were marked by the symbols /╱, ∧, ╲, ‿/. Because oral reading is sequential and continuous, the stress patterns were lighter than they would have been for single words and sometimes they were very weak indeed.

Stress in oral reading is closer to oral language usage than it is to dictionary stress and frequently it is lighter.

Procedure

The passages were read aloud by each child, recorded on tape, and timed. The instructions were: 'I want you to read some stories for me. Read them as well as you can.' The test booklet of typed passages was opened, the title of Story 1 was pointed to and read slowly by the experimenter: 'The first story is "Nobody Listens to Andrew". Go ahead.' The children read for 10 minutes or until they had finished the Four Stories. This relieved the poor readers of the hurdle of reading the difficult passages. Children were prompted after a 3-second pause at a word. Taped records were replayed to obtain four sets of scores— accuracy rate, juncture, pitch, and stress. A reading score of the number of *words read correctly per minute* had a mean of 47.0 (*SD* 35.9). At this level of reading attainment after 2.5 years of reading instruction the accuracy plus speed score was considered necessary for discriminating between inferior and superior readers, although it was recognized that at some point beyond this level speed would cease to be an indicator of good oral reading. From these accuracy-plus-speed scores the children were allocated to four quartile groups called High (H), High-Middle (HM), Low-Middle (LM), and Low (L).

Data Analysis

As the child read, the experimenter recorded errors in full and the time in seconds. For analysis of the linguistic variables according to the criteria and categories listed above, tape-recordings were replayed as often as necessary, first to mark pausing, then pitch, and finally stress on the original behavior protocol of error and accuracy. The second author completed all the analyses and no statistical checks were made on the reliability of his categorizing. As both authors had received training in this aspect of descriptive linguistics they assumed the psychological reality of the phenomena, but if study of these variables were taken beyond the exploratory stage of this research it would be essential to establish that the behavior could be reliably categorized by persons of appropriate and equivalent training or experience.

Results

Accuracy and Error

The total sample of reading behavior was large (49,547 running words) and predominantly correct (44,804 words). As can be seen in Table 2, the quantity of reading and the speed/accuracy scores fell from High to Low groups, and the median error rate per 100 words increased markedly (Table 2). These quantitative data showed differences between groups in the level of reading efficiency without indicating any qualitative differences.

Table 2
The Quantity and Accuracy of Reading[a]

	Reading group			
	H	HM	LM	L
Median age: (years)	7.6	7.5	7.8	7.7
Running words	907.0	492.0	309.5	212.0
Correct words per minute	100.0	46.0	25.0	14.0
Number of errors	9.5	35.0	49.5	72.0
Error rate per 100 words	.9	7.1	12.7	33.9

[a] All scores are medians.

Juncture

The mean number of words read between pauses was 4.3 but the behavior varied greatly (*SD* 5.9). Results are reported in Table 3.

Table 3
The Variables of Pausing or Juncture[a]

	Reading group			
	H	HM	LM	L
Running words	907.0	492.0	309.5	212.0
Corrected juncture[b]	–59.0	+56.0	+68.0	+103.0
Words per juncture (average)	7.4	3.0	2.1	1.3
At punctuation (%)	75.9	57.1	47.5	41.6
Not at punctuation (%)	23.9	42.8	52.4	58.3
J1 (very brief)	104.5	113.5	84.5	63.5
J2 (mid)	11.5	36.5	47.5	67.5
J3 (long)	.5	6.5	21.5	23.0

[a] Except for percentages, all scores are medians.
[b] Corrected juncture is the number of pauses made by the child minus the number of punctuation points in the text he read.

The H group paused at punctuation but not at all punctuation (the median Corrected Juncture Score was –59). They used short rather than long pauses and read 7.4 words between pauses. Conversely, the

L group had many more pauses than the punctuation signaled (the median Corrected Juncture Score was + 103). They used long pauses frequently and read only 1.3 wors between pauses. These differences occurred despite the fact that the H group was readng more of the texts and more difficult texts than the L group in the 10 minutes allowed. The children in the HM and LM groups followed these trends that distinguish the H and L groups.

Pitch

As shown in Table 4A, the H group read confidently with appropriate pitch behavior for punctuated segments and little pitch movement that was not at punctuation. All other groups used a rising pitch or a sustained pitch proportionately more often than the H group at punctuation marks, as if they expected their sentences to be unfinished. When juncture was not at punctuation, sustained pitch was usually appropriate. While H group scores were low on this variable HM, LM, and L groups had a high incidence of inappropriate behavior.

Table 4
The Variable of Pitch: Type, Spread, and Change[a]

	Reading group			
	H	HM	LM	L
A. Pitch movement prior to juncture				
Juncture at punctuation				
Falling	61.5	47.5	36.0	26.0
Sustained	20.0	24.5	13.5	20.5
Rising	9.0	19.5	18.5	16.0
Juncture not at punctuation				
Falling	5.5	14.0	13.5	6.0
Sustained	7.5	26.5	36.5	37.5
Rising	7.0	20.0	26.0	30.5
B. Pitch change after fullstop				
Up 2	8.0	3.0	—	—
Up 1	40.0	36.5	14.0	7.0
Same	54.5	95.5	89.0	102.5
Down 1	3.5	4.0	4.0	7.0
C. Spread of pitch				
Extra high 4	8.0	—	—	—
High 3	63.0	55.5	30.5	13.5
Mid 2	41.0	39.0	34.5	30.0
Low 1	1.5	—	—	—

[a] Medians are for each group per category.

Pitch movements from the end of one sentence to the beginning of another were classified as moving Up 2, Up 1, or Down 1. Changes in pitch were surprisingly slight in all groups, mostly in the Up 1 and Same Pitch categories. These data are shown in Table 4B. As sentences usually end with a falling pitch the next word tends to have a higher pitch and the importance of the Up 1 category is clear. It was used often by the H and HM groups but not by the LM and L groups. The Same Pitch category is the highest for every group but the reason for its size differs from group to group. For the fastest readers the flattening of pitch was probably a function of the speed of their reading, as the faster the rate of reading the more even the pitch became. The L group who also had a high Same Pitch score read slowly in a monotone.

A few H group children used a wide variety of pitch but this was exceptional rather than usual, as is shown in Table 4C. When an analysis of pitch movements took type of juncture into account the pattern changed little.

The pitch pattern used for punctuated segments and the change of pitch following a fullstop were found to be two variables which showed differences between reading progress groups.

Stress

The results of the stress analysis are given in Table 5. In this continuous prose reading task the contours of intonation tended to be flattened. Heavy or primary stress did not occur very frequently; weak stress was low for HM, LM, and L groups, but high in the good readers.

The behavior of the H group on stress was very different from the other groups. They stressed one word in every 4.7 words, which was appropriate behavior for phrasing within sentences. The HM group had one stress for every 1.2 words, but the lower 50% of children were reading with a pause between almost every word and often with more than one stress per word (1.1 per word). There is a similarity between such behavior and the reading of words in a list, where the words tend to be heavily stressed. Children in the LM group read faster than the L group, but still with syllable and word-by-word stress. The HM group was only slightly more sparing with heavier stresses.

Summary

The variable of juncture or pausing was correlated with reading ability. The children who made few pauses were found to be the best readers. On the average, they read 7 words between pauses, compared with 1.3 words for the poor readers. The best readers paused briefly while the poorest readers used the longer pause categories most often. The best readers completed a sentence with a fall in pitch but the poorer reader was more likely to use a rising or sustained pitch,

Table 5
The Variable of Stress

	Reading group			
	H	HM	LM	L
Totals for:				
Primary stress	63	50	119	21
Secondary stress	2,556	5,053	4,503	3,432
Tertiary stress	2,240	6,078	4,644	3,258
Weak stress	17,838	2,210	973	769
Proportions: stress/words read				
Primary stress	.00	.00	.01	.00
Secondary stress	.11	.37	.55	.61
Tertiary stress	.09	.45	.58	.58
Weak stress	.79	.16	.12	.15
Words read	22,697	13,491	8,146	5,624
Words or syllables stressed (omitting weak)	4,859	11,181	9,271	6,711
Words per stress	4.7	1.2	.9	.8

implying uncertainty. The best readers read 4.7 words per stress and there was a sharp drop to the HM group who used 1.2 words per stress and to LM and L who used 1.1 *stresses per word* as if reading a list of words.

Discussion

The H group with 1% of error retained the rich context of syntactic and semantic cues. They gained in speed by reduction of pause and stress time, yet as a group they showed the greatest range of variation in pitch, in that some H children were the only users of the extra high category. The incidence of weak stress may indicate that they were ready for the transition to 'silent' reading. There can be little doubt that this group was reading out the processed message in syntactic chunks, and their frequent disregard for punctuation signals suggests that, in addition to phrase and sequence chunks, they were also looking for cues and processing them at the discourse or intersentence level. The median score for the L group was 140 correct words and 72 errors. Such error rates would destroy contextual cues and leave the child reading a "string of words." Each of the juncture, pitch, and stress analyses supports this interpretation for the L group.

Two explanations of these differences are possible. The lower groups may have acquired a word-by-word or phrase-by-phrase habit, with sustained or rising pitch so that the motor task of saying the words was pacing the reading. Alternatively these groups may have failed to establish contextual anticipation, an ability to predict ahead, that would enable them to gain in processing time and increase the reading span by sensing what linguistic construction might occur and what semantic items might fill it. These suggestions may both be true, for if contextual anticipation is not fostered word-by-word habits could well be consequent learning. (Attention is drawn particularly to the differences between the top two groups in these respects because it could be argued that the behavior of the lower groups probably results from the cumulative effects of many handicapping behaviors, including lack of language facility.)

The consistency with which the three different suprasegmental variables studied in this research were related to the reading of connected prose suggests to the investigators that the psychological processes are complex, rather than simple. It seems likely that the suprasegemental variables indicate something about the organization of the response repertoire of the reader. One is tempted to suggest that the best readers can work through a sequence of possibilities guided by story, intersentence, and sentence cues, and can drop to the levels of phrase, word, and letter probabilities if necessary, whereas the other groups work at best on the two- and three-word phrase and more usually at the word, syllable, and letter level.

It is not our claim that letter and word discrimination are not significant in the progressive accumulation of reading skill but that for fast accurate sequential decoding of texts a hierarchy of reading responses places the linguistic cues from large stretches of structure and meaning in the most facilitating position, or top gear as it were, with the other levels of cues available if there is a need to drop gear.

The results of this research point to a clear relationship between large language chunks, reduced processing time, and increased accuracy on the one hand and language detail, increased processing time, and decreased accuracy on the other, but they do not explain the nature of that relationship.

8   An Increasing Effect of Disorientation on the Discriminaton of Print: A Developmental Study

It is interesting to remember where a research question arises. This study, which teachers may feel they can pass over, began when I watched my daughter, in her first year at school, practicing her 'words' from a tin which contained those written for her by the teacher on separate cards. Fascinated with what I saw, and not convinced I was getting it right, I asked her to repeat the exercise. What I noticed was that she read the words just as well upside down as right way up. Unwilling to accept an obvious rationale that at this early stage of learning to read she was particularly competent, I explored this further with a range of children and found beginning readers less disturbed by disoriented print than older readers. These first exploratory steps into a research hypothesis developed into an experiment which was repeated on the same children at 5:6, 6:0, 7:0 and 8:0 to capture change over time, and using the easiest words in their first reading books printed in normal, reversed and inverted print.

In the reversed and inverted orientation conditions, children who were normally competent readers stumbled, paused for long periods, offered no response as if nonplussed, squinted at the words, backed away from the print, and tried to apply some strategy for unravelling the words that were easily read in normal orientation. The cues that good readers commonly used to identify words and discriminate one response from another appeared to be seriously disrupted by changed orientation, particularly in the reversed condition. In contrast, and perhaps remarkably, very little of this concern was shown by poor readers.

Attentional expectations, perceptual scanning, or search-and-check strategies have some explanatory relation to the results. It is reasonable to suggest that strategies change throughout the 3-year period.

This study comes close to the metatheoretical issues of my initial question. Does behavior become organized in different ways? If so, can different types of organization be characterized as self-improving and others as self-limiting? Reading instruction regularly produces its failures. We blame the type of programs, the educational system, the

material resources, or the children; but almost never do we attribute
the result to the sequence of instruction itself creating in the particu-
lar child a set of behaviors that are self-limiting rather than self-
extending.

The author observed that beginning readers seemed to be less disturbed over reading word cards upside down than older readers.
Adults report multiple-letter displays in a manner which suggests that
learning to read English creates perceptual scanning or serial organization habits which induce the perception of printed stimuli from left
to right (Howard & Templeton, 1966; Bryden, 1966; Harcum, 1966).
Spong (1962) found left-to-right reporting of square, four-letter displays at the age of 6:6 in children who began reading at 5:0 and made
good progress but not in children who were retarded readers. Elkind
and Weiss (1967) showed the left-to-right survey habit to be dominant
in first graders who explored a triangular arrangement of pictures
from left to right rather than in triangular order. Retarded readers in
that study continued to report the pictures from left to right in the
second grade after the average progress readers had given up that
practice.

A related issue is whether poor readers read letters and words
without apparent heed to the position they occupy in space (Fildes,
1923; Davidson, 1935; Newson, 1955; Goins, 1958). Four-year-old
children classify as equivalent, stimuli which vary in orientation,
although they are sensitive to orientation (Wohwill & Wiener, 1964).
Perhaps all readers encounter directional problems and good readers
overcome their difficulties better than poor readers (Bond & Tinker,
1957). Howard and Templeton (1966, p. 320) state as a general
hypothesis that if objects were viewed repeatedly in only one orientation (mono-oriented) this would lead to an increase in the effects
of relative disorientation on discrimination. This should apply to
the perception of print, and the present research sought to test the
hypothesis in a longitudinal study. Children were asked to read 15
words in each of three treatments, Normal, Reversed, and Inverted.
These treatments are illustrated in the following examples (Figure 1).

The effect of disorientation on discrimination was operationally
defined as a significantly lower word list score for one treatment
compared with another at the .01 level. Quality of reading progress
and age were independent variables and number of words read correctly in each treatment were dependent variables. Six hypotheses
can be stated.

Figure 1
Examples of Three Treatment Conditions

Normal	Reversed	Inverted
this	ziʜɟ	ɟʜiƨ
help	qlɘʜ	pɘ|b
boys	ƨʏod	poʎƨ
meet	ɟɘɘm	ɯɘɘɟ

1. *Trend with Age: Total Group and Four Reading Progress Groups*

There will be increasing trends:
(a) for normal scores to exceed reversed scores with age;
(b) for normal scores to exceed inverted scores with age; and
(c) for inverted scores to exceed reversed scores with age.

2. *Timing of Onset of Effects*

The number of words read correctly will be higher in each age-progress comparison:
(a) for normal compared with reversed lists;
(b) for normal compared with inverted lists; and
(c) for inverted compared with reversed lists.

Method

Subjects

From 100 children who entered school on their fifth birthday 87 were available at 8:0. They were representative of urban intelligence, parent occupation groups, and of national distributions for sex, reading-readiness scores, and age of entry to school. The sample was drawn from five schools, in districts classed as middle class (2) working class (2) and decaying city center (1). The teachers, who were rated slightly above average on a national comparison by five school inspectors, followed a published reading scheme and a standard series of reading books, but each had freedom in the prereading, supplementary reading, and creative writing programmes, and in the detailed methodology of lessons. The reading scheme emphasized grammatical and semantic cues in natural language texts and minimized instruction in letter-sound correspondence. Children were grouped and regrouped by teachers according to their rates of progress at any time throughout the three years of this study (Clay, 1966).

Word Lists

The 48 most frequently used words in the first-year reading books (Department of Education, 1963) were alloted systematically to three lists, and the most frequent words, *the, said,* and *is* became practice words. (Internal consistency reliabilities of lists for 100 children aged 6:0 were 0.90 for Normal, 0.84 for Reversed, 0.89 for Inverted lists.) Because (a) no difference between means of list scores in Normal treatment was significant at the .05 level, and (b) a Chi-square test for differences between Treatments × Lists was not significant ($X^2 = 1.50$, $df = 4$), it was felt that the three lists could be considered of equivalent difficulty. Treatments were rotated across the three lists to minimize any effects that changed orientation might have on the difficulty level of lists.

Procedure

The words (printed on 4- by 1-in. cards with Uno stencils, Size VL6) were presented singly, in decreasing order of frequency, and without timing. The treatment order was fixed as N, R, and I, for reasons of rapport with young children and poor readers. The children were encouraged to try, but no prompting or verbal reinforcement was given after the practice item. A general comment on good effort was made following the completion of one list. To clarify the timing of effects, chldren were tested within 2 weeks of 5:6, 6:0, 7:0, and 8:0. At 6:0 the sample was divided into quartile groups on the basis of a word reading test which correlated 0.93 with accuracy of book reading at 6:0 and 0.85 with a word reading test at 8:0. The groups were referred to as H, HM, LM, and L groups.

Data Analysis

Difference scores were calculated for each two-list comparison. Mean difference scores between treatments are reported for inspection (Tables 4 and 6). They are *not* the basis for the tests of significance for two important reasons. Firstly, the distributions of scores are far from normal at the younger ages close to the beginning of reading instruction. Secondly, the means are not considered to be comparable across ages or within ages because one cannot be certain that the increase in difference score is not an artifact. The child who reads more words may merely have more room to make a larger difference score. Consequently, significance tests are reported for each separate age-progress group (Wilcoxon signed-ranks test in Tables 3, 5, and 7). A monotonic test of the increasing trend for scores to differ recorded change at the coarse level of plus or minus, taking every child's set of scores into account (Table 2).

Results

Figure 2 presents actual scores for one child from each of the reading progress groups, selected because the scoring illustrates the general trends reported below. There was, however, considerable variation among children within progress groups.

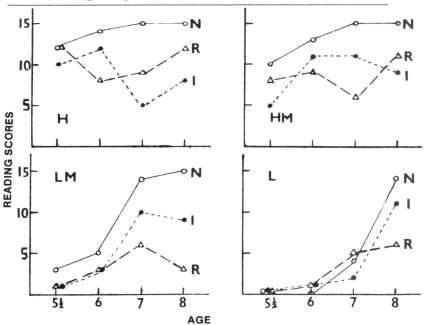

Figure 2
*Typical Learning Curves for Individual Children
From Four Levels of Reading Progress:
High; High-Middle; Low-Middle; and Low*

Table 1
*Mean Word List Scores for Total Sample:
Age × Treatment*

| | Age | | | |
Treatment	5:6	6:0	7:0	8:0
Normal	3.50	7.35	13.57	14.22
Reversed	2.57	5.24	9.10	10.00
Inverted	2.67	5.90	10.72	10.98

Trend with Age

1. Mean word list scores for the normal treatment exceeded reversed scores at every age, although the massive exposure to mono-oriented stimuli in school did not prevent considerable gains in reading reversed words (Table 1).

A test for an increasing trend for normal scores to exceed reversed scores was significant for the total group ($z = 8.74$, $p > .005$) and for each progress group (Table 2). The significant but lower z score for H was caused by a drop in difference scores at 8:0 to below the 6:0 level running counter to the trend tested (Table 4).

2. Normal scores exceeded inverted scores for the total group, ($z = 8.78$, $p > .005$) and for each reading progress group (Table 2).

3. Inverted scores did not exceed reversed scores in the total group, and reading progress groups differed markedly on this comparison with opposite trends cancelling each other out in the total group test. The L and LM groups showed the I > R trend at the .01 or near .05 level but the HM group showed no trend, and the H group showed a nonsignificant trend in the opposite direction.

Table 2
Tests for the Increasing Effect of Disorientation on Discrimination of Print Across Ages 5:6 to 8:0: z-Scores for Total Group and Four Reading Progress Groups[a]

Reading progress	n	Hypothesis[b]		
		N > R	N > I	I > R
Total group	87	8.74[a]	8.78[a]	1.1
High	21	2.59[a]	3.61[a]	−2.00
High-middle	22	4.75[a]	3.53[a]	−0.1
Low-middle	22	5.21[a]	3.71[a]	3.0[a]
Low	22	4.65[a]	4.43[a]	1.5

[a] Monotonic test for trend in correlated samples (Fergusson, 1966); significant at 2.33 for .01 level in one-tailed test.
[b] N = normal; R = reversed; and I = inverted.

Timing of Onset of Effects

1. At age 5:6, after 6 months of instruction, the H and HM groups showed significant differences in favor of the N treatment in the N > R comparison, the LM group showed no difference, and insufficient of

the L group were scoring above zero for the statistical test to be applied (Table 3).

2. At age 6:0, after 1 year of instruction, the three top groups showed significant differences in favor of the N treatment and the L group did not.

3. Differences were significant for all groups at ages 7:0 and 8:0.

4. A similar, later, and more variable change was found in the $N > I$ comparison (Table 5). The L group did not show significant disorientation effects until 8:0, compared with 5:6 for the H group. Tables 4 and 6 show that the mean difference scores are smaller for the $N > I$ comparison than for the $N > R$ comparison. For 13 age/group comparisons the reversed condition creates more difficulty: in only 3 comparisons is the mean difference score for the $N > I$ equal to or greater than the $N > R$ comparison.

Table 3

Tests of the Hypothesis that Normal Scores Will Exceed Reversed Scores[a]

Reading progress	Age			
	5:6	6:0	7:0	8:0
H	.01	.005	.005	.005
HM	.005	.005	.005	.005
LM	NS	.005	.005	.005
L	—	NS	.005	.005

[a] Significance level reported as Wilcoxon signed-ranks test.

Table 4

Mean Difference Scores of Words Correct in the Normal Minus Reversed Comparison Calculated from Lists of 15 Words

Reading progress	Age			
	5:6	6:0	7:0	8:0
H	1.62	5.00	5.42	4.01
HM	1.59	2.23	4.64	4.82
LM	0.62	1.43	4.86	4.24
L	0.05	0.16	2.10	4.32

Table 5

*Tests of the Hypothesis that Normal Scores Will
Exceed Inverted Scores[a]*

Reading progress	Age			
	5:6	6:0	7:0	8:0
H	.005	.005	.005	.005
HM	.005	(.025)	.005	.005
LM	(.025)	.005	.005	.005
L	—	(.025)	NS	.005

[a]Significance level reported as Wilcoxon signed-ranks test.

Table 6

*Mean Difference Scores of Words Correct in the
Normal Minus Inverted Comparison Calculated
from Lists of 15 Words*

Reading progress	Age			
	5:6	6:0	7:0	8:0
H	1.46	2.50	4.50	4.17
HM	1.36	1.86	2.95	3.82
LM	0.57	1.09	2.66	2.29
L	0.05	0.32	0.05	2.63

5. In the I > R comparison there was no consistent trend (Table 7). When a difference was significant it was in favor of the inverted treatment, except for the L group who preferred the reversed treatment at 6:0!

6. The change was related to successful reading rather than exposure to print for equivalent periods of instruction. Mean difference scores tended to be larger for better reading groups in terms of either level or age. The differences represent a 30 to 50% loss of efficiency.

7. At 8:0 two reading groups showed a drop in difference scores, which may mean that the children were gaining some control over the effects of disorientation, but the statistical evidence was weak.

8. The nonsignificant differences in the I > R comparison increase one's confidence that the trends found in the N > R and N > I

comparisons are not artifacts of the experimental situation.
9. The data on timing of onset are not explained by intellectual ability. The mean Stanford-Binet IQ's for the reading progress groups were H 123, HM 118, LM 108, and L 106. The difference between the LM and L groups is not interpretable in terms of intelligence, and the similarities between the HM and LM groups could not be so interpreted.

Table 7

*Tests of the Hypothesis that Inverted Scores
Will Exceed Reversed Scores[a]*

Reading progress	Age			
	5:6	6:0	7:0	8:0
H	NS	.005	NS	NS
HM	NS	NS	NS	NS
LM	NS	NS	.005	.01
L	—	.01	NS	NS

[a]Significance level reported as Wilcoxon signed-ranks test.

Discussion

In a word recognition task, unsupported by semantic or grammatical context, the child had to search a store of familiar and frequently-used words. Under untimed conditions, differences in favor of normal orientation were found for good progress readers after 6 months of reading instruction. Behavioral evidence showed that children who were normally competent readers stumbled, paused for long periods, offered no response as if nonplussed, squinted at the words, backed away from print, or tried to apply some strategy for unravelling the words which were easily read in normal orientation after the first year at school. The cues that good readers commonly use to identify words and discriminate one response from another appeared to be seriously disrupted by changed orientation, particularly in the reversed condition. Very little of this concern was shown by poor readers. The strategies that children use to solve the disoriented words would make an interesting study and one might expect young high progress readers to be able to verbalize their solutions.

The trends were related to successful reading progress and active processing of information rather than mere exposure to print. Directional cues were involved. Reversed orientation was at first the most difficult but inverted became more difficult as reading improved which suggests a two-state learning sequence of visual scanning. The first stage, having a left-to-right, horizontal, directional component with a set to start at the 'left end' would be in conflict with reversed presentation of word stimuli. At a second stage, when a subschema to scan and categorize individual letters was added, inverted presentation could interfere with performance. If the lower case alphabet is written in reversed orientation, only five letters change their identity, i.e., can be categorized as another known letter (b, d, p, q, g), but if the alphabet is written in inverted presentation fifteen letters could be readily identified as other letters (b, d, f, g, h, k, m, n, p, q, r, t, u, v, w), give or take some variations which allow h and k to approximate y when inverted. The examples in Figure 1 were chosen to illustrate how a different identity could be assigned to some inverted letters.

If attentional expectations, perceptual scanning, or search and check strategies have some explanatory relation to the results, it cannot be assumed that the mechanisms involved are the same at each age. It is reasonable to suggest that strategies change throughout the 5:0- to 8:0-year period. In the organization of early reading behavior, directional behavior and the perceptual analysis of symbols are important, but the preceding argument would imply an earlier attention to directional behavior and a later attention to letter identity. The strategies required for reading normal print and disoriented words may be different at each of these two hypothesized stages. One cannot assume that the low progress groups were following the same track as the high progress groups 1 or 2 years later. It is more likely that qualitative differences exist between children who interweave perceptual, cognitive, and motor learning into a coherent functioning whole within a year and children who learn directional behavior, choose strategies based on meaning and grammar, and visual discrimination behavior in various different sequences.

One fact is clear from this study. The high progress reader must be studied close to the beginning of instruction if we are to be able to understand more about the perceptual consequences of learning to read. If the left-to-right habit of reporting visual displays and the hemifield differences are products of the culturally standard task of learning to read, perhaps there are other aspects of perceptual functioning in adults which are unwittingly induced in young children by massive exposure to mono-oriented stimuli when they enter school. It is obvious that careless or inadequate training in orientation to print is likely to be a source of difficulty in the early years of learning to read.

The Howard and Templeton hypothesis that the effects of disorientation on discrimination should increase with repeated exposure to mono-oriented stimuli was very strongly supported, but with age and progress children also gained in ability to read disoriented print. Overall, reversed print tended to create more difficulty than inverted print at the ages studied. The results of statistical tests do not suggest a liberation from the effects of disorientation for this age group, but it would not be inconsistent with the data presented if this were to occur beyond the 8-year age level.

9 The Spatial Characteristics of the Open Book

In my books I have discussed in some detail the many concepts about the printer's code that may confuse the child. Directional conventions are among these. To explore the insights from the first longitudinal study in this area I took the opportunity to follow the development of a set of identical quadruplets through this early reading period. In the following brief report teachers may find the analysis of complex pointing behavior interesting. In the discussion I am trying to ask 'But what if . . . ?' questions because for the researcher there is some teasing information in the results. What if the use of the hands in pointing to early reading texts could provide cues to neurological organizations that were occurring? That question packages together two different questions. Can the observable data be reliable as an indicator? And if so, how do we interpret what is occurring?

One of the first code-breaking activities for the beginning reader to discover concerns arbitrary conventions of how books are presented.

Where should he start?

What direction should he move?

Where should he look on reaching the end of a line?

Most discussions of beginning reading ignore this early learning of orientation to visible language, and yet a test of these 'Concepts About Print' (Clay, 1979b) has discriminated reliably between children in their first six months of school instruction.

An opportunity to observe this learning was provided for the author by four identical girls. Despite an unusual degree of similarity in hereditary and environmental histories, they approached the problems of orientation to visible language on different time schedules and in different ways.

Background information was available from an earlier study of 100 children who had been observed each week during their first year at school. All behavior was recorded by the researcher as each child read his reading book for which the teacher had prepared him in the past week. A note was made of all occasions on which children pointed to the text and the direction of movement that they made. To externalize this 'direction of movement,' the child was asked to 'Read it with your finger' after a warm-up period on two or three pages. An unexpected finding emerged. When the children were divided into progress groups, the top two quartiles used either right or left hand for pointing to texts. In 892 observations recorded at weekly intervals during the school year, 459 were right-hand responses and 423 were left-hand responses. It was as if the children were flexible in their hand approach to the printed text. The two lower quartiles (i.e., the slow progress readers) used their left hands more often and were different from the top 50% in this respect. Only three of the 100 children were left-handed. It happened that the reading books being used by all the children had been published with the text invariably on the left page and the pictures on the right page. Thinking of the open book as the visual field with the target to be located on the left page, the results suggested that the high progress readers approached this target with either hand, while the low progress readers used their left hands often as if drawn to this by the location of the text on the left. They matched their body response to the visual field characteristics. In the lower 50% of children, body and field seemed to be linked; in the top 50% they seemed to be independent (Table 1).

These results report the summed records of hand behavior observed during the first year of instruction. It is possible that such a summary masks important changes that occur during that year.

The movement possibilities as a person with two hands approaches an English book with two pages were plotted diagrammatically. Suppose that simple text occurs on each page. Records must be kept of (1) which hand was used, (2) to move in which direction, (3) across which page. This complex orientation problem related to the acquisition of the directional schema, for the printed form of a particular language is not covered by the simple question, 'Which hand does the child prefer to use?' In the diagram at the top of Figure 1 the solid arrows plot several appropriate movements using a left hand or a right hand, and the dotted arrows show a few of the inappropriate movements. My research records show that observations close to the onset of reading instruction will produce each of these movements and others even more strange.

The diagram records some behavior that can occur when either hand is used on either page in either of two horizontal and two vertical directions. Constraints on such variety must be established. Are there any common factors as the child comes to behave within these constraints?

This problem was explored further with a longitudinal record of change in identical quadruplets. Observations were made at intervals during their first year at school. The girls obtained average intelligence test scores and average scores on visual perception tests. Baseline observations of handedness during the first week at school showed that one subject was left-handed and three were right-handed in self-selected classroom activities. This was explained in

Table 1
Pointing Behavior During Reading Observations

Quartile	Right-hand pointing	Left-hand pointing	Interpretation
H	216	206	Independent of perceptual field
HM	243	217	
LM	163	284	Dependent on perceptual field
L	157	235	

Figure 1.
Hand used to point to text. ■ = *left hand;* ○ = *right hand.*

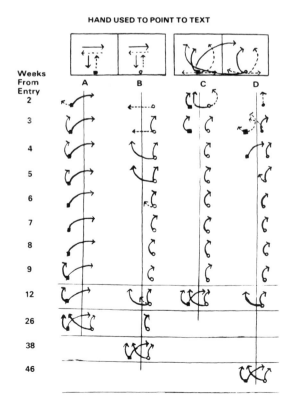

the medical history by the fact that a later subdivision of cells could produce one mirror pair. During the first year at school many observations of finger-pointing to simple texts were recorded.

After two weeks at school one right-handed subject B and one left-handed subject A were consistently using one hand for pointing to caption book texts. The other two right-handed subjects, C and D, took four and five weeks respectively to reach this stage. This behavior was not specifically trained in the classroom program. After that period the subjects used their preferred hand consistently and without lapse to point to both right and left pages; and asymmetrical response to the directional schema of English had been established on the basis of hand behavior. Variety occurred in the text stimuli and its placement on a page; consistency occurred within the individuals' orientation to that stimuli.

Observations continued. At twelve weeks right-handed subject C — who was making the best progress in reading — began to use either hand again. This behavior was different in several respects from the initial behaviors at the beginning of the study. The approach was always correct, and either hand could be used to produce this correct response despite variation in the stimulus or visual field. The change was in the direction of flexibility. Variety in the stimuli could now be consistently and correctly approached from either of two asymmetric responses in the individual. Would this be true of the other three subjects?

Left-handed subject A, making good progress in reading, reached this flexibility stage at 26 weeks. The other two subjects arrived at a similar state at 38 and 46 weeks respectively, although they showed occasional lapses from consistent performance.

In this particular group of five-year-olds a developmental progression in the orientation to the spatial characteristics of written language was recorded.

1. There was a period of orienting to print and the difference between subjects would probably be due to past or concurrent learning.
2. There was a period in which an asymmetrical hand response was consistently applied.
3. There was a later movement to alternate use of either hand whatever the format of the text.

The sequence held true for both right- and left-handed subjects, and the timing of acquisition differed for individuals of identical heredity and similar environmental histories.

The subjects of this study were learning to operate effectively within the directional conventions of written language. They were bilateral humans seeking to master an arbitrary directional approach to a bilateral source of stimuli. They could use either of two hands, but must read one of two pages first and move horizontally, not vertically in a left-to-right direction only, with a return sweep rather than returning right to left.

Theoretical explanations of the observed behavior touch on bilateral systems, handedness and reading, and perceptual strategies for visual analysis of stimuli. The bilateral symmetry of the nervous system in animals creates difficulty for discriminating between forms and displays and their mirror images (Corballis and Beale, 1971). If one is to develop asymmetry in a symmetrical system (that is, a preference for one particular type of response rather than an alternative one), then one may learn a tilt of the head to one side, the predominant use of one hand, or a particular directional approach to surveying print. Asymmetrical responding is most obvious in man's vehicle driving. He does not sit in the center of the road and respond randomly to any possibilities. His responding is constrained to one of two sets of rules, keeping to the left or keeping to the right. Returning to the example of written language, the directional constraints to be learned are a starting position, sequential movement along (or down) a line, and return on the diagonal to a new starting point. This is quite arbitrary and the directional schema for Hebrew or Japanese are quite different from the schema for European languages. Each requires the establishing of asymmetrical responding in the interests of efficiency.

It therefore appears that if one is a young child, the learning of an arbitrary directional convention for approaching written language may be a matter of movement or placement of one's body relative to the visual field. There is a motor component to the learning. If the approach is made by eye scanning movements only, it is still a motor activity though less easy to observe (Elkind and Weiss, 1967). Eventually it becomes a brain scan, so that during a fixation of the eyes sequential attentional scanning without apparent movement gives little sign of the motor activity which was probably necessary during the acquisition stage.

If the school entrant has a firm preference for a particular hand, one could predict that such an asymmetrical response would be used to guide the asymmetric eye scan movement needed in reading. Either hand could be used to orient the body and so bring the eyes to the appropriate starting position (Clark, 1973).

For a long time there has been repeated reference in the literature on learning to read to left-handedness and its possible link with reading difficulties. Once such a notion appears in print, there occurs a selective referral problem. Children referred to the clinician or neurologist are children who have the characteristics which the literature describes. The specialist is then able to say with some certainty that the children he sees with reading difficulty have handedness or laterality differences. When a sample of children from the whole community is studied rather than a clinical sample, such a selection bias disappears. Clark (1973) has found in community surveys of handedness and reading difficulties that the association does not hold up. If 4% of the population are left-handed and 33% are left-eyed, there must be a large group of the population of mixed laterality, and many are successful readers.

The school entrant to a reading program in English has to learn how to approach an open book.

The child may scan the pictures as he scans the world, from a focal point of high interest or information in a criss-cross of visual search patterns as he links up ideas (Luria, 1966). Perhaps by such 'open search' he first locates the print of the text. Russian developmental psychologists have been interested in the development of eye and hand searching as young pre-school children explore novel stimuli (Lynn, 1966). Before the age of five they found that children attended better to the stimuli if the tracing of new shapes involved hand and eye together, and that it was only the older children who were able to carry out effective exploration of new shapes with their eyes alone.

The child must first learn something about the placement of his body in relation to an open book (Benton, 1959).

The child reading English must learn to locate the left side of the text and proceed left to right according to the directional schema of the English he is reading. This learning is relative rather than fixed because the placement of texts in books changes in size and layout. Detailed study of the emergence of this directional control has shown that children demonstrate all manner of variations in learning these arbitrary conventions, but that within about six months of entry into formal instruction the *average* child has become consistent in the use of an appropriate asymmetrical response. The quick learner may take less than a month; the slow learner may take a year to stabilize an appropriate schema or set of responses.

Although a child beginning to grasp this directional learning may operate within the general pattern required by printing conventions, he may not read a left page before a right page or he may not scan the letters within the word from left to right even though he sweeps along the line in the correct direction (Clay, 1972a).

How is the hand action related to visual scanning? The mechanisms of perceptual analysis are duplicated within each cerebral hemisphere, although visuo-spatial functions relate primarily but not uniquely to the right hemisphere. Dimond (1972) believes that 'it would appear to be misleading to attribute the capacity for analyzing the events of the three-dimensional world to one hemisphere only.' He has studied performance when both the right and left hand were required to respond at the same time and has devised a model according to which an asymmetrical pointing response to print would not mean that the brain organization on one side had exclusive control over the behavior. He proposed a centrencephalic movement system receiving instructions from either the right or left cortex and passing impulses back to hemispheric control of muscular activity.

How does this relate to the observations on the identical subjects reported above? Interpreting these observations ontogentically in relation to Dimond's model, 'cortical instructions' to point to print were perhaps executed at first by the preferred hand and an established motor localization pattern. Over time the subjects came to perform as if a centrencephalic movement system had been created, possibly by cross-talk between hemispheres, so that the organized response pattern could initiate the response to print by *either* hand.

Such a view is consistent with Luria's position (1966) that 'writing and reading are functional systems of complex composition . . . (and) the psychophysiological composition of these acts changes in the successive developmental stages. . . . ' The differential timing of the acquisition of this behavior implies that the apparently similar environments produced different learning histories in the subjects and points to a differential interaction of subjects with environmental opportunities.

The technique of asking a child to 'Read it with your finger' will only reveal the directional orientation to the gross schema of line scanning. Beyond this there must be some very important visual perception learning relating to the attentional scanning of letters and clusters of letters. One might anticipate that further steps in the developmental progression described above occur, but some further devices for externalizing what is happening would be needed to observe these. A closer analysis of motor activity in the young child's orienting to print and its relation to attentional scanning during fixations of the eyes seems warranted.

10   Concepts About Print

Reviewed by Yetta M. Goodman

In the next paper a reviewer, Yetta Goodman, introduces some of the techniques developed for observing one aspect of the progress of the young reader. As I do not necessarily agree with the reviewer's arguments I have replied to some of them.

Many teachers of young children have found that traditional reading readiness measures provide little insight into the knowledge children have about books and the written language in books even though children will be using books as part of literacy development. Before coming to school, many children have been involved actively with various reading experiences at home and in preschools, developing knowledge about books, the print in books, and the functions of books. Children are read to from books; they read with older care givers; they play school with siblings; they pretend to read to themselves, to dolls, or to stuffed animals. It is the knowledge which young children develop through these varied experiences that Marie Clay believes is important for teachers to understand in order to plan appropriate beginning reading experiences for children.

Clay rejects standard reading measures for children, stating that 'Preparation for reading can be done more directly with written language' (1979a, p. 7). Her 'Concepts about Print Test' is her contribution to aid teachers, diagnosticians and researchers gain insight from a child's involvement with written language. Her main objectives for this test include: (1) observing precisely what a child is doing; (2) uncovering the processes a child controls; and (3) discovering reading behaviors which need to be taught.

Description of the Test

The full details for the administration of the 'Concepts about Print Test' are given in a book called *The Early Detection of Reading Difficulties: A Diagnostic Survey with Recovery Procedures* (1979b) and must be accompanied by one of two test booklets, *Sand* (1972) or *Stones* (1979c). Originally published in Auckland, New Zealand, they are all available in the United States. Additional insights into Clay's views are provided in *Reading: The Patterning of Complex Behaviour* (1979a). *The Early Detection of Reading Difficulties* is a text on reading measurements including error analysis in book reading, letter and word recognition tasks, analysis of writing samples, as well as a program to overcome reading difficulties. This review deals only with the 'Concepts about Print Test', which is a unique contribution to the evaluation of beginning readers.

Concepts about Print is concerned with observing and evaluating the following:

1. *Concepts about book orientation.* Items related to these concepts provide insights into whether children know how to open books and know when a book, pictures and print are right-side up or upside down.

2. *Concepts about whether print or pictures carry the text message.* These are observed by asking the child to point to where the observer is reading as the observer reads aloud to the child.

3. *Concepts about directionality of lines of print, page sequences and directionality of words.* These are evaluated by asking the child to follow along with a finger and point as the teacher is reading and also by asking a child to say what's wrong with a page that has lines of print, letters or words out of order.

4. *Concepts about the relationship between written and oral language.* The child is asked to follow along with a finger as the observer reads. This provides insights into the child's awareness of what is being read and its relationship to specific text items.

5. *Concepts of words, letters, capitals, space and punctuation.* These are obtained by asking the child what the conventions are or to point to such items.

The *Sand* and *Stones* booklets used to administer the 'Concepts about Print Test' are 20 page paperbacks that resemble children's picture story books. The picture and print are arranged so that it is easy to observe whether the child is responding to the print or to pictures.

The pictures in *Sand* show a little boy with a shovel and pail on a beach. Waves come in and fill up the hole. The child plays in the hole. He has a playhouse and a play tree. His mother calls him. In the final picture he is seen looking over the beach.

The pictures in *Stones* show a little girl dragging a stick up a hill. She stops to look at a bird and some stones. She dislodges the stones. One stone rolls down the hill and into a pond. The language of both texts is in first person and accompanies the pictures appropriately. Most of the sentences early in the texts consist of independent clauses, some connected with *and*. The last few pages include more complex sentence structures, questions, and dialog.

Analysis of the Test

I believe the 'Concepts about Print Test' is a significant beginning in evaluative measures that provide insight into what children know about written language. It is the first instrument I have seen which uses a real reading experience with very young children to provide information to an observer about their knowledge of how to handle books and of the written language in the books.

Clay has made a significant contribution to those who work with beginning readers by providing a more natural measurement to help in understanding how children interact with a real book in a real situation. She has achieved her objectives so that indeed, a teacher can: (1) observe what a child is doing in response to print as a teacher reads; (2) determine what needs to be taught by examining the actual behavior of a child interacting with print in a book; and (3) gains insight into aspects of written language over which a child is developing control.

I believe that the 'Concepts about Print Test' should be explored by all professionals working in beginning reading. It provides a base for discussion about what aspects of reading are involved in the beginning reading process. It raises many questions about the measurements used in tests of reading readiness which have little to do with reading behavior. It provides insights for teachers about what kinds of activities should become part of beginning reading programs. It also provides a way of getting at a child's knowledge without relying on question/answer, paper/pencil tests that may be testing knowledge other than that which a teacher or reading specialist wants to know. Clay has provided an innovative foundation which should be used to develop more natural kinds of observational devices.

Interpretation and Use

Although Clay has provided norms, reliability and validity measures for her test, these need to be used with caution since the test was standardized in New Zealand. In our use of the test, my colleagues and I found that some parts of the test which New Zealand children passed at 6.6 years of age were passed by some of our subjects at 5.9, while items passed at 5.6 by 50% of Clay's population were missed by our children. Some children who were reading in books already, according to their teachers, missed items that, according to the norms, they should control.

This test is best used to gain insight into the individual child. It need not be used to obtain norm-referenced scores but may be used very profitably for developmental insights into the individual. Clay herself cautions: 'Items should uncover concepts to be learned or confusions to be untangled . . . items are not in a strict difficulty sequence . . . '(1979b, p. 18).

From my point of view, the test's greatest value lies in it innnovative approach to evaluation. I believe researchers and teachers should explore using the test booklets in different ways. One adaptation might have the researcher read the whole story to the child first and then do the tasks. Some children wanted to hear the whole story without interruptions and so were impatient with the questioning. After teachers use the 'Concepts about Print Test' and become comfortable with it, they may be able to adapt the procedure for use with any picture story book. Except for the upside down print and words and sentences out of order, which are part of *Sand* and *Stones,* most picture story books provide the child with the same opportunities that the test booklets provide.

The upside down print and pictures, and the words, sentences and letters out of order, such as 'I sat the in hole,' are not natural to text and even good readers may miss those because they don't expect such aberrations. Other good beginning readers miss the aberrations because they are reading for meaning and they miscue on the 'mistakes' embedded in the test booklets. The use of those items relates to the view about reading development which Clay holds. She believes that at some point in development, a child should notice certain misorders and misspellings. In my view, this is not a necessary part of reading development.

Other reasons I suggest using picture story books other than *Sand* and *Stones* are related to cultural relevance. *Sand,* the test booklet, shows a blond haired boy playing on a beach while *Stones* shows a blond haired girl climbing a hill, so they may not be culturally relevant to the diverse populations and settings in many countries. In fact, *Stones,* the most recent edition, may have been added to expand the cultural opportunities in the pictures and texts. From among children's literature, however, teachers can select a text more relevant to the experience of their own children than the beach theme in *Sand* or the hill climbing in *Stones.*

In administering *Sand* and *Stones* we found other problems. For the sequences in the test booklets that are not presented in their natural states (e.g., upside down print, lines out of order, misspelling), the directions suggest asking the children, 'What's wrong with this?' or 'What's wrong on this page?' The children replied most often by reacting to the story line or the meaning of the story itself rather than to the written forms. We believe this does not mean the child does not realize that something is wrong with the print. Rather, it suggests that children are concerned more with the truth of the story than they are with problems in the form of the written language.

Summary

Depending on the view of the reading process one holds, there may be other aspects of the 'Concepts about Print Test' which might be criticized. However, the procedure itself is dynamic. Teachers who use this instrument a great deal learn to adapt the instrument to their own needs. But for all teachers, it is a fine observational tool which provides information about what the child knows about print.

Comment

I do not entirely agree with this characterization of the observation potential of the Concepts About Print technique. I prefer not to have it called a test, and I have never described it as a readiness test. I think that it reveals some of the behaviors that are related to reading progress but only a very few of them.

It is the Interpretation and Use section which I want to focus on in detail and I want to try to point out what teachers or researchers lose if they chose to use a non-standard situation.

To share the story with the child first changes the situation to the extent that it provides the child with more meaningful background and frees that child to concentrate on other features of the printed message. The question for the observer to decide is whether they want to know what the child typically does when faced with a new book (i.e., with an overload of conventions to process) or what the child knows if we first establish the context of the story.

The second comment also provides the teacher with a choice. In the process of sharing books with children, teachers who are comfortable with the procedures will check or teach about concepts. What is lost in leaving out the items in which letter, words and sentences have been placed out of order is the section of the test which captures the behaviors described in the article on 'An Increasing Effect of Disorientation on the Discrimination of Print'. They provide a way to observe which of the critical visual messages in the printed code the child is attending to. It is not necessary for the teacher to understand theories of visual perception, or developmental changes in learning to perceive, to be able to observe from the child's behavior that the child notices changes in line order and word order and initial letter order in words but is as yet unable to detect a reordering of letters within a word. The teacher may find that a valuable piece of information to help her planning of instruction.

My only real argument with the reviewer is a possible difference in our assumptions about what teachers want to know. I think Yetta Goodman is saying that teachers do not need to use a standardized observation situation, that they do not need to be concerned about the reliability of their data, and that the intricacies of visual perception learning are beyond them. Contrary to that position I would want to argue that using the observation situation as suggested gives the practicing teacher the assurance that, in addition to what she is able to observe, she can be assured that her data will be reliable (that it is not just a chance thing that the child was a high or low scorer), she will have a good basis for judging that change has occurred when she retests the child later, and it is possible that those sections of the instrument in which she does not see much value at first might just provide her with opportunities to discover some new insights when other aspects of the instrument have become familiar and she is free to puzzle over these other behaviors.

I would not want to say that teachers should not have access to conditions of observation that researchers find essential for making their judgments.

III Observing Oral Language and Early Reading Progress

This section begins with a short extract which was part of a contribution to a symposium in The Rotarian *which pointed to literacy issues around the world. It is included here as an introduction to the educational issues associated with the ethnic groups which were studied in the reports in this section. The New Zealand multicultural situation is described in more detail in extracts from* 'Early Childhood and Cultural Diversity' *which was published in* The Reading Teacher.

The papers in this section all arose from the second longitudinal research I carried out, reported in 'Language Skills: A Comparison of Maori, Samoan and Pakeha Children Aged Five to Seven Years'. *Further reports of that study are the extract from* 'Sentence Repetition: Elicited Imitation of a Controlled Set of Syntactic Structures by Four Language Groups' *and the papers on* 'Morpheme Completion' *and* 'The Polynesian Language Skills of Maori and Samoan School Entrants'.

The 'Record of Oral Language' *was a further development of the work on sentence repetition but was carried out by an interdisciplinary research team. It has proved to be a useful technique for the observation of children's language.*

11 Extract from 'Literacy Around the World: In Oceania'

Oceania includes Polynesia, Micronesia, and Melanesia, countries of many languages and many different cultures, from Papua New Guinea to Tahiti, from Western Samoa to Norfolk Island. There has been a tendency for many island people from all over the Pacific to seek a congenial life and financial support through work in neighboring developed countries. Relatively open immigration policies have led to a valuing of education by Pacific Islanders as a way to survive in the larger societies.

In the Pacific Islands bilingual situations create problems for education and for the teaching of reading in particular. All the questions are raised to another level of complexity when children are faced with learning both their mother-tongue and the metropolitan language of their territory (in this case English or French). The countries that may be able to solve the problems of bilingual education are those with a strong cultural tradition, a homogeneous population and control over their own affairs — countries like Western Samoa, Tonga, some aboriginal communities in Australia, and some trust territories. If a culture is clear about its goals for language learning, the problems of teaching children to read either in the mother tongue or in the metropolitan language can be faced. But in multilingual settings, among the large migrant populations of Australian cities, or in the large Polynesian populations of some New Zealand cities, or in Fiji, the schools are not clear what languages should be learned at which stage. Questions about the improvement of reading take second place to these major language issues. And what should the schools do about the Maori language? Ten percent of New Zealanders are Maoris who are in danger of losing their ability to use their language.

There is every reason to take a hard look at the teaching of English as a second language in this area.

At its 1978 conference, the South Pacific Commission asked how well education is suited to the real-life needs of the children in these territories. We could also ask what is known about these children. How are their minds challenged by their respective cultures, and what do they learn at home and in their communities about the world around them? Those questions will find little in the way of answers. Nowhere in Oceania, in the developing or developed countries, is there one research institute whose purpose is to study how children of the area grow and learn.

Information about how languages are acquired and how children learn and develop in the cultures of Oceania, Australia, and New Zealand, would provide a sound foundation for further improvements in reading instruction.

12 Extract from 'Early Childhood and Cultural Diversity in New Zealand'

New Zealand is a small country of three and a half million people. It became a British colony in 1840, although missionary settlements began in 1814. New Zealand has always been separate and different from Australia, including having a different educational system. New Zealand is small scale with a centralized education system, whereas Australia is large scale with separate state systems of education and a Federal Government.

When the settlers arrived in New Zealand, it was already populated by one particular group of Polynesians called Maoris. The Polynesians of the South Pacific have developed in different ways in the various island groups. The Maoris in New Zealand number a quarter of a million and they have a high rate of natural increase which doubled the population between 1945 and 1966. The educational tradition of the Maoris was an oral one; they selected people from within the tribe who had excellent memories to learn the important information that had to be passed from generation to generation; the genealogies, the historical facts, and the intertribal histories (Best, 1974). With this well-developed oral tradition, the Maoris took readily to the education that was offered them by the missionaries in the nineteenth century and they had no difficulty in learning to read and write (Biggs, 1968).

Auckland, the largest city in New Zealand, is an entry point for other people coming to New Zealand from the Pacific. It has been called the largest Polynesian center in the world. The immigrants come from Western Samoa, the Cook Islands, Nuie, Tonga, Fiji and the Tokelaus. Of all the 60,000 Polynesians now in New Zealand, 64 percent live in Auckland.

New Zealand has historically accepted some responsibility for education in the South Pacific and has tried to maintain a fairly open policy for either immigration or for temporary work permits. Some Pacific Island children in New Zealand schools have been born in New Zealand, some have been sent to New Zealand by their parents to get an education.

Each of these island groups has its own language, its own culture, and a different style of child-rearing related to a particular value system which makes for different reactions on the part of the children to what happens in schools. The teachers must know the characteristics, the values and type of child-rearing which the Western Samoan people are likely to provide for their children and how this differs from that of the Nuiean children, or the Tongan children, or the Maori children.

The three major groups in New Zealand schools are minority groups of Maori and Pacific Island children and majority groups of Pakeha (White) children. A challenge is being offered to our teachers to find improved procedures for the instruction of the large minority groups. Some Auckland schools have 10 percent non-Pakeha children, other schools have 10 percent Pakeha children and there is every combination between these, varying from district to district according to residential characteristics. Artificial mixing has not been used. It is rare to find a class in Auckland that has no Polynesian children in it.

The Maori people are passing through a crisis in their history. There is a danger that the Maori language, which is the real basis of the Maori culture, will be lost, dispersed by policies about assimilation, by the drift into the cities that has split Maori communities, and by an attitude in the past that Maori language and culture were things to be perpetuated by the people themselves and not by a school syllabus. Maori leaders have pressed for advances in health, welfare, housing, education and economic advancement but they have also pressed for continuation of language, culture, land inheritance, and the marae or meetinghouse focus of the tribal groups.

In a time of rapid social change when even the ways in which language is used undergo rapid shifts, education systems may be insensitive to the changing needs of children unless careful observation and recording of what young children are doing is carried out. The research study I wish to comment on was designed to look at these five-year-old school entrants and their progress over two years of schooling.

13 Language Skills: A Comparison of Maori, Samoan and Pakeha Children Aged Five to Seven Years

This research explored the oral language and reading behaviors of Maori, Samoan and white New Zealand children (referred to in these reports by the Maori word for white people, Pakeha). The Maori children were monolingual in English and most of the Samoan children were bilingual.

For the researcher, the design of the study, in 1967, was novel. Drawing upon the well-known article by Campbell and Stanley (1963) and using the fact that New Zealand schools have continuous intake of students, this study used a cross-lagged longitudinal design. Children were only followed for six months, but intake groups were aged 5:0, 5:6, 6:0, 6:6 and 7:0 and every child was within two weeks either way of one of those ages. At the end of the six months the level reached by the five-year-olds could be compared with the level attained by the original group aged 5:6, and so on throughout the sample. Another feature of the research was that the sample was divided in half for analysis of the results providing two equivalent groups and the two analyses were compared one with the other, yet gathered in the same period of historical time.

This research was planned to describe differences and age trends in the language performance of children between five and seven years. One purpose was to record the actual progress of Maori and Samoan children who might require compensatory instruction for language deficits, but of equal importance was a description of the performance of average Pakeha children, and of a 'ceiling-performance' group of Pakeha children who had experienced optimum language learning conditions.

Assessments were made in the following areas:

1. Oral Language in English: (a) articulation, (b) vocabulary, (c) sentence repetition, (d) inflections.
2. Auditory Memory: (a) digit span, (b) memory for words.
3. Visual Perception of Print: (a) Conventions of Written Language (such as directional behavior, and concepts of letters, words, sequence,

	punctuation, etc.), (b) identifying letters.
4. Reading:	(a) Word Test (from basic readers), (b) Schonell R.1, (c) Daniels and Diack Standard Reading Test.
5. Oral Language in Maori or Samoan:	(a) vocabulary, (b) following instructions, (c) answering questions.

The results presented here are from an analysis of the performance of four groups of 5- to 7-year-old children on the combined scores of the major variables Oral Language, Auditory Memory, Visual Perception of Print, and Reading,

Design

It is a feature of this research that results were obtained from two independent samples simultaneously thus providing a check on any unusual findings.

Sample

The project used two samples of 160 children from the total available population in 10 urban primary schools. Staff at each school were asked to list every child whose parents met the language requirements of the research under age and sex categories. The youngest group were between 5:0 (age of school entry) and 5:3, and the remainder were grouped 5:4-5:9, 5:10-6:3, 6:4-6:9, 6:10-7:3. From these lists children were allocated by random numbers to Samples A and B so that there were for each age group, eight children from each of the four different language backgrounds, usually four boys and four girls. This provided 32 children per age group, (Figure 1) 40 children per language group and 160 children per sample, (Figure 2).

Figure 1
Sampling Plan of One Age Group

	P	E	M	S	
Boys	4	4	4	4	16
Girls	4	4	4	4	16
					32

Figure 2
Sampling Plan for Samples A and B

			Age Groups			
Language Groups	5:0-5:3	5:4-5:9	5:10-6:3	6:4-6:9	6:10-7:3	
Professional						40
English (Average)						40
Maori						40
Samoan						40
	32	32	32	32	32	160

5 Age groups = 5 × 32
4 Language groups = 4 × 40
2 Samples = 160 + 160

Language Groups

Criteria for admission to the language groups were as follows:

1. *Professional Group:* Children with an optimum model of English language available from professional fathers or mothers. (Two assumptions were made. A mother or father with tertiary education would speak English fluently in all its richness, and would also provide a good psychological environment for the child's development.)
2. *English Group:* All other children in the same schools who had two parents with English as their mother-tongue.
3. *Maori Group:* An Auckland urban Maori group with two parents who claimed to be Maoris. This group was drawn from schools in the city centre (3), urban Maori communities (2), a state housing area (1) and two suburbs where Maori families tended to own their homes (2). These children, tested for knowledge of Maori by an experienced infant supervisor of their own ethnic and language group, who was also a lecturer in Maori Studies, were all found to be monolingual in English.
4. *Samoan Group:* An Auckland urban Samoan group with two parents who claimed to be Samoans. They were found in the same schools as the Maori children although few were found in the two schools serving Maori settlements. These children were tested by five Samoan teachers and three-quarters were found to have considerable knowledge of the Samoan language.

Procedure

Both Samples A and B were tested in September-October, 1968 by a team of nine trained assistants, one of whom was Maori. Three assistants received six training sessions on the precise procedures for administering tests. The battery of tests required two sessions with each child so that effort would be maintained and fatigue reduced. Testers were given freedom to vary only the order of presentation to suit the dual aims of maximum rapport with, and effort from, the child, and minimum wastage of the five hours available in a school day.

Data Analysis

Scores were normalized (T-scaled) for each single test using all scores of Samples A and B (N = 320). Combined total scores for each major variable, Oral Language, Visual Perception, Auditory Memory and Reading, were normalized again. Two-way analyses of variance for five age groups by four language groups were made.

Results

Within Language Groups: Age and Major Test Variable Differences

The results of an analysis of variance for each language group in Sample A are recorded in Table 1.

Table 1
Analysis of Variance of the Four Major Test Variables for Each Language Group
F ratios and significance levels for Sample A

	Professional F	p	English F	p	Maori F	p	Samoan F	p
Age	24.29	< .001	35.59	< .001	35.45	< .001	34.50	< .001
Tests	0.67	ns	2.97	ns	6.29	< .001	4.40	< .01
A × T	1.28	ns	1.56	ns	0.57	ns	1.31	ns

1. The results showed highly significant changes with age on test variables in all language groups.
2. The professional and English children did not show significant differences *between* test variables being located at comparable scoring levels on each variable.
3. The Maori and Samoan groups each had significant differences in the level of scoring on the four major test variables.

Within Major Test Variables: Age and Language Group Differences

1. In the analyses of variance, differences of high magnitude were found between age and language groups on the major test variables for both Sample A and Sample B (Table 2).

Table 2

Analysis of Variance of Language and Age Differences for Each Major Variable

F ratios and significance levels for Samples A & B

		Sample A		Sample B	
		F	p	F	p
Oral Language	L	31.35	< .001	40.45	< .001
	A	19.95	< .001	24.52	< .001
	L × A	0.44	ns	0.22	ns
Auditory Memory	L	7.40	< .001	4.84	< .001
	A	9.26	< .001	10.71	< .001
	L × A	1.34	ns	1.35	ns
Visual Perception	L	37.58	< .001	19.91 < .001	
of Print	A	64.13	< .001	50.99	< .001
	L × A	0.88	ns	0.41	ns
Reading	L	20.20	< .001	9.58	< .001
	A	79.69	< .001	67.75	< .001
	L × A	1.39	ns	0.91	ns

Age: The increase in scores between 5:0 and 7:0 for the total group produced a main effect for age which was highly significant ($p < .001$), in all four variables for both Samples A and B.

Language: The differences in scores between language groups produced a main effect for language which was highly significant ($p < .001$) in all test variables, for both Samples A and B.

Interaction: The interaction effect was not significant for any test variable.

The T-scaled scores of Samples A and B are also presented in graphs for three age groups, (Figures 3 to 6) although the results are discussed in terms of five age groups used in the statistical analysis.

2. *Oral Language:* The language groups were ranked in the same order at all ages, Professional, English, Maori and Samoan, (Figure 3).

3. *Auditory Memory:* The auditory memory of digits and words did not follow the pattern of the oral language scores, (Figure 4). Differences between groups were much smaller on this variable. Lan-

FIGURE 3

*Comparison of Language Groups on the Combined Scores
for Four Tests of Oral Language at Ages 5:0, 6:0 and 7:0*

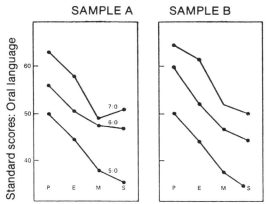

guage group ranks changed differently in Samples A and B with the Maori group in Sample B beginning high and ending low. A limitation of span seems evident in that all groups cluster around a relatively low ceiling of scores at 7:0. It is not clear what is happening in this variable but it is possible to state that the Polynesian groups suffered no specific limitation.

FIGURE 4

*Comparison of Language Groups on the Combined Scores
for Two Tests of Auditory Memory at Ages 5:0, 6:0 and 7:0*

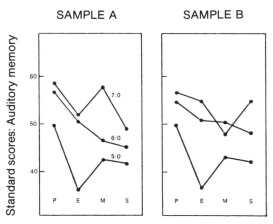

4. *Visual Perception of Print:* On this variable the language groups were ranked in the order Professional, English, Samoan, Maori, (Figure 5) and the largest amount of change took place in the first year of school.

5. *Reading:* The ranking of groups did *not* follow the oral language pattern. By 6:0 the order tended to be Professional, then English and Samoan about equal, and Maori last. By 7:0 the English were scoring higher than the Samoan groups so that the order was Professional, English, Samoan, Maori, (Figure 6).

FIGURE 5
Comparison of Language Groups on the Combined Scores for Two Tests of Visual Perception of Print at Ages 5:0, 6:0 and 7:0

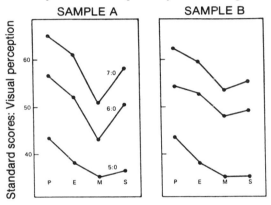

FIGURE 6
Comparison of Language Groups on the Combined Scores for Three Tests of Reading at Ages 5:0, 6:0 and 7:0

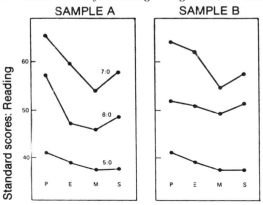

Discussion

Although the analysis so far deals only with major variables and combined test scores the problems have been set in perspective. The children from professional homes, assumed to have had the greatest advantages in pre-school language experience, continued to gain in oral language skills and maintained a clear lead over other groups up to the age of 7:0. In the visual perception of print and reading variables these children from professional homes began school with relatively low scores, ahead of, but close to, the performance of other five-year-olds. In these areas their behavior changed markedly during their first two years at school.

The usefulness of an optimum group has therefore been demonstrated. The spread of abilities in oral language at five years is very much greater than the spread of visual perception of print or reading behaviors. These latter achievements become differentiated *after* entry to school. Action aimed at the reduction of oral language deficits should be aimed at the preschool years, but measures to prevent early reading failure can be taken after entry to school.

The English (average) group fell below the Professional but above the Polynesian groups on oral language, reading and visual perception of print variables as would be expected, but they were the lowest scoring group at school entry on the auditory memory variable. However, findings on this variable were confusing.

The Samoan group *began* with the lowest scores on oral language tests and *remained* in the lowest rank throughout the first two years. Yet in the visual perception of print and on the reading variables the Samoan average is higher than the Maori average at every age after 5:0.

Since the Samoan child has less control over English and yet makes better progress in reading, the visual perception variable seems to be very important. Early reading progress may depend more upon progress with visual perception of print than upon a high level of sophistication in oral language skill. This conclusion applies (1) to the first year of school and (2) under current methods of instruction. A causative relationship has not been demonstrated, and other factors such as motivation to learn could be related to this finding. The outstanding feature of these results is that they are at variance with a current emphasis on the problems of the oral language deficits of the Maori child as a major cause of early school failure.

In two previous studies of Pakeha children the visual perception of print tests also showed high relationships with reading progress. After one year at school identifying letters showed the highest correlation (0.83) of 8 variables with reading progress (Clay 1966) and in a followup study this was maintained at 7 years (0.86) and at 8 years (0.81) (Clay, 1968). The Conventions of Written Language test had shown a moderate to high relationship with reading progress in the first year of school (0.79), but lower correlations at 7 and 8 years (0.73, 0.64). What was surprising in this research was the finding that differences between *language* groups existed on these visual perceptions of print variables.

Does the Maori preschool child have an accumulated lack of visual exploratory experiences in comparison with the average Pakeha child with play materials? or with books? Do auditory rather than visual stimuli dominate in his home environment? The auditory perception scores of the five-year-old Polynesian groups would lend weight to this hypothesis as the mean scores were usually better than those of the English group. However, the Maori and Samoan children show a similarity at 5:0 which is not maintained. Does the Samoan child make a quicker adjustment to school than the Maori child so that he readily gains from his experiences, thus learning to perceive print, and to read? This might be related to either home or school factors. Selective migration from Samoa to the city environment may be operating to produce a Samoan group with more ability and/or initiative. Comment is also heard that Samoan parents urge their children to work hard at school because education is valued, a motivational factor. The Maori child may suffer emotionally from the impact of school to a greater extent than his Samoan classmate for some reason hidden in child-rearing practices. A teacher's expectation of the potential of Maori and Islander may differ. For example, Benton's assumption that Pacific Island children start from behind and pass Maori children before long, has been widely accepted in Auckland schools but this has commonly been associated with language background variables rather than school-learning as this present research suggests.

Unfortunately, this research was not designed to answer any of these questions because the visual perception differences were not anticipated. However, it is hoped that in subsequent reports a finer analysis of language and reading behavior may clarify the particular difficulties that the Maori children are having, so that compensatory activities in special programs may be implemented within the schools.

To conclude with a practical recommendation, it would appear that teachers of Maori children in their first years of school should pay as close attention to the visual aspects of early school learning, the ability to 'see' letters and words, as they would to a Pakeha child with considerable immaturity in the development of appropriate visual perception and directional behavior.

Note

This research was financially supported by the Maori Education Foundation and the Kelliher Maori Economics Foundation as part of a continuing study of language development in Maori, Samoan and English-speaking children. The points of view expressed do not necessarily reflect the opinions of these organizations.

14 The Development of Morphological Rules in Children of Differing Language Backgrounds

Because of the complexity of language there are some problems for the observer who wants to capture change in language learning. With little confidence in any global assessment of 'language ability' for helping us to understand the interrelationships of language learning and learning to read we assessed different aspects of language learning with separate instruments. Research reports had shown how the changes in children's control of the inflections in the language could be demonstrated so we adopted those procedures and designed an instrument that would be sensitive to the changes that occurred in five- to six-year-olds.

There was one feature of our reasoning which should be made explicit. Among white New Zealand children there would be two groups. One would have been fortunate enough to hear a model of English spoken in elaborated and flexible ways making use of the richness of the language. There would be no limitations of their language learning set by the model from which they had had the opportunity to learn. Other white children would have heard a more restricted model of the language and therefore their own use would be limited by the characteristics of that model rather than by their own capacities to learn the language. So, in this research, we made use of both these comparison groups, an optimum learning group, and an average group. This would enable us to say that the most advanced users of language at five years were using language in this or that way, and so to gain some measure of the distance behind this that other language groups fell, be they Caucasian or Polynesian. I accept the argument that we should focus on language differences and not claim that these are language deficits, but one also has to take into account that there are language differences between what five-year-olds and what three-year-olds can do with the English language and such acquisition differences have to be considered.

The inflectional rules of English are sometimes used by older Maori and Samoan children in non-English ways. A study of older children aged 8:0 to 10:0 is included in this report along with the results from the first study.

Introduction

A child experiments with the morphological rules of English when he makes sentences like 'We goed to town', making a past tense ending which matches with *showed* and *mowed*. Other aspects of the inflections that might be traced developmentally are plural forms, *bird birds*, changes in verb tense, *sit sat*, the verb form used with the third person singular, *run runs*, the ways of indicating possessiveness, *baby's coat*, and so on.

Several studies of children's ability to inflect words correctly and to apply other rules like the use of pronouns, have been reported for the 4-7 year age group. Berko (1958) showed that the child of this age could apply some of the morphological rules of English to nonsense words. Her groups showed an improvement within this age group in the direction of perfecting knowledge of simple plurals and possessives, and the progressive tense. The children performed best when inflectional endings were most regular and had fewest variants. If there were several alternative endings they handled the most common of these before they could deal with those which appear in more limited distribution. Kirk and McCarthy (1966) presented statistical information for a subtest of this kind in their test of psycholinguistic abilities. They used words with which the child would be familiar. Working with 700 children from to 2:6 to 9:0 they found that raw score means increased regularly with age, with rare exceptions, for their 22 item test and that standard deviations remained relatively constant. The following points arise from these two reports .

1. Behind the traditional aspects of speech behavior such as vocabulary, articulation and standard grammatical usage there is an important linguistic skill which shows a clear pattern of change as experience with language accumulates.
2. This skill seems to operate with central nervous system control at the level of automatic habit mechanisms and not at the conscious level.
3. The child's control over inflection is an important facet of his general linguistic ability, showing a moderate and a consistent relationship with a more extensive battery of psycholinguistic ability.
4. These grammatical features are important carriers of meaning.

In a developmental overview Dale (1972) places the first appearance of inflections soon after the beginning of grammatically structural speech. The young child, who has no difficulty with the general notion of suffixing, behaves as if he were a pattern learner, and once a pattern is acquired he applies it as generally as possible, over-regularizing the inflections. He is divided between his tendency to extend patterns as widely as possible and his desire to match the patterns of the language about him. However, he takes some years to master particular inflections. Selby (1972) reports a replication of Berko's technique with Scottish children using 100 children at every age group 4-14 years. She found that most of the rules tested by Berko showed a steady improvement towards a ceiling value at about 12 years.

The two studies to be reported here have looked at changes in the morphological rule behavior of New Zealand children aged 5-10 years. The test contained both real word and nonsense word items, provided a wider sampling of rules than Kirk and McCarthy's test, and was applied to English, Maori and Samoan groups of children. The Samoan groups were bilingual (in English and Samoan) and although the urban Maori children had English as their mother-tongue, these children may use a dialect of English which might be called Maori-English. (This point is the subject of current research in New Zealand.)

Design and Procedure

Subjects

Two samples each of 160 children were drawn from the total available population in 10 urban primary schools. In February 1968 staff at each school were asked to list according to age every child whose parents met the language requirements of the research. The youngest group were between 5:0 and 5:3 and the remainder were grouped 5:4-5:9, 5:10-6:3, 6:4-6:9, 6:10-7:3. Four boys and four girls from each of four language groups were selected. This provided 32 children per age group, 40 children per language group, 160 children in all, in each of 2 samples. The criteria for admission to language groups has been published in a previous report (Clay, 1970). The groups were called Optimum English (because they had maximum opportunity to learn the rules of English), Average English, Maori and Samoan.

The Morpheme Completion Test

A 36-item test was constructed after piloting items with 40 children of mixed ethnic groups and eliminating items of similar difficulty level. One has to choose between a test instrument which surveys all the types of inflections that exist, or a test which yields a distribution of scores and a reliability which permits the use of statistical treatments to establish whether differences between groups are significant ones. A third factor is that the test must be of suitable length for the subjects so that motivation and attention are retained. For these reasons items of similar difficulty level were dropped from the pilot test and the Kuder-Richardson reliability coefficient for the final form was 0.95 for 40 children, aged 5:0-7:0 years.

In its final form the test explored the child's use of plurals, possessiveness, adjectives and verbs, and the use of pronouns with a selected rather than an extensive range of examples. It tested whether the child could inflect real words, and nonsense words. The range of items tested was:

Plurals, Regular	girls	guns	wugs	
	hats	books	biks	
	houses	pouches	gutches	
Irregular	men	feet	calves	
Uninflected	seaweed	hay		
Possessive Nouns	father's	girl's		
Pronouns	his	her	their	mine
Pronouns	you	them	himself	
Noun Agent	painter	climber		
Adjectives	happy	happier	happiest	
	old	older	oldest	
	kwerki	kwerkier	kwerkiest	
Verbs	is climbing		is opening	
	climbs	shuts	watches	
	climbed	opened		

Administration

The child was shown a picture and the tester would introduce the item as follows:

The children said to the lady, 'Open the door'.
And that's what she's doing.
The lady is o........the door.
But she is careful when she o........it.
Yesterday she nearly knocked the little girl over, when she o........the door.

In the presentation of nonsense words the child was shown a picture of a calf kicking up its back legs.

This is a calf who knows how to naz.
What is he doing?
Yes, he is nazzing.
Every day he does this.
Every day he...........
Tomorrow he will do it.
Tomorrow he...........

Light articulation of the initial consonant of the response word was permissible if this was necessary to stimulate a child's response.

Results

Total Language Score

A report has already been published of the differences between the four language groups when a total language score was obtained from four different tests of oral English, namely, articulation, vocabulary, sentence repetition and inflections (Clay, 1970, p. 157). On entry to school the Optimum group had high language scores which they maintained through 6 and 7 years. The Average English group improved at a similar rate approximately 1 year behind the Optimum group in their control of language. The Maori group was a similar distance from the Average English. The bilingual Samoan group had the lowest scores at every age tested. These results were similar for Samples A and B.

The changes in test scores between 5 and 7 years reflected the large amount of language learning taking place in the first two years of school in *each* of the four language groups. However, the rates of progress were similar and the graphs of progress parallel. If this parallel progress is to be turned to an accelerated rate of progress in order to close the gaps between any of the groups, then further insights into the process of language learning at this age must be gained.

The Morpheme Completion Scores

The scores of two different samples of children were analyzed for the effects of language group and age on the scoring level of the subjects. In Table 1 the Samples A and B were two different samples each of 160 children (see Clay, 1970); that is, they were separate cross-sectional groups. Samples B[1] and B[2] come from longitudinal testings of Group B six months apart. Each of the analyses of variance applied

Table 1

Three Two-way Analyses of Variance of Language and Age Group Differences on Morpheme Completion Test Scores

F ratios for three different samples.*

Sample	Sample A		Sample B[1]		Sample B[2]	
	F	p	F	p	F	p
Language	41.77	.001	42.33	.001	54.57	.001
Age	18.07	.001	13.57	.001	18.33	.001
L × A	0.89	ns	0.34	ns	0.58	ns

* Samples A and B are separate cross-sectional groups. Samples B[1] and B[2] are longitudinal testings of Group B six months apart.

to these three groups separately shows that the language groups and the age groups were significantly different in performance on the Morpheme Completion test at or beyond the .001 level of confidence. It should be noted that the age group results refer to groups six months apart, pointing up the rapid change in language skill which takes place at these ages. The differences between language groups are of greater magnitude.

The rate and direction of change in the test of morphological rules was similar to that of tests of other aspects of language acquisition. The language groups at each age level were in the same order as that discussed above for Total Language Score.

Relative Ease and Difficulty of Items

This section refers to a more detailed analysis of the responses of Sample A.

1. Table 2 arranges the features tested into a difficulty sequence for the Average English group. The left-hand column shows the number of errors made. Classes of words have been placed in separate columns across the table. The easy items are grouped at the top of the table and are not repeated in subsequent tables.

The third way of forming the plural in English, /ez/ in *houses* was more difficult and so was the phonologically similar verb form, *washes.* When children were required to apply these two rules to nonsense nouns or verbs the items were amongst the most difficult in the test, *gutches nazzes.*

The present participle and the simple past tense of regular verbs were easier to apply to real words, *opening opened,* than to nonsense words, *bodding bodded.* (The relative difficulty of *opened* and *opening* was the reverse of what would be expected from other research and this is perhaps due to a phonological feature of the word *opening,* the two unstressed syllables.) Two very difficult items are the irregular past tense verbs *wrote* and *swept.* The future tense was of moderate difficulty. The two pronoun items suggest a range of difficulty within this class of item. The superlative form of the adjective is easier than the comparative form.

2. No table has been constructed for the Optimum English Group because the sequence of acquisition or control duplicates, with only minor exceptions, that of the Average English group. Error scores were much lower.

3. For the Urban Maori group it could be hypothesized from sociolinguistic studies that these children learn a Maori/English dialect from their parents. Such a dialect might have its own rules for signalling the meaning changes equivalent to those tested in this research. It is an observation of teachers that Maori children seem to use the inflections of English in flexible ways rather than being constrained by the restricted rules of English morphology. If the dialect hypothesis were valid one

might expect to find systematic differences in the error patterns of urban Maori children when compared with children speaking a standard dialect. If what the teachers are reporting is a more haphazard phenomenon then one might expect to find unsystematic differences in the two groups.

Table 2

A Difficulty Sequence for Inflections for the Average English Group (N = 40)

			Type of Inflection			
No. of Errors	Plurals	3rd Pers. Sing. Verb Present	Verb: Simple Past	Present Participle	Future	Pronouns Possessives Adjectives
Easy items	girls, hats	climb, sit fish, sweep wait, write	climb, fish wait, wash	climb, fish wash, wait write		mine, her you, his, them, dirty
2	guns					
3						father's
4	book-s	paint-s				
5	bik-s					
6	feet	open-s				
7	houses					
8	seaweed					their
9						old-est
10	climb-er					
11	wug-s		open-ed			
12		wash-es		open-ing		old-er
13		mot-s				happi-est
14		bod-s				
15	men				will naz	
16			sat		will sweep	
17			paint-ed		will paint	
18				bod-ding		himself
19						
21	paint-er	naz-zes				
21	cal-ves					
25			swept			
26	gutch-es					
28						happi-er
29			wrote			
30			bod-ded			

The plural phoneme /s/ or /z/ is relatively easy and so is the possessive *father's*. The present tense of the third person singular verb is also relatively easy, *paints opens;* it requires only the addition of the same /s/ or /z/ phoneme. This rule can be generalized to nonsense words with relative ease, *bods, mots.*

Table 3
*A Difficulty Sequence for Inflections for the
Maori Group (N = 40)*

No. of Errors	Plurals	3rd Pers. Sing. Verb Present	Verb: Simple Past	Present Participle	Future	Pronouns Possessives Adjectives
			Type of Inflection			
4	gun-s					
6	book-s					
8	bik-s					their
9						father's
13		paint-s				
14	seaweed	open-s	open-ed			
15				open-ing		
16	climb-er					old-est
18	feet	bod-s				
21	wug-s	mot-s		bod-ding	will paint	happi-est
22	houses				will naz	old-er
23	cal-ves		paint-ed			
23			sat			
27						himself
28					will sweep	
29	men	wash-es				
30	paint-er					
34						
35		naz-zes	wrote			happi-er
35			bod-ded			
36	gutch-es		swept			

Neither of these positions was indicated by the results. The Urban Maori group made higher error scores and there were slight variations in the order of difficulty (particularly for irregular plurals and the /ez/ phoneme group) but on the whole Table 3 duplicates the sequence reported in Table 2. The variations could be due to chance variations. A rank order correlation of item difficulty in the two groups supports the impression of similar difficulty sequence.

4. The bilingual status of 75 percent of the Urban Samoan group was established (Clay, 1971) so that a viable hypothesis would be that rules from the mother-tongue, Samoan, might create interference with the acquisition and use of English morphological rules and alter the difficulty sequence for Samoan children. The error scores of this group were very high but the difficulty sequence is again similar to that of the Average English children.

Further Development After Seven Years

Presland (1974) reports the application of this same test to English, Maori and Samoan children at 8:0, 9:0 and 10:0 years using 90 children from 12 Auckland schools. His mean scores showed an improvement with age for all three groups, with a fairly satisfactory level of scoring by the Urban Maori and Urban Samoan groups from 9:0 years onwards on the real word items. Yet at 10 years both the Maori and Samoan mean scores were lower than those of the Average English children of 8 years; that is, an achievement lag still exists in this limited aspect of language development.

Table 4

A Difficulty Sequence for Inflections for the Samoan Group (N = 40)

			Type of Inflection			
No. of Errors	Plurals	3rd Pers. Sing. Verb Present	Verb: Simple Past	Present Participle	Future	Pronouns Possessives Adjectives
12	book-s					
14	gun-s					
15						their
17	seaweed		open-ed			
20						father's
21	climb-er	paint-s				old-est
22	feet					happi-est
23				open-ing	will naz	
24	bik-s					
25	houses	open-s	sat		will paint	old-er
26	paint-er			bod-ding		
27	wug-s	mot-s				himself
28		bod-s				
30			paint-ed		will sweep	
32	men					
32	cal-ves					
33						happi-er
34		wash-es				
35			wrote			
37		naz-zes	swept			
37			bod-ded			
38	gutch-es					

Table 5

Mean Morpheme Completion Scores in Clay and Presland Studies for Three Language Groups

	Clay	Age		Presland		
	5.0	6.0	7.0	8.0	9.0	10.0
Average English	19.6	21.9	29.6	32.9	33.3	35.0
Maori	9.8	14.9	23.2	22.1	28.3	28.6
Samoan	6.1	11.2	19.9	20.4	29.4	30.5

Discussion

Tables 2, 3 and 4 report the pooled scores of children who were between 5 and 7 years. They do not in any sense establish in which order the items are acquired. It is an assumption yet to be tested with longitudinal data, that the difficulty order of items in the report is related to a difficulty order of acquisition. The error patterns among different language groups suggest a gradual learning process over the period 5-10 years. The Average English group made more errors than the Optimum English group but the pattern of errors suggests that both groups were responding to a similar sequence of difficulty but that the Optimum group were mastering each rule earlier than the Average group.

When all four language groups are considered, error scores indicate that they had different degrees of control over the inflection rules of English, but within each group the pattern of difficulties was similar. For children of this age the difficulty sequence appears to be determined more by factors within the English language, such as frequency, regularity, or phonemic shape, than by factors within the child, such as interference from the rules of another dialect or language. Because none of the groups showed peculiar or different patterns of responding this does not in itself imply that special instruction is unnecessary. If tuition is necessary it seems as though the same teaching sequence could apply to all language groups.

This report is a descriptive one and does not lead to conclusions as to what is causing the higher error rates of the Maori and Samoan children. Presland found that in 48 percent of his error scores his subjects made no change in the stem word. It would be tempting to link this with the fact that nouns are generally uninflected in the plural in Maori as plurality is indicated by a change of article, but it is also true that young Average English children also adopt this strategy. Thus further exploration of this learning, particularly trial programs designed to accelerate the rate of acquisition, should include an Average English group.

There is an experiment which seems to have a useful pointer for instruction programs on these morphological rules. The first group of children were provided with the uninflected forms and were asked to inflect them while a second group received the opposite treatment. They were given the full form and asked to give the uninflected form. The second group made the greatest gains in learning the appropriate use of both forms (Osser, Wang and Zaid, 1969). Intuitive judgment might lead teachers to go from singular to plural, or uninflected to inflected, or present to past. There is strong evidence that the teacher's example should be the 'hard' one and the child's response the 'easier' of the two paired items.

15 Sentence Repetition: Elicited Imitation of a Controlled Set of Syntactic Structures by Four Language Groups

In my first longitudinal study I had used a sentence repetition test to test the articulation of sounds within a linguistic context rather than in isolated words. Within a short period of time it was obvious that this test was measuring something else. Sentence repetition might be used to check on a child's imitative control of language structures he might need to use in his schoolwork. A research student carried out a project to try to write harder items which would discriminate well among all five-year-olds, both those who were advanced and those who were slow. She had some success. A new research instrument was then designed and used in the second longitudinal study with white, Maori and Samoan ethnic groups, and the results were published in a monograph. The summary of that report is reprinted here. Not reported but of interest to the text or test designer, are the difficulty sequences of various phrase structures in the appendices of the earlier report. Readers should note that the report does not refer to the Record of Oral Language, *an observation instrument which was developed as a result of the insights gained in this study.*

Purpose and Design

The general purpose of this research was to clarify the relationship between the psychology of language acquisition and teaching procedures, programs, and texts at the beginning of schooling across ages 5:0—7:0. The specific problem was to examine what control over English grammar was revealed in a test of sentence repetition. If a child is required to listen to and repeat a sentence which is longer than his short-term memory span for single units, he will be forced to group the units in some way and will presumably refer the input to his personal grammar. His success on carefully constructed sentence-repetition items should reflect the structures over which he has imitative control, and his failures should reflect, in part, those structures he cannot control. Mingled with these effects will be errors made for other reasons, such as inattention.

The 10 urban schools used sampled a wide area of Auckland city and suburbs according to a demographic description of the urban area. Four groups of children were selected to sample different experiences with the English language. An Optimum experience group came from Professional homes where, it was assumed, good models of English and good preschool experiences would reduce any likelihood of handicapping cultural effects. An Average English group was drawn from the remaining children in the same schools. Two groups of Polynesian children were used with the requirement that each had two parents of the selected ethnic group. The Ss in one of these groups were the indigenous Maori children who, in this urban sample, were found to be monolingual in English. The other group was composed of immigrant Samoans, and 75 percent of these were found to be bilingual.

Two independent samples, A and B, were randomly drawn from the available populations in each language group. There were 320 children in all, 160 per sample. Within one sample there were 40 per language group and eight per age group—at 5:0, 5:6, 6:0, 6:6, and 7:0.

The test consisted of six sentence types with a common syntactic description of noun phrase plus verb plus X, where X could be either one or two following structures, which varied the number and type of syntactic rules. Each sentence type was written out in six variant forms, which varied the type of psychological operation applied to the basic description—transformation, preposing, expansion, and embedding. There were also four sentences with conditional clauses, making a total of 40 sentences.

The child's task was introduced by the instruction 'Say this. Say "Isn't the shop open, yet"?' 'Now say, "My next picture is going to be prettier".' And so on. After 20 sentences the tester moved to other tasks. The second half of the test was completed when the child was fresh at a second session.

Three types of data analysis were used: (1) To establish age and language group differences on tests, analyses of variance were made. (2) To record the relative difficulty of sentences allowing for an interaction of type and variant effects, a two-way classification table was constructed. (3) For 16 children aged 5:0 and 24 aged 7:0 in each language group, a comparison was made of performance on the syntactic segments of sentences.

General Trends

A marked increase in ability to repeat sentences was typical of each language group, including the Professional group, between 5:0 and 7:0. There were marked differences in the ability to repeat sentences *between* language groups with the proficiency order being Professional, Average English, Maori, and Samoan, but the graphs of progress were parallel rather than divergent. Graphs plotted for three other tests of language (inflections, vocabulary, and articulation) showed similar trends.

Sentence Type

An order of difficulty for sentence types in both Samples A and B, from easy to difficult, was: (1) N, be +; (2) NVN; (3) NV+; (4) Here, be +; (5) NVNN; (6) NVN+. This order of difficulty is relatively close to that found in Barham's (1965) or Loban's (1963) studies of spontaneous utterances, and an analysis of item-difficulty statistics *for each item* showed the same sequence of language groups—Professional, Average English, Maori, and Samoan—on almost every comparison. Only four of 108 comparisons failed to maintain the difficulty relationship.

Sentence Variants

An order of difficulty for sentence variants in both Samples A and B, from easy to difficult, was: (1) simple questions (transformations including negatives, passives, and tag questions), (2) preposed phrases, (3) expanded phrases within declarative sentences, (4) preposed clauses, (5) relative clauses, (6) infrequently used expansions within declarative sentences.

Item analysis again showed the same sequence of language groups— Professional, Average English, Maori, and Samoan—at the individual item level.

Type X Variant Analysis

A difficulty matrix was constructed of sentence type X sentence variant. From tables like this a teacher or text writer could select an easy variant of a difficult sentence type (for high-progress children), or an easy variant of a new sentence type (for an average group), or an easy variant of an easy sentence type (for a slow group). The matrix also showed interactions between sentence type and sentence variant which were not consistent with the general pattern. A tag question made a 'here, be +' sentence difficult ('There's a train to Wellington tonight, isn't there?'), and double embedding of two relative clauses in the relatively easy 'NV+' sentence type ('The boy who saw the car hit the bicycle ran to a policeman') made it one of the most difficult for all children. This demonstrates that it is possible to complicate a familiar sentence type so that it becomes unrepeatable by the young child, and, conversely, it is probably possible to simplify unfamiliar structures so that they are repeatable and can become familiar.

The Polynesian groups differed only in minor ways from the Pakeha groups in the rank order of difficulty for sentence types and sentence variants.

Contractions of Verbs

Contractions of the verb 'to be' were relatively easy to repeat, but in conditional clauses contractions were more complex and difficult.

Errors Within Sentences

When errors within sentences were considered, language and age group differences were found, decreasing from 5:0 to 7:0 and increasing from Professional, to Average English, to Maori, to Samoan.

The 'no response' category of failed sentences was always small, and the 'begun but not completed' sentences were relatively few. Children tried to give a sentence response. Even if they reduced the sentence to something shorter they tended to sample across the phrases rather than selecting first or last items.

At age 5:0 the proportion of error in any position in the sentence tended to be about the same, with the possible exception of the last syntactic segment or phrase which tended to be easier. At age 7:0 the most proficient group, linguistically, showed a slight but consistent trend for less error to occur as more of the sentence was repeated. For them, the beginning of the sentence to be repeated had greatest uncertainty because, as information built up and predictability increased, there was less and less error. This could be interpreted as indicating the development of new information-processing strategy. A progressive reduction of uncertainty by cumulation of linguistic cues across the sentence did not take place for the Maori children, who were almost all monolingual in English.

However, it is not certain that the change noted for age groups is necessarily age related. The sentences were rather long and difficult for young children. If easier sentences had been used, a beginning-to-end processing effect may have been found at age 5:0. It is not clear, therefore, whether the changes noted in this study were related to changes in cognitive or memory factors in the 5:0-7:0 period or whether it is a difference that depends upon prior familiarity with the structured nature of the stimuli.

Error Strategy

Errors were described as reductions, expansions, transpositions, and substitutions of morpheme or syntactic sequences within sentences. A reduction-type error was more common among the lower-scoring groups. Expansion varied from long-way-round attempts to render something that had been expressed succinctly, to filling out contracted verbs to their full citation forms, to inventive attempts to fill out intonation or rhythm contours following a reduction. Transpositions occurred when semantically similar nouns or verbs occurred within a sentence, but they were few in number. Perhaps reduction is a better strategy for language learning than substitution because it leaves a clear path to the acquisition of new structures or items, whereas prolific substitution could amount to practicing incorrect structures or cluttering the channel with noise. The bilingual Samoans tended to use a reduction strategy most frequently, while the monolingual Maoris used more substitution. Such differences could account for more efficient performance in the language of instruction by bilingual children compared with monolingual groups whose adult models use a nonstandard dialect.

Grammatical and Ungrammatical Substitutions

Expansions, transpositions, and substitutions were combined as substitutions, and these were classified, together with reductions, as grammatical or ungrammatical. While rates or proportions of *grammatical* substitution or reduction did not differ markedly across language groups, the rates and proportions of *ungrammatical* reductions and substitutions varied with language proficiency. The poorer language performers used ungrammatical reductions and substitutions at rates that were equal to or greater than their production of 'grammatical errors.' According to the 'spew hypothesis' of language learning, this would tend to increase the likelihood of ungrammatical segments recurring in language production.

This may indicate that Polynesian groups practice ungrammatical language, while the English groups increase their awareness of the flexibility and variety of English by substituting grammatical alternatives to the syntactic segments of the stimulus sentences. If this were true, the best would get better and the worst would get poorer with exposure to the same educative experience.

Substitutable Immediate Constituents

An interesting theoretical problem arose in the analysis of error, particularly in the analysis of contracted verb forms. How does the child equate a reduced form he says with an expanded form in the stimulus, and how does he match a contracted form in the stimulus with an expanded or citation form in his response? This behavior seems to have some analogy to reversibility in cognitive operations which emerges at about age 7:0. But the very young child has been using such a reduction strategy from his earliest attempts at naming and at two-word sentences and has been increasing his skill meanwhile. The problem deserves investigation. Contracted verb forms may be an experimental task that could be used to explore this problem. Perhaps the 'match' between an emitted reduced phrase and a stimulus expanded phrase is related to the speed with which the S receives auditory feedback from his own language production to match with a fading input memory of the stimulus.

Repetition of Noun Phrases and Verbs

The noun phrases of this limited set of sentences were analyzed in some detail at ages 5:0 and 7:0, and an order of difficulty, from easiest to hardest, can be suggested: (1) pronoun, (2) determiner class, (3) one adjective, (4) three morphemes, (5) four morphemes, (6) unusual usage. Repetition of the noun phrase was more accurate for some syntactic functions than for others, which suggests selection along the following lines for the introduction of new features of the noun phrase in a teaching program: *(a)* 'Here, be +' sentences may be a little easier at age 5:0. *(b)* The indirect object, however simple, is relatively difficult at age 5:0. *(c)* Initial noun phrases or preposed phrases have no prior distractions, but if the difficulties are placed here they can affect subsequent processing.

From the analysis of verbs, a tentative order of difficulty can be suggested for tenses: (1) present continuous, (2) simple past, (3) simple present and future, (4) past and future continuous. In single-clause sentences, difficulties were in the order: (1) the verb 'to be' despite its frequency, (2) contractions ('there's'), (3) two to four morphemes ('was getting'), (4) verb plus infinitive ('likes to get'), (5) auxiliary 'have' and modal 'can'. In two-clause sentences verb difficulties occurred *(a)* less in main verbs and more in subordinate verbs, *(b)* less in initial positions and more in subsequent ones, *(c)* when a main verb was separated from its subject by apposition or relative clause, *(d)* when there were three verbs per sentence, *(e)* when two or three verbs were similar ('hit', 'catch', 'throw'), *(f)* when tense changed across two clauses.

Theoretical Issues

Assuming that increasingly accurate performance on a sentence-repetition task reflects increasingly precise control of grammar, there was strong statistical evidence of marked change over the 5:0-7:0 period for all language groups, with the best children not yet in full control of the syntax of English.

Overall, the similarities of language behavior in all four language groups were predominant, from the linguistically rich or advanced Optimum group to the bilingual group. The sources of similarity would be the linguistic processing capacities of the human brain and the linguistic characteristics of the English language.

Despite a recurring finding of similarity between groups on several levels of analysis, some differences were found. There were differences *between* the monolingual-in-English Maori group and the bilingual Samoan group, in error rates and in the proportions of reduction and substitution strategies. There were differences between English and Polynesian groups in the rates of ungrammatical substitution and reduction, such that the Polynesians emitted ungrammatical 'errors' as often or more frequently than grammatical 'errors'. There were further differences in control over noun phrases and verbs. It was at the level of linguistic (or grammatical or cognitive) operations that any limitation on linguistic growth seemed to exist. Further study of the psychological processes of reduction and substitution at the level of the immediate constituents of sentences is required.

A basic question for research is how children of different linguistic status equate reduced or substituted constituents of sentences to longer or shorter stimulus inputs. Within this broad question more specific queries are raised. What is the effect on language of increasing cognitive mobility between 5:0 and 7:0? Does this imply a change in *(a)* the strategies for categorizing inputs into subjective units, *(b)* the type of edited construction process that is used, *(c)* dependence on semantic as opposed to syntactic cues (allowing more substitution and less syntactic matching by reduction)? Do such changes affect children of different linguistic status in different ways?

What is the relation between language growth and the three conditions of *(a)* omitting new features, *(b)* substituting optional ones, and *(c)* substituting nonoptional or ungrammatical for obligatory ones? Specifically, how does rate of emitting such responses relate to their later accessibility in productive language? Do the nonoptional forms remain in free variation with the obligatory ones? Whatever the performance in experimental or educational settings, does language usage in the child's home contribute to the viability of the nonoptional forms?

Practical Issues

From the educator's point of view, the linguistic status of an individual child may be observed by some carefully planned systematic probes of his ability to repeat the sentences of his reading texts and of other children's written expression. Where the child's language skill is found to be limited, it would probably be wise to respect the complexity and irregularity of the English language and introduce new difficulties slowly. Anchor the child's competence securely in the simple sentence structures of English before attempting to develop flexibility. Limit the number of words, phrases, clauses, and embellishments. Introduce novel features within a familiar linguistic context, with rhythm, intonation, markers, and meaning all directing attention to the feature and minimizing complexity elsewhere in the sentence. (This does not mean reducing sentences to the 'Come, John, come' variety, because this type of text reduces the cues available from the supporting linguistic context and does not tap the wide range of linguistic cues which the child already uses skillfully.) Particular attention should be paid to the relative ease with which the research children repeated imperative and short, simple declarative sentences, and to the relative accuracy with which phrases in the last position and the preposed position in a sentence were repeated. The use of such linguistic environments or positions for the introduction of *new* features will probably be least disturbing to the total linguistic context. A teacher must somehow strike a balance between a natural, spontaneous use of language which can facilitate growth, and a fluent, flexible, varied, and literary language which may force her language-limited groups to practice grammatical errors. Breaking through any self-limiting strategies may depend upon preventing and reducing the occurrence of ungrammatical utterances by simplification of the language used in the early education of language-limited groups, together with respect for a sequential order of difficulty in various aspects of the English language not unrelated to the number of morphemes in each phrase.

16   Extract from 'The Record of Oral Language'

Marie Clay, Malcolm Gill, Ted Glynn, Tony McNaughton and Keith Salmon

As a result of the interesting results in the cross-ethnic study, I worked with a team of colleagues to produce a practical instrument that could be used by teachers. This endeavor was a response to a request from the teachers themselves, through the executive of their professional union, and it was funded by them. Our purpose in designing the Record of Oral Language was to provide practicing teachers who had little or no knowledge of the study of linguistics with a means of observing very closely what children actually said. The ROL was designed, piloted and normed on a large random sample of Auckland children aged five to six years, and has been used with several English-speaking groups, in South Australia, Queensland, USA, Liverpool, Glasgow and Edinburgh. Apart from minor alterations to a word or two it moves across to other countries where English is spoken without losing its measurement qualities. It has all the statistical characteristics of a well-designed test and the somewhat surprising feature is the stability of the difficulty sequence of the items. However to put an emphasis on teacher and child development and on teacher observation we tried to eliminate the word test in the ROL manual.

Readers have chosen to use the ROL in different ways. It has been used to train teachers in language observation, to develop guidelines for programs arising from the protocols it produces, to monitor the size of changes that have occurred in the language of immigrant non-English-speaking children placed in special classes after their arrival in New Zealand, to assess one type of language difference in statistical studies which relate language status to other variables, and as an experimental tool in a study in Scotland (reported later in this section).

From a theoretical point of view the stability of the item difficulty is of greatest interest. The difficulty sequence found in the study of inflections appeared to be determined more by factors within the English language such as frequency, regularity or phonemic shape than by factors within the children such as dialect or language difference. Two studies of sentence imitation, the cross-ethnic study and the ROL development study, again point to a difficulty sequence applying across very different groups of children with different levels of performance ability. For this reason an extract from the ROL manual, and two pilot study reports from Australia, and from Fiji are included next.

Construction of Test Items

The items compiled for the pilot study were designed to represent cells in the following matrix of structures.

Type	Basic Structures	Declar-ative	Imper-ative	Yes-No Question	Nega-tive	Preposed Phrase	Relative Clause	Adverbial Clause
				Transformations				
A	Nbe +							
B	NVN							
C	NV +							
D	NVNN							
G	NVN +							

Supplementary sentence types in addition to those in the matrix were

Here be. . .
Wh-questions
Tag questions
Multi-predicated clauses
Noun clauses — 2 sets

Thus there were 35 structures in the matrix and 6 supplementary types giving a total of 41 sets. Each set had 3 levels of difficulty (123 subsets) and each subset contained 3 equivalent examples. This gave 369 items in all.

Origin of the Items

Examples of child utterances were compiled from the literature on language acquisition and from a pilot study. However as very few structures needed in the matrix were well represented, the majority of the items were made up using a frequency list of child vocabulary (Edwards and Gibbon, 1964) and an Australian research study of sentences used by 5-year-old children (Harwood, 1959).

The Linguistic Difficulty of the Items

No single linguistic criterion has been devised for predicting reliably the difficulty of sentences. A combination of factors was used in the creation of the item sentences. There are many factors which influence the difficulty of any sentence. An unusual word or ambiguity of meaning could easily cause an increase in difficulty greater than that produced by a change in grammatical structure or an increase in sentence length. The most reliable guide to difficulty is the nature of children's responses.

The following factors were used to control the difficulty of sentences in the ROL and should be borne in mind when creating new examples.

1. *Morpheme Counts* may not provide a reliable guide to the difficulty of encoding and decoding utterances. For example, in:

He is coming	4 morphemes
I come	2 morphemes

the first sentence has greater frequency in speech and is probably less difficult for the child to repeat than the shorter second one. Also the problems introduced by affixes and by fused morphemes make a measure of morpheme count very difficult to apply in a systematic way. However, an attempt was made to keep the morpheme count relatively consistent within each level. Where a sentence has a markedly different morpheme count from other sentences of that type or level it is because other factors have affected its difficulty to a greater extent.

2. *Phrase Count.* The number of phrases in a phrase structure description of the basic sentence must vary because that number is determined by the sentence type. For example, the imperatives necessarily do not have a subject phrase. Sometimes a phrase was added (e.g. as a qualifier of a nominal group). Nevertheless the difficulty level of a particular item could be increased by including additional phrases such as a qualifier of a nominal group. Sentence difficulty was varied by such additions.

3. *Difficult Features.* From research reports it was found that children of this age found the following features difficult: words not often used (nurse); words of greater complexity (shopkeeper); contracted forms, infrequent tenses, irregular forms of verbs and nouns; complex verbal groups; coordinated groups; final rather than initial placement of adverbial phrases or clauses. To achieve a progression from easy Level 1 examples of a sentence type to Level 2 or 3 examples some of these difficult features were introduced.

4. *Number of Actors.* Equivalence was sought with respect to the number of actors appearing in paired sentences. Compare —

May I play with Bill at his house?

May I play with Bill at Jim's house?

In the second sentence 'Jim's' introduces an extra person and thus an extra semantic element to handle.

5. *Ambiguities.* To avoid ambiguities in sentences with two or more actors when pronouns were used, the actors were differentiated by sex. Also sentences were avoided where the syntax could be misinterpreted momentarily during decoding.

e.g. That lady teacher...

teach   initially classed as a verb

The footballers

ers /əz/   *misinterpreted as 'is'.*

6. *Syntactic Structure of Items.* It was the aim that each clause in a multiclause sentence should conform to the structure type. Certain exceptions were allowed in order to produce natural sentences.

Nominal groups serving a syntactic function in two clauses were regarded as fulfilling the qualification for the basic clause type in each clause; the same consideration applied to relative pronouns.

7. *Semantic Acceptability.* The Australian and English word frequency lists used did not guarantee that the high frequency words used would be known to New Zealand children and the only other means of controlling for meaning was to have the sentences checked by two trained infant teachers.

Hence, in summary: if the test items were intended to probe syntactic control then ideally, phonological, morphological, lexical and semantic aspects of the sentences should not increase the sentence difficulty. One approach would be to use only a limited list of words and morphemes. However, there is also the need to gain the child's cooperation and therefore the sentences should maintain a reasonable level of variety and naturalness. Thus, at the stage of item writing, the difficulty of the items was manipulated by:

1. using a detailed matrix of structures,
2. counting morphemes,
3. counting phrases,
4. noting the difficulty of features,
5. avoiding ambiguities,
6. matching clause structures in multi-clause sentences,
7. keeping the meaning as simple as possible, and
8. using high frequency words.

Pilot Study

Sample

The selection of the actual items for the ROL necessitated the administration of the 369 items forming the item pool, to a random sample of children of the types for whom the instrument was intended. Thus, from a sampling frame of the 238 State and Private schools of the Auckland metropolitan area, a random sample of approximately one tenth (24 schools) was selected. This was done with probability of selection being proportional to size, and with replacement. From each of these sample schools, a second stage random sample of 10 children was chosen. The sampling frame within each school was all those children who were between 5.0 and 6.0 years at testing.

Testing Procedure

As 369 items were considered to be too many for any child to be given, a procedure was devised so that no child was given items unnecessarily. No easy items were given to a child who passed the items of average difficulty, and no difficult ones were given to children failing those of average difficulty.

Testers started each sentence structure at a level of average difficulty — specifically at item 4 of the 9 written. Items 5 and 6 of each structure were subsequently presented. But, in order to prevent the possibility of a structure being learned simply through the successive presentation of its items, other structures were used to separate that structure's item trio at that level of difficulty. Where any error occurred on items 4, 5, or 6 of any sentence type, the easier items — namely 1, 2, and 3 — of that structure were given to the child. However, whether or not the easiest items of a pattern were administered, if any of the average difficulty items of that type were responded to correctly, the harder items 7, 8, and 9 were subsequently given. After three consecutive failures on a sentence structure, testing on that structure stopped. For scoring, *any* deviation from the sentence given for repetition was marked as an error. Thus 'I will' for 'I'll', 'on to' for 'on', 'is' for 's', 'his' for 'its', and so on were all treated as errors.

In standardizing the procedures for the ROL it was necessary to decide on a consistent way of scoring such responses. While the use of either 'is' or ''s', for example, may indicate that the child has control over the grammatical structure, the statistics for the ROL have been calculated on the basis of the scoring method described, that is, exact repetition. In a trial rescoring, analysis allowed both full and contracted forms to be scored as correct, the difficulty level of the items changed only minimally.

The sequence of types and variants was designed not only so that items of a structure were separated from each other, but also so that easier forms were interspersed between more difficult ones. Further, similar structures were separated from one another.

Analysis

For each item, the following statistics were calculated:

(i) the difficulty index
(ii) a discrimination index, based on top and bottom 27% groups
(iii) the point biserial correlation between that item and the test as a whole.

Further, the sample was split at the median, and the statistics were recalculated separately for the top 50% and bottom 50%.

Selection of the Items

The basic form of the ROL was planned to be of three levels of difficulty. Thus, the difficulty of an item, as demonstrated by the pilot study, was a core concern when its inclusion in the instrument was being considered. However, other criteria also had to be satisfied.

(i) The ROL had to be of practical use to teachers, and therefore its components had to be ones which separately and together were pertinent to the classroom situation.

(ii) The set of items to be selected for the ROL had to make linguistic sense. That is, there had to be clear linguistic rationale for the item statistics of the items making up the ROL.

(iii) Each item had to satisfy certain statistical criteria:

a) It had to be comparatively easy for children who turned out to be above the median on the final instrument and comparatively difficult for those below the median.

b) It had to discriminate well among the children ranked at the top on the instrument and among those ranked at the bottom end.

c) It had to measure the same underlying ability as the instrument as a whole measured.

d) It had to have a difficulty appropriate for the sentence type and consistent with the other items at that level.

The levels sentences deliberately are selected at varying difficulty levels. The difficulty indices range from .15 to .89. There is no overlap in difficulty from level to level in the Field Trial data.

An examination of the item statistics from the pilot study showed that it was indeed possible to construct a test with three levels of difficulty, *and* satisfy all the above criteria. This was done by using the declarative form of the five basic sentence types, one of the noun clause structures, and the 'here be +' sentences to select a form other than the declarative in order to get satisfactory item statistics. Instead of the declarative form of NVNN structure in the middle difficulty set of items, the one actually used contains a preposed phrase, *For his birthday Kiri gave him a truck.* Similarly, of the more difficult items, the declarative form of an Nbe + item was not suitable according to the statistical criteria, and the imperative form *Be as quiet as you can when your father's asleep* was included.

It was possible to find two items of each structure at each difficulty level which satisfied the criteria, appropriately tempered for the level concerned. Thus, the core of the Levels Sentences consists of two examples of each of seven sentences types at each of three levels of difficulty. That is 42 items constitute the Levels Sentences section of the Record of Oral Language.

There were, however, many other statistically sound items. These then formed the pool of items from which further selection resulted in the construction of the Diagnostic Sentences. The three groups of levels sentences and the diagnostic sentences used 123 of the original 369 items.

Main Study
Sample

In order to test the instrument generated by the pilot study, and obtain valid item statistics on all 123 items of the test, it was necessary to sample randomly from the Auckland metropolitan schools again, this time using the information gained from the pilot study in regard to (i) mean school size, (ii) variation within schools, (iii) variation between schools, (iv) mean cost to visit a school for testing pupils, and (v) cost of testing a child. When these factors were weighed appropriately using an optimum allocation formula, it was found necessary to test 3 children from each of 131 schools.

As with the pilot study, the 238 state and private schools in the area constituted the sampling frame, and 131 of these were randomly selected, with probability of selection being proportional to size. Each school was returned to the sampling frame after selection. From each of the sample schools a second stage random sample of three 5.0 to 6.0 year olds was taken and tested.

Testing Procedure

The testers visited one school each day. At the beginning of the school day they obtained their random sample of children who were between 5.0 and 6.0 years on that day, and then spent the rest of the day testing them. Each child was called back three or four times in order to have him complete all 123 items of the instrument.

The order of presentation of the items was as follows:
(i)   The Level 2 items
(ii) The Level 1 items
(iii) The Level 3 items
(iv) The easiest Diagnostic items
(v)   The hardest Diagnostic items.

However, within each of the above sets, the sentences were sequenced in the same way as they had been in the pilot study. That is,
(i)   similar items were separated from one another
(ii) item pairs were separated maximally, and
(iii) easier forms were interspersed between more difficult ones.

Analysis

Using the whole sample, the same basic item analyses as for the pilot study were undertaken.

Item difficulties ranged as follows:

Level 1	.68 – .87 except for one item .56
Level 2	.42 – .63
Level 3	.15 – .38

Figure 1
ROL Item Difficulties from Field Trial

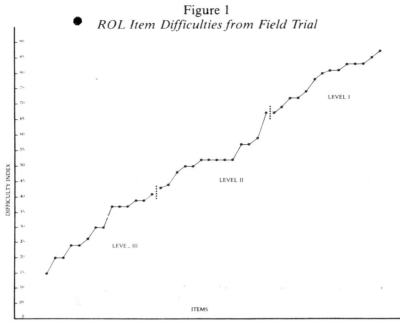

The mean score for 42 sentences was 22.3 for an ethnically mixed random sample of Auckland school children, the SD was 9.2 and the Kuder Richardson 20 reliability coefficient was .93.

Field Trials

Further trials were conducted with the assistance of speech therapists in the Auckland area. Two samples were used. The first consisted of 100 children drawn at random from all 5-year-olds while the second was also of 100 5-year-olds but was drawn only from children who had been referred for therapy.

Analysis of the item difficulties from these studies confirms that three distinct levels of difficulty have been obtained. A teacher can therefore start the administration with items from the middle difficulty level. If these are repeated correctly it is unnecessary to administer the sentences from the lower difficulty level. Since the Level 1 sentences are of lower difficulty than those of Level 2 it can safely be assumed that the child would pass those items also. This saves considerably in administration time.

An additional outcome of the analysis was to establish that the 42 items of the Levels Sentences have a reproducibility coefficient of 0.83. This was established by Guttman Scalogram analysis. With a perfect scale one could say that if item X were repeated successfully by a child, then all the items below it would also be correctly repeated by the child. (Such a scale would have a scalability coefficient of 1.00). The scalability of the ROL items means that very often one would be correct in predicting that a child who has demonstrated competence with grammatical structure X will also be competent with all structures which precede X on the ROL.

The trials using Speech Therapists as recorders are of importance in the development of the ROL. They confirm that the findings obtained under research conditions with one sample and only two recorders can be replicated with different groups of children using many different recorders under field conditions.

17 Australian and Fijian Pilot Studies using the ROL

Australia

In Brisbane Toohey and Miller (1978) decided to trial the Record of Oral Language as an assessment tool for establishing language differences and for providing the basis of an intervention program in the first year of school. They noted that the ROL was designed to assist teachers to:

- *observe aspects of a child's control over oral language*
- *assess a child's ability to handle selected grammatical structures.*

For their study they used only the Levels sentences. These consist of two examples for seven different types of sentences presented at three levels of difficulty so that there are 42 sentences in all.

The seven types of sentences are listed in Table 1 and an example of the different levels is given in Table 2.

Table 1

Sentence Types Used In The Levels Sentences

Type A	subject	verb 'to be'	simple statement	
Type B	subject	verb	direct object	
Type C	subject	verb	additional construction	
Type D	subject	verb	indirect object	direct object
Type E	subject	verb	noun clause	
Type F	adverb or relative pronoun		verb	subject
Type G	subject	verb phrase	object	additional construction

The Brisbane study used one Grade One class from each of six schools in the district under study. Apart from retardates and three children who refused to co-operate, all the children in these classes formed the total sample. There were 84 boys and 84 girls with an age range from 4 years 11 months to 7 years 0 months (mean age 5 years 6 months, SD 4 months).

The children were tested by experienced remedial/resource teachers before noon during the children's second week at school. All responses were tape-recorded and these tapes were used to correct any errors in the test scoring. All the Levels Sentences were administered following the directions in the manual.

The difficulty index was calculated for each of the Levels Sentences. In Table 3 these were compared with the indices reported in the ROL manual for New Zealand children from five to six years of age. In Table 4 the three schools in the southern part of the district (S) are compared with those in the north (N).

The analysis suggests that the order of item difficulty in this study is similar to that obtained during the New Zealand test construction. *In only one case* was a high level item easier than a lower level one. This occurred in:

For the holidays, Grandpa bought us a ball.

A similar result was reported in a Glasgow study (Clay, 1976).

Table 2

Levels of Difficulty for Type D Sentences

	Subject	Verb	Indirect Object	Direct Object
Level 1	John	is buying	me	a boat
	Mary	is giving	me	a book
Level 2	(For his birthday) Kiri	gave	him	a truck
	(For the holidays) Grandpa	bought	us	a ball
Level 3	The shopkeeper	sold	my mummy	some fresh cream
	The new teacher	read	our class	a fairy story

Note: The Level 2 sentences contain a preposed noun phrase (in brackets) because this proved to be the best item in terms of statistical criteria for the difficulty sequence.

Apart from two items at Level One, the New Zealand sample performed better than the Brisbane sample, which was to be expected. In New Zealand the sampling was randomized from the Auckland urban population whereas the Brisbane study was undertaken because a language intervention program was considered necessary.

The comparison of ROL results for different schools agrees with observations made by the teachers who administered the test. The children from schools in the southern part of the district appeared, to the teachers, to have more difficulties with language than their coun-

Table 3

Item Difficulty Indices
Brisbane, Australia and Auckland, New Zealand

Sample		Example 1							Example 2					
	Level	A	B	C	D	E	F	G	A	B	C	D	E	F	G
Brisbane	one	.79	.82	.85	.89	.87	.88	.80	.78	.82	.88	.78	.79	.63	.73
Auckland	one	.74	.87	.89	.85	.86	.87	.68	.72	.84	.85	.76	.56	.70	.70
Brisbane	two	.38	.42	.48	.63	.49	.50	.56	.53	.36	.46	.29	.49	.52	.42
Auckland	two	.52	.50	.51	.63	.52	.48	.63	.49	.44	.50	.42	.47	.45	.59
Brisbane	three	.32	.07	.25	.23	.10	.13	.26	.18	.10	.04	.08	.16	.18	.07
Auckland	three	.32	.20	.37	.38	.20	.32	.35	.26	.15	.21	.24	.18	.30	.30

Table 4

Item Difficulty Indices for Different Schools
Brisbane Project

Schools		Sentence Type													
	Level	A	B	C	D	E	F	G	A	B	C	D	E	F	G
S	one	.76	.78	.82	.89	.85	.85	.74	.76	.82	.84	.76	.78	.53	.68
N	one	.81	.85	.89	.89	.89	.90	.86	.80	.83	.91	.80	.79	.73	.78
S	two	.37	.38	.44	.62	.39	.45	.52	.49	.33	.40	.21	.49	.48	.39
N	two	.38	.47	.52	.64	.60	.56	.60	.57	.40	.52	.38	.49	.57	.44
S	three	.31	.05	.21	.17	.09	.14	.21	.16	.08	.01	.08	.14	.15	.06
N	three	.32	.09	.30	.30	.10	.12	.31	.20	.12	.06	.09	.19	.21	.07

terparts in the northern part and this is supported in the ROL results.

The project team concluded that the ROL could be a useful tool in identifying groups whose language development needed special attention. Minor changes to three items were found desirable for Queensland use.

Fiji

A study was conducted in 1973 of the English language skills of Fijian primary school children. This study has not been reported and I wish to thank the researcher, Isikeli Nacewa for permission to publish these results. The study demonstrated one way in which the ROL could be used with groups of children who were learning English as a second language. It provided results which showed that not only were the declarative sentences in the Levels Test sensitive indicators of changes that occurred in the learning of English but that the other types of structures listed for diagnostic purposes — imperatives, negatives, questions, and sentences with particular phrase and clause structures — were each sensitive to the gains in language control.

The study was designed to compare the performances in English sentence repetition of children who spoke a home dialect and who attended:
(a) Church schools in which they learned English from school entry onwards and in which English was the medium of instruction. Formal Fijian was taught as a subject.
(b) District schools where formal Fijian was the medium of instruction and oral English was taught as a subject for the first three years.

From the fourth year the programs were similar. Children were randomly selected—five girls and five boys from each class group in the two types of schools and the two provinces (N = 100). The mean ages of children in these five groups were 6.4, 7.10, 8.9, 10.1 and 12.4.

In the main part of the Sentence Repetition Test, the Levels Test, the scores increased with age indicating growing command of English language structure. There was an early advantage for the Church (English Instruction) schools but this had diminished by Class 6 (Table 1).

Table 1

Sentence Repetition Levels Test (42 items)

		Class 1	Class 2	Class 3	Class 4-5	Class 6-7
Type of School	Church*	5.45	10.80	18.65	26.40	31.55
	District*	1.75	5.20	10.55	17.15	28.40

* English was the language of instruction in Church Schools, Fijian in District Schools.

An analysis of variance showed that differences between years at school and types of school were both highly significant at the .001 level.

This result was confirmed for each of five specific types of variants on the declarative sentence forms of the Levels Test. Statistically significant differences for years at school and type of school at the .001 level were found for:
  Imperatives
  Questions
  Negatives
  Phrases
  Clauses.

If only data from the first three years of school had been gathered a very strong case for the early start in English might have been made. After Class 3 the differences decreased so that by Class 6-7 the differences had been reduced drastically.

Questions to be raised in attempting to explain these differences would be the effect of the trilingual situation of most children (two-dialects plus English) the language of the home, the language of the playground, the multi-lingual population of the church schools compared with the two dialect situation for the District school children, the training and quality of the teachers, the methods of instruction, the availability of reading materials and so on.

The study demonstrates the value of a simple, but hopefully valid, test of language acquisition for checking on the control being gained by these children over the English language. The control of the average New Zealand school entrant over this set of repeated sentences was reached in the 3-4th year of Church schooling and 5-6th year of District schooling. Time in tuition, as in many other studies, seemed to be important for language learning.

18   The Effect of Two Educated Dialects on Sentence Repetition Scores of Five-Year-Old Scottish Children

This paper reports a study of the effect of the speech or accent of the person who gives the sentence repetition items on the way in which young children repeat those items. One would imagine that a very different accent would create problems for five-year-olds. The solution sometimes advocated is that a standard administration using taped examples is preferable but this is debatable when young children are being tested. Personal contact can ensure attention, holding the child to the task, and providing encouragement to continue. The results of the study suggest that there may be other factors operating.

Methodologically there are two points of interest in this paper. Because there are two items of equivalent structure and approximately equivalent difficulty at each level and for every structure in the Record of Oral Language the observation instrument can be split in half. That opportunity, and the fact that the two experimenters had Glaswegian and New Zealand accents provided us with the opportunity to ask a question which probably is of interest to those who wonder what effect a teacher's accent has on young children's ability to understand what the teacher says.

Questions to be raised in attempting to explain these differences would be the effect of the trilingual situation of most children (two-dialect plus English) the language of the home, the language of the playground, the multi-lingual population of the church schools compared with the two dialect situation for the District school children, the training and quality of the teachers, the methods of instruction, the availability of reading materials and so on.

The study demonstrates the value of a simple, but hopefully valid test of language acquisition for checking on the control being gained by these children over the English language. The control of the average New Zealand school entrant over this set of repeated sentences was reached in the 3-4th year of Church schooling and 5-6th year of District schooling. Time in tuition, as in many other studies, seemed to be important for language learning.

Introduction

Dialect is defined in this study according to McDavid (1969) as any habitual variety of a language, regional or social. He states that '... we do need a term sufficiently inclusive to describe the fact that educated Britons do not talk the way educated Americans, or Canadians, or Australians or New Zealanders or South Africans do ...' (pp. 91-2). The research explored the influence of an educated Scots model and an educated New Zealand model on the sentence repetition scores of young Scottish children. In this test situation the language register would be described as Careful English (Dale, 1972). In the stimulus sentences, which were acceptable usage for both speakers, the lexical and syntactic aspects of language were controlled. Any differences occurred at the level of phonology—in pronunciation, intonation, accent and timing.

Several research studies have shown that children's control over the structure of English seems to be reflected in the types of sentences that they can repeat in an elicited imitation task (Menyuk 1969; Graham, 1968). When children are asked to imitate a set of sentences which are graded in different ways for syntactic complexity, imitative control has been shown to be in advance of comprehension or language production (Brown and Fraser, 1963). A test of this skill might be said to tap the growing edge of a child's control over language structure. However, it seemed highly probable that if a tester using a very different pronunciation from the child's home dialect were to present the sentences to be imitated this would affect the child's performance. The question of interest was the extent of this effect.

Method

The Test

A test was available which used 7 sentence types in declarative form (NVN, Nbe+, NV +, NVNN, NVN +, Here be + and NVC_{noun}). From 369 items tried out in a pilot study two declarative items were chosen representing each sentence structure at each of three levels of difficulty. Difficulty level was first hypothesized by the linguist and developmental psychologist who constructed the items and was confirmed (or rejected) after the pilot study on the basis of statistical evidence on item difficulty. The 2 examples on each of 3 difficulty levels for 7 sentence types gave a 42 item test.

Statistical results for this test were satisfactory and are presented in the results section of this report.

Examples of the sentences used are:
Pussy is drinking some milk.
Sally is riding her bike.
The boy by the pond was sailing his boat.
The cat next door was chasing a bird.
My aunt and uncle want to start building a new house.
That dog and the one next door like to chase the postman.

When this test was used in Scotland an opportunity arose to study two questions. Firstly, would New Zealand and Scottish children perform in a similar way on this sentence repetition test or would the item difficulty statistics vary in any systematic way in the two samples? Secondly, would the educated dialects of a New Zealand and a Scottish tester be related to the scoring level of the Scottish children?

Because the test contained two examples of every structure matched for syntax and item difficulty it could be divided in half and be administered as two parallel forms by two different testers.

As the sentences were constructed to exceed the memory span for digits of five-year-old children, it was hypothesized that the language signals emitted by the New Zealand tester would lead (1) to significantly lower scores on items administered by her or, alternatively (2) to a significantly lower scoring at the level of the test that was of moderate difficulty for a particular child but not on items that were very easy or very difficult for him.

Subjects

The 64 children tested in Scotland in December 1972 had entered school aged 5 years to 5 years 3 months in 1971 and 1972. They were randomly chosen in four selected schools after stratification for age and sex, 4 boys and 4 girls being chosen from each age/sex/school group.

The schools were selected to provide 2 lower socio-economic (LSE) and 2 higher socio-economic (HSE) samples. The 2 LSE schools were selected from Glasgow because the Scottish tester was Glaswegian. The 2 HSE schools were in Edinburgh.

Procedure

The testers visited each school at the same time and carried out a program of reading and language testing in separate rooms. Each administered half the battery and so it was natural for the child to receive half the sentence repetition items from one tester and at a later stage while performing other tests for the alternate tester to complete the parallel set on sentence repetition items. The record forms were marked as the child repeated the item, error responses were recorded in full and ticks were recorded for the correct parts of the sentences. Both testers were educational psychologists with extensive clinical experience in testing children. A preliminary training period to standardize administration was arranged but no statistical check was made on tester reliability for the recording.

Results

Total Scores

The mean Scottish score was 26.95 ± 7.18. The KR20 reliability co-efficient was 0.90 and the scalability co-efficient for 42 items was 0.84. These figures imply that the test was moderately easy, that there was a wide range of scoring throughout the scale, that it was internally consistent and that there was a gradient of difficulty within the scale. Table 1 reports these results together with comparative data from other samples.

Item Difficulty

In each school children were able to score close to the possible score of 112 on Level 1 (7 sentences per tester × 16 children).

The marked drop in scores at Levels 2 and 3 suggests that the difficulty sequence derived from children's performance in New Zealand was appropriate for Scottish children. This was confirmed when item difficulty in the Scottish sample was compared with both the New Zealand random sample (including many non-Europeans) and the New Zealand European sample. Only one item was more difficult for the Scottish children. It was:

For the holidays Grandpa bought us a ball

administered by the New Zealand tester.

Table 1
Sentence repetition test: results for four samples

Sample	Scottish: Total	Scottish: N.Z. Tester	Scottish: Scottish Tester	Liverpool	N.Z. Random	N.Z. Dutch
N	64	64	64	34	389	40
Mean	26.953*	13.484**	13.547	24.118	22.293	26.200
SD	7.182	3.750	3.857	9.731	9.217	8.165
K2D	0.901	0.819	0.831	0.957	0.934	0.933
Scaleability co-efficient	0.837	0.837	0.845	0.871	0.829	0.880

*No. of items in total test = 42
**No. of items in half test = 21

The comparison between Scottish and New Zealand speakers (S and NZ) showed little difference in scoring level (Table 2). The tester totals per school were so close that tests of the significance of the differences were inappropriate. Five and six-year-old children from Glasgow and Edinburgh found it no more difficult to repeat the sentences presented by a New Zealand tester than by a Glaswegian tester.

A test of significance of differences between schools was applied to the mean score for each Level Test. The differences between schools were not significant when the items were easy (Level 1) or difficult (Level 3) but there was a significant difference when the two low socio-economic schools were compared on Level 2, the level that was of average or moderate difficulty. While schools 1, 3 and 4 had similar totals, the children in school LSE2 had a much poorer control over sentence repetition items.

In Table 4 it can be seen that when the task was easy the child was likely to respond consistently to the two parallel items one from each tester, passing both. When the task was difficult the child tended to fail both parallel items, one from each tester. When the task was of moderate difficulty in terms of the level of the child's total test score, inconsistent scoring on parallel items occurred much more frequently. However as the scores obtained with either tester are not significantly different (Table 2) the inconsistency is more likely to be related to the item difficulty than to the tester accent variable.

Table 2
Sentence repetition: comparison between testers and schools

School	Tester	Test Level 1	Test Level 2	Test Level 3	Tester Sub-total	School Total
LSE 1	S	104	82	34	220	
	NZ	104	77	38	219	
	Total	208	159	72	439	439
LSE 2	S	99	61	17	177	
	NZ	96	66	10	172	
	Total	195	127	27	349	349
HSE 3	S	109	81	45	235	
	NZ	110	88	47	245	
	Total	219	169	92	480	480
HSE 4	S	107	82	36	225	
	NZ	111	80	36	227	
	Total	218	162	72	452	452

Table 3
Comparison between schools on mean scores

School	Sentence Repetition Test Level 1	Level 2	Level 3	Total
LSE 1	13.0	10.0 ± 1.7	4.5	27.4
LSE 2	12.2	$8.0 \pm 3.9*$	1.7	21.8
HSE 3	13.7	10.6	5.7	30.0
HSE 4	13.7	10.1	4.5	28.2

*Significantly different beyond 0.001 level from all other means.

Table 4
Inconsistent scoring on parallel items presented with different accents

	No. of Inconsistencies: using an individual criterion of moderate difficulty.		
School	Easy	Moderate	Difficult
LSE 1	12	54	33
LSE 2	12	48	22
HSE 3	3	45	16
HSE 4	2	60	26

Discussion

A sentence repetition test was administered by testers with two different accents, a New Zealand tester and a Glaswegian. The test appeared to discriminate between five-year-old Scottish children as effectively as it did in its country of origin, New Zealand. Of the four schools tested it was found that children in one school scored considerably lower than in the other three schools, and this might be considered to be a school at risk and needing intensive language programming if the school entrants were to be successful in their early reading progress. The test could have value as a screening instrument, selecting schools for special programs.

The evidence seems to indicate that the accent of the speaker made very little difference to the scoring level of the children in this research. Differences might have emerged because the two educated dialects of the testers were interacting with the effects of region (Scotland, New Zealand) district (Glasgow, Edinburgh), or social class (LSE and HSE). The results showed no effect for region, and as one LSE school in Glasgow scored similarly to the children in Edinburgh, the district and social class variables were not clearly distinguished. The only significant difference found was *between* the LSE schools in Glasgow. This suggests either a difference in level of language acquisition over-riding the phonological variation in the speech of the testers or a significant difference between the educated dialect of both the test and the testers, and the particular dialect found in one LSE school.

The New Zealand tester found she had great difficulty in understanding the Scottish children in any school in the classroom setting when they were clamoring around their class teacher. She had no difficulty understanding them in a one-to-one testing situation. Although her dialect did not make any difference in a one-to-one situation or in conversation with a five-year-old child, it could still be a considerable handicap in classroom teaching. Children trying to listen to a teacher who speaks very differently from the speech that they are used to in their homes before they come to school, may have great difficulty, and the limited task used in this research does not allow the results to be generalized to that situation.

There may be something different about the one-to-one situation, and that difference might lie in the speaker's adaptability. The speaker in a one-to-one situation matches his language in some ways to the comprehension of his subject. Perhaps the speech is slowed, perhaps it is delivered with greater clarity, better articulation, and possibly these variables change as the tester monitors the signals from his subject and works to retain rapport and attention.

Speitel (1981) explored the variations of dialect and Standard Scottish English (SSE) and concluded that many five-year-old children enter school with dialect forms learned in their homes but that 'they have more often than not also learned at that age that while it is all right to perform in the dialect in a play situation, when faced with some kind of superior person who speaks English, one has to suppress dialect forms.' This implies an adaptability on the part of the child as well as the tester. Shatz and Gelman (1973) have provided support for this view. Their four-year-olds adjusted their language in response to the 'receiving capacities' of their two-year-old listeners.

It is only possible to conclude from the results presented in this study that in the situation where the speech of a New Zealand tester and a Scottish tester were compared, five-year-old children were not handicapped by the differences in educated dialect in an individual testing situation. Whether this situation is different from a situation in which the speaker with a strange accent confronts a class of children is not answered.

Perhaps there are variables of adaptation and flexibility operated by the adult in the one-to-one situation which makes it a valuable tutorial situation for the child. It does seem that such adaptation on the part of adult speakers may be elusive to study but may be a very important variable to be considered in any explanation of language acquisition.

19   The Polynesian Language Skills of Maori and Samoan School Entrants

Tests of Maori and of Samoan language were administered by native speakers to two Polynesian groups in the study described early in this section. The Maoris were an urban group with two parents who claimed to be Maori. The Pacific Island groups in New Zealand were represented by the urban group of Western Samoans with two parents who claimed to be Samoan. (These tended to be recent immigrants.) The study investigated the children's understanding of their ethnic language, using the simple tasks of following directions and answering questions. It was assumed that a child was entitled to be assessed for language performance not only in English but also in his mother tongue so that credit could be given for being able to use more than one language. The contrast between the two groups was marked. The Maoris tended to score nil and the Samoans tended to get perfect scores. The vital factor seemed to be a decision of Samoan parents that Samoan would be the language of the home. The Maori children heard Maori spoken occasionally but were rarely called upon to use it.

If compensatory teaching programs are directed to children's deficits in the language of instruction, the first two years of schooling must be of prime importance. It is a widely accepted principle that a child should be instructed at first in his mother tongue while he gains oral control of the language of instruction but such a policy is impracticable in multilingual settings where children of several ethnic groups enter one school system. In Auckland schools many languages of the Pacific, such as Samoan, Tongan, Niuean, Fijian, Cook Island Maori, and Tokelauan, are found and English is the language of instruction. The principle 'to teach in the mother tongue' provides no guidance where an ethnic language has almost disappeared and has been replaced by a dialect or creole version of the language of instruction such as the West Indian dialect of English found among recent immigrants to Britain. The development of the language skills of young school entrants is of current research interest but one point is clear: intervention programs cannot be effectively based only on the analysis of the target language and the error patterns commonly observed. Programs must also take into account the total language competence the child already has; that is, the languages or dialects he already speaks. At school entry no child has more than a partial command of any language and the bilingual child has partial control over two languages.

These issues were explored in a research which compared a group of school entrants, immigrants from Western Samoa, with an indigenous Maori group. Avoiding estimates of how much either Polynesian language was spoken in the homes (as in the use of the Hoffman Bilingual Schedules, 1934) an attempt was made to record the child's understanding of either Maori or Samoan as well as his understanding and use of English.

The Research Design

An extensive study of young school entrants compared the progress in oral and written English between five and seven years of Optimum English, Average English, Maori and Samoan groups of city children (Clay, 1970). The present report deals with the language skills of the two Polynesian groups in the period October to December, 1968.

Subjects

To secure adequate numbers of Samoan children three city center schools were used and those selected were considered to have good teaching programs. For the Maori sample it was important to add two schools serving urban Maori settlements, plus one from a new state housing area, and two from own-your-own home suburbs, one established and one new. Samoan children were also drawn from these schools. The study was limited to urban children but every effort was made to obtain a sampling of schools that was representative and scattered widely throughout the urban area.

In each of the schools, teachers were asked to list under age and sex categories every child whose parents met the ethnic group requirements of the research. The Maori group had two parents who claimed to be Maoris and the Samoan group had two parents who claimed to be Samoans. The new entrants to school were aged 5:0 and 5:3, and the other age groups spanned 6 months each, so that the group aged 5:6 had children with ages between 5:4 and 5:9, and similarly for the 6:0, 6:6 and 7:0 groups. Subjects were selected by random numbers from these lists, 4 boys and 4 girls for each age and language group, giving 40 Maoris and 40 Samoans for Sample A, and a second independent sample, Sample B, drawn by identical procedure.

Language Performance

Three aspects of language were assessed: Vocabulary Recognition, Following Directions, and Answering Questions.

1. *Vocabulary recognition*
English vocabulary. The Peabody Picture Vocabulary Test was used (Dunn, 1959). It has four pictures per page and the child is asked to 'Show me the fish', 'Show me the one that's jumping'. Any culturally

relevant set of pictures could be used for a similar comprehension task. Because the child is required to 'show' rather than 'say' the task has advantages with subjects who are socially, culturally or linguistically shy. Co-operation and rapport was no problem and the Polynesian children attempted 50 to 100 words without tiring. The advantage of the Peabody Test over any set of pictures was that the items were pre-arranged in an order of difficulty appropriate to American children of similar ages.

Maori vocabulary. A Maori linguist who was also the father of young bilingual children prepared new Maori items that were appropriate for the same pictures but which were not translations of the English items. It was usually possible to find 2 pictures per page for which culturally relevant words existed in Maori. An intuitively-selected gradient of difficulty in the items was used because, as most of the Maoris were grouped at the low-score end, the usual techniques of item analysis could not be applied to the results. This may well be true for other combinations of dominant and non-dominant languages. The usual test design techniques may not be applicable to data from young bilingual subjects who have been randomly selected.

Samoan vocabulary. Samoan items were prepared in a similar manner with the assistance of both a linguist and a Samoan teacher. The items were new items appropriate to the pictures and to translations of either the English or the Maori items.

Following directions
Eleven simple instructions like 'Go to the door', and 'Put the pencil on the book', were administered in Maori. These were translated and administered to the Samoan group.

Answering questions
A set of 7 questions that could be answered readily if they were understood were written in Maori and translated into Samoan. In this task an item was passed if the child gave a correct or possible answer in English or Maori or Samoan. Thus high scores indicate only comprehension in the language and not the child's ability to generate utterances in that language.

Administration of Tasks

As the ethnic and language characteristics of the research worker in cross-cultural research are important (Vaughan, 1964) a tutor of Maori Studies, who was experienced with school entrants, worked with the Maori children. When she was given freedom to develop her own method of introducing the tasks she established rapport sensitively, and rapidly gave the child permission to speak Maori by instructions like these.

> *Do some of the people you know speak Maori?
> Who are some of them? 'My father.'
> *Daddy is clever. Anybody else? 'Mummy.'

Are you clever like Daddy? 'Yes.'
*Are you lucky like Mummy? 'Yes.'
*Shall we see how clever you are?
You and I are going to play a game.
See this book?
Look at these pictures.
*They all have English names.
*They all have Maori names too.
This is a moenga.
Which is the picture of a *moenga*?

The starred instructions were thought to be very important in the cross-language situation. The research worker was free to give her instructions in either Maori or English but found English the appropriate language in every case. It was believed that the Maori children had every opportunity to perform without handicap in this situation.

Assessing the performance in the Samoan language was not so satisfactory. The people located as fluent speakers of Samoan and skilled in working with little children were all classroom teachers. The co-operation of headteachers who made the teachers available within their own schools was greatly appreciated but it did mean that five different testers were used, and no-one was available to travel to distant schools to which isolated children had transferred. Therefore 8 of the 80 Samoan children in the research sample were not tested in the Samoan language compared with 4 of the 80 Maoris. However, these factors, which would normally introduce variability and inconsistencies into the results, are of little significance because of the high scoring of most of Samoan children. Although the investigator could not check on the Samoan conversation between tester and child she felt (as an observer and an experienced clinician) that the procedures were valid ones for testing (and not prompting) and were comparable to those used with Maori children. Research assistants had freedom to give the instructions in either language and frequently did so in Samoan. They were shown the style of introduction used by the Maori assistant and asked to use a similar one. Their introductions were judged by the investigator to be much briefer than those used with Maori children and *less* reassuring. Despite this most Samoan children obtained high scores. (This also defeated the item analysis techniques).

Results

English Language

The Maori and Samoan groups were below the Average English group at school entry and two years later. Combined scores for English articulation, vocabulary, inflections and sentence repetition were expressed as T-scaled scores for samples A and B, and were plotted for all language groups, Optimum English (children with professional parents), Average English, Maori and Samoan. With only one exception the groups at every age in both Samples A and B were ranked in the order Optimum, Average English, Maori and Samoan (Fig. 1).

An analysis of variance yielded significant main effects for age, and for language groups ($p < 0.001$, Table 1). At 7 years in Sample A the Samoan group exceeded the Maori average which agreed with a claim by teachers that the Samoans do, in time, draw ahead of the Maori children in school achievement (Benton, 1966) but this was not a significant difference in this research and was not supported in Sample B. However, the progress of *both* Polynesian groups at 7 years placed them well above the Average English child at 5 years. The parallel progress of all groups was satisfactory but efforts could be made to accelerate the progress of the Polynesian groups.

Figure 1
*T-scaled Scores of Four Language Groups at Three Age Levels
on a Combined Score for Tests of Oral English
(P: English (Professional Parents); E: Average English;
M: Maori; S: Samoan).*

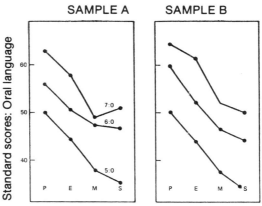

Table 1
*Analysis of Variance of Language and Age Differences for
Samples A and B on a Combined Score for Oral Language*

Sample	Source	df	F	p
A	Language	3	31.35	< .001
	Age	4	19.95	< .001
	L × A	12	0.44	ns
B	Language	3	40.45	< .001
	Age	4	24.52	< .001
	L × A	12	0.22	ns

Table 2
*Raw Scores for Vocabulary in Maori, Samoan
and English for Samples A and B[1]*

	Sample A				Sample B			
Vocabulary score	Maori × Maori PPVT	Samoan × Samoan PPVT	Maori × English PPVT	Samoan × English PPVT	Maori × Maori PPVT	Samoan × Samoan PPVT	Maori × English PPVT	Samoan × English PPVT
No items	43	58	100	100	43	58	100	100
67-100			3					
61-66			3	1			1	2
55-60		3	10	10		5	3	3
49-54		11	14	13		6	10	5
43-48		10	8	8		8	14	6
37-42		3	1	3		4	5	4
31-36		0	1	2		3	3	5
25-30	3	3		1	1	2	3	2
19-24	**15**	2		1	**14**	2	1	2
13-18	17	4			22	4		
7-12	4	1						
0-6								
Mean score	18.57	40.36	53.27	50.25	17.59	40.90	44.85	46.05
All scores above	19	23	35	35	19	23	35	35

[1] Bold-type figures indicate the cut-off point for guessing.

Maori Language

A limited control over Maori vocabulary was shown in each Maori sample with mean scores of 18.57 and 17.59 for Samples A and B, when the possible score was 43 (see Table 2). In the 4-choice task a score of 19 or more had probably not been obtained by guessing ($p < 0.01$) and if children only scored on those items which were transliterations of English words they would be placed below this cut-off point for guessing. Mean scores for the longer test of English vocabulary were 53.27 and 44.85 for Samples A and B. To overcome the problem of comparing a shorter test in Maori with a longer one in English the significance of the difference was calculated between the proportion of Maoris scoring better than chance in each test of vocabulary. A significant difference was found in favor of performance in English over performance in Maori vocabulary in each sample (Table 3).

Table 3
*Differences in Proportions Scoring Better Than Chance
in Samples A and B*

	Language groups	Peabody Pic. Voc. Test in	Number above chance	Scoring below chance	Proportion above chance	*p*
Sample A	Maori	Maori	18	21	.46	< .01
	Maori	English	39	1	.97	
	Samoan	Samoan	30	8	.79	< .01
	Samoan	English	35	4	.89	ns
Sample B	Maori	Maori	15	22	.42	< .01
	Maori	English	33	7	.83	
	Samoan	Samoan	28	6	.82	< .01
	Samoan	English	30	9	.77	ns

Table 4
Following Directions in Maori and Samoan

Test score	Sample A		Sample B	
	Maori	Samoan	Maori	Samoan
	High scorers:	Median > 10	High scorers:	Median > 10
11		21		18
10		5		4
9		2		3
8		(28)		(25)
7				
6	1			
5	Low scorers:	Median < 1	Low scorers:	Median < 1
4	1			
3		1		1
2	1	2	1	1
1	14	3	5	3
0	22	4	31	3
		(10)		(8)
Total	39	38	38	33

For Following Directions the mean score for both Samples A and B was less than 1 correct out of a possible score of 11 (Table 4).

On Answering Questions only 3 of 39 Maori children in Sample A and 4 of 37 in Sample B answered one question and the remainder did not score (Table 5).

The Maori group knew some items of Maori vocabulary but were unable to understand spoken Maori. They were also below average in their control of English.

Table 5
Answering Questions in Maori and Samoan

Test score	Sample A Maori	Samoan	Sample B Maori	Samoan
	High scorers:	Median = 7	High scorers:	Median = 7
7		16		18
6		7		4
5		4		1
4		(27)		(26)
3	Low scorers:	Median = 0	Low scorers:	Median = 0
2		1		1
1	3	3	4	1
0	36	7	33	5
		(11)		(7)
Total	39	38	37	33

Samoan Language

For Samoan vocabulary, a task of 58 items, scores were relatively higher. Samples A and B had mean scores of 40.36 and 40.90, with a range from 6 to 38. Samoan scores for English vocabulary were 50.25 and 46.05 but the Samoan and English mean scores cannot be related meaningfully to each other because the total number of items differed. When the proportions of children scoring better than chance on the English and Samoan vocabulary were compared (Table 3) there were no significant differences. The Samoan child had a useful control of vocabulary in each language.

On Following Directions the Samoan sample split into 2 groups (Table 4). The top-scoring group of 28 and 25 children had mean scores of 10.88 and 10.30 while the bottom-scoring groups of 10 and 8 children had means of 1.73 and 0.83. The same pattern was observed for Answering Questions (Table 5). With a possible total of 7, scores of 5 or more were obtained by 27 and 26 children in Samples A and B respectively. The bottom-scoring group contained 11 and 7 children who scored 0 to 3.

The Samoan group can be classed as predominantly bilingual in understanding both languages, although about 25% scored higher in English than Samoan.

Comparison of Maori and Samoan Groups

The Samoans had better performance than the Maoris in their ethnic language ($p < 0.01$). On Vocabulary the Samoan proportion scoring above chance was 0.79 and the Maori proportion was 0.46. For Sample B comparable proportions were 0.82 and 0.41. Differences that were significant were also found for Following Directions

(X^2 = 41.54 and 43.57, df = 1, p < 0.001) and for Answering Questions (X^2 = 42.67 and 51.01, df = 1, p < 0.001).

A high proportion of the bilingual Samoan group had better than chance scores in *both* English and Samoan Vocabulary. They had good control of Samoan although they made the lowest scores in English. Samoan children were not significantly lower than Maori children on English vocabulary and performed comparatively better on their ethnic language test. Their total language competence was, in a sense, greater than that of Maori children who performed better than the Samoans on English vocabulary but scored poorly on the Maori Vocabulary, Following Directions and Answering Questions.

Discussion

This research began with the simple assumption that a young child's total language skill at school entry consisted of his control over the language of instruction (English) plus his control of his 'other' language. At this age, the child would have only partial command of either language. The child's understanding of the two languages was tapped by simple tasks of Following Directions and Answering Questions which provided a clearer division of those who knew the language from those who did not than did vocabulary tests. Some assessment of language production would be desirable in future studies. The development of tests for these purposes will face problems of item analysis, reliability and validity, and research variables which must be sensitively controlled are the ethnic status of the researcher and the cultural sanctions on the use of the non-dominant language.

Language planning for school entrants in a multilingual environment may have one of several aims. 1. To improve performance in the language of instruction (*e.g.*, Australian for immigrants, Hebrew in Israel, American English in Pago Pago); 2. To add a standard dialect to a non-standard dialect (*e.g.*, West Indian or county or lower class dialects in Britain); 3. To improve performance in two or more languages (*e.g.*, in India adding Hindi and English to the mother tongue); 4. To revitalize a minority language (*e.g.*, Maori in New Zealand, Gaelic in Scotland).

In New Zealand language planning to meet the needs of Maori and Pacific Island children in urban classrooms has been directed towards their relatively poor command of English and the search has been for 'Non-European' or 'Polynesian' difficulties with the English language. There has been an increasing faith that the techniques of teaching English as a second language will provide educational solutions. Such a solution will not solve the educational dilemma which arises if the society has chosen to keep alive the home language as well as ensure a high level of functioning in the language of instruction.

The language problem for the Maori emerges from this study as teaching a standard dialect to children with a non-standard dialect and of revitalizing a minority language. Historically educational policies forbade Maori children to speak their ethnic language at school. The aim was to improve performance in the language of instruction by speaking in English (Biggs, 1969). This report has described what can happen when such a policy is applied over a long period of time. The Maori child has been given a restricted dialect of English that is spoken by his parents in place of the Maori language. Better solutions are required.

Should the Maori language be taught to school entrants as part of a campaign to reinstate the ethnic language and improve the Maori child's self-concept and ethnic pride? The author believes that this study of a city sample provides some strong evidence *against* the introduction of Maori language teaching at this level for the following reasons. 1. The children do not know Maori and could face an entirely new language which was not the medium of conversation in the home environment and not the language of instruction. 2. Public education systems do not teach second languages very successfully to children *of this age*. 3. Reports have shown that Maori pupils had three other areas of deficit in their early school learning — in oral English, in visual perception of print and in reading (Clay, 1970). Diverting teaching time to Maori language seems likely to increase rather than decrease the opportunities for failure unless the language can be reactivated in the home environment also.

These are arguments against *formal instruction* in Maori language for English-speaking five-year-old Maoris. They do not preclude the recognition and fostering of Maori in other ways. Bilingual preschool activities, culture clubs in schools, story books for young children in both languages, and parent-teacher-child contacts planned to foster the Maori language and culture in informal ways and so remove the sanctions on Maoris speaking in Maori with children may have desirable effects for revitalizing the language that Maori scholars have said is necessary for Maori identity. The teaching of Maori to older children might be considered.

For the Samoans in Auckland the educational task is to improve performance in the language of instruction. There appeared to be no continuing disadvantage to the Samoan children in their bilingualism. Although their control of English was relatively poor on entry to school at 5 years and their progress slow in the first year at school, an overall control of two languages emerged at 7 years. It was suspected that bilingual Samoan children had learned two languages because their parents had required home conversation to be in Samoan, but had been equally insistent that progress be made at school. The first language was supported by a strong ethnic culture, the second by the school and parents, both urging the child to do well. What may be crucial for success in two languages may be parents who value and speak two languages, providing for the continuous development of language beyond the limits of the classroom. This would be consistent with reports of French-English success in Canada, and English-Gaelic difficulties in Scotland.

To test this hypothesis it would be desirable to go beyond the approach of this research and to study parents' conversations with their preschool children and school entrants, analyzing on the one hand for frequency, context and topic, and on the other for linguistic features. If bilingual facility depended upon bilingual competence of the parents, and a society aimed to foster both a minority language and the language of instruction, there would be reason to plan educational programs which brought parents and children together in the school for language activities. In countries where literacy is being increased such practices could serve the purpose of oral language learning and of reading and writing.

A further discussion point relates to the concept of a 'passive bilingual.' In attempts to sample bilingual and monolingual groups a difference is said to exist between those subjects who hear and understand a second language but do not speak it with any fluency and those who are able to generate new utterances in that language. If a question in Samoan were put to a passive bilingual he would be unable to answer in Samoan but, comprehending the question, would answer it in English. In the course of this research the doubt arose in the mind of the author that passive bilinguals exist among young children, but that this is a concept applicable to (a) the subject who has had the opportunity to learn from the written language, or (b) the subject who is addressed in one language and permitted to to reply in another.

It would be consistent with much in the developmental psychology of language to hypothesize that the young child's understanding of a language will depend on his active use of it in conversation with a model who is expanding his utterances. Therefore both condition (a) and condition (b) would not apply to young children up to 5 or 6 years. Such a view is consistent with the Samoan language skill of the urban Samoan child and the absence of Maori language skill in the urban Maori child in this research.

Finally, a tentative hypothesis is raised by the relative success of the Samoan children in total language competence compared with the Maori children. The bilingual adult is always aware of which language he is speaking, and some research evidence suggests that by 6 years a child can keep two languages clearly apart (Leopold, 1949). The differences are gross. When two dialects are involved the differences are far less obvious, especially for the child whose articulation, vocabulary and grammar are all, as yet, immature. It may be easier for a child to master two languages from two difference sources or settings (Smith, 1935), than to develop two dialects that are independent of each other, one for the neighborhood and home and the other for the school. Even if one condition is not easier than the other, each may require different educational programs.

The simple assumption that language planners should know what languages or dialects the child speaks on entry to school has raised important issues relating to the education of two Polynesian groups in urban Auckland. Direct analogy to other countries would be improper. What has generality is the principle that programs should arise from descriptive accounts of the linguistic environment and the total language competencies of particular groups of school entrants.

Note

The research was supported by the Maori Education Foundation and the Kelliher Maori Economics Foundation. The opinions expressed by the author do not necessarily reflect the opinions of these organizations. The author acknowledges with gratitude the valuable assistance received with aspects of test construction, administration and interpretation from Dr. P. W. Hohepa, Dr. A. K. Pawley, Mrs. Heath, Mrs. M. Penfold and Mr. P. Sharples who are associated with the Department of Anthropology at the University of Auckland.

IV   Tangled Tots and Reading Knots

This group of papers describes the development and implementation of an early instruction program that undercut a high proportion of reading difficulties in the second year of school.

Between 1963-9 the progressions in reading behavior made by infant school children in New Zealand were observed, recorded and described. Several ways in which teachers could observe their children's progress were made available to teachers who were encouraged to set aside time for observation of reading behavior and changes in reading behavior, as distinct from teaching of reading. Writing was considered an integral part of gaining control over understanding messages in printed language.

1969-72. Teachers were encouraged to arrange for a thorough observation of all children who were not making satisfactory progress after one year of instruction. (In New Zealand this would be at the time of the child's sixth birthday).

1972-6. To facilitate a wider understanding among teachers of the procedures available, the State Department of Education provided an inservice program of rather unusual form, a tape-slide program, for teachers to take individually, to learn the latest ideas about infant reading instruction and ways of observing and recording reading behavior.

1976-7. As a result of implementing observation procedures teachers asked for further help. They wanted more guidance on what to do with the children caught in this six-year-old 'net' who were having unusual degrees of difficulty getting started on reading. We began at the workface. We observed good teachers of children having difficulty, and we observed the children. Gradually we articulated what we thought were some of the children's problems, and what seemed to be efficient, helpful and economical procedures. We encouraged the teachers to make the children independent of them, avoiding a major hazard of remedial education when the child becomes dependent on the teacher. We urged the teachers to accelerate the children's progress so that they could rejoin the mainstream of their class and survive (even with a poor teacher!). Acceleration was achieved by starting always from the child's universe of knowledge (not the teacher's) and judging what would be the next most profitable step for that child to help him to read more complex printed texts. Almost all the work occurred on story texts. Every lesson had a story writing section. Every child had a lesson every day by himself.

1978-9. The scheme we developed was field-trialed in five schools with success. It was then tried in 49 schools in 1979, another 48 schools in 1980 and 24 in 1981. There is an on-going inservice training scheme for the teachers which runs for an entire year. The follow-up study showed that the gains of the children who completed the program were retained a year later.

20 Learning Disorders

I have not attempted to bring this 1972 paper up to date. My reading of research and review literature in the last five years has not led me to change my position markedly. The paper is included in its original form because of the important relationship it has to the development of the Reading Recovery program. It shows the position from which we began that work.

When each group of children for whom special education was traditionally provided has been diagnosed there remains a group which has great difficulty in learning. Such children seem intelligent, but they fail in school. They may use language well, or show high problem-solving ability with practical tasks, but their performance in school subjects is miserably low. They seem to have poor concentration, but one must remember that for hours every day the activities of their class are too difficult for them. They seem to attend poorly, but who can persist for long with meaningless symbols and failure tasks? What could be the reasons for this school failure?

First, the children may not have had appropriate opportunities to master basic and necessary learning skills. This could occur because they have lived in depriving environments outside school itself, or because of absences from school, changes of school, poor teaching, or unhappiness in the child at a critical point of education, especially during his early schooling.

Secondly, the child may have been learning, more or less, throughout his years at school, but because of many misconceptions, wrong associations and faulty approaches to his work, not detected by teachers with large classes, he may have tangled the teaching into a web of distorted learning and have acquired less than adequate strategies for learning which block his school progress.

Thirdly, the child may have been unable to learn because of inefficiencies in his nervous system: not a lack of intelligence, but pronounced difficulty in applying visual and auditory perception or language or motor responses to the cumulative task of complex learning.

Because some children who came to psychological clinics with learning problems seemed to have a difficulty of this last kind it was thought that there could be blocked nerve pathways in the brain (as a result of slight brain damage) or, alternatively, that there could be some disturbance within the brain as it operates (analogous to interference in communication systems), which disrupts the inward and outward transmission of messages (described as minimal brain dysfunction).

Children who have pronounced difficulty with school learning may therefore be divided into those who have missed important opportunities, those who have tangled their learning and those who have possibly suffered from some organic limitation. Can those three sources of learning problems be separated one from the other, and from the flux of inefficiency in normal development that goes with being young and immature? The answer to that question is critical for the new concept of learning disorders which is discussed in the literature of special education today.

Although this concept has not yet made a significant impact on New Zealand education, the popular press has begun to explore reading problems labelled as 'dyslexia' and publishers have advertised special materials for children with learning disorders. New Zealand educators have an opportunity to view from afar the blooming and fading of new concepts in other Western countries and to apply critical analysis to the evidence. It is an appropriate time to examine the concept of learning disorders in order to weigh its utility. This chapter evaluates the earlier concept of minimal brain dysfunction, explores some problems inherent in the learning disorder concept, discusses the clinical tests used for diagnosis, and examines some of the dilemmas about teaching programs.

The Concept of Minimal Brain Damage or Dysfunction

Between 1945 and 1960, the attention of special educators was drawn to a group of children suspected of having minimal brain injuries. When brain damage could not be detected by neurological examination a psychologist might still conclude that damage of a minor degree existed because the child's behavior and test scores resembled those of children known to have brain injury. As the manifestation of minimal brain injury would be solely in learning or behavior disorders, the diagnosis was not open to proof or disproof. It relied upon a consensus of expert opinion based on agreed-upon definitions.

The modified concept of minimal brain dysfunction, according to which unusual but testable behaviors were assumed to be the product of a brain functioning in unusual ways, was a step in the direction of objectivity. This concept, unlike that of brain damage, has not come to be widely accepted.

Either concept was non-specific in that it embraced different learning — problems in reading, speaking and writing or in social and emotional learning. Yet, each was specific in the sense that a child's particular set of difficulties could be unique. Defined in general terms, the concepts subsumed a large variety of difficulties; defined

in any precise way, they covered particular types of disorders.
It is a symptom of the diversity and confusion within this area
that the concepts tended to be redefined by each writer on the
subject.
A typical and recent definition of minimal brain dysfunction is
provided by Weiner (1970):

> . . . children of near average, average or above average intelli-
> gence with certain learning or behavior disabilities ranging
> from mild to severe which are associated with deviations of
> function of the nervous system. These deviations manifest
> themselves by various combinations of impairment in percep-
> tion, conceptualization, language, memory and control of
> attention, impulse or motor function. . . .

There are difficulties with this and similar definitions; these are
outlined in the remainder of this section.

1. Children with below-average intelligence are excluded, although
this would possibly remove at least 50 percent of those who suffer
from minimal brain dysfunction from special treatment. Yet the
cut-off point has been necessary to exclude children with other types
of handicap.

2. The disabilities are associated with deviations of *function* of
the nervous system. That definition does not separate out:
(a) functioning that has never been organized by appropriate experience;
(b) functioning that has been organized by experience into a distorted or inefficient system;
(c) functioning which is deviant for organic reasons.

3. The disorders are described as mild to severe. The diagnosis of
atypical conditions is always more reliable and valid if the disparity
with normal is large. One can be less sure that mild degrees are not
merely fluctuations within normal development. Also, when the
disorder is mild the elimination of competing diagnoses like emotional causes and poor teaching becomes difficult.

4. The impairment may arise in any area of functioning and in
various combinations. Children diagnosed may have few symptoms
in common.

5. Minimal brain dysfunction is not observable. The psychologist
makes a diagnosis by inference from a pattern of past history and
current functioning, according to his personal understanding of brain
functioning. The diagnosis is arrived at because . . . "it seems logical
to infer . . . that subtle organic bases . . . reflect minimal brain dysfunction". . . . The inference is made on the basis of carefully-assembled,
complex data of varying degrees of reliability and in this there is
scope for error.

6. Minimal brain dysfunction may arise from genetic or biochemi-
cal irregularities, birth injuries, or other illnesses or injuries sustained

in early childhood. Later in childhood the symptoms are confounded by a developmental variable. Behavior and learning problems may be diminished in later years by increased emotional control, satisfactory social development and improved cognitive skill so that many characteristic features may be no longer apparent. The sole manifestation may be poor academic performance, a sympton held in common with half the school population whose difficulties arise from other sources. Alternatively, behavior disorders which stem from organic causes may be aggravated by the developmental challenges of particular age groups. The child with minimal brain damage or dysfunction has a developmental history of interactions with his environment which contribute to his present style of functioning. There is little documentation of the effects which experiences have on the symptoms.

Two decades of critical analysis did not diminish these problems with the concept of minimal brain damage or dysfunction. The sum of such criticisms is not that this diagnosis should not be made if it has practical value, but that one should always be aware of the limitations of the concept. The diagnosis is merely an inference which can be drawn from careful evaluation of a comprehensive case study by trained experts, and tentativeness is appropriate considering the reliability and predictive value of our present procedures.

Reaction and redefinition

A search for a more satisfactory concept produced the new terms 'learning disorders', or 'learning disabilities', in the literature of special education, but juggling with the label has done little to clarify the concept. As mentioned, the new concept has not yet been accepted in New Zealand but in the United States parents, publishers, teachers, psychologists, clinicians and special educators welcomed the redefinition in terms which appeared to relate to what could be done for the child. Parents felt schools should provide special programs for the child who has trouble learning. Publishers produced special materials which teachers thought might solve the learning problems. Education authorities set up special programs and used itinerant tutors, and university courses were established to prepare teachers of the learning disabled.

The child's problem was said to be described in a behavioral rather than a medical frame of reference. He was a learner with a difference; some children learned poorly, but he learned differently. It was claimed that a behavioral description of learning style would give more chance of selecting appropriate instructional techniques and materials than would a diagnosis of dysfunction or damage. In short, the analysis of the learning disorder would lead to remedial procedures.

Bateman (1967) defined a learning disability as 'a demonstrated inability to perform a specific task normally found within the capability range of individuals of comparable mental ability', and she used the term 'learning disorder' for cases with a known impairment of the nervous system. Her four criteria for selecting children with learning disabilities were:

1. They manifest an educationally significant discrepancy between their estimated intellectual potential and actual level of performance.

2. This is related to basic disorders of 'the learning process'.

3. There may or may not be demonstrable central nervous dysfunction.

4. The condition is not secondary to generalized retardation, educational or cultural deprivation, severe emotional disturbance or sensory loss.

The first criterion undermines the possibility of prevention, because it is an 'after the fact' definition. To detect children we must let them fail for two years to create the educational discrepancy that can be reliably measured by tests.

The discrepancy is presumed to stem from a basic disorder of the learning process which is not observable. A model or an analogy which describes the learning process is required and the one most frequently used refers to (a) input to the brain through visual and auditory senses or channels, (b) becoming associated, linked or integrated in the brain and (c) resulting in verbal or motor output in action. This output can be observed and therefore one looks for disorders, distortions, deviance or deficiencies in the language or movement behavior of the child. How this behavior came about *is inferred from the model* which may or may not reflect the actual process of brain functioning.

The inclusion of demonstrable and not demonstrable central nervous system effects in Bateman's definition probably strengthens the concept because it allows for children who have disorders in 'the learning process' which cannot be linked with dysfunction to be included in the definition.

The fourth criterion defines learning disorders by exclusion of several other handicapping states. This tactic depends for its usefulness on the validity of diagnoses in the excluded categories such as cultural deprivation and severe emotional disturbance. How clearcut are these? The placement of autistic children inside or outside the 'learning disordered' group, for example, would depend on one's preferred explanation for the etiology of that condition in brain dysfunction or in emotional origins.

The homogeneity of the learning disordered group rests on the fact that they show a deficit in learning in the presence of average or superior ability. To identify them, some learning or behavior which is demonstrably different from normal must be observed.

Disordered learning

Children with specific learning disorder are divided arbitrarily into categories which describe disorders of perceptual-motor activity, symbolization and attention. The categories are not mutually exclusive as a child may have a combination of disorders, and there is little agreement about this inclusion-exclusion problem. One author will include reading disability and language problems while another will exclude either or both. At other times the focus is on behavior problems. The decision seems to be an arbitrary one.

Perceptual-motor disorders. Gibson (1969) recently summarized six *types* of contemporary theories of perceptual development and she emphasized that the topic of perception abounds in controversial issues. When there is little agreement in the theory of normal perceptual functioning one must doubt whether disorders of perception can be reliably detected.

A developmental test of visual perception was prepared by Frostig (1964) with norms for middle-class children aged three to seven years. She recommended it as a screening test for children up to school entry and as a clinical, evaluative instrument for *older* children who suffer from learning difficulties, but specifically stated that 'the test does not presume to measure organic dysfunction.' Children who made low scores on Frostig's five tasks which were selected to translate visual perception into motor planning on non-verbal material, may have missed opportunities to learn, may have poor strategies for attending to or carrrying out the task, or may have some organic limitation. Frostig developed a set of training exercises which presumably would raise performance on her test. Does improvement in Frostig test scores have any relation to later reading progress? Her correlations of 0.40 and 0.50 at the end of first grade are not high and the relationship drops subsequently. Uhl and Nurss (1970) suggest that visual perception-motor planning is only one of four factors in early reading achievement, and that letter and word perception represent a second and separate factor.

There is much immaturity in the visual perception and motor coordination of normal children in the five to nine year period. This makes the differential diagnosis of learning disorders very difficult. However, it is no solution to conclude that a child must fail for two to four years before available tests can give a clear indication of the child's disorders.

Language disorders. A similar relationship exists between language development and language disorders. The preschool years are most important for language learning, but language skill increases throughout the primary school years with a large amount of change in language performance between five and seven years. It may be difficult to measure a skill reliably when rapid change is taking place and even more difficult to make differential diagnoses.

The Illinois Test of Psycholinguistic Abilities (ITPA) was designed to assess nine aspects of language functioning. A child's score is recorded on a profile of high and low abilities. Remedial work proceeds by pairing a high scoring ability with a low one until strength in the low one is increased. While the test results may permit this general approach to a program, the test does not describe the child's actual language skill and does not suggest what aspects of language to teach in the program. Process rather than content is prescribed.

Does the concept lead to programs? Does defining the child as a learner with a difference lead to instructional programs matched to a child's particular needs? This view seems to be too optimistic. A test is constructed from some hypothetical model of the learning process. A child, given that test, obtains a profile of scores which the examiner interprets. The examiner prescribes certain methods and materials for the training program, which are usually derived from the same hypothetical model. Under these conditions the training program should increase the learner's scores on the test. What remains uncertain is the manner, direction, and amount of effect that will transfer to learning other material. The availability of new assessment techniques accounts for some of the current emphasis on learning disorders (see Myers and Hammill (1969), but their relationships to progress in school learning is seldom successfully demonstrated.

A contrary opinion has been strongly stated by Reed, Rabe and Manikinen (1971) who reviewed the literature on the teaching of reading to brain-damaged children. From the nine rigorously-designed studies which they located, they found little evidence to suggest that children with chronic neurological impairment benefited from teaching procedures which differed from those used for teaching retarded readers without brain damage. If children with detectable organic impairments do not benefit from special procedures, it would be hard to argue that those with minimal damage would.

To date, the evidence that the available tests lead from learning disorders to procedures for reducing the problem is very slight. Tests tend to predict with considerable error from one kind of psychological functioning to performance on a new and different learning task (e.g. Frostig's training exercises are preliminary to, and do not necessarily carry over into, school learning). Tests may indicate areas of difficulty or neglect in the older child who has failed in school subjects, but they cannot specify the modifications or the likelihood of success of the remedial program.

Translation from the theoretical concept to the diagnostic test, and again from the test to the teaching program creates two areas of confusion, and programs which are articulated to the test profiles have yet to be developed.

Instructional problems

There are many tuition dilemmas in the education of children with learning disorders, and it is to these that attention will now be directed.

Behavior versus content. The child with a learning disorder may be active, fidgety, inattentive, emotional, uncoordinated and casual. Should the teacher befriend him, motivate him or coerce him before teaching begins? Studies suggest that her task is to program his work individually, in small assignments within his capacity and to reward him each time he works satisfactorily for a few minutes. He may gain ticks or counters to exchange for treats at the end of the day, or he may be praised or rewarded by the teacher's attention. In this way both the program of work and behavior receive attention.

Rich stimulation versus austerity. A child who has difficulty attending to a task is easily distracted. In the 1950s, it was recommended that rooms be stripped of distracting stimuli like pictures, toys and corners of interest. To reduce distractions further, tables were turned to the blank grey wall or children were placed in separate and soundproofed booths. Today, for the same children, a different psychological theory encourages teachers to have richly stimulating rooms, full of color, crowded with interesting and unusual activities and changing patterns of decor. Both extremes relate to getting and holding the child's attention on the task from which he will learn.

High skill versus low skill. When a test produces a profile of abilities, some normal and others low, to which should the program be directed? Does one teach to strength or build up from weakness? It can be argued that using the child's high skill gives him confidence because he feels competent. He can produce a result worthy of praise which he badly needs. However, by definition, the learning task requires the low skill also. If attention is given to this, no matter how expert the tuition, the gains will be slow, the learning process tedious and hard to motivate. One compromise is to provide opportunities for both in the lesson—some activities directed to the high skill and some to the low. For maximal gains, it is advisable to design activities which require both skills so that the high *supports* the correct functioning of the low skill until the low can be strengthened, weaned from support and practiced alone.

Prior skill versus new skill. When a child cannot read and has low scores on perceptual-motor tasks, should teaching effort be directed first to the visual-motor tasks with real objects, pictured objects, geometric forms and letter-like symbols? A preferable alternative is to train new habits of visual analysis on the stimuli required in reading—on letters and words. This is economical in time and avoids one problem of having to teach for transfer of one kind of learning to a new task.

Complex versus simple tasks. It is usually assumed when a complex learning task defeats a child that it was too difficult for him to analyze and that it should be broken down into manageable segments. The fast learner readily does this for himself, and yet keeps the total structure of the learning intact. Whenever the task is broken into simple steps there are three dangers:

1. The steps will result from an adult's logical analysis of the task which may not relate to the child's psychological acquisition sequence.

2. Learning the simple steps will make progress slow.

3. The simple steps may be difficult for the child to integrate into a smooth, on-going process.

The irony of this miniscule of learning approach is that it depends upon only a few cues and associations, and memory must be precise and accurate. In a more complex activity, cues from different sources prop up and support uncertain memories and the same associations might be triggered by several different cues. In this sense, sentence reading can be easier than phonic associations.

The spontaneous, integrative activity of the child who learns easily falls apart for the child with learning disorders. The teacher's challenge lies in devising tasks that will put the on-going behavior sequence together, not merely isolating and stamping in items of knowledge.

Slower rates of learning versus acceleration. The child with learning disorders will need more repetition of more detailed exercises for longer periods of time than the normal child. The dilemma here is that such a program will retard the child more and more. Individual tuition will counter this trend, but the program is even more effective if every effort is made to accelerate the child in the remedial program. This can be achieved by dealing directly with his learning difficulties, moving as rapidly as his observed progress allows, and avoiding activities he has already mastered. There is a need for tailoring the program to his specific needs. This is why commercially produced programs can be merely supplementary in the hands of a sensitive teacher.

The no-skill problem. When there is no behavior to observe or test—for example, when there is no reading achievement or when speech is incomprehensible—diagnosis is made on the basis of related behaviors which give no indication about tuition needs. In a way, the more severe the problem, the less useful the learning disorder concept may be! It is usually hoped that developing the related behaviors will lead on to the desired skill. A more direct approach is to analyze the task into its smallest segments and elicit some relevant behavior in that child, however minute. For example, if there is no reading behavior, instead of turning to geometric shapes the teacher can, as a first stage, build words and sentences out of the letters of the child's name.

The balance sheet

Not a great deal has been gained by the shift from medically-based to learning-based descriptions of disorders, a conclusion which is endorsed by the way in which both concepts have been defined and redefined during the past decade.

There has been a gain in encouraging teachers to think seriously and specifically about the input of stimuli, the output of behavior and the integrative processes in the brain as elements of the learning process. However, the fact that most of the process is not observable leaves room for valid theories and personal schemata of understanding that are, one suspects, a long way from actuality.

There has been a gain in the movement towards controlling unwanted and unnecessary behaviors by reinforcing the appropriate and wanted behaviors, and by gaining the child's attention by rewarding attention. This specificity is an improvement over generalized solutions like the reduction of stimulation in the environment.

But with these gains sources of error have emerged. Tests which help a clinical child psychologist to guide teachers in planning programs for children with learning disorders have been given diagnostic qualities relative to instructional tasks which they do not possess. Neither the Frostig test nor the ITPA adequately conceptualizes the developmental aspects of visual perception, or of language, and to the extent that each test samples these behaviors in limited ways, so they reflect in limited ways performance in these important aspects of learning. By using these tests well up the age scale one can increase the reliability with which they distinguish deviant functioning from developmental immaturity. But children with learning disorders should be diagnosed in their first year at school.

The concept of learning disorders has not been therapeutically gainful. It has not clarified the problem of matching programs to profiles of disability. One book records the approaches of 16 authorities in learning disorders. The authors relate all the teaching methods to a composite model of language and visual perception which they have constructed from Osgood's model and from Wepman's model. This composite model they claim to be a 'theoretical frame of reference' within which to view learning disabilities from assessment through to remedial procedure. All deductions from such a theoretical framework depend in the end on the veridicality of the model, and the error variance that is accumulated as each suppositional step is taken from the model to the diagnosis and the selection of program.

Authors who survey both normal and clinical populations stress again and again the diversity of disabilities which do not exist in neat, tight compartments since each child appears to exhibit his own unique syndrome. Clark's statement relating to severe reading disability is typical of this view: 'The striking finding was the diversity of disabilities and not an underlying pattern common to the group which could have provided a basis for one single remedial method for all these children.'

If little or no homogeneity exists among children with learning disorders, there will be no consensus on programs and materials. This means that a teacher should be able to select from a wide range of approaches several which he and the diagnostic team of specialists predict will have greatest pay-off.

If the concept of learning disorders leads to a reduction of error in the decision-making of teachers and psychologists, then it is a useful tool, but it should not be mistaken for a syndrome of behavior that exists among children.

In prospect

A good school system should provide for the individual instruction necessary for remedying learning disabilities, as children with disabilities will occur throughout the primary school because of (1) missed opportunities, (2) tangled or disorganized learning, and (3) organic limitations.

The expense of creating a sense of failure in children, and of providing for individual treatment within the educational system, can be reduced only by the very early detection of difficulties achieved by accurate monitoring of the earliest stages of learning. After the detection of difficulties, teaching effort must immediately be intensified and individualized to establish fundamental skills.

For older children, the magic is to individualize instruction and to motivate the child to re-enter the area of previous failure and try again. Given these conditions, the chances of success are increased by having well-trained, sensitive teachers with a respect for the complexity of psychological functioning and for the diversity of paths which can lead to the same achievement. This eschews a misplaced faith in one type of program and one theoretical explanation for the disorder.

Will research and practice move to the more precise conceptualization of learning disorders? The concept is inherently imprecise because it covers children who have marked trouble with learning for different reasons. If well-designed research could separate on the one hand children who become functionally disorganized because of their experiences with learning tasks and, on the other hand, children with known neurological impairment, the description of learning disorders from these two different and researchable sources might be a forward step towards formulating more precise hypotheses about the third and in-between group with minimal organic limitations.

21   An Emphasis On Prevention

In 1977 the Journal of Special Education *published a symposium for which Phyllis Newcomer wrote the lead article. She argued against the conventional diagnostic-remedial model. She saw this as being based on five premises all of which she thought were false. She did not believe that:*

- *children with mild reading problems are deviant*
- *that their deficits are discrete*
- *that we can isolate the underlying problems in our diagnosis*
- *that present instruments are adequate to detect these problems*
- *that remediation can be provided in isolation from everything else.*

She qualified her condemnations of testing programs followed by remedial lessons as irrelevant for most children but not for all children. Among the five responses to her paper was 'An Emphasis On Prevention' in which I argued for the value of careful observation of the child's day-to-day reading behavior to ensure the early detection of difficulties. This is consistent with Newcomer's position that too many children are being treated within a medical model when their difficulties are acquired, and that by carefully unpicking those learning tangles early and putting children back into the mainstream of learning we will arrive at a much more effective program for the few children who have organic deficits.

Most educators and education systems have yet to learn that you can teach a child into a reading problem very easily.

I can accept the arguments in Newcomer's excellent and timely article as valid, with two reservations. First, the ratio of one special educator to five regular teachers would, in many countries, be considered utopian and unachievable. Second, without a major shift in thinking towards early detection of school-created problems, we will not diminish the size of the problem of mild handicap but merely re-arrange our provisions for it. To prevent academic failure, more responsibility must be placed on the regular teachers of the reception classes, using the special educators as teacher consultants.

The mildly handicapped children discussed by Newcomer are those who share nonachievement in academic subjects, particularly reading, and who have a tendency to engage in disruptive behaviors. They do not respond well to group instruction and are sometimes described by terms such as 'slow', 'immature', and 'poorly motivated'. They become increasingly deviant as their stay in school lengthens, which is a good reason to propose earlier intervention. Common sense suggests that a school-created problem should be detected early. The diagnostic-remedial model based upon testing has been an obstacle to early intervention. Newcomer has put a strong case for limiting assessment tests and for prescribing instruction, since any value most standardized tests do have diminishes rapidly the closer one moves towards the beginning of schooling. The reliability and validity of tests dwindles when there is little achievement to sample and measure. Are there alternatives?

Developmental guidance

If the reception class teacher can identify a child as very different, adaptation to that child's program should begin at that time. This point is more clearly illustrated by the case of the severely handicapped child.

A severely handicapped child will be identified in infancy or during the early preschool years and can be given intermittent help so that he enters formal education better prepared. However, the child who is unusual meets each developmental hurdle in unusual ways. Parents of ordinary children who listen to the cultural folklore gather ideas about how to raise their children. But the development of the severely handicapped child makes even the most sensitive parents perplexed. When should they push for certain behaviors? And when should they patiently wait? Society does provide developmental guidance for perplexed parents of children with special needs to minimize problems that might otherwise be a consequence of the handicap. In this way, the tutoring force of parent interaction with the child throughout his preschool years can be enlisted for better quality experience rather than for more and more inappropriate experience. Such services are often available for the blind, deaf, or cerebral-palsied children in the preschool years.

When the severely handicapped child enters school and begins his formal education, the special educator, acting as a consultant to the regular classroom teacher, can help monitor the child's transition into formal instruction. With help, the child may succeed in regular class placement. Similarly, any child in preschool or kindergarten who is found to have particular difficulty with reading-relevant behaviors (e.g., in the motor coordination, visual discrimination, or language areas) could have an adapted program *from the start*. The nature of the adaptation would be worked out by the regular and special educators, each with their particular competencies.

One longitudinal study of 100 school entrants in Auckland (Clay, 1966a, 1966b) showed some children making slow progress because of poor language development. Their real problem lay in the limited range of syntactic forms that they could control. Other children wavered for some months trying to establish a consistent directional approach to print. Some children with poor coordination found the matching of words and spaces in print to words and pauses in speech a very difficult task. Other children had very fast speech and mature language, but could not achieve success because they could not slow down their speech to their hand-pointing or visual matching speed. They needed help to coordinate their visual perception of print and their fast speech. There were unhappy children who were reticent about speaking or writing, and there were rebellious and balky children. There were children of low intelligence who made slow progress with enthusiasm, and there were others with high intelligence who worked diligently and yet were seldom accurate. There were those who lost heart when promoted because they felt they were not able to cope, and others who lost heart because they were kept behind in a lower reading group. This is what individual differences amount to. No prior screening or tutoring program would set as its goal the elimination of such individual variability, but it is the pattern of individual variability interacting with the standard program of the classroom that creates differential responsiveness and differential progress. A flexible program which respects individuality is required.

Children differ not only in the timing of their readiness but also in the pattern of readiness skills which they are able to develop. The solution is not to be found in selecting a different program of instruction. It is necessary to discover ways of handling the variability among children more effectively. A child with a difficulty in one area will avoid performing in that area and may manage to avoid the very opportunities which would help him improve. His particular difficulties will call for special insights and successive adaptations of program by his teachers.

When a learning problem is thought of as a deficit in the child, researchers often turn to surveys to detect children likely to fail before they enter school. Special programs are produced to remediate the deficit before the child begins reading instruction. These children suffer from the problems outlined by Newcomer. The developmental programs are related to improved scores on the tests but not in school achievement. Such surveys try to predict that an individual child is likely to fail in an experience which he has not yet encountered but, by and large, predictive correlations are far too small for success in such detection. At best, a prior-to-school entry survey will only detect conspicuous problems, the severe rather than the mild disabilities. This approach also raises the problems of labeling children and creating preconceptions—in the minds of the school authorities who receive the children—about what they are capable of doing.

If the learning problem stems from a failure of the child to learn from the program, then this failure must be detected in the classroom situation, as Newcomer suggests, and this is where the impact of any program designed to reduce reading failure must be felt.

We are never likely to be able to diagnose in advance whether a child will attend to the distinctive features of print or whether, faced with a text, he will be able to discipline his language, visual, and directional learning into that smooth, on-going, integrated activity that makes up successful reading. These important aspects of the reading process are unlikely to be predicted by prior testing.

Sensitive Observation of the Reading Process

The concept of diagnostic teaching has been advocated among reading educators. Strang (1964) described it as an attitude, a set of techniques and a diagnostic approach to be carried out in the classroom by the teacher observing the child in his interaction with the learning environment. She advocated a movement of traditional diagnostic insights into the classroom. More recently this approach has been expanded by Harris and Smith (1972).

However, because I agree with Newcomer's appraisal of the diagnostic model, I am led to question the wisdom of moving 'traditional diagnostic insights' into the classroom. Recent emphases in reading research indicate that the reception class teacher may soon be able to observe the acquisition of strategies in the reading process rather than the products of reading as measured by criterion tests. Miscues (Goodman, 1970) and self-correction behavior (Clay, 1969) seem to be reliable indicators of how the child is responding to reading instruction. The strategies to be observed will vary with emphases in the instruction program, and a description of behaviors appropriate to progress in that program must be written.

In New Zealand, these have been derived from research which recorded in detail, at weekly intervals for the period of a year, the behaviors of gifted, average, and slow children learning to read. The observable reading behaviors which showed high relationships with reading progress were defined. These have been recommended to teachers for use in the observation of the day-to-day progress of pupils and for check testing during the year (Clay, 1972a, 1972b, 1972c). An analysis is made by the teacher as the child reads any continuous text that his class teacher has been using for instructional purposes. The best example of this approach I can cite is not from a regular classroom, but it does provide research evidence that the approach works in a special education setting.

Two research projects were carried out in a special class for young subnormal children using behavior modification procedures (Glynn & McNaughton, 1975). The consultants worked in a special classroom with the teacher; the teacher worked on individual programs with each child. An individual contingency program was operated for academic responses during reading time (mornings) and writing time (afternoons), and the programs were operated for an entire school year. The reading responses selected for reinforcement included correct directional behaviors and self-correction behavior (Clay, 1969). In writing, reinforcement was given for new words used and for complete sentences written (Clay, 1975). Results showed distinct gains in level and stability of on-task behavior in the class during lessons and substantial gains in reading and writing over baseline levels. In one year, reading ages increased 1 year on the average and 2 years for the best of the nine children. Towards the end of the year, back-up reinforcers were withdrawn completely and high levels of on-task behavior and academic gains were maintained. The program was operated by the class teacher.

The children's behavior responded quickly to the program, but the teacher's attitudes were less easy to change. She was reluctant to move her pupils from individually prepared interest books with little gradient of difficulty on to a graded sequence of little books used in normal classrooms. She showed renewed reluctance to move the children from the early reading books on to the bigger, harder, and more substantial texts of the series. There was a suggestion that such fast rates of progress were 'not right' for subnormal children and that they would suffer in some way. Yet the children's final attainment was not unusual for their intelligence level, and the teacher acknowledged that they read their books well. Her reaction to the marked progress of the children which did not match her low expectation for them illustrates a situation where a special educator could act as a consultant and provide continuing support for the program.

Observation of the child's responsiveness to a good school program is required. Time for recording what children are saying and doing is needed. Only from such records can one know, in the early stages, whether the child is moving comfortably through the program or becoming confused.

Sensitive observation of the reading process during the first year of instruction must be primarily the responsibility of the regular teachers, but if the teacher becomes perplexed by the child's response to her teaching, the insights of special educators will be needed. If the teacher has techniques available which allow her to sensitively observe her children's response to the program she is running, she will often appeal for a second opinion on what she herself has found. An appeal could be made to Newcomer's teacher consultant. Classroom teachers who become very sensitive observers of young learners tend to share what they find and ask for help.

Individual Instruction

The child who begins to fail in group tuition may be recovered by learning the same things as his classmates in the tutorially more powerful setting of individual instruction. Such provision is made in Swedish education (Malmquist, 1973a). The classroom teacher's own program is used on an individual basis with the child who is not keeping pace with the class. The return of the child to the classroom would be monitored by the teacher in consultation with the special educator. This procedure makes use of the obvious fact that in the individual situation the learning contingencies can be those that are right for a particular child. The complex difficulties may need the skills and creativity of the special educator; the simpler ones may be handled by a class teacher released to take her own children for individual instruction. Coordination of individual and class instruction is essential, as Newcomer argues, because the problems of the young child and the inefficient learner are very easily confused.

A survey of progress should be the responsibility of an experienced teacher—to catch in a 'diagnostic net' those children who have escaped other procedures. This survey can be applied systematically to every child after he has had sufficient time to adjust to school, to respond to the program, and to progress through the early stages of reading. For five-year-old New Zealand school entrants, the opportune time to survey, which is neither too soon nor too late, is not before 6 months in school and not later than 12 months.

A year at school will have given all children a chance to settle down, to begin to try to read, to be approached by several programs, to be forming good or bad habits. It is not hurrying children unduly to take stock of their progress a year after their introduction to formal instruction. Indeed, special instruction must then be intensified for those children who have been unable to learn by the standard teaching practices. That proportion of children deemed to be at risk in their further development within the school program may be selected for special programs. A teacher with much experience in early reading instruction should work with a special educator consultant to try to change the early pattern of failure.

I have not wanted to alter the arguments put forward by Newcomer but to suggest some further implications of her position. If a shift occurs from a diagnostic–remedial role to a teacher–consultant role for the special educator, then the effectiveness of the change should be increased by the reception class teacher and the special educator working together on the early detection of school failure. It has been claimed that such an approach in Sweden prevented more than 80% of the cases identified as potential cases of reading disability at the beginning of first grade (Malmquist, 1973b).

22 Reading Recovery: A Follow-Up Study

It was at the request of teachers that we began a research and development program aimed at helping young children with reading difficulties. We spent two years observing children and teachers in tutoring situations and then a year in field trials of the procedures that we considered had worked well. The program was to be implemented in schools by ordinary teachers released for individual teaching. A year later we checked on the progress of the children tutored in those field trial schools.

There are several interesting strands to this project. Firstly, the study of teacher-child interaction involved theories from developmental psychology and focused on the interaction of child and task, and of teacher and child, rather than on either child deficits or teaching procedures, taken separately. Secondly, for the field trials we took care to consider how to add an effective intervention to the on-going organization of the schools. Thirdly, when the success of that program was supported by the follow-up study we had to think about theories of effecting changes in the education system as a whole, to capitalize on the potential of the scheme. The body of theory relevant to the first stage would not help us with the second or the third. Getting research into practice, it seems, must take us through several different kinds of theory.

A research program was undertaken with a preventive aim. This was to explore the extent to which it is possible to undercut reading failure by a program of early intervention. The approach to this problem, the development of the conceptual framework and the teaching procedures, the outline of those procedures and the success with which they were used by teachers in the first year of field trials have been reported (Clay, 1979b). An analysis of follow-up data one year later and of three replication samples will be reported here and some implications for the theoretical assumptions that underlay the whole project will be discussed.

Terms and Concepts

To avoid cross-cultural confusions some terms require clarification.

Fifth Birthday Entry. In New Zealand schools a child enters school on his/her fifth birthday, not before and rarely after. This brings a continuing flow of new children into the first class where reading instruction begins and time at school can be calculated from the child's birthday. To understand the research data the reader must keep Fifth Birthday Entry clearly in mind.

Diagnostic Survey After One Year of Instruction. A check on progress has been recommended after one year in a reading program for the slowest 50 percent of children in any school. To prevent too many false diagnoses the critical timing cannot be earlier than the reliability and validity of the observation or measurement techniques will allow. It should not be later than one year after the reading instruction begins so that inappropriate learning is not firmly established. Previous research suggests that for New Zealand schools this timing occurs on or about the child's sixth birthday and this makes it feasible for class teachers to observe their own children on a staggered schedule of testing that is entirely practical.

Reading Recovery. Some colleagues refer to this set of procedures as remediation; others think that the term is ill-chosen and that it is 'an attempt to implement sound instruction on an individual basis'. An examination of the guidelines for the use of the procedures will show that most children do not need these detailed, meticulous and special recovery procedures or any modificaton of them. The procedures are special and therefore the aim is corrective. The aim is to develop in the children behaviors which appear spontaneously in most children. However the term *recovery* implies a return to average classroom performance levels rather than mere improvement which is what many remedial programs achieve. (See also the discussion of self-improving strategies below.)

Preventive Intervention. Any preventive program must treat more subjects than a remedial program which starts after the problems have developed to an advanced and obvious stage. That is one of the costs of prevention. (An immunization program for an entire population treats more people than would contract the target infection.) It is always difficult to show that what has been prevented would, in fact, have ever occurred in the treated subjects. For example, it is not easy to answer the challenge that our tutored children were late starters but strong finishers, unless we were to deprive some children of the treatment to act as control subjects and that presents an ethical problem.

Self-Improving Strategies. Parents, teachers, researchers and theorists have long recognized a state or stage which they call 'independence' in reading. The children at this stage can read suitable material on their own and although they need less teacher attention than children who have not reached this stage, they continue to increase in reading skill.

The Reading Recovery program focuses on cognitive, perceptual and language processes which are part of this independence. It is believed that the child who makes good progress begins to acquire such processes early in the instruction program, applies them tentatively and unevenly at first, but comes to push the boundaries of his own learning by using these strategies. When the strategies are well-established and used effectively we recognize the child as an independent reader. A rare child can perform in this way on entry to school; the fastest learners can reach this stage in their first year of school. Most of the slow-learning children we tested were not acquiring these self-improving strategies. If a program could be designed to facilitate this learning it must operate as an insurance against later difficulties with group or class instruction. The child who could teach himself something from his own interactions with print must contribute to his own progress.

Profiting From the Class Program. Teachers can diversify their programs to meet the needs of children of different levels of learning. Teachers in small rural schools teach all elementary classes effectively in one classroom. However, teaching is undoubtedly easier if groups are homogeneous rather than very diverse in their needs.

The Reading Recovery research sought to answer a particular question about this. Could individual tutoring aimed to develop self-improving behaviors in children with lower attainment levels raise some of these children to the average performance levels of their classmates, making the day-to-day teaching and learning interactions more rewarding for both teachers and pupils? For what percentage of the children would this be possible and would they retain the behaviors learnt under these special 'hot-house' conditions? What percentage of children would continue to need further help?

Background

In 1978, 5 teachers gave individual tutoring using special procedures to 122 children. They worked in 5 schools where attainment ranged from below average to average. *Schools with high attainment levels were excluded from the study;* this must be kept in mind when evaluating the results obtained. A teacher tested each child in her school with a Diagnostic Survey (Clay, 1979b) after the child had been at school for one year (i.e., when each child reached his or her sixth birthday).

Every child who was not selected for tutoring was used for the control group. These children attended the same schools as the tutored group and were taught in the same programs by the same teachers. They were not matched on attainment as that was to be the dependent variable. Individual tutoring according to specified procedures (Clay, 1979b) should *reduce the differences.* (Treatments usually seek to increase differences). Using such a control group establishes a stringent test of the results, since the aim would be to show that the lowest scorers in the tail of the normal distribution could be moved to a level where they would not be significantly different from the control children. This design does not control for the possibility that these children would have improved without help. This seems an implausible hypothesis because the poorest performers were selected and children and teachers worked extraordinarily hard during the individual tuition. (This was observed every second week when two teaching demonstrations were arranged by the teachers in the field trials for their colleagues, and is evident on the videotapes of three typical lessons. A comment often made by visitors to the program was that you can't expect teachers and children to work that hard!)

At the end of the main study (December, 1978) the tutored group was divided in two. One group (DISCONTINUED) reached present criterion levels of performance and left the tutoring program before the end of year. (Phase 2 in Figures 3 and 4). The other group (NOT DISCONTINUED) had not reached these levels when the program ran out of time at the end of 1978.

In the following year these children did not receive any further help from the Reading Recovery program. Their progress was assessed again in December, 1979.

The Research Questions in 1978

Could teachers use the recommended teaching procedures in schools of different sizes and characteristics? What differences in organization would be needed in the timing of the program, the numbers of children taught, the scheduling of lessons? At this level the questions posed for the field trials of the Reading Recovery Project aimed simply at descriptive data about the ease or difficulty schools had implementing the program. It proved to be flexible in a variety of schools. We were also interested in the progress made by the children and how the gains and relative status of the groups could best be described. This was also descriptive data. We were able to record change in scores and change in rates of improvement. At a theoretical level the explanatory value of the concepts of strategies or operations used while reading was being put to the test. Was this a satisfactory way to account for what children need to learn? The concepts were used to generate an operational framework for work with children with the lowest achievement. The answers to these questions have been reported (Clay 1979b).

The Research Questions in 1979

Three different sets of questions were posed in 1979. Firstly, was the improvement obtained for the total group in 1978 (Clay, 1979b) an effect that occurred in each school? Secondly, a Reading Recovery program operated in forty-eight schools in 1979. Teachers were prepared for the work by an inservice course which ran throughout the year but they were allowed only ten hours a week for tutoring. Under such conditions and without the close supervision given to the field trial schools in 1978 what magnitude of improvement would they be able to achieve? Thirdly, if children in 1978 were taken from the tail of the normal distribution of attainment in reading and were tutored to perform at average levels in their classes (the DISCONTINUED children made such a shift) what happened when tutoring was no longer available over the next year? Did the children lose skills they had gained? Did they fall back in level relative to other children because they were unable to maintain a high rate of improvement?

These questions are discussed in this paper.

The Research Phases

The Preresearch Period (One Year). The children entered school on their fifth birthdays and were tested one year later on their sixth birthdays. As this birthday occurred anywhere between September 1977 and September 1978 the next phase began on variable dates throughout the year for individual children.

The Tutoring Phase (Phase I). The tutoring phase began soon after a child's sixth birthday and continued as long as necessary to meet preset criteria of performance based on reading strategies. On the average a period of 12-13 weeks was needed. Children were discharged from tutoring when they demonstrated a set of behaviors thought to be related to surviving in the ordinary classroom program. If children did not demonstrate these behaviors they continued in the program. Of necessity the tutoring phase ended for all children at the end of the school year, December 1978.

Back-In-Class (Phase 2). The decisions about discontinuing tutoring and the staggered timing of the children's entry to the tutoring phase created three groups of children by the end of 1978. One group of 53 children were tutored (Phase I) and had a period back in their classroom (Phase 2).

The Follow-Up Phase (Phase 3). No contact was made with the children during 1979. Some moved to other schools. In December, 1979 all children who could be located in the Auckland area were retested. Of the original 291 children tested at 6:0, 282 were retested in December, 1978 (97 percent) and 270 in December, 1979 (93 percent). The subjects across the group for the follow-up phase were CONTROL 160 (153), DISCONTINUED 53 (51), DISCONTINUED WITHOUT PHASE 2, 27 (25) NOT DISCONTINUED 42 (41).

The Research Subjects

The CONTROL children were all children in the age cohort not selected for tutoring. They were too competent to be included in the tutoring program. A few with September 1972 birth dates needed help but

could not be admitted to tutoring because there were no vacancies—
an end of year problem.

DISCONTINUED children had received individual tuition and had
been discharged on individual schedules when according to observational and test data they were expected to survive in the ordinary
classroom. The group was made up of two subgroups—the Dis
group, DISCONTINUED-WITH-PHASE 2 (53)/and another group who
reached criterion behaviors by the end of the year, the Dd group who
were DISCONTINUED-WITHOUT-PHASE 2 (27).

The NOT DISCONTINUED children had received individual tuition
but had not been discharged because they did not have the strategies
needed to survive in their classrooms. However, their program had to
be terminated at the end of the school year.

The Tests Used

Measures of reading applied in the 1978 study were used again at
Follow-Up. These were:
1. *Book Level*, on a 32 step scale, was assessed with a running record
   of the highest level book the child could read with 90 percent
   accuracy from the reading series in use in the schools. For the six
   final steps in this scale the Neale Analysis paragraphs 2-7 were
   used. Step sizes were smaller in the lower part of the scale and
   larger in the higher parts. There are obviously some limitations
   with this 'stretchy' measuring scale for subsequent calculations.
2. *Reading Vocabulary* combined the Clay *Word Test* with the
   Schonell R1, an instrument shown to be reliable, valid, and sensitive from early reading through to later reading levels for children
   taught in the New Zealand reading program (Clay, 1966).
3. Other tests included *Concepts About Print* and *Letter Identification*, *Writing Vocabulary* and *Dictation* (Clay 1979b). Some
   results from the last two tests are reported.
Two new measures were used.
4. The *Slosson Oral Reading Test* (Vocabulary) standardized in USA
   and perhaps a guide to establishing comparative levels of performance for New Zealand children. Its use has not been reported in
   New Zealand before.
5. The *Peters' Spelling Test* (1970) an indicator of performance in a
   cognate area.

Results

For the Total Group. Questions about the level and the spread of
attainment at 6:0 and at the end of the school years in 1978 and 1979
could be answered by examining the scores of the total group.

Results in Table 1 show that the mean score for BOOK LEVEL (with
90 percent accuracy) rose under instruction and the Standard Devia-

tion narrowed, probably as an effect of the uneven steps in the scale being used. READING VOCABULARY mean scores increased and so did the Standard Deviation. This means that the better readers drew further away from the poorer readers.

Results for the 5 Schools in 1978. The mean scores for each of the 5 schools on Initial, Final and Follow-Up tests for BOOK LEVEL and READING VOCABULARY are given in Table 1. Follow-Up scores for each school on the SLOSSON ORAL READING test, the SCHONELL R1 test and the PETERS' SPELLING test are given in Table 2. The trends reported for the Total Group can be seen in each of the schools.

Table 1
*Mean Scores for Research Groups and Schools
on Book Level and Reading Vocabulary*

TEST	GROUP	6:0	MEAN End of 1978	1979	6:0	SD End of 1978	1979	Correlation Initial to Follow-up
	TOTAL	9.40	18.51	24.39	6.22	6.42	4.92	.61
Book Level	CONTROL	12.54	20.86	26.36]*	5.86	5.47	3.29	See
	DISCONTINUED	6.33	18.53	24.66]*	3.67	3.96	3.10	Table
	NOT DISCONTINUED	2.48	8.21	16.23	1.61	2.76	4.75	5
	School 1	7.97	19.82	26.00	6.71	6.29	3.53	.51
	School 2	12.68	20.73	26.18	5.51	4.72	2.62	.66
	School 3	11.96	21.44	25.23	5.59	4.46	3.70	.72
	School 4	7.84	17.44	23.73	5.99	5.52	5.32	.61
	School 5	6.49	12.80	20.59	4.85	6.87	6.48	.71
	TOTAL	16.20	28.86	41.52	10.40	11.29	13.13	.71
Reading Vocabulary	CONTROL	24.03	33.53	47.07]*	16.78	11.51	12.11	See
	DISCONTINUED	9.25	27.63	39.09]*	9.32	6.46	7.36	Table
	NOT DISCONTINUED	4.76	14.76	24.59	2.96	5.20	8.99	5
	School 1	14.02	30.10	44.31	11.38	11.10	13.71	.65
	School 2	19.18	30.71	44.88	9.59	9.67	10.86	.79
	School 3	19.60	33.15	43.26	9.54	8.80	11.13	.73
	School 4	15.40	27.38	41.24	9.74	9.60	12.92	.71
	School 5	12.65	23.24	33.67	9.80	14.20	13.89	.79

* Differences are significant at p < .01 level.

Table 2
Mean Scores for Five Schools at Follow-Up

	SLOSSON		SCHONELL Reading		SPELLING (Peters) Spelling	
	Score	Grade	Score	Age	Score	Age
School 1	74.46	3.7	29.6	8.0	23.95	7:7
School 2	74.74	3.6	28.6	7.9	23.47	7:6
School 3	73.00	3.6	29.7	8.0	22.88	7:6
School 4	67.60	3.3	26.0	7.6	21.64	7:5
School 5	51.37	2.5	20.5	7.1	16.47	6:7

At Follow-Up the children had been at school from 2.3-3.3 years and were aged 7.3-8.3 years. The levels of attainment for tutored children were close to average for their age group. It should be noted that schools with higher attainment levels had been excluded from the study. School 5 had a highly mobile Polynesian population and many of the parents in School 4 were solo parents.

Results from 48 Schools in 1979. An inservice course in 1979 guided 48 new teachers in the running of Reading Recovery programs in their schools. These teachers worked at individual teaching for 10 hours a week, a considerable reduction on the 25 hours available in the 1978 field trial schools. Consequently the 1979 teachers taught and discontinued fewer children per teacher, and lesson time was reduced from 40 to 30 minutes. For the analysis of results the 48 schools were listed alphabetically and divided into three groups (B C D) providing 3 replication samples. The question here concerns the average levels of scoring at Initial and Final testing for the 1979 groups (B C D) compared with the 1978 (A). The Initial and Final scores for the four samples in Table 3 cluster within a narrow range. The samples A, B, C, D are plotted left to right in Figures 1 and 2. Results for CONCEPTS ABOUT PRINT and LETTER IDENTIFICATION tests were similar. It is possible to conclude that teachers guided by a year-long inservice course were able to replicate the results of the 1978 field trials in regard to the level of most scores although they were not working full-time and therefore helped fewer children. F-tests for each set of scores suggest the following qualifications to the above conclusion (Table 3).

Children taken into the program in 1979 (samples B C D) had lower scores in READING VOCABULARY and BOOK LEVEL but similar Final scores compared with the 1978 sample. Teachers presumably retained them in the program until they reached satisfactory levels of performance.

Final WRITING VOCABULARY scores tended to be lower for the 1979 groups. There is a strong possibility that teachers in 1979 with less tutoring time available gave less time to writing.

Overall the results in 1979 fairly replicate the field trials of 1978 and variations between samples are small. Time for tutoring emerges as an important variable and lower entry scores imply more individual tutoring time.

Table 3

Comparison of the 1978 Sample (A) With Three Replication Samples in 1979, (B, C, D) on Initial and Final Scores

		INITIAL			FINAL		
READING VOCABULARY							
		Dis	Dd	Not D	Dis	Dd	Not D
	A	11.79	8.15	4.76	29.54	22.19	14.76
	B	8.39	9.53	5.85	29.98	22.42	13.73
	C	8.71	9.50	4.62	28.52	24.65	11.90
	D	8.65	6.71	4.38	28.29	23.13	12.16
	F ratios	3.87*	1.22	0.92	0.74	1.16	1.68
BOOK LEVEL							
	A	6.94	5.07	2.48	20.17	15.04	8.21
	B	4.69	6.78	4.02	20.52	16.89	9.31
	C	5.19	7.15	2.82	19.29	17.15	8.03
	D	5.14	4.13	2.25	19.51	15.00	7.75
	F ratios	3.46*	2.91	4.67**	1.59	3.34*	1.12
WRITING VOCABULARY							
	A	11.02	9.11	5.64	51.02	39.96	24.05
	B	8.63	10.26	7.05	49.56	38.74	25.07
	C	9.08	11.55	5.15	48.10	39.10	18.77
	D	8.67	7.88	5.43	42.79	35.21	16.66
	F ratios	2.09	1.38	1.48	2.87*	0.81	4.62**
DICTATION							
	A	16.25	13.89	8.29	34.38	31.07	24.52
	B	11.58	12.74	9.33	33.73	33.63	25.40
	C	12.65	14.90	5.61	33.63	32.85	20.72
	D	13.00	11.29	6.50	33.65	32.96	21.81
	F ratios	3.19*	0.61	2.71	0.68	2.91	2.59

* Differences significant at .05 level
** Differences significant at 0.1 level

FIGURE 1

READING VOCABULARY and BOOK LEVEL for four samples,
A (1978) BCD (1979). *Mean Scores of* Initial, Discontinuing (Dis only)
and Final *tests for* DISCONTINUED-with-Phase 2 (Dis)
DISCONTINUED-without-Phase 2 (D) *and*
NOT DISCONTINUED (Not D).

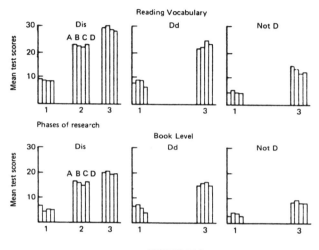

FIGURE 2

WRITING VOCABULARY and DICTATION for four samples
A (1978) BCD 1979). *Mean scores of* Initial, Discontinuing (Dis only) *and*
Final *tests for* DISCONTINUED-with-Phase (Dis),
DISCONTINUED-without-Phase 2 (D) *and* NOT DISCONTINUED (Not D).

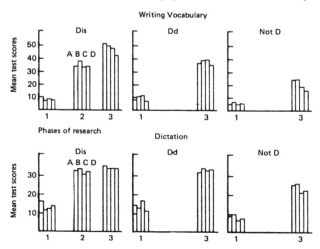

FIGURE 3

Mean scores for READING VOCABULARY *at Initial, Discontinuing, Final and* Follow-Up *testing for* Control, Discontinued *and* Not Discontinued *groups.*

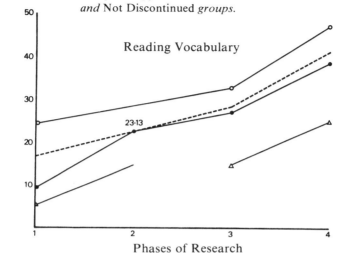

FIGURE 4

Mean scores for BOOK LEVEL *at* Initial, Discontinuing, Final *and* Follow-Up *testing for* Control, Discontinued *and* Not Discontinued *groups.*

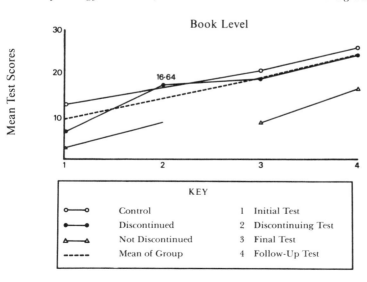

The Follow-Up Study of the 1978 Group. In the follow-up Phase children were not receiving extra attention outside the classroom program. Many things may have occurred in this intervening period to upset the trends established with tutoring in the previous year. DISCONTINUED children might be unable to build on their gains and so slip back. CONTROL children might forge ahead at a faster rate once the early reading skills had been mastered as they profited from wide-ranging individual reading. NOT DISCONTINUED children might have slipped further behind or they might have been able to accelerate their progress.

Table 1 and Figures 3 and 4 summarize the comparisons between the 1978 research groups at Initial, Final and follow-up testing.

The CONTROL group scored above the mean of the total group at each of three testing times (Initial, Final and follow-up) on two test variables BOOK LEVEL and READING VOCABULARY.

The DISCONTINUED group of children had low Initial scores. Final scores were well within one standard deviation of the CONTROL group's Final means, and they retained that position at follow-up testing. It would be reasonable to claim that children in that position should be able to profit from the usual classroom instruction. This applied to both the BOOK LEVEL and READING VOCABULARY measures.

The NOT DISCONTINUED group of children had the lowest Initial Mean score and although they continued to improve their scores they remained more than a year below the main-stream of class instruction by th end of 1979 on both measures of progress.

There was little change in the relative positions of the three groups during the follow-up year (Table 1 and Figures 3 and 4). This adds weight to the theoretical argument that the attainment of strategies during the early reading period gives the child a firm foundation for further progress. T-tests applied to the mean scores at follow-up testing are significantly different for the three progress groups but the difference in the CONTROL and the DISCONTINUED groups would not lead a teacher to treat them differently in the classroom program. The NOT DISCONTINUED group would, on the other hand, find difficulty reading much of the material which the other two groups could cope with independently. It should be noted here that the CONTROL group used as a standard has the top 66 percent of the 6-year-old readers in it and therefore the comparison is a stringent one.

Similar follow-up results were obtained for the Slosson and Spelling tests.

The test scores for groups at follow-up are given as reading and spelling ages in Table 4, for summary purposes only. These are a type of score which the author considers unhelpful for teaching purposes because they provide no guidance for teachers about the child's instructional needs.

Table 4
Follow-Up Scores as Mean Reading and Spelling Ages

	TOTAL	CONTROL	DISCONTINUED	NOT DISCONTINUED
Slosson Oral Reading (U.S. Grade Level)	3.4	4.1	2.9	1.4
Schonnel R1	7.7	8.2	7.4	6.1
Spelling	7.4	7.9	7.2	6.1

Two conclusions about the follow-up Phase can be drawn from all these results.

The DISCONTINUED children were functioning in reading at levels which should permit them to profit from the instructional programs of their classes.

The NOT DISCONTINUED children would not be able to participate fully in class activities and would require further tutoring to accelerate their progress.

Correlations Between Initial, Final and Follow-Up Scores. Correlations of Initial and Final scores for the CONTROL group were higher (0.64 and 0.74) than correlations of Initial scores with Follow-Up scores (0.50 and 0.63, Table 5) suggesting that some re-ordering of children occurred. However, the correlations are moderately high for such longitudinal data.

For the DISCONTINUED group the correlations of Initial scores with Final and Follow-Up scores were low, as one would predict following an intervention program (0.53, 0.30, 0.42, 0.20, Table 5.)

For the NOT DISCONTINUED group the correlations of Initial scores with Final and Follow-Up scores were higher than for the DISCONTINUED group (they were not so influenced by the program) but lower than those of the CONTROL group (0.48, 0.48, 0.47, 0.50, Table 5).

Do Initial Scores Predict Final and Follow-Up Scores? To answer this question steps were taken that would take account of regression to the mean effect. Pupils who score lowest tend to make the greatest gains on a second testing. It was necessary to show that any movement of the children with low reading attainment towards the mean of the group was greater than would be predicted by a regression effect. The correlation between two sets of scores for the total group was used to establish a predicted Final, and a predicted Follow-Up score for each value in the scale of scores. For every child a difference score was calculated between (a) the predicted Final and the actual Final score and (b) the predicted Follow-Up and the actual Follow-Up score. Mean difference scores for CONTROL, DISCONTINUED and NOT DISCONTINUED groups were compared by t-tests.

Table 5

*Correlations Between Initial Scores and Final Scores (3-11 Months)
and Follow-Up Scores (15-23 Months)*

	TIME	CONTROL	DIS-CONTINUED	NOT DIS-CONTINUED	TOTAL
Book Level	Final	.64	.54	.48	
	Follow-Up	.50	.30	.48	.61
Reading	Final	.74	.42	.47	
Vocabulary	Follow-Up	.63	.20	.50	.71
Book Level/ Slosson	Follow-Up	.58	.22	.39	.69
Book Level/ Spelling	Follow-Up	.52	.14	.30	.62
Reading Vocabulary/ Slosson	Follow-Up	.63	.18	.29	.71
Reading Vocabulary/ Spelling	Follow-up	.56	.12	.32	.65
Writing Final/ Spelling	Follow-Up	.70	.53	.54	.74

Table 6

*Difference Scores Between Predicted and Follow-Up Scores
for Book Level and Reading Vocabulary*

| | | | | MEAN | | SD | |
TEST	GROUP	N_1	N_2	FINAL	FOLLOW-UP	FINAL	FOLLOW-UP
Book	CONTROL	160	153	0.14]*	0.44]*	4.26	3.07
Level	DISCONTINUED	80	76	2.34]*	1.66]*	3.44	3.10
	NOT DISCONTINUED	42	41	-5.02]	-4.84]	2.45	4.44
Reading	CONTROL	160	153	0.94	0.45	7.69	9.48
Vocab-	DISCONTINUED	80	76	2.26]*	2.33]*	5.16	8.19
ulary	NOT DISCONTINUED	42	41	-6.56]	-6.36]	4.50	8.07

* t-tests yield significant differences at the .01 level.

The results of these analyses are given in Table 6 for BOOK LEVEL and READING VOCABULARY. On both variables the CONTROL group were close to predicted scores on each variable, and on both occasions, the DISCONTINUED children were consistently higher than would be predicted, i.e., their gains were greater than would be predicted by regression effects on each variable and on both occasions. The NOT DISCONTINUED children were consistently lower than would be predicted on each variable and on both occasions.

The results of the t-tests between the mean difference scores for groups show that the DISCONTINUED group made significantly better progress than the CONTROL group relative to their Initial scores, and this trend was maintained at Follow-Up. The DISCONTINUED group made significantly better progress than the NOT DISCONTINUED group relative to their Initial scores and this trend was maintained at follow-up.

Further information which supports these trends was obtained by predicting final scores on two new tests administered only at follow-up, the *Slosson Oral Reading Test* and the *Peters Spelling Test*. Each of these was correlated with the Initial scores on the two reading measures and then the groups were compared (See Table 7). The mean difference scores of the CONTROL and DISCONTINUED groups were not significantly different, but the NOT DISCONTINUED group was in every case significantly different from and lower than the DISCONTINUED group, i.e. the results were consistent with those of the repeated tests.

Table 7

Difference Scores Between Predicted and Follow-Up Scores on Slosson Oral Reading and Peters Spelling Test

TESTS Initial/Follow-Up	GROUP	N	Mean Difference	S.D.
Book Level/ Slosson	CONTROL	153	3.00	25.84
	DISCONTINUED	76	1.90]*	21.90
	NOT DISCONTINUED	41	-15.04	-11.86
Book Level/ Slosson	CONTROL	153	0.78	7.81
	DISCONTINUED	76	0.87	7.67
	NOT DISCONTINUED	41	- 5.17	- 4.92
Reading Vocabu-lary/ Slosson	CONTROL	153	- 1.83	24.54
	DISCONTINUED	76	3.37]*	22.38
	NOT DISCONTINUED	41	-13.80	-12.95
Reading Vocabu-lary/ Spelling	CONTROL	153	.057	7.55
	DISCONTINUED	76	1.18	7.70
	NOT DISCONTINUED	41	- 4.70	- 4.90

* t-tests yield significant differences at the .01 level.

In summary, the results above may be said to support the interpretation that the children who were tutored until it was judged that they could survive in their classrooms were at Follow-Up one year later scoring above predicted scores while the children who were judged not to be ready for the termination of their individual tutoring program were in every comparison below predicted scores. This is taken to be support for two theoretical arguments. The first is that the operational criteria used for judging that children were using certain processing strategies while reading were successful in separating out the two groups of children who subsequently maintained their trends of progress. The second is that the theory upon which the instructional program was based (that gains in reading can be described in terms of operations carried out by children rather than items of knowledge gained) has received endorsement.

Supplementary Analysis 1: The Transfer Group. During the Follow-Up phase when no Reading Recovery program was available to the schools 36 children of the same age cohort transferred into the research schools. They were tested at Follow-Up as a group who had not been in contact with the Reading Recovery program. Their scores on four test variables were significantly lower than those of the total group, and lower than the DISCONTINUED group (see Table 8) but higher than those of the NOT DISCONTINUED group.

Table 8
Follow-Up Test Scores for Children
Who Transferred Into Research Schools

	N	Book Level	Reading Vocabulary	Slosson	Spelling
CONTROL	153	26.36	47.07	82.90	25.91
DISCONTINUED	76	24.66	39.09	59.43	19.86
NOT DISCONTINUED	41	16.44	24.59	27.70	9.82
TRANSFERS	36	21.44	36.11	53.33	15.83
TOTAL (without transfers)	270	24.39	41.52	68.17	21.84

Supplementary Analysis 2: The NOT DISCONTINUED Group. A comparison of the NOT DISCONTINUED groups with the DISCONTINUED-WITHOUT-PHASE 2 groups is shown in Table 9. Children in both groups entered tutoring later in Term 2 or 3. At the end of the tutoring program teachers placed the children in two groups on the basis of performance. Retrospective inspection of their READING VOCABULARY scores at entry to the program shows that in all four samples A, B, C, D the NOT DISCONTINUED groups had lower entry scores than the DISCONTINUED groups. Further information was available for Sample A. The 1978 groups were not significantly different in age at entry or mean weeks in tutoring, although the children with lower scores did have more tutoring sessions. The obvious conclusion is that children with higher entry scores are ready to leave the program earlier than children with lower scores on entry who need more tutoring to bring them to satisfactory levels for classroom performance. The slightly accelerated progress of the 1978 NOT DISCONTINUED children during the Follow-Up phase suggests that they could as a group profit from further tutoring. The data render unlikely the interpretation that most of the children in the NOT DISCONTINUED group were in some way different in learning ability from the DISCONTINUED group. However, in the conceptual outline of the intervention it was suggested that the intervention would identify a very small group of children who would need to receive remedial help from a trained clinician. None were so referred by their schools during the program so any that existed remained in the NOT DISCONTINUED samples.

Table 9
Comparison Discontinued-with-Phase 2,
Discontinued-without-Phase-2 and Not Discontinued Groups

	DISCONTINUED-WITH-PHASE-2	DISCONTINUED-WITHOUT-PHASE-2	NOT DISCONTINUED
READING VOCABULARY AT ENTRY			
A	11.79	8.15	4.76
B	8.38	9.53	5.85
C	8.71	9.50	4.62
D	8.65	6.71	4.38
AGE AT ENTRY—A			
	6.31	6.25	6.18
TIME IN TUTORING—A			
Mean Weeks in Tutoring	14.26	14.11	13.48
Mean Tutoring Sessions	22.45	27.78	30.14
SCORES AT FOLLOW-UP—A			
Book Level	24.66	22.28	16.33
Reading Vocabulary	39.09	34.92	24.59
Slosson Oral Reading Test	59.43	48.64	22.70
Spelling	19.86	16.00	9.82

Discussion

The program has been shown to be workable under field conditions and to have some merit as a package of several variables all of which were considered to be important. Critics have tended to attribute the effectiveness to single variables like individual instruction, or the extra time given to the child, or the school's enthusiasm for the program, and the implication in the criticisms is that the other variables are not important. The research design was suited to answering practical questions like 'Does it work in field conditions?' and '. . . with various replication groups?' but it did not provide a basis for answering the critics about the relative importance of these variables.

The intervention was planned to work for children in the education system and to be used by non-specialist class teachers. To work in a practical situation the program package had to give prior attention to factors in the system which could neutralize its effectiveness. It must be a school project because teachers would not be able to work effectively in isolation. It could not be operated with fixed requirements for numbers of children per school, levels of entry scores, time in tutoring because in the real situation schools differ markedly in terms of the population they serve. In the New Zealand setting where research resources tend to be limited this type of practical research was likely to gain support: while a carefully designed study to test inferential questions would have been much harder to 'sell' to teachers.

A survey of previous research on remedial programs which provided individual instruction produced no confidence that this variable alone would bring children with reading difficulties to average levels of performance in a short time. Although the research literature reporting time available for learning shows good results from increased time for children with average attainment the remedial reading studies suggest that this effect is much less with children who have low reading attainment.

The school's enthusiasm for a program may raise performance levels because of a Hawthorne effect. This was controlled by the method of selecting the CONTROL group. Other children better than the tutored children might profit from the insights gained by teachers discussing their poor readers with the Reading Recovery teachers but this made the research hypotheses harder to test.

One interpretation of the changes in scores from Initial to Final testing (Clay, 1979b) was that the DISCONTINUED group was probably a more competent group at entry than the NOT DISCONTINUED group. (This was initially reported to be a chance difference such as might be expected when several samples are drawn from the same population). Further comparisons of the NOT DISCONTINUED group with the DISCONTINUED-WITHOUT-PHASE-2 group for several samples have shown them to be not comparable on the Initial test scores. They were similar in age at entry, and in time of tutoring.

A strong challenge to the theoretical bases of the program comes from critics who claim that any procedures used under similar conditions (daily, individual tuition) would achieve similar results. This argument is not easily answered but the following points can be made. The DISCONTINUED group survived in the classroom for a further year making gains at what appear to be similar rates. The theoretical bases of the program, articulated prior to implementation, provided a rationale for this. In many remedial programs only small gains are made after the tutoring program has ended. The critical variable in this research was not whether the program was intensive, or had a high time allocation but rather whether the program fostered dependence on the remedial teacher or whether it fostered independence. Independence was operationalized as behavioral strategies used by the child while reading which were observed and recorded by the teacher during lessons. The results of the NOT DISCONTINUED group can be interpreted to support both sides of the argument. They continued to gain during Follow-Up perhaps even increasing their rate of improvement. Critics could say that this shows the tutoring program was not necessary. Advocates (and the tutor teachers would be among them) would claim that such progress would not have been possible but for the impetus provided by tutoring which developed new strategies in their earliest forms. The forward thrust in the next year could be the result of this change rather than a widening gap as attainment fell further away from the average which is the more common outcome for the lowest group in any distribution. Only a control group study can address this question.

In attempting to evaluate the contribution of the teaching procedures to the results some attention must be paid to the 'blind' nature of the discontinuing decisions in the first year of the field trials. The project aimed to bring the tutored children to levels of performance which enabled them to profit from mainstream instruction in their classroom. These levels were described in behavioral terms as operations and strategies used by the child and observed by the teacher. At the time the judgments were made to discontinue children the research team had no knowledge of the performance levels of the CONTROL children and had no way of checking whether the judgments about ability to survive in the classroom were likely to hold up. Judgments were made on the basis of the theory, the child's behaviors and where his classroom program seemed to be. It was only after the completion of the study when the test scores were analysed that the researchers had any idea of where the average children or CONTROL children were during the year. Tutored children had been discontinued at levels that were later shown to be average for the age group and close to the average levels of the CONTROL group. Children who were NOT DISCONTINUED because they did not demonstrate the appropriate operations and strategies were later found to be performing at lower levels, forming a 'low group' compared with their age mates. (Data were available for the replication groups B, C, & D which showed the same results.)

Conclusion

The research design does not allow for the isolation of several variables to ascertain their contribution to the intervention effect. It does show that the package achieves results and is workable in a wide range of schools. There is a strong likelihood that the conceptual bases of the program are not unrelated to the effects gained.

23 An Inservice Program for Reading Recovery Teachers

Marie M. Clay and Barbara Watson

We prepared teachers for the Reading Recovery program in a novel way, but a way which had many advantages. The key word in the development and implementation of this inservice program was again observation and the unique feature was the potential for multilevel observation and learning that was embedded in the situation. One teacher taught one child. On the other side of a one-way screen the teacher's peers watched intently the child's behaviors and the teacher's decisions. When the child struggled the observers anticipated the teacher's next move.

These observing teachers were themselves being tutored, at the same time. Their tutor asked questions about the child's difficulties, and the teacher's decisions. That tutor was herself in training and how she ran the session was analysed later with her tutor-trainer who had been present.

Visitors to the program, parents and other family members, school inspectors or principals, administrators and politicians sat on high stools behind the teachers and watched the three levels of training proceeding at one and the same time — teacher with child, tutor with teachers, and the tutor with tutor-trainer. That was how we shared the nature of the program with anyone who wanted to know about it.

This training situation might be used for developing teaching competence for other one-teacher-one pupil situations such as speech therapy or music education. Like micro-teaching it might also play a part in the preservice training of new teachers.

The Reading Recovery Project was developed to answer the question, 'How can teachers provide a second chance for young children who have not responded to the reading program in their first year at school?' In that project, teachers helped children from the bottom third of the achievement distribution in their schools to participate at or near an average level in their classrooms. Interest in the teaching procedures used to train these teachers has mounted, so it has become important to report on the in-service program which supported them and which presently supports the continuing Reading Recovery Project.

Selection of the Teachers for the Reading Recovery Project

It was planned originally that the program should be implemented by experienced teachers informed about reading instruction in junior classes. Schools were asked to select a teacher who was a permanent member of staff, was able to work with the teachers of the children selected and had good relationships with staff members, was prepared to demonstrate her teaching to members of the in-service course, was able to commit herself to the program for an entire year, and had some experience with the *Diagnostic Survey* procedures, particularly running records.

We thought that teachers would probably not spend more than three to four years in teaching individual children in this way, and that the teacher's everyday instructional activities in her classroom would benefit from this course.

Introducing Schools to the Program

Consultation was a keyword in our planning; we did not want to prescribe how teachers would operate the scheme. We recognized that school populations are very different and that any new program must allow for different solutions in different settings.

We were also convinced that the reading recovery teacher would not work effectively in isolation, but should be part of a team aiming to raise the lower levels of reading achievement for the school. So an initial meeting was held at the beginning of the school year for all principals, teachers in charge of junior classes and reading recovery teachers of the participating schools. The Deputy District Senior Inspector explained the arrangements for substitute teaching and in-service attendance for the year-long course. The tutor for the course gave a historical synopsis of the development of the reading recovery program, and explained the scope of the reading recovery teacher's work and the ground rules for participation.

It should be mentioned that, during the first two years of the course, two models have been tried, a full-time and a part-time model. Each had its strengths and its difficulties. Teachers working on the course part-time had only two hours a day for individual tutoring and taught a class for the rest of the time. They could only tutor the most needy children, and other members of their staff helped them with testing and assessment. They had to be given extra time to attend the in-service sessions which met once a fortnight. For these sessions, teachers were divided into small tutorial groups of twelve teachers with one tutor.

The full-time teachers did not have the divided loyalties and the other problems of switching from one job to another. They did, however, feel the loss of reinforcement from not teaching a class of children who were progressing normally, and they found the concentrated individual tutoring very demanding. Probably twenty hours of individual teaching per week is an optimum. This means that more than one reading recovery teacher is required in a large school or in a district where children are ill-equipped for reading when they enter the junior school.

Valuing the Teacher's Experience

We wished to minimize the feelings of insecurity that teachers might initially feel about changing their teaching patterns and thinking differently about reading instruction. Teachers were invited to teach. They were reminded that they were experienced teachers and were urged to draw on their own experience when working with the children. It was considered economical to move both children and teachers gradually from their existing competencies rather than to demand at the outset new behaviors which might cause confusion and disrupt established and efficient responses.

New concepts and activities were demonstrated and discussed, and these became part of the teachers' procedures. As the course continued, it became obvious from the teachers' discussions that their views of the child's task and of their own roles were changing. Our teachers, at first, had their own theories about the task and the characteristics of their pupils. By the end of the year and after the in-service course, they had acquired new theories about how they and their pupils performed and how they should perform. They were now able to question, challenge, discuss, work out courses of action, and explain their decisions in ways they could all understand because these new theories were shared and explicit.

Training in Assessment

Teachers were trained to administer the running records and tests of the *Diagnostic Survey*. They observed and recorded exactly what the children were doing, and were forced to make these observations more explicit by writing a diagnostic summary report. This careful analysis of precisely what children could do was considered a sound basis for leading the teacher into the program she needed for a particular child. Teachers brought these test results to sessions for discussion of perplexing points or alternative interpretations, and they submitted a diagnostic summary of two cases for detailed appraisal by the course tutor.

Before they began tutoring children individually, teachers wrote predictions of what changes they would expect to see in the children's reading behaviors as they improved. Teachers were given two tasks: to complete a statement such as, 'At the end of the tutoring program the child will be able to . . . '; and, following this analysis of the child's expected achievements, to answer the question, 'Are there any priorities among these?' This helped them to specify the program goals for each child and begin to grapple with some of the conceptual issues, although at a rather superficial level.

Selection of Children

Children selected for individual tutoring were not chosen by setting a particular attainment level. *They were the lowest scorers on text reading in that particular school.* The lowest scorers in school C might be better than some of the higher scorers in school E. A teacher in each school was trying to raise the performance of the low progress readers *in that school.* Consequently, the teachers had to learn to make their own decisions about whom to admit to the program.

The teachers tested all children at 6:0 who were considered not to be making good progress. (Some schools already carried out such identification procedures). Information was sought from three sources: class teachers, supervising teachers, and the *Diagnostic Survey* results. One source of information was checked against the other. Within the *Diagnostic Survey,* teachers considered book level, and stanine scores (the method of grouping normalized test scores into nine groups).

The number of children who were individually tutored differed from school to school because of the different sizes of the schools and because of the variations in the needs of the children. The working week of the teacher set limits on the number of children who could be included in her program. The responsiveness of each child to individual tuition determined the time allocated for lessons and for the weeks the child remained in tutoring. Factors which tended to lengthen time in the program were language problems, family mobility, unsettled family circumstances, sickness or absence, general retardation, and unusual learning problems.

The children who were admitted to individual teaching had learned very little about reading and, after more than twelve months at school, were still reading caption books or the red or yellow books of the *Ready to Read* series. Sometimes in the smaller schools the teachers could also tutor 'gap-fillers'. These were children, able to read at higher levels, who had low scores in particular areas, i.e., on one or more of the tests. Part-time teachers selected four children, full-time teachers began with six and increased this to ten within a short period.

Beginning the Teaching Program

Tutor-trainers then had to support teachers through a brief but difficult period. For two weeks they were to teach only within what the child could do. The idea was to develop fluency on things that were easy for the child. By the second week, teachers were keen to introduce new material. However, they were held to the time limit to give them some experience of the value of consolidating what children already knew. The children were allowed time to become fluent with the familiar, to habituate their responses so that they no longer needed attention, and to enjoy the creative and exploratory payoffs of roaming around the known. A teacher's tendency to drag her student into new territory, into harder work, was being challenged. The value of reading quantities of easy material began to be obvious. These are some of the important principles of the reading recovery program which were established in these two weeks.

The diagnostic summary report gave the teacher an analysis of the behavior that should relate directly to her teaching program, and she arranged to see children on any timetable that suited both her and the school. Sometimes this was once a day for thirty minutes; sometimes it was twice a day for two sessions of twenty and ten minutes, or some other variation of this. Most of the instruction was individual. Very occasionally, towards the end of their program, children would come to her in twos and threes in preparation for returning to group instruction in the classroom.

Records

Teachers were asked to keep the following records: a test record sheet, a diagnostic summary, a lesson plan or summary for each session with the child, detailing the teaching sequences and providing a record of the changes or persistent difficulties in the child's responses, a running record of the text read at every session, and a graph of the progress made on book level, plotted once a week.

Some teachers liked to pre-plan their lessons. All recorded during the lesson what actually happened, noting especially the child's responses to new tasks. As lesson summaries were mandatory, full notes were completed immediately after the lesson ended.

Fortnightly Demonstrations and Group Discussions

The critical parts of the in-service training were probably the demonstration and discussion sessions held every other week. The in-service training program made extensive use of a one-way window between two rooms. Children were taught in one room. In the other, teachers observed and discussed a teaching demonstration while it was in progress, and visitors observed the program. The one-way viewing facility was an essential part of the in-service training, allowing for discussion of what the child was doing and why the teacher might have responsed as she did. Delayed discussion would not have been as effective. Video-taped replays lost the excitement of the on-task question and commentary. A teacher had to act when a teaching decision was required and these training discussions attended to such decision points as they arose.

During early training sessions, a tutor demonstrated testing or teaching and another modelled the discussion procedures for the new teachers. Demonstrations by the tutor were kept to a minimum and the first demonstrations by the teachers themselves began after six weeks. Children were brought to the in-service center, and a typical lesson was conducted for the teacher's peers. This provided several opportunities: the teacher's techniques were evaluated, gently, by her peers; the watching teachers had a chance to observe, from the outside, the tutorial situation which they usually worked inside, either as a teacher being tutored, or as a teacher tutoring a child; and the situation induced an objectivity among teachers in evaluating their own work.

None enjoyed giving a demonstration lesson but almost all commented on its value. They described their ordeal as 'a very nerve-wracking experience', which they dreaded, but a profitable one because 'one was reinforced for some things and was shown ways of improving'. They felt the sessions made them more aware, as teachers, of their own choices and assumptions, and more self-critical. The discussion among the observers as the child and teacher worked was described by the teachers as 'invaluable'.

Under such close scrutiny, strong pressure was on the teacher to make sound judgments which had massive payoffs in terms of learning gains for the child. If the children were to return to an effective functioning level near to the average for their class, they had to make accelerated progress; yet they were the very children who should not be pressured. Teachers were asked to take every necessary step warranted for a particular child. They were to waste no time on instruction that was inappropriate for any one child. Short-cuts were fine; detours away from text reading were suspect. The teacher's peers were quick to criticize any indulgent wandering into unnecessary activities once they appreciated the importance of acceleration.

The emphasis in the in-service sessions shifted, in the latter part of the year, to the reading recovery children who were proving the most difficult to teach. Teachers taught in their demonstrations in ways deliberately chosen to expose the child's peculiar problem to the group, and, in discussion, the resources of the group were directed to exploring the problem and searching for a solution.

After two demonstrations, each of which lasted for half an hour, the teachers spent a further hour discussing their work. Issues were raised by the tutor or by the teachers. Teachers' comments on these sessions were:

- A major percentage of learning takes place here. The in-service sessions extend and consolidate one's understanding of reading processes and recovery procedures.
- They kept me thinking about ways to improve my teaching and gave me a good opportunity to discover whether I was approaching problems in the best way.

- Your demonstration of how to increase writing vocabulary suddenly made it all go clear.
- Seeing X take a lesson was far more valuable than a video because it was alive and not static.
- The one-way window was invaluable and could never have been taken over by videotapes. Being able to see someone working and being able to discuss and question as they went along was really good.
- I learned so much by just observing the children at work. Each one is so different and how they operate on print can vary so much.
- The most difficult pupils are very interesting to watch.
- The last term when we saw people working with very difficult children was extremely helpful.
- One of the early demonstrations should be with a child who knows almost nothing. Where do you start? What do you do? How do you build on nothing?
- Reading Recovery teachers have no-one else at their school to discuss problems with and need to meet other Reading Recovery teachers to air problems and find possible solutions.

At all times, the in-service sessions aimed to enrich the teachers' understanding of their children and to sharpen their use of special teaching procedures in order to maximize their effectiveness. Some of the discussion centered on the difficult problem of finding appropriate resources, especially easy reading books.

Throughout the year, teachers were introduced gradually to the new teaching procedures and concepts. The book describing these procedures did not provide a simple set of instructions that could be read and then implemented, but was a reference source and a basis for the discussion and clarification of concepts. Some activities were introduced to teachers before others (to reduce the load of newness). The text and book reading, text writing with cut-up stories, letter identification and new vocabulary were the first to be introduced. A concept of teaching children to make use of reading strategies was introduced early. By the beginning of April, procedures for helping children hear the sound sequences in words were introduced, with videotapes, demonstration and discussion.

As the program continued, the teachers became more adept at discussing the children, the teaching they observed, their own programs, and the directions and explanations in the written account of the procedures. Other aspects of reading which were discussed included ideas about the reading process, syntax, semantics, visual analysis, over-learning and habituating responses, word learning, memory, integration and cross-relating of cues, and independence.

Topics raised by the teachers in these discussions suggested that their attention to the reading process was shifting from teaching for items of knowledge (letters known, words remembered), and from getting the child to habituate a skill or memorize a new element, to developing in the child the confidence and willingness to use a variety of strategies. Another feature of the shift in teaching was movement away from having the poor reader dependent on the teacher and towards teaching in such a way that the children had many opportunities to teach themselves.

Tutor's Visits to Schools

The tutor paid on-site visits to programs running in the schools as often as her busy schedule allowed. These had three purposes: to communicate with the school about the running of the project; to talk over new techniques recently introduced with the teacher and answer any queries; and to observe the reading recovery teacher at work, to demonstrate some procedure, or to work with a particular child at the teacher's request.

Discontinuing Teaching

When the teachers judged from the children's work that they were able to work with, and survive in, an appropriate group in their classroom, they recommended the children discontinue special teaching sessions. It was not uncommon for a fast learner to be ready to leave the program before the end of the first term. Reading recovery teachers were now faced with a new set of decisions, for which they were prepared. Initial discussion dealt with what a teacher would look for in a child prior to discontinuing, and what information she would ask for about the class the child was going back to. The dangers of dependency on the recovery teacher were emphasized as threatening a child's survival in group work back in the classroom.

Teachers were asked to make recommendations that a child discontinue sessions on the basis of: the setting a child would be working in (the teacher, the other children, book levels and groups available for placement, class teacher's style and demands, etc.); the observed behaviors of the child that would make him or her likely to cope; and the evidence from the child's accumulated running records of book reading.

Retesting the child was carried out in order to cross-check the decisions to discontinue, not to initiate them. Decisions to discontinue were always checked by the course tutor. Occasionally a child was not ready to discontinue the sessions. In most cases, however, the teachers had carried the children for longer and to higher levels than may have been necessary. They were conservative in their recommendations for discontinuing.

Continuing Support for Teachers

The teaching procedures were carefully designed to help children with specific problems make fast progress. Because of this, there was little room for changing the procedures. Innovation was welcomed, but top priority was always given to accelerating the child's progress, and, in practice, teachers' suggested variations in procedure were often ineffective because a crucial skill was no longer included. In-service training usually encourages teachers to innovate, to apply new ideas in creative ways. In this program, strict adherence to most procedures seemed necessary. In the year following their training, we watched some of our teachers veer away from appropriate practices in their demonstrations when they were not attached to the program for regular meetings.

To foster a critical approach to non-productive variations and an open mind on productive changes to the program, it was agreed that some continuing support for teachers might be useful. Teachers met at least once a term to learn what new things each had discovered, to demonstrate to their colleagues and to discuss their programs. Demonstrations and probing questions tend to prevent practice drifting away from the most accelerating procedures. Teachers welcomed these meetings. Without the training course, they found their role in schools in subsequent years was sometimes a lonely one.

In-service Program for Tutors

The key person in running the in-service program is the course tutor. Her role is seen as a complex one which requires a wide range of skills in diverse areas. It is essential that she have a thorough and academic understanding of the theoretical concepts upon which the program is based, a sensitive awareness of the organizational, professional and child development issues associated with the innovations in the program, and extensive practical experience of the everyday workings of the junior school.

The first training course for a group of tutors was provided in 1980. Strengths considered in their selection were: effectiveness as class teachers and as reading recovery teachers; a thorough knowledge of the theoretical basis of the reading recovery program; and the ability to work supportively with teachers.

The course moved through several patterns of organization to meet the changing needs of the tutors throughout the year. It was an intensive course demanding flexibility.

Effective dissemination of reading recovery programs on a national basis, then, will require two levels of in-service training support, one for the teachers of children, and another for the tutors of teachers.

V   Observing Writing Behavior

This is a short section because it is an area which has interested me most recently. For the longitudinal study of reading reported in the first section of this volume I had collected many interesting samples of children's writing. It took me some years of searching to find order within these and the results of that struggle came together in a book, What Did I Write? *That title was intended to capture the puzzlement and searching of little children facing the complexities of print.* Exploring With A Pencil *covers briefly some of the discussion from that book of the possible interrelationships that exist between reading and writing in the preschool years and around the time the child begins formal education.*

In the Reading Recovery project we tested out some of these interrelationships as the program contained an important component of writing activities. These are discussed in Early Writing and Reading: Reciprocal Gains, *although it is in the Reading Recovery follow-up study that the evidence of writing progress is given. I have completed this year a major review of early writing which is in press, and in that review I have explored further the interrelationships of oral language learning, early reading and early writing. The last paper in this section,* Writing From A Developmental Perspective, *summarizes some of the thoughts that emerged from that review.*

24 Exploring With A Pencil

In the Early Detection of Reading Difficulties *(Clay, 1979) I have reported some of the ways in which the child's current status in writing behaviors can be sampled, but those procedures are enriched by access to a series of dated samples of the child's work collected over a period of time. Those who observe the changes that occur in the early writing samples of individual children will find them very informative.*

Somewhere between three and five years most children in a literate culture become aware that people make marks on paper purposefully. In imitation those children produce scribble, mock writing or mock letters. The linear scribble that fills the lines of a writing pad has, for the child, all the mystery of an unfamiliar code. It stands for a myriad of possible things but does not convey a particular message. The child seems to say, 'I hope I've said something important. You must be able to understand what I've said. What did I write?'

One such sample was presented to a mother by a four-year-old. Seriously, the mother sounded out the first line. 'SAHSPNO.' Natasha, thoughtful and satisfied, said, 'I did it.' What had she done? To her mind she had used the code that adults use to send messages and her mother had been able to respond to the messages but she was beginning to gain control over a few, first signals.

It would be possible for a child to move from here, using alphabet blocks or plastic letters, to the invented spelling that has been described by Read (1975), and Carol Chomsky (1976), making his or her own discoveries about the way we put the sounds we use in speech into written language. Those children who do this complete a fascinating analysis of the sounds they hear in the words they speak, and this can be an excellent preparation for learning to read. The children I observed approached their early creative writing in other ways because of two kinds of opportunities.

Opportunities Before School

Some children are introduced to written language by adults or older siblings in their preschool years. The following example is a diary record for Penny, a child aged 4 years 11 months, who entered school two weeks later. She had not learned to read, she could write only one word and that was her name, and she could produce a few single letters. Yet she was quite certain that her writing conveyed messages.

She received a party invitation by mail from Mary. She whipped it out

of her mother's hand, retreated to her bedroom, and then brought it
back to display the writing in the center and asked for it to be read to her.
She seemed to assume that it contained a message that her mother could
read.

Later that day Penny asked for paper saying, 'I want to write to Mary.'
No suggestion of replying had been made because that part of the
invitation had not been read out. She complained about the first piece of
paper that she was offered. 'Too scrappy', she said. Obviously this was
an important message. 'How do you write "come"?' she asked after she
was given a more elegant piece of paper. The assumptions in the next
piece of dialog are interesting:

Mother: (puzzled) What do you want to say?
Penny: I would like (pause) to come to your party.
Mother: Don't you want 'I' and 'would'?
Penny: (Shrilled in excited irritation) But I will have to write COME!

Come was the significant message; it was the first thing she wanted to
write.

Penny went to the cupboard and tore off a white strip from the
newspaper edge for her mother to write a copy on. She repeated the
message. It was written and she read it word for word, although this
was the first time she had been asked to read words. It was not
surprising that she could do this because it was her message and she
had already stated it twice. The message was from within her and
she was merely matching it to the marks on paper. She began to
write 'I' at the top right corner of the page. 'That's the wrong side',
her mother corrected. She then copied the words carefully and correctly with good spacing because she could copy letters quite well.
No further help was given until she realized she had skipped the
second 'to' and asked for help. She completed the task and then
asked for 'from Penny'. She was given 'from' and insisted on getting
'from Penny' although she could write her name. Was this to delin-
eate the relationship of one word to the other? She asked for an
envelope, and copied Miss Mary B . . . on it putting the surname on
the next line. Her mother was quite satisfied but Penny seemed to be
searching for a word. 'Put (pause) the address.' She got a copy of
this and added it to the envelope showing concern when she thought
the line would clash with the previous one.

This episode seemed to provide a great leap forward in the child's
concepts of written language coding. It was a first request for a
coherent message to be conveyed in written words to someone else
and was in response to a written invitation. Two prompts were
given; one was about the order of words in the message and the
other was about placing the first word on the page. Both relate to a
critical set of learning *that is central to understanding the relationships of speech and written language,* the relationship of temporal to
visual ordering. The episode demonstrated a skill for letter-by-letter

copying, maintaining direction once it is established, spacing words, keeping somewhat in lines. Although she could re-tell the message pointing accurately there was no frustration, and the request for the address surprised her mother. The emotional tone was not one of achievement; she did not display this to the rest of the family, but treated it rather as a social communication task which had to be carried out.

The preschool experiences of some children will have already introduced them to concepts about written language before they get to school.

School Opportunities

In most of the New Zealand schools where I have been observing children the creative urge of the child to write down his own ideas was considered to be the important thing to be fostered in written language. During the first year of school, teachers did not place much emphasis on penmanship, on separate lessons in how to print because this was thought to inhibit the spontaneous efforts of children to make written statements. Then how did the children learn to print?

They drew pictures and the teacher wrote their dictated captions.
They traced over the teacher's script. (There was a good model.)
They copied underneath the teacher's captions.
They copied words and captions from around the room.
They remembered some word forms and wrote them independently.
They invented word forms, often correctly.
They asked the teacher for unknown words only.

Marshall (1974) described the first sentences that children are asked to write as 'a scrap of individual personal news inscribed in a diary or newsbook.' Perhaps creative writing is too grand a term for this but I will use it.

Children proceeded through the sequence at very different rates. The transfer from tracing and copying behavior that is dependent on a model, to self-initiated, self-organized sequences of behavior carried out without any outside support is a complex set of learning. Ignoring for the moment the letters or words that the child is learning, and the quality of the messages that he is writing, we can note that a very important psychological change occurs. Behavior that is at first dependent on external control becomes entirely controlled by the child. He generates the messages, breaks them up, codes them into written language, arranges them on the page so that they comply with the adult reader's assumptions about written messages, re-reads or checks his message, detects some of his own errors, and recognizes what he does not know and when he has to seek outside help. Very early such creative writing becomes a child-generated, a meaning-transmission activity with in-built checks for accuracy, sharpening the child's discrimination of what he knows and does not know and leading to his using of his teacher as a resource in an efficient manner.

Individual Differences

This approach can be adapted to different classrooms and to individual differences.

The teacher of school entrants must work with a wide range of individual differences which can be discovered by studying the children's early writing samples. At school entry one child will draw a picture but write nothing. Another may draw, invent writing, talk well and copy well. Yet another may have a small vocabulary of words that can be written into simple stories or sentences. In these circumstances, brought about by ability differences, preschool opportunities, program differences and individual motivations, it is not useful to look for age norms and descriptive sequences of which step comes before which. Unlike language acquisition where the evidence that certain forms are learned before others is very strong, the written language task permits a more varied entry. It may be the visual sense that accounts for the difference. I doubt whether there is any fixed sequence of learning through which all children must pass in early writing and this raises doubts in my mind about any sequenced program that proceeds from the adult's logical analysis of the task and not from observation of what children are doing. Eventually as each convention is mastered the children acquire a common fund of concepts but the point of entry and the path of progress may be different for any two children. The usual starting point is the child's own name which suggests how varied that initial attainment may be. From there one child's passion for escalators and another's curiosity about elephants may take them in different directions, temporarily.

Approximations, Early Concepts, Strategies and Principles

Two features of the learning process warrant some special emphasis. The first things learned will be gross approximations which later become refined: weird letter forms, invented words, make-believe sentences. Such creative efforts suggest that the child is reaching out towards the principles of written language and any instruction should encourage him to continue to do this.

Yet this knowledge is very specific. 'Ian' reflects that spelling of his name, claiming that it is spelled 'IAN.' Jenny has developed the habit of writing 'Jehhy' and refuses to acknowledge the correct spelling as her own name. Because early learning is both approximate and specific any one new insight may change the child's grasp of the activity drastically, and may even disorganize it.

These two characteristics of gross approximations on the one hand and specificity on the other demand that the teacher of school entrants know an individual child's progress to date if she or he is to understand the significance of the child's current creative writing product in the scheme of development. All the teacher needs is a collection of samples of work arranged chronologically. But she must work hard at understanding what the child is trying to say in his written expression. The jumbled story written from right to left or the weird letters should be read for their message. Those who make the effort will find a rich commentary on each child's learning encapsulated in his accumulated attempts to write (Clay, 1974).

One early and easy concept is that signs carry messages. The child demonstrates an understanding of this when he produces signs you cannot interpret and expects you to read them.

When the child realizes that the messages we speak can be written down he has grasped the main concept required for reading and for writing progress.

Much later in his work with written language he will come to acknowledge the space concept. A space is used to signal the end of one word and the beginning of another. But what is its equivalent in speech? Some children take a long time to learn to hear the word as a segment of their spoken sentence and so cannot 'see' the function of the space in print.

I was surprised to observe that copying was not a very productive strategy. Some words, some letters and some word groups must be imitated to get novel behaviors into the child's repertoire but I observed it to be a slow and laborious way to establish the first units in printing behavior. One frequently observes how quickly the child tires of a copying task and how he turns then to the easier task of inventing forms for himself. It seemed that careful copying was a check on wayward inventing, but inventing was a quicker way to new discoveries for the children I observed.

Until I began observing five-year-olds closely I had no idea that they took stock of their own learning. They spontaneously and systematically made lists of what they knew. They consciously ordered or arranged their learning — or should I say, some of them did. Perhaps they were the brighter ones, and possibly self-generated inventories are evidence of some meta-memoric strategies devised by the child for arranging and interrelating his categories of information.

When I began to work on the writing samples I had collected I had no organizing ideas in mind. The samples themselves suggested that children were assuming certain things about the language and the task. I have called these implied assumptions, principles. They are important because when the child operates according to one of these principles for the first time his work takes a leap forward in complexity. However, these principles may have an existence only in my analysis and there may be no analogous function in the child's cognition. As illustrations of these principles I will discuss flexibility, recurrence and the generating principle.

The flexibility principle. Children experiment with letter forms creating a variety of new symbols by repositioning them. They explore the limits within which each letter form may be varied and still retain its identity. When is a sign not a language sign? When is a sign a new sign? Can you turn a letter around? The answer is usually no. Can you change the letter order around? Again the answer is usually no. Can you begin on the right hand side of the page or at the bottom? Sometimes established habits seem to become disorganized when a new feature requires attention. It is as if the old habits regain their flexibility to admit the new learning before settling to a new organization of the habitual response. Such flexibility may be of critical importance to the early stages of complex learning. Too early and rigid patterning might prevent later modification.

The recurring principle. The tendency to repeat an action has the obvious advantage of helping in the establishment of quick, habitual response patterns and it probably produces pleasant feelings of competence. The recurring principle makes an even greater contribution to the child's progress when he realizes that the same elements can recur in variable patterns for this is how we use the alphabetic principle in language, and how we can make many sentences from different arrangements of a few words.

The generating principle. An easy way to extend one's repertoire is to know some elements and to know some rules for combining or arranging these elements. One can then produce many new statements in an inventive way. Generating statements seems to suit the young learner better than the laborious task of copying. After all he has been generating speech for several years and would not want to merely imitate speech. Generating written language, accurately and inventively is facilitated by the flexibility principle and by the recurring principle.

Some Risk Areas

These are two things which have been considered important in early reading and writing that could become neglected in this approach. Teachers have often found it necessary to guide children manually and verbally in forming letters, calling for an approved sequence for starting and forming letters. This motor activity is sometimes seen by teachers as necessary for emphasizing the distinctiveness of somewhat similar letters such as *m* and *n*. If this is important, and it certainly is for a few children, then it might be overlooked in a creative writing program. But this need not be so.

The other area of learning that may be overlooked warrants closer attention. Carol Chomsky describes the invented spelling that children have been encouraged to use in some Grade 1 classrooms, and she describes how the children are being encouraged to listen to their speech, to discover relationships between speaking and writing with the focus on the way the code represents the sounds. To have children do this effectively, one must withhold much of the teacher's example in modelling and in writing words for children. It is not clear whether there is a better payoff from learning something about the sounds of English in the analytic way which invented spelling provides before one learns to read, or whether there is an equal or greater benefit in placing the emphasis on the creative writing, meanwhile using alphabet corners with invented spelling activities as an extra activity. I have seen creative writing used in all types of schools in an urban center with five-year-olds, some of whom used English as a mother tongue and others who did not. Vast differences existed between these children in their preschool learning experiences. I am not sure how many or which children would find invented spelling difficult.

The Contributions of Writing to Reading

Observing children in classrooms has led me to the understanding that in the informal infant room program where child discovery is valued and creative writing encouraged, the writing plays a significant part in early reading progress. It provides for synthetic experience where letters are built into words which make up sentences, reinforcing the left to right principles, and an understanding, however, intuititive, of the hierarchical nature of language.

Some reading programs can allow children to overlook these important insights. Creative writing in New Zealand schools provides complementary, and corrective, experience for a reading program there which focuses on the messages of continuous text, and depends less on learning words and letter-sound relationships. A measure of writing vocabulary was found to be equally good as a predictor of reading progress after 6 months of instruction as letter identification. I am confident that the program that emphasizes early creative writing, and succeeds, will produce at least as good readers as the program which emphasizes letter knowledge.

The young child seems to derive a sense of mastery when he writes a word which is recognized by an adult. To achieve this he had to attend to the detail of the letters he wrote and the correct letter order. Far more important than this, he had to organize his own behavior into appropriate sequences of actions, he had to reach into his language stores, into his sound segmentation strategies, into his associations of graphemes with phonemes, into his motor skill for creating a specific letter from his 'mental programs' for letter formation, and into his reading knowledge to check on the written sequences he had created.

How is this different from reading? The marked difference is in having the motor skill to produce the letters and words instead of what seems the easier route of saying the words. Here we must consider the goal of the instruction. If the goal is to have a child see a word and name it correctly the writing act might be seen to be a tedious detour. But if the point of reading and writing at this level is to have the child eager to search his stores of knowledge about written language, reaching out for new information to supplement them, meanwhile working slowly and carefully enough for the complex processes to become interrelated, for awareness of error to occur by feedback processes, and for self-correction to occur, then it may be appropriate that some of these activities are performed at slower speeds. In addition, the motor performance adds another way of knowing about wrtten language and allows one more way in which error may be recognized, providing another source of error detection. When the learner is a novice with only tentative strategies for responding correctly he needs more sources of error detection. As the child becomes a better reader, aware of more of the redundancies in the written code, he can afford to forget movement as a way of checking on the correctness of a response but in those early unsure days his memories for the words which he has tried to write may provide feedback to both early writing and early reading.

In the early stages of learning to read it is not the child's repertoires of items of knowledge, that is the letters identified or the words learned, that interest me most. It is the strategies that the child acquires that permit him to bring his knowledge of the world to bear on building up those stores of items, strategies he gains for searching and checking upon the accuracy of what he has so far said or written.

I am impressed with the potential of early writing, as a highly satisfying experience for young children, for complementing the early reading program. The more this is organized by the child the greater value it will have. The more the teacher feels compelled to direct, sequence, correct and oversee this learning the less value for reading it will have, although it might produce children with excellent letter formation.

If a child knows how to scan letters and words, how to study a word in order to write it and how to organize his writing of that word he has the skills to deal with the detail of print. It is probable that early writing serves to organize the visual analysis for print, and to strengthen important memoric strategies.

The child's written work also provides us with objective evidence of what the child has learned. We have an opportunity to see how the child organizes his behavior as he writes. From the correct copying of a word carried out in an appropriate sequence we may assume some functional organization in the brain which permits that sequence of actions. If we see a child write a new word without a copy we can assume the capacity to synthesize information from several sources.

My aim in early writing instruction would be to provide many interesting activities to establish and stabilize these strategies for analyzing words. I think I would want to precede them by some invented spelling with alphabet letters to ensure that the children were hearing sounds in words, listening to their own articulation of words, but given that the first successes with this had been established I would encourage creative writing. Once the child's writing with only a limited vocabulary had shown me that the child could search, find, and check on his own information as he worked with words, use directional cues, and respect letter and word order, then I would assume that these strategies would remain in the child's repertoire and be called into action when needed. Once the basic visual scanning, memoric and self-correction strategies were established, practice in writing would have its own value and would not contribute directly to reading progress. The goal for the child learning to read would shift from flexible organization of complex activites to automatic, speedy responses on the basis of partial cues. The older reader would be learning how to build shorthand processes on the basis of the foundation he had already established.

For the foregoing reasons I would want to take issue with all who wish to save little five-year-olds from the tedium of writing.

But, some will say, there are many children who build efficient visual scanning and speedy recognition systems, who self-correct and progress well, who read first and write much later. True, for the complex process of learning to read can be successfully approached from many points and by different routes. This must not be forgotten in one's enthusiasm for recommending any procedure in reading instruction. How does the teacher know that these strategies are being created in a sound manner? The answer is of course because the child is successful. How does she know what is wrong when the child is not being successful? This has been our problem. How do we help the less successful children to perform as the successful ones do? Perhaps we have to find a highly motivating way of slowing up the processes, so that we can monitor the products and procedures with care, reinforce the tentative inching towards an efficient search and check procedure and then think about encouraging fast automatic responding.

I am not saying that a child should not be asked to read until he writes. I think he should have reading and writing programs which are complementary until he is secure in reading and making good progress.

And Finally . . .

Luria, an eminent Russian neuropsychologist, has described how a study of injuries to the brain provided him with a theory of complex brain functioning in speech and writing (1970). He stresses that particular zones of the brain are responsible for the synthesis into a coherent whole of collections of information from memory and from different senses. Every complex form of behavior depends upon the joint operation of several areas located in different zones of the brain. It is a combination of cues 'out there,' of memories and of expectations of what might happen next which enables the person to perform complex actions, to understand the complex grammar of a sentence spoken to him. In Luria's analysis there is a similarity between reading orally and writing because both require motor action: to speak is as much to organize movement as to write. The difference for the young child is that speech is already well organized and the movements in writing are not. Those who wish to bypass early writing will be right if they can ensure that reading behavior does become intricately organized without it. I see writing as a means of slowing up the complex activity so that all the pieces can be interwoven. The musician, skilled though he be, will slow up the intricate passage to ensure control; the chorister may be asked to sing the notes of a difficult passage very slowly before he combines them in what seems to be a rapid and intricate cadenza. Luria poetically describes a skilled sequence of movement as a kinetic melody of interchangeable links.

Luria possibly provides an explanation for the fact that adults find it difficult to analyze the problems of very young children as these children approach the task of learning about written language. He has concluded that training and practice change the organization of the brain's activity so that the brain comes to perform an accustomed task without having to analyze this task. That is to say the final performance of the task may be based on a network of cell connections in the brain which is quite different from the network that was originally called upon when the performance was new and required the help of analytic processes.

However, if a teacher's conception of writing is governed by standards of penmanship and correctness of grammar then these demands may certainly detract from a concept of early writing as an exploratory activity to accompany early reading. There is nothing to be gained unless the teacher reacts as one advocate of early writing did when he wrote, 'Their writing may not be good, but they know and I know what a huge effort lies behind it and I let them feel my pleasure.'

25 Early Writing and Reading: Reciprocal Gains

This paper represents my thinking on this topic when it was undergoing a transition. For What Did I Write? *I had thought about the ways in which early exploration with a pencil, and early creative writing (in the sense of simple composed messages put into print) interacted with early reading experiences to sharpen learning in each. The possible interactions were explored further in the Reading Recovery program where every lesson had a writing component. Reviewing recent literature on children's writing I would now go further than the position taken in this paper, and would develop hypotheses about the interplay of all experiences with language — spoken, read or written by the child — for enriching performance potential in any one of those activities. This paper relates to the section on reading difficulties but it also points to new kinds of rationales for whole language approaches in the last paper.*

Reading

At school entry old learning must be transformed into useful ways of dealing with print, a new medium which has its own special characteristics. At this time we begin the production of our reading problems because some children build inefficient systems of functioning which keep them crippled in this process throughout their school careers. Reading behavior becomes organized into a complex system of functioning during the first two years of instruction, in a way which sets the pattern for subsequent gains in skill. If the system functions efficiently the child reads fluently without much error and adds to his skill with every exposure to this task. If the system functions inefficiently the child establishes habits of inefficient processing of cues with every extra reading lesson he has.

Children who fail in reading do not all have damaged brains. Most have developed inefficient behavior responses for finding, using, checking, and correcting the information they gain as they read. The child who cannot read appears to lack certain skills with letters, sounds, and words, and remediation is often only directed towards the teaching of those missing items of knowledge. A different remedial approach proceeds on the assumption that children who fail to learn to read stop producing many of the responses which are used by successful readers. They specialize rigidly in particular kinds of responses usually associated with item learning. Good readers explore print more than poor readers. It is also noticed that good readers have both writing and reading vocabularies but that poor readers have little or no writing vocabulary. Naive explanations of these differences in reading and writing vocabularies might run like this — 'Children learn words by seeing them over and over again. They gain a visual memory for the words; they see them in their heads. Then they will be able to write them.' Yet I can write down names I have never seen written and attempt to spell words I have only heard which are too long for me to visualize. Readers have assumptions about English orthography that lead them to predict how sounds are represented by letters, how common clusters of sounds are written, and even when peculiar spellings might occur. The probabilities of English orthography guide our attempts. Another way of stating this is to say that we operate on the problem, constructing a solution. Young children who are encouraged to explore the possibilities of print create words. To think that we have to impress a visual record of a word in the child's brain before a child can write it is to conclude that we must teach a child to read before he can write. Turning that assumption upside down I would suggest that if the child begins to record some simple ideas in writing the action he carries out to construct the message will build a 'knowing' of the ways of words that is more comprehensive than any visual impress method can achieve. So with problem readers we encouraged them to write from the beginning, and ours was not the first remedial scheme to do this.

This approach is not inconsistent with the way authorities describe early reading, or practitioners approach it. Carol Chomsky (1971) said, 'The child enters the classroom equipped to learn language and able to do so by methods of his own.' He has constructed a complex system of language rules which enable him to understand and produce sentences in his language. He builds these rules by a process that is as yet little understood, but his language-learning is already innovative and rule-governed.

There are critical aspects of learning to read which the child must teach himself because we do not yet understand them. The child has to discover the distinctive features that can be used during reading to distinguish letters and words. He has to discover the sources of redundancy in language so that he knows what to attend to and what to ignore. This knowledge is not accessible to our conscious level of thinking and yet we acquire it and use it (Smith, 1971).

The best British schools have long been admired for the teacher's ability to act as a facilitator or consultant and not as a didactic expert.

> Where the teacher's expertise really counts . . . is in knowing what the child is going to want. . . . There are two ways in which

we can help a child to learn. One of them is by attempting to teach him; the other is by facilitating his attempts to teach himself. We need to give the child freedom to explore and to learn on his own.... The child is self-stimulating and self-starting provided conditions are right for him. (Cashdan, 1976 p. 82, 83).

It is the aim of most reading programs to bring children through the beginning reading scheme to a stage of independence in reading. At this point the teacher has to do less teaching. She provides the structure, the time and acts as a resource but the child pursues a large amount of the activity himself, pushing the boundaries of his own skills as he tries more and more material of increasing difficulty. The child reading to himself knows when he is more or less correct. Smith (1978) considered that one of the beautiful advantages of reading sense is that it provides its own feedback. One way to describe this independence is that the child has found out how to read novel texts all by himself. He finds this activity rewarding. Once the child learns to search for cues the reinforcement lies within the reading process, in the agreement he can achieve between the signals and the messages in the code. He no longer needs as much outside help to confirm whether his response is right or wrong. The activity of making cues fit, of eliminating any misfit, is rewarding to the child who succeeds. Independence in reading is a much larger cognitive enterprise than being able to decode words. The independent reader reads and because he reads he improves his reading ability. Why is this? An unthinking answer might be that he is repeating the words so often that they become his automatic responses. That is a small part of the story. His responses do get speedier, and more often correct but he becomes able to read more difficult text. How does he improve his own skill? What accounts for the *rise* in level of performance?

At the moment of making an error a child, reading for meaning, will notice the error; it will become self-evident. This is a monitoring activity. The reader takes some action. At this moment he is observing his own behavior closely because he will have to decide which response is the best fit. He chooses which to retain and which to discard. As he searches and selects he must carry out two further types of self-regulatory action. He observes his own behavior closely and he assesses his own behavior. Has he solved it? Has he got it right? Do all the sides of the jig-saw piece fit that particular slot? By using self-observation, self-assessment and self-reinforcement the young reader discovers new features of written language, new instances of things he learnt earlier, new relationships and best of all for fluent reading, new short-cuts to storing and retrieving information.

The child's contribution is quite considerable.

Writing

Graves (1978) has been studying writing in the U.S.A., and what children think is expected of them.

> People want to write. The desire to express is relentless. . . . Yet most of us write less and less . . . writing is perceived as a form of etiquette — to be properly attired, demonstrated in correct manners, saying as little as possible. This view of writing was taught us in school. In the classroom learners are viewed as receivers, not senders. A far greater premium is placed on a student's ability to read and listen than on their ability to speak and write. . . . (p. 4, 5).

He asked children 'What does the teacher want?' They said, 'It has to be long, not too messy and have no mistakes.' Graves likened this to seeing writing as a method of moral development in which the eradication of an error is more important than the encouragement of expression. So, when seven-year-old children were asked, 'What do you think a good writer needs to do in order to write well?' children who had a difficult time with writing responded, 'To be neat, space letters, spell good and know words.'

Very little is written about early writing. I found a few lines in Sybil Marshall's *Creative Writing* (1974), nothing in *Children and Writing in the Elementary School,* which is a collection of articles on theories and techniques edited by Richard Larson (1975). David Holbrook in his 'sampler for student teachers', *Children's Writing* (1967) is referring to older children. Two authors of books on English infant school methods mention it briefly: Joy Taylor in *Reading and Writing in The First School* (1973) spares the topic eight pages, and Nora Goddard in *Literacy: Language-Experience Approaches* (1974) weaves the discussion of writing into the total language-experience approach and spares four pages for the activities a teacher should have in 'the writing area.' Brief reference to the American context is made by Edward Fry (1977) in a chapter called 'Writing: Language Experience Approach, Readability.'

There has recently been a renewed interest in writing which arose from a concern that children now have fewer opportunities to write and that schools may not be sufficiently hospitable to such activities (King, 1978; Graves, 1978). King concluded that significant work on the composing process was already completed or underway which could encourage teachers to allow more spontaneous writing in their classrooms but that we do not have a theory of how children learn to write in their first years at school. The new interest is generating a new set of competing ideas. Florio (1978) suggested that teachers may best serve the acquisition of writing by structuring social occasions which require the children to write purposefully, such as letters of invitation and request. One of the children studied in her ethnographic approach said that he made his own words and he didn't copy people and that the more he learned to write good letters, the better they got. This suggests to me that the power of making one's own statement and getting better at it was, for the child, a real reward in itself. The need to communicate does not emerge strongly in the child's comment. This is the position that Frank Smith supports in his recent work on how writers write. He argues that writing is a constructive and expressive activity for the individual and not a communicative one.

Durrell expressed a similar view in an interview with Graves (1978):

> Writing is active; it involves the child in doing and is important. Teachers make learning too passive. We have known for years the child's first urge is to write and not to read, and we haven't taken advantage of this fact. We have under-estimated the power of the output languages like speaking and writing . . . (p. 8).

Writing also contributes to reading. When a child writes she has to know the sound-symbol relations inherent in reading. Auditory, visual and motor systems are all at work when the child writes and all contribute to greater skill in reading. Between three and five years of age most children in a literate culture become aware that people make marks on paper purposefully. In imitation those children produce scribble or mock writing. To the child the scribbles have the mystery of an unfamiliar code with a myriad of possible meanings. The child seems to say, 'I hope I've said something important. What did I write?' (Clay, 1975). It is possible for the child to move from here in several different directions. The invented spellings described by Read (1975) and C. Chomsky (1976) allowed children to complete a fascinating analysis of the sounds they hear in words which is an excellent preparation for learning to read. Some children are introduced to written language by adults or older siblings in their preschool years (Clark, 1976; Butler and Clay, 1979).

In the informal infant classroom where child discovery is valued creative writing plays a significant part in early reading progress and schools avoid the situations which Graves described. They support the creative urge of the child to write from the beginning. Teachers do not emphasize things which might inhibit the spontaneous efforts of children to write. There is a minimum of stress on penmanship and lessons on how to print. The first sentences that children write are 'a scrap of personal news' (Marshall, 1974). Creative writing may be too grand a term for this but it captures the expressive nature of the activity. The usual starting point is the child's own name which suggests how varied the initial attainment may be. From there one child's passion for escalators and another's curiosity about elephants may take them in different directions.

Tracing and copying behavior may be the child's first steps and such behavior is dependent behavior requiring a model. Withing a few months a very important psychological change occurs. The child takes control of the task. He generates messages, breaks them up, codes them into written language, arranges them on the page so they comply with the adult's assumptions about written messages, re-reads or checks his message, detects some of his own errors, and recognizes what he does not know and when he must seek outside help. Such creative writing of child-generated meanings has in-built checks for accuracy, sharpening the child's discrimination of what he knows and does not know, and leading to his use of his teacher as a resource in an efficient manner. Perhaps that sounds like the description of a very competent upper primary school child. Careful observation of competent pre-schoolers who are trying to write will uncover such behaviors in their formative stages (Butler and Clay, 1979).

Although teachers often want to have the young child write there is a prior problem of his not being able to write letters (not knowing them), and not knowing from sight, or from memory, the words he wants to write. Four of the many approaches that have been suggested for teachers to use are:

- the teacher acts as the child's scribe, taking his dictation
- the producer of the reading books provides a compendium of already-written words
- the child is given plastic letters and helped to build words and sentences from them
- the child is taught, first, to hear the sound sequence in words and to move counters representing sounds before he is allowed contact with letters or words in print.

There is an inevitable hurdle for the child in the transcription side even if he can compose messages he wants to write.

Some Myths About Writing

There are myths associated with children's writing; they explain why children cannot be expected to write. Let me provide some examples.

In the *Breakthrough to Literacy* program a compendium of words is intended to save the child the struggle of writing a word and allow him to build sentences early and easily. However the approach places great demands on the child's very immature visual scanning of print skills. The scheme implies that children will learn more easily if they are saved the effort of writing words, or if they have opportunity to copy words correctly spelt. Yet a child who enters a creative writing program and writes the simplest message like *I am Belinda* has coordinated a host of behaviors — the movements, the ordering, the visual scanning, and the sound analysis. In saving the child the effort of attention to these things we may have withheld the opportunity to learn important constructive behavior.

The second myth is that competent children may be able to learn in a creative writing program but less competent children need to be saved from the tedium of creative writing. They can copy and trace and fill in spaces in ditto sheets. If the analytic tasks associated with writing are difficult but facilitative of reading progress then the less competent child has greater need of help because he is unlikely to put himself through this learning. More difficulty means greater need; avoidance is not an appropriate instructional strategy.

The third myth is that although writing and reading may start together there are physical reasons why hand-coordination slows the whole process and makes it tedious. (I want to ask 'Tedious for whom?'). The hand coordination problem forces a slow careful analysis bringing detail into focus. The child who has something to say in print can be unusually persistent, and there are many supports that a teacher can bring to this situation. A class of new entrants can run their teacher off her feet with their demands for help at writing time.

Many older children who have difficulty with reading can write very little. It is not a motor problem; it is something else. Grace Fernald (1943) had remarkable success with her remedial treatment. One facet of her program was the saying and tracing of new words in script writing. It is another myth, in my opinion, to believe that the explanation of success lay in kinesthetic imagery, the memory for the movement carried out, the feel of the words. In the Fernald method the reader dictates a story which is written for him. He rereads this. He must trace new words saying them slowly in parts and repeat this until the word can be written without looking at the copy. Slowed by the need to carry out the movements the reader establishes a scanning order, attends to detail in correct sequence, and carries out a drawled but not distorted sound analysis. More recent publications have provided insights into the reasons for Fernald's success. Her procedures anticipate Lashley's ideas on learning sequential order and Elkonin's account of learning to hear the sound sequences in words.

Writing and Reading: Reciprocity

In the early stages of learning to read the child acquires strategies which permit him to build great stores of items, and strategies for searching and checking upon the accuracy of what he has so far written.

I am impressed with the potential of early writing as a highly satisfying experience and for complementing the early reading program. The more this is organized by the child the greater value it will have. The more the teacher feels compelled to direct, sequence, correct and oversee this learning the less value for reading it will have, although it might produce children with excellent letter formation.

If a child knows how to scan letters and words, how to study a word in order to write it and how to organize his writing of that word he has the skills to deal with the detail of print. It is probable that early writing serves to organize the visual analysis for print, and to strengthen important memoric strategies.

The child's written work also provides us with objective evidence of what the child has learned. We have an opportunity to see how the child organizes his behavior as he writes. From the correct copying of a word carried out in an appropriate sequence we may assume some functional organization in the brain which permits that sequence of actions. If we see a child write a new word without a copy we can assume the capacity to synthesize information from several sources.

We must consider the goal of the instruction. If it is to have a child look at a word and name it correctly the writing act might be seen to be a tedious detour. If the point of reading and writing at this level is to have the child eager to search his stores of knowledge about written language reaching out for new information to supplement them, meanwhile working slowly and carefully enough for the complex processes to become interrelated, for awareness of error to occur by feedback processes, and for self-correction to occur, then it may be appropriate that some of these activities are performed at slower speeds. The motor performance adds another way of knowing about written language and allows one more way in which error may be recognized, providing another source of error detection. When the learner is a novice with only tentative strategies for responding correctly he needs more sources of error detection. As the child becomes a better reader, aware of more of the redundancies in the written code he can afford to forget movement as a way of checking on the correctness of a response but in those early unsure days his memories for the words which he has tried to write may provide feedback to both early writing and early reading.

My aim in early writing activities to support reading acquisition would be to provide many interesting activities to establish and stabilize strategies for analyzing words. Practice in writing could be critical at an early learning stage and of much less value for reading progress once the basic visual scanning and memoric processes are established. However the reader must work hard at understanding what the child is trying to say in his written expression. When the jumbled story or the weird letters are read for their message those who make the effort will find a rich commentary on each child's learning in his accumulated attempts to write (Clay, 1975).

A Program for Children Having Difficulty

We developed a program for children who had been in instruction for a year and who were getting left behind by their classmates. By giving them individual instruction, daily, we hoped to return them to average levels of functioning in the classroom. The program was successful, but that was probably because it had 'system impact'. It addressed the organizational issues within schools, professional issues like the experience, role and supply of teachers, child development issues, broader than reading progress alone, and even issues related to social change and political interest (Clay, 1979).

The Reading Recovery project in its first years set out to describe the range and variability of reading behaviors in children with marked difficulty in beginning reading, who had been at school one year and who were about six years of age. The project also sought to explore the range of teaching responses made by teachers to such children taught individually. Procedures for dealing with the diverse difficulties in the referred children were evolved by observing teachers at work, challenging, discussing and consulting in an effort to link teacher and pupil behaviors with theory about the reading process. A large number of techniques were piloted, observed, dis-cussed, argued over, written up, modified and related to theories of learning to read. Some were expanded, others were discarded. As a result some carefully graded sequences within each technique were described. During the discussions the implicit assumptions of the teachers' decisions were explained verbally rather than remaining intuitive hunches. The process of articulating the basis of teaching decisions was always difficult, sometimes uncomfortable and embarrassing. The process of evolution and refinement continued over three years and the written accounts were edited, discussed and revised many times. A component of the package involved writing. It was a vital segment of the daily lesson, not a casual extra or a late extension. We asked the child to write messages from the first day in the program. He read these messages in several ways. He accumu-lated visible records of his growing control over the writing of mes-sages. Most important of all, in order to write he had to carry out a detailed analysis of how you put speech into print, and he began to predict some of the consistencies.

Let me go back to the characteristics of our clientele. They were children who had failed to engage beginning reading instruction for a whole year. They could write perhaps three words. This was hardly enough knowlege to begin reading even the simplest of books. Observing them carefully and recording what they said and did we noticed something which was new to us. Children who could look at a letter and find some sound equivalent for it had a complete block in doing the reverse. They could not find a letter to represent a sound in a word they were saying. Our first insight was that to be able to go from letter-to-sound does not mean that you can go from sound-to-letter. Why was this? We observed the children again. Slowly the reasons became very clear. Most of our children with reading difficulties could not hear what they were saying. They could hear the word as an entity but they could not hear most of the components within the word. If they could hear any it was rarely the sound that occurred first in time. Some were fairly adept at isolating the last sound, and sometimes a prominent consonant in the middle, but never the sequence of sounds in the order they occurred, and the vowels dropped out of existence.

Normal progress children, we presumed, were flexible enough to do a reciprocal analysis. Taught something about the sounds that letters can have, their active brains had done the reciprocal learning task — finding sounds that they could then put down in print as letters. But most of our non-readers had been unable to do this on their own.

Elsewhere in the program for a few minutes a day the pupil's letter knowledge was being extended. A good way to increase the active use of that knowledge was, in the same lesson, to have the child write letters. Instead of copying, used in many programs to back up learning to scan letters visually in appropriate ways, we linked this use of letters to two other things, (1) writing messages you want to write and can use as further reading material, and (2) doing a sound sequence analysis of words you don't know how to write. We were conscious of the need to cut out all unnecessary practice and to save the child's time by drawing as much payoff as possible from each task in this recovery program (Clay 1979b).

In a typical individual tutoring session the teacher selected the reading books and the content of the activities to suit the current needs of a particular pupil. Lessons for different children used different books, and emphasized different aspects of the reading and writing processes. Every lesson had, however, a standard format in that seven activities were to be included. These activities were:

- re-reading two or more familiar books   __ Text
- letter identification (magnetic letters)   __ Letters
- writing a story   __ Text
- sound analysis of words for that story   __ Sounds
  (using Elkonin's techniques)
- cut-up story to be re-arranged   __ Text
- new book introduced   __ Text
- new book attempted   __ Text

The emphasis on text reading and writing was deliberate. To function at average levels in classroom activities children would have to be able to read and write text. It was argued that developing children's reading and writing vocabularies by extensive experience with words in isolation would not develop the searching, sequence and self-monitoring behaviors that are needed when one writes or reads messages. The cut-up stories provided many opportunities for these behaviors.

Three areas of these Reading Recovery procedures relate to early writing — writing stories, hearing the sounds in words, and cut-up stories. The focus in these activities was to get the child to produce his own written stories so that he could work somewhat independently back in his classroom on this type of activity.

Hearing the Sounds in Words

Russian psychologists had provided us with a teaching sequence for the sound analysis of words, well-thought-out to cope with the initiate's difficulties. The difference between our children and theirs was that our children had already been exposed to print, so we had to adapt the Russian procedures. The guiding principles were these:

- Provide the child with a structure for the words (squares to represent sounds, and later letters).
- Ask the child what he hears and record this for him in the squares, wherever it occurs in the sequence.
- Ask him what else he hears. And what else?
- Fill in the remainder as he watches and says the word slowly.
- Let him use it in his story.

Select only words that are appropriate for his level of achievement and write for him any words which it would be too difficult for him to analyze (Clay 1979b).

These activities help the child to hear the sounds in words. They create a sense of competence and achievement. The onus for finding out how to write the word is the child's and the activity helps the child to get to new words he wants to write in his stories. Sometimes the teacher will work for fluency with a commonly occurring word. Usually the emphasis will be on the construction — how you can write the words you want.

Writing Stories

Teachers used unlined exercise books turned sideways. The child drew his picture and wrote his story on the page nearest him; the teacher's model or his own trials or any practice attempts, repeated several times to gain fluency, were written on the top page.

The child constructed a statement, usually only a sentence, a personal bit of news, a recent interesting observation. He was encouraged to write whatever he could. An easy word which the child should know was often written for him on the top page and the child invited to copy it there. Then he was asked to write the word again, and again, and again, becoming fast and fluent and not dependent on the copy. Difficult words were written into the story for him. Words suitable for sound sequence analysis were worked out on the top page in squares.

This sentence writing occurred every day, so that a bookful of his 'own stories' was built up and used for re-reading. They were also used for home reading. The child was producing his own reading material. In the re-reading the purpose of letter formation, layout and spacing, and error-free products became obvious to the child without teacher attention. *He could not read his own message* if he made a messy job of writing it. Self-set standards have functional value for him.

As the child re-reads his sentence self-monitoring behaviors emerge.

Cut-up Stories

The first cut-up stories were written by the teacher at the child's dictation but later the teacher asked the child to re-read his story from his unlined book so that she could write it again on paper (another purpose for the reading). The story was then cut up, somewhat ceremonially, into language units which the teacher knew the child would be able to reassemble. Larger segments were used for poorer readers. The descending order was phrases, words, structural elements, clusters of letters or particular letters.

The child now reassembled the story, constructing it for the second time. This induced careful self-monitoring and checking. The difficulty of the task could be increased in several ways. The child was invited to scan for any errors by a prompt like, 'Something is not quite right, calling again for a self-monitoring response.

Cut-up stories provided the child with practice for assembling sentences, one-to-one correspondence of printed and spoken words, directional behaviors, self-monitoring and checking behavior, breaking oral language into segments, and word study. Yet it all seems to be just an elaboration on the invitation to the child to write his own story, and it is a puzzle-type task on a personal text that can be used for home reading when it is placed in an envelope.

Research Evidence

The research evidence that was obtained on this teaching has already been presented in *Reading Recovery: A Follow-up Study*.

Conclusions

The strongest arguments for the writing recovery program are
- its facilitation of very early reading progress when skills were minimal

- the visible record of progress it provides for the teacher
- its strong motivational potential because of the sense of power it gives (which we overlook when the frustration is highlighted)
- the reciprocal nature of its payoff for letter learning, word recognition, and cue-finding in new words
- the sense it creates in the child that he, himself, can find ways to work on the task
- and the sense of personal control over difficulties that arises from this.

I have not yet thought of an alternative and equally profitable way of helping the child who cannot go from sound sequence to letter sequence except perhaps using a plastic alphabet. This approach creates words or stories that are then broken up and lost. It does not achieve the same sense of control and continuing gain described above, unless a written copy of the array is made by the child in a book that he keeps.

26 Writing From A Developmental Perspective

I recently reviewed all the literature that I could find on early writing for a chapter in a book on writing (Wells and Kroll, in press). That review took me towards new concepts of the interrelationships between oral language learning, learning to read and learning to write. There is a need for theorists to explore more extensively the possibility that each draws on and contributes to the other, building a central store of communicative competence, a concept described by Johanna DeStephano (1978). When she asked me to write a brief review of the developmental aspects of early writing it was not easy to distill a short paper from the wealth of material that is now available on how children learn to write. What follows is no more than an invitation to go far beyond this introduction.

Some years ago I found myself searching for some order in hundreds of scrappy pieces of writing which five-year-olds had produced, their scripting merging into drawing and aptly described by Robert Southey's term, the scribblative arts. I knew there was some order in the products because I had watched the children change in their first year of school. I identified some principles which allowed me to group the children's products and which I hoped teachers would look for in their children's work (Clay, 1975). I was reluctant to talk about stages in development. For one thing I had only the products to analyze: I had not actually observed the children in the process of producing them. And for another I was particularly impressed with the alternative routes to better writing that seemed to exist. In the program that I observed new school entrants were encouraged to write from the beginning, when they knew only a few letters of the alphabet!

Since that time many insights have emerged in research on writing.

Adults often focus on a consumer view of writing. When we have difficulty understanding another's written message this confirms our assumption that writing must be legible, grammatically correct, with clear messages. We are less analytic about our own difficulties with composing which lead us to draft and redraft our letters and reports. I look forward to Frank Smith's forthcoming analysis of how a writer writes, and applaud the work of the writing workshops which have encouraged teachers to become writers and to observe the processes they use as they write. Too often what teachers believe about children learning to write stems from old ideas about school subjects and curricula sequences. Some of these assumptions have resulted in less and less demand on children to do this difficult task because it is seen as an aversive activity. There has been a call for an end to this downward spiral and, in the last decade, a new set of questions have been asked about children's writing.

When we observe children in classrooms we begin to uncover some of our assumptions. I asked New York students to collect samples of writing from five-year-old children. They suggested, politely, that although New Zealand children of that age might write, they would not expect to find American children producing writing. I insisted, pointing out that American children of that age know far more letters than New Zealand children, so they went out and observed some children and were delighted with what they found.

- Writing was not a difficult activity.
- Children did like to write, if encouraged to try.
- Writing was occurring before and alongside early reading and did not wait for a reading vocabulary to be learnt.
- Motor coordination did not limit the young child's attempts to write if one was not too demanding about the shape and form of the script.

However, if teachers insist on clean, readable, error-free samples of work in beautiful script then they will quickly convince children that the task is too difficult for them.

Let me illustrate how teacher assumptions enter into classroom writing activities. I observed this teacher myself. She used a delightful filmstrip called 'Finding Room For A Sassafroon'. The story was about an imaginary creature which could only be seen by children but not by adults. The creature changed its form and color from one exciting thing to another. After the filmstrip had been shown the teacher checked the children's understanding and helped them to recall important ideas. Eagerly they drew pictures of sassafroons, drawings that were rich in ideas and showed that the story had been understood. Drawing was a spontaneous production needing no constraints and the teacher left them free. The teacher moved around the room helping the children to write their stories. Notice the constraints that were applied. No child began to write without lines to write on, nor without the teacher's copy. Every story began with the same phrase, 'My Sassafroon . . . ' even for the most able group. The teacher seemed to assume that children would need help to put their ideas into spoken language and that they would need a full copy of the sentence they were writing. A perfect copy was expected, and the children would learn that it was wrong to make mistakes. One cannot make discoveries without making errors, so the children's theory of writing would be that the correct form lay somewhere outside them, and that the initiative would not be theirs.

How do we know that children can write? Attention has been directed to young children before they get to school. Evidence suggests that the preschool child seems to say 'I think I can make some sense of print.' Jacqueline Goodnow (1977) provided an analysis of the young child's drawing and writing. In several studies of Spanish-speaking and Swiss children Emilia Ferreiro (1978) described the discoveries made by preschool children from illiterate and highly literate families. For both groups she concluded that her children developed simple hypotheses about writing like:

- it has shape (circles)
- shapes are separated (several circles)
- shapes go in lines (several circles in linear arrangement)

and that children shifted to new hypotheses as their present theories conflicted with new things they encountered. We would copy an unfamiliar script in Russian or Hebrew for example. Little children do this sometimes but they also invent and compare their inventions with samples of print in the real world. Ferreiro described a series of shifts in children's ideas about what writing is before these children even arrived at the alphabetic principle of letter-sound relationships.

Ferreiro's children were not exceptional. If we accept the products that children give us when we ask them to write, just as we have learned to accept their drawing, we can find a wealth of information in them and some exciting insights emerge. Products alone are not enough, however and we have to take a close look at the way children go about their writing. What children finally arrive at is not necessarily a guide to how they got there.

How do these primitive efforts contribute to the child's understanding of the writing process? Eleanor Duckworth (1979) provided us with a powerful Piagetian statement of explanation. Only if the child has a theory can one instance contribute to the development of understanding. Once s/he has a theory, no matter how primitive, s/he can pay attention to results that confirm or contradict this theory. Noticing a novel feature in someone else's print or his/her own inventions may confirm or contradict this theory. A contradiction may lead the child to figure out some other theory that would take the new features into account. In this way a few examples can raise the child's understanding to another level. This is a cognitive theory of development which applies to oral language learning also. It is close to what Frank Smith has said about learning to read, and I think it is very applicable to early writing. The work of Charles Read (1975) and Carol Chomsky (1979) confirm this.

There is evidence from several countries that children's literacy knowledge or concepts about print when they enter school is highly related to progress in learning to read two years later. At first it was thought that this knowledge came from the books that were shared with children (Clay, 1979a) but studies of children who wrote before they entered school have led us to a more general statement. Children are constructing theories about print from diverse experiences — seeing print in the environment, putting pencil to paper, thumbing through magazines, and receiving birthday cards, invitations and letters. This broader concept of developing a knowledge of literacy accounts for the high scores obtained by Samoan school entrants in New Zealand on a Concepts About Print test. They came from Samoan-speaking homes and they did not have story books in their own language. Probably their immigrant parents received letters from Samoa, and the strong church affiliations of this group with bible-reading as a family activity led the children to some awareness of the importance of print by quite a different route (Clay, 1976) from the book-sharing found in the homes of middle-class whites.

These early discoveries of the child interact with our teaching. There are some tough research questions to be answered about the interaction of teaching with the child's discoveries. One approach to these questions has been classroom observation studies such as those at the Writing Process Laboratory at the University of New Hampshire. Not only have we learnt more about the effects classrooms have on children from these and from ethnographic studies, but also the reports describe procedures which individual class teachers can use to get a window on the child's hypotheses and strengths as a guide to teaching. A new respect for how teachers can facilitate or constrain children's writing activities has emerged from such research. The whole class is now seen as a functional context which provides some opportunities and imposes certain restriction on what children can discover (Florio, 1978).

The most simple question has been 'How much writing do children do?' and following the answer 'Very little' the question then became 'How do we get children to write more?' The obvious answer is to accept their approximations with more respect especially at the kindergarten to Grade 2 level. Classrooms can become more hospitable places for children's writing (King & Rentel, 1979; Graves 1978; Henderson, 1980). If we do not set out to convince first graders that writing is difficult they will not arrive at Grade 2 convinced of it.

James Britton (1970) described the expressive forms of writing as the earliest forms because they arise out of the writer's experience and take less account of audience. Sowers (1979) has suggested that the earliest expressive forms are non-narrative personal accounts rather than fiction. Children's little bits of news, their journals, their personal accounts of experiences, or of a class activity, tap their willingness to write out of their experience in an expressive mode. Perhaps we should let them discover the need to take audience into account rather than hurry them into forms of social communication or writing stories, or books for others. Early writing can begin with the teacher as a scribe, helping the child to attempt all he can by himself as soon as possible. Classes that accept invented spelling find that children produce quantities of writing before very long.

One of the writing forms that children like to engage in is story writing. How do children write stories? Research has shown that children who have books read to them develop a sense of the conventions of stories, formal beginnings and endings, central characters, plot and climax, and even for the structures in particular types of stories like fairy tales or folk tales (Applebee, 1978). Work in progress attempts to look at what elements in a story retell and what elements of story structure appear in their written stories (King & Rentel, 1979).

Children's writing is facilitated by a sense of framework or a supporting fence along which their story can be trained, the framework providing reminders of what comes next, as well as support for holding what has already been completed and a sense of how far there is to go. If sharing stories with children facilitates writing progress then the children's literature lobby and whole-language approaches to education will have stronger arguments for their curricula than the oral language acquisition research has already given them. There may be alternative routes to frameworks. For the linguistically different child for whom the language of children's story books could be too big a leap into the standard written dialect, story-telling might be more appropriate. We have yet to discover an easy route for children into transactional writing. My favorite example of transactional writing is a letter from some twelve-year-olds who had completed a research survey for us and who were invited to respond to it in some way. They had some questions which they expressed so clearly that they drew a serious and carefully thought-out reply from our research team:

> Dear Sir,
> Our class has just finished your questionnaire and we would like some answers to the following questions.
> A. What is the purpose of this questionnaire and what did you hope to learn from it?
> B. What will you do with this information?
> C. Why did you pick those particular questions?
> D. Why did you pick the twelve-year-old age group?
> E. How did you pick our school for the questionnaire?
> We would be very grateful if you have time to answer our letter as we would like to know why we did this questionnaire.
> Yours truly,
> Pupils of Room 15.

In answering these questions we had to write a twelve-year-old's version of our research design. They had asked the right questions in a very clear form, which readers who have designed research will recognize. We have no indication of the class activity that preceded this letter but we admired the product. We, as audience, knew exactly what the writers wanted. Their writing was on target.

How do children write before they can read words and have been taught spelling? A series of studies reported by Henderson and Beers (1980) explored the shifts that children make from invented spelling at entry to school to conventional spelling. As more is written about the consistencies in English orthography some teachers have become aware that programs based on sound to spelling-pattern correspondences may create some problems. What the good speller learns is a much more useful and complex set of consistencies of how words relate to other words not only in spelling patterns but also in derivations. Studies show that as children learn more about words in their writing, reading and spelling, their errors change. Working out how to write a word by listening to yourself say it becomes meshed with remembering having seen the word (or one like it) in reading. Over an extended period children construct tentative rules for spelling new words.

In many spelling programs there is slight recognition of the frequency principle in language. Some units occur more frequently than others — letters, letter sequences, words, spelling patterns, sentence patterns and writing forms. If the child speaks, reads and writes language which retains the natural frequencies that occur in language then some things which occur more often than others will come to the child's attention, and will continue to be confirmed until they are well and truly learned. This is one reason why one can say that a child learns to talk by talking, to read by reading, and to write by writing. It is because of the frequency principle in natural language sequences that it is possible for language programs to support and foster the child's own efforts to learn to read and write.

Writing is writing wherever it is done especially as the young child views it. One American study reported that time on writing journals or stories varied from no time to 8 minutes a day while reading time was allocated an average of more than 120 to 200 minutes a day. I would want to ask how much writing was being done in reading time, and was it gap-filling, finding words, crossing out or circling letters, and copying spellings? How much of the 120 to 200 minutes was given to workbook activities and ditto sheets and what does such massive exposure do to the young child's view of writing? Would writing be seen by the child as puzzle-solving, copying letter by letter, or at best finding words on a page out of which to build a sentence? Does such activity prepare one for composing or does it compete with what children will need to do when they write? Our well-intentioned division of learning into subject compartments can build up competing concepts.

I have another question about journal writing. It is seen as highly motivated because children write of their own experiences. My reaction to some work of this kind was that this can be a very tedious activity for many children. I would contrast it with work from classrooms where young children's work is treated as special productions to be admired, illustrated, colorfully mounted for display and replaced at frequent intervals by new works.

In a developmental view young writers move by various routes across several strands of language learning:

- trying to get a theory about written language.
- trying to express their experience in writing.
- trying to construct stories.
- exploring sound to spelling patterns.
- developing new language options.
- developing a range of writing forms.

There is evidence that in a whole language program the responsiveness of the children increases as their learning in one area is facilitated by what is happening in another area. Carol Chomsky (1972) wrote about the effect of reading on oral language. Charles Read (1975) showed how children used their knowledge of the alphabet to invent spelling systems for recording their messages. An early intervention program to undercut reading difficulties had an important writing component in it (Clay, 1979b). There can be a payoff for any language area of what is learned in another type of language performance.

I have a theory about language learning and as I encounter new examples I will test out my theory and modify it in the face of new evidence, just like the five-year-old trying to invent a script to convey a message. Whatever the correct usage of the child, in oral language, reading or writing, the developmental direction is always to increase the range of operation. The child extends an effective control of his mother-tongue dialect to include a standard spoken dialect and the dialect of written prose, and other specialized forms of language. From the concrete reference of language the child comes to understand the metaphoric and the poetic. Writing at first out of his experience the child frees himself from being context-bound and can learn to write for audiences of different kinds.

A common feature of such learning must be tentativeness, a position from which it is easy to change. Increasing flexibility that allows one to select from a variety of language options must be a feature of any aspect of language learning. This then provides us with some important questions to ask ourselves about our writing programs.

- Have we observed what our children actually do?
- Are we sensitive to what their writing can tell us about them?
- Do our procedures prevent them from making their own discoveries?

- Have we made unnecessary assumptions about teaching sequences?
- What kinds of teacher-child interactions will foster tentativeness, change and flexibility in language use?

Bibliography

Applebee, A.M. *The child's concept of story: Ages two to seventeen.* Chicago: University of Chicago Press, 1978.

Ashton-Warner, S. *Teacher.* New York: Simon & Schuster, 1963.

Austin, Mary G. & Morrison, C. *The first R. The Harvard report on reading in elementary schools.* London: Collier-Macmillan, 1963.

Ausubel, D.P. *Maori Youth.* New York: Holt, Rinehart & Winston, 1965.

Barham, I.H. *The English vocabulary and sentence structure of Maori children.* Wellington: N.Z.C.E.R., 1965.

Bateman, B. Learning disabilities – yesterday, today and tomorrow. In E.C. Frierson and W.B. Barbe (Eds.), *Educating children with learning disabilities,* New York: Appleton Century Crofts, 1967.

Benton, A.L. *Right-left discrimination and finger localization.* New York: Paul B. Hoeber, 1959.

Berko, Jean, The child learning of English morphology. *Word,* **14,** 1958, 150.177.

Berlyn, D.E. *Conflict, arousal and curiosity.* New York: McGraw-Hill, 1960.

Best, E. *The Maori school of learning.* Wellington: New Zealand Dominion Museum Monograph No. 6, 1974.

Biggs, B.G. The Maori language past and present. In E. Schwimmer (Ed.), *The Maori people in the nineteen-sixties.* Auckland: Blackwood & Janet Paul, 1968.

Birch, H.G., & Lefford, A. Intersensory development in children. *Mono. Soc. Res. Child Dev.,* 28, Chicago: University of Chicago Press, 1963.

Birch, H.G. & Lefford, A. Visual differentiation, intersensory integration and voluntary motor control. *Mono. Soc. Res. Child Dev.,* **32,** 1967.

Birch, J.W. & Birch, Jane R. *Preschool education and school admission practices in New Zealand.* Pittsburgh, Pennsylvania: Center for International Studies, University of Pittsburgh, 1970.

Blank, Arapera, One, two, three, four, five. In E. Schwimmer (Ed.), *The Maori people in the nineteen-sixties.* Auckland: Blackwood & Janet Paul, 1968.

Bloomfield, L. and Barnhart, C.L. *Let's read: A linguistic approach.* Detroit: Wayne State University Press, 1961.

Bolinger, D.L. Identity, similarity and difference. *Litera,* Vol. 1, 1954.

Bond, G.L., & Tinker, M.A. *Reading difficulties: Their diagnosis and correction.* New York: Appleton-Century-Crofts, 1957.

Britton, J. *Language and learning.* London: Allen Lane Penguin Press, 1970.

Bruner, J.S. On perceptual readiness. *Psychological Review,* **64**, 1957, 123-152.

Bruner, J.S. Going beyond the information given. In J.S. Bruner (Ed.), *Contemporary approaches to cognition.* Cambridge: Harvard University Press, 1957.

Bruner, J.S., Olver, R.R. & Greenfield, P.M., et al. *Studies in cognitive growth,* New York: Wiley, 1966.

Bryden, M.P. Left-right differences in tachistoscopic recognition: directional scanning or cerebral dominance? *Perceptual and Motor Skills,* **23**, 1966, 1127-1134.

Campbell, D.T. and Stanley, J.C. Experimental and quasi-experimental designs for research on teaching. In N.L. Gage (Ed.), *Handbook of research on teaching.* Chicago: Rand McNally, 1963.

Cashdan, A. Who teaches the child to read? In Merrit, J.E. (ed.), *New horizons in reading.* Newark: IRA, 1976.

Cherry, C. *On Human Communication.* New York: Wiley, 1957.

Chomsky, C. Reading, writing and phonology. *Harvard Educational Review,* **40** (2), 1970, 287-309.

Chomsky, C. Write first, read later. *Childhood Education,* **47** (6), 1971, 396-399.

Chomsky, C. How sister got into the grog. *Early Years,* 1975, 36-39.

Chomsky, C. Invented spelling in the open classroom. In von Raffles Engel, W. (Ed.) *Word,* Special issue entitled *Child Language Today,* 1976.

Chomsky, C. Approaching reading through invented spelling. In Resnick, L.B. & Weaver, P.A. (Eds.) *Theory and practice of early reading.* Hillsdale, N.J.: Erlbaum, 1979.

Clark, Margaret M. *Reading difficulties in schools.* Harmondsworth: Penguin, 1970. Second edition, London: Heinemann Educational Books, 1979.

Clark, Margaret M. *Young fluent readers.* London: Heinemann Educational Books, 1976.

Clay, Marie M. Emergent reading behavior. Unpublished doctoral dissertation, University of Auckland, 1966.

Clay, Marie M. The reading behavior of five-year-old children: A research report. *N.Z.J. educ. Studies,* **2**, 1967, 11-31. (Reprinted in this Vol., p. 12)

Clay, Marie M. A syntactic analysis of reading errors. *J. of Verbal Learning and Verbal Behavior.* **7,** 1968, 434-438. (Reprinted in this Vol., p. 30)

Clay, Marie M. Reading errors and self correction behavior. *British J. of Educational Psychology,* **39**, 1969, 47-56. (Reprinted in this Vol., p. 37)

Clay, Marie M. An increasing effect of disorientation on the discrimination of print: A developmental study. *J. of Experimental Child Psychology,* **9**, 1970a, 297-306. (Reprinted in this Vol., p. 65)

Clay, Marie M. Research on language and reading in Pakeha and Polynesian groups. In Bracken, Dorothy K. & Malmquist, Eva (Eds.) *Improving reading ability around the world.* Newark: International Reading Association, 1970b.

Clay, Marie M. Language skills: A comparison of Maori, Samoan and Pakeha children aged five to seven. years. *N.Z. J. Educ. Studies,* **5**, 2, 1970c, 153-162. (Reprinted in this Vol., p. 94)

Clay, Marie M. The Polynesian language skills of Maori and Samoan school entrants, *International Journal of Psychology,* **6**, 2, 1970d, 135-45. (Reprinted in this vol. p. 142)

Clay, Marie M. Sentence repetition: Elicited imitation of a controlled set of syntactic structures by four language groups. *Mono. Soc. Res. Child Dev.,* 1971, **36**, No. 143. (Reprinted in this vol. p. 113)

Clay, Marie M. Learning disorders. In Havill, S.J. & Mitchell, D.R. (Eds.) *Issues in New Zealand special education,* Auckland: Hodder and Stoughton, 1972a. (Reprinted in this Vol., p. 156)

Clay, Marie M. *Sand: Test booklet.* Auckland: Heinemann Educational Books, 1972b.

Clay, Marie M. The development of morphological rules in children with differing language backgrounds. *N.Z. J. Educ. Studies,* **9**(2), 1974a, 113-121. (Reprinted in this Vol., p. 103)

Clay, Marie M. The spatial characteristics of the open book. *Visible Language,* **8**, 3, 1974b, 275-282. (Reprinted in this Vol., p. 76)

Clay, Marie M. *What did I write? A study of children's writing.* Auckland: Heinemann Educ. Books, 1975.

Clay, Marie M. Early childhood and cultural diversity. *The Reading Teacher,* (January) 1976a, 312-333. (Reprinted in this Vol., p. 92)

Clay, Marie M. The effect of two educated dialects on sentence repetition scores of five-year-old Scottish children. *Language and Speech,* 1976b, **19**, 244-250. (Reprinted in this Vol., p. 135)

Clay, Marie M. An emphasis on prevention. *J. of Special Educ.,* **11**, 2, 1977a, 183-188. (Reprinted in this Vol., p. 167)

Clay, Marie M. Exploring with a pencil. *Theory Into Practice,* **16**, 5, 1977b, 334-341. (Reprinted in this Vol., p. 202)

Clay, Marie M. *Reading: The patterning of complex behavior.* Auckland: Heinemann Educational Books, 1979a.

Clay, Marie M. *The early detection of reading difficulties: A diagnostic survey and reading recovery procedures.* Auckland: Heinemann Educational Books, 1979b.

Clay, Marie M. *Stones: Test booklet.* Auckland: Heinemann Educational Books, 1979c.

Clay, Marie M. Early writing and reading: Reciprocal gains. In Clark, M.M. and Glynn, T. (Eds.) *Reading and writing for the child with difficulties.* Educational Review: Occasional Publications No. 8, University of Birmingham, 1980a. (Reprinted in this Vol., p. 211)

Clay, Marie M. Reading recovery: a follow-up study. *N.Z. J. Educ. Studies,* **15**, 2, 1980b, 137-155. (Reprinted in this Vol., p. 173)

Clay, Marie M. and Watson, Barbara. An inservice program for reading recovery teachers. *Education,* **4**, 1981, 22-27. (Reprinted in this Vol., p. 192)

Clay, Marie M. Writing from a developmental perspective: research update. *Language Arts,* **59**, 1, 1982. (Reprinted in this Vol., p. 226)

Clay, Marie M. Looking and seeing in the classroom, *English Journal,* Jan. 1982.

Clay, Marie M., Gill, M., Glynn, E. and McNaughton, A.H. *Record of oral language,* Wellington: NZEI, 1976.

Clay, Marie M. and Imlach, R.H. Juncture, pitch and stress as reading behavior variables. *J. Verb Learn. & Verb. Beh.,* **10**, 1971, 133-139. (Reprinted in this Vol., p. 54)

Corballis, M.C. & Beale, I.L. On telling left from right. *Scientific American,* **96**, 1971.

Dale, P.S. Language development: Structure and function. Hinsdale, Illinois: The Dryden Press, 1972.

Department of Education. *Ready to read.* Wellington: School Publications Branch, 1963 (18 titles).

De Stephano, J.S. *Language, the learner and the school.* New York: Wiley, 1978.

Dimond, S. *The double brain.* London: Churchill Livingston, 1972.

Duckworth, E. Either we're too early and they can't learn it or we're too late and they know it already: the dilemma of "applying Piaget". *Harvard Educ. Review,* **49**, 3, 1979, 297-312.

Dunn, L.M. *Manual for the Peabody Picture Vocabulary Test.* Nashville: American Guidance Service, 1959.

Durrell, D.D. First grade reading success. *J. Educ.,* 140 (Feb), 1958.

Edwards, R.P.A. and Gibbon, V. *Words your children use.* London: Burke, 1964.

Elkind, D. Developmental studies of figurative perception. In Lipsitt, L.P. & Reese, H.W. (Eds.), *Advances in child development and behavior,* Vol. 4. New York: Academic Press, 1969.

Elkind, D. & Weiss, J. Studies in perceptual development. III Perceptual exploration. *Child Development,* **38**, 1967, 553-561.

Entwisle, Doris R., Forsyth, D.F., & Muus, R. The syntactic-paradigmatic shift in children's word associations. *J. Verb. Learn. Verb. Behav.,* **3**, 1964, 19-29.

Ervin, Susan M. Changes with age in the verbal determinants of word-association. *Amer. J. Psychol,* **64**, 1961, 361-372.

Fellows, B.J. *The discrimination process and development.* Oxford: Pergamon Press, 1968.

Fergusson, G.A. *Statistical analysis in psychology and education.* New York: McGraw-Hill, 1966.

Fernald G. *Remedial techniques in the basic subjects.* New York: McGraw-Hill, 1943.

Ferreiro, E. What is written in a written sentence: a developmental answer. *J. of Education,* **60,** 4, 1978.

Festinger, L. The motivating effect of cognitive dissonance. In Lindsley, G. (Ed.) *Assessment of human motives.* New York: Grove Press, 1958, 65-86.

Fildes, Lucy G. Experiments on the problems of mirror-writing. *British J. of Psychology,* **14** (July), 1923, 57-67.

Florio, S. The problem of dead letters: social perspectives on the teaching of writing. East Lansing: University of Michigan, Institute for Research on Teaching Working Paper, 1978.

Fraser, C., Bellugi, U. and Brown, R. Control of grammar in imitation, comprehension and production. *J. Verb. Learn. Verb. Behav.,* **2,** 1963, 121.

Fries, C.C. *Linguistics and reading.* London: Holt, Rinehart and Winston, 1963.

Fry, E. *Elementary reading instruction.* New York: McGraw-Hill, 1977.

Gates, A.E. *The improvement of reading* (3rd edition). New York: Macmillan, 1947.

Gibson, E.J. and Levin, H. *The psychology of reading.* Cambridge: MIT Press, 1975.

Gibson, E.J., Osser, H., & Pick, A.D. A study of the development of grapheme-phoneme correspondences. *J. Verb. Learn. Verb. Behav.,* **2,** 1963, 142-146.

Gimson, A.G. The transmission of language. In Quirk, R. (Ed.) *The use of English.* London: Longmans, Green, 1962.

Gleason, H.A. *An introduction to descriptive linguistics.* New York: Holt, Rinehart & Winston, 1961.

Glynn, E.L., & McNaughton, S.S. Trust your own observations: Criterion referenced assessment of reading progress. *The Slow Learning Child* (University of Queensland), **22**(2), 1975, 91-107.

Goddard, Nora. *Literacy: Language experience approaches.* London Macmillan Education, 1974.

Goins, Jean T. Visual perceptual abilities and early reading progress. *Suppl. Education Monographs.* Chicago: University of Chicago Press, 1958.

Goodman, K.S. Analysis of oral reading miscues: Applied psycholinguistics. *Reading Research Quarterly,* **5,** 1969, 9-30.

Goodman, K.S. Readings: A psycholinguistic guessing game. In Singer, H. & Ruddell, R.B. (Eds.) *Theoretical models and processes of reading.* Newark: International Reading Association, 1970.

Goodman, Yetta. Review of Concepts About Print. *The Reading Teacher,* **34,** 4, 1981.

Goodnow, J. *Children's drawing.* Glasgow: Fontana/Open Books, 1977.

Graham, N.C. Short term memory and syntactic structure in educationally subnormal children. *Language and Speech,* **11,** 1968, 209.

Graves, D.H. *Balance the basics.* New York: Ford Foundation, 1978.

Gray, W.S. The teaching of reading and writing. Paris: UNESCO, 1956. (Handwriting).

Harcum, E.R. Visual hemifield differences as conflicts of direction of reading. *J. of Experimental Psychology,* **72,** 1966, 479-480.

Harris, L.A., & Smith, C.B. *Reading instruction through diagnostic teaching.* New York: Holt, Rinehart & Winston, 1972.

Harris, Z.S. From morpheme to utterance. *Language,* **22,** 1946, 161-183.

Harris, Z.S. *Methods in structural linguistics.* Chicago: University of Chicago Press, 1951.

Harwood, F.W. Quantitative study of the speech of Australian children. *Language and Speech,* **2,** 1959: 236-271.

Henderson, E.H. & Beers, J.W. *Developmental and cognitive aspects of learning to spell.* Newark, International Reading Association, 1980.

Hill, A.A. *Introduction to linguistic structures.* New York: Harcourt Brace, 1958.

Hoffman, M.N.H. *The measurement of bilingual background.* New York: Columbia, 1934.

Hoffman, Mary. *Reading, writing and relevance.* London: Hodder & Stoughton, 1976.

Holbrook, D. *Children's writing.* Cambridge: Cambridge University Press, 1967.

Howard, I.P., & Templeton, W.B. *Human spatial orientation.* London: Wiley, 1966.

Imlach, R.H. Juncture, pitch and stress as reading behavior variables. Unpublished M.A. thesis, University of Auckland, 1968.

King, M. Research in composition: A need for a theory. *Research in Teaching English,* **12,** 1978.

King, M. and Rentel, V. Toward a theory of early writing development. *Research in the Teaching of English,* **13**(3), 1979: 243-253.

Kirk, S.A., & McCarthy, J.J. The Illinois Test of Psycholinguistic Abilities. *Amer. J. Defic.,* 1966, 399-412.

Larsen, R. *Children and writing in the elementary school.* New York: Oxford University Press, 1975.

Lefevre, C.H. *Linguistics and the teaching of reading.* New York: McGraw-Hill, 1964.

Leopold, W.F. Speech development of a bilingual child. A linguist's record. *Northwestern University Studies in Humanities,* 1949.

Lieberman, P. *Intonation, perception and language.* Cambridge: M.I.T. Press, 1967.

Loban, W.D. *The language of elementary school children.* Champaign, Illinois: National Council of Teachers of English, 1963.

Lunzer, E.A. *Recent studies in Britain based on the work of Jean Piaget.* London: Nat. Foundation Educ. Res. in England and Wales, 1960.

Luria, A.R. *Higher cortical functions in man.* London: Tavistock, 1966.

Luria, A.R. The functional organization of the brain. *Scientific American,* March, 1970.

Lynn, R. *Attention, arousal and the orientation reaction.* New York: Macmillan, 1966.

Malmquist, E. In Downing, J. (Ed.), *Comparative reading.* New York: Macmillan, 1973a.

Malmquist, E. Perspectives on reading research. In Karlin, R. (Ed.), *Reading for all.* Newark, Del.: International Reading Association, 1973b.

Marshall, Sybil. *Creative writing.* London: Macmillan Education, 1974.

McCullough, Constance. The language of basal readers. In Staiger, R.C. & Andresen, O. (Eds.), *Reading: A human right and a human problem.* Newark: International Reading Association, 1969.

McDavid, R.I. Dialects: British and American standard and non-standard. In Hill, A.A. (Ed.), *Linguistics, Voice of America Forum Lectures.* U.S. Office of Information Service, 1969.

McGrath, P. An Irish schooling. *Education.* **22,** No. 7, 1963. (Wellington: School Publications)

McKinnon, A.F. *How do children learn to read?* Toronto: Copp Clarke, 1959.

Macnamara, J. *Bilingualism and primary education: A study of Irish experience.* Edinburgh: Edinburgh University Press, 1966.

McNeil, J.D. and Keislar, E.R. Value of oral response in beginning reading. *Brit. J. Ed. Psych.,* **33,** 2, 1963.

Menyuk, Paula. Syntactic rules used by children from preschool through first grade. *Child Developm.,* **25,** 1964, 533-546.

Menyuk, P. *Sentences children use.* Cambridge: M.I.T., 1969.

Metropolitan Reading Readiness Test. Wellington: NZCER, 1943.

Miller, G.A. (Ed.) *Linguistic communication: Perspectives for research.* Newark: International Reading Association, 1974.

Myers, T.I. and Hammill, D.D. *Methods for learning disorders.* New York: Wiley, 1969.

Nacewa, I. Acquisition of English language among Fijian children at primary school level. Unpubl. report.

Neisser, U. The multiplicy of thought. *Brit. J. Psychol,* **54**, 1, 1963.

Neisser, U. Visual search. *Scientific American* June, 1964.

Neisser, U. *Cognitive psychology.* New York: Appleton-Century-Crofts, 1967.

New Zealand Council for Educational Research. *Metropolitan reading readiness test,* 1943.

Newson, E. The development of line figure discrimination in preschool children. Unpublished doctoral dissertation, University of Nottingham, 1955.

Osser, H., Wang, M.D., & Zaid, F. The young child's ability to imitate and comprehend speech: A comparison of two subcultural groups. *Child Development,* **40**, 1969, 1063-75.

Presland, I.V. Inflection skills: A comparison between Maori, Samoan and English children aged eight to ten years. Unpubl. Dip. Ed. Thesis, University of Auckland, 1974.

Read, C. *Children's categorization of speech sounds in English.* Urbana, Illinois: National Council for Teachers of English, 1975.

Robinson, H.M. News and Comment. *Elem. Sch. J.,* (May) 1963: 417-426.

Russell, D.H. and Fea, H.R. Research on teaching reading. In N.L. Gage (Ed.), *Handbook of research on teaching,* Chicago: Rand McNally, 1963.

Ryan, E., & Semmel, M.L. Reading as a constructive language process. *Reading Research Quarterly,* **5**, 1969, 293-9.

Schonell, F.J. *Diagnostic and Attainment Testing.* London: Oliver and Boyd, 1956.

Selby, S. The development of morphological rules in children. *Brit, J. Educ. Psychology,* **42**, 5, 1972, 293-9.

Shatz, M. and Gelman, R. The development of communication skills: Modification in the speech of young children as a function of listener. *Mono. Soc. Res. Child Dev.* **38**, 5, 1973.

Simpson, M.M. *Suggestions for teaching, reading in infant classes.* Wellington: Department of Education, 1962.

Skinner, B.F. *Verbal behavior.* New York: Appleton Century Crofts, 1957.

Smith, F. *Understanding reading.* 1st edn. 1971; 2nd edn. 1978. New York: Holt Rinehart and Winston.

Smith, M.E. A study of the speech of eight bilingual children of the same family. *Child Development,* **6**, 1935, 19-25.

Solley, C.M. and Murphy, G. *Development of the perceptual world.* New York: Basic Books, 1960.

Sowers, S. Young writers' preferences for non-narrative modes of composition. Paper available from Writing Process Laboratory, University of New Hampshire, 1980.

Speitel, H.H. Dialect. In Davies, A. (Ed.) *The problems of language and learning.* London: Heinemann Educational Books, 1981.

Spong, P. Recognition and recall in retarded readers: A developmental study. Mimeograph report, University of Auckland, 1962.

Strang, R. *Diagnostic teaching of reading.* New York: McGraw-Hill, 1964.

Taylor, J. *Reading and writing in the first school.* London: Allen & Unwin, 1973.

Thorndike, R.L. *Reading comprehension education in fifteen countries.* New York: Wiley, 1973.

Toohey, M. and Miller, S. The Record of Oral Language: A preliminary report on a Brisbane project. In P. Gunn (Ed.) *Learning problems: A collection of conference and workshop papers.* Brisbane: Schonell Centre, Univ. of Queensland, 1978.

Vaughan, G. The effect of the ethnic grouping of the experimenter upon children's responses to tests of an ethnic nature. *British J. of Social and Clinical Psychology,* 2, 1963, 66-70.

Walsh, R.D. (Ed.) The new English - how to . . . *J. Primary English Teachers Assoc.,* N.S.W., 1976.

Wells, C.G., & Kroll, B. *Explorations of children's writing development.* New York: Wiley, in press.

White, S. Evidence for a hierarchical arrangement of learning processes. In Lipsitt, L.P. & Spiker, C.C. (Eds.), *Advances in child development and behavior,* 2. New York: Academic Press, 1965.

Weiner, M., & Cromer, W. Reading and reading difficulty: A conceptual analysis. *Harvard Educ. Review,* 37, 1968, 620-643.

Williams, B. The oral reading behavior of standard one children. Unpublished M.A. thesis, University of Auckland, 1968.

Wohlwill, J.F. Developmental studies in perception. *Psychological Bulletin,* 57, 1960, 249-288.

Wohlwill, J.F., & Wiener, M. Discrimination of form orientation in young children. *Child Development,* 35, 1964, 1113-1125.

DATE DUE

STAYING ALIVE
in Alaska's Wild

By Andy Nault
Transcribed and Edited by Tee Loftin

Photographs by Andy Nault

True Adventures

with
Bears, Wolves, Wolverines, Beavers,
Seals, Dogs, Volcano, Williwaws

on
Kodiak Island, Contact Point,
Kamishak Bay and River,
Tugidak Island

ISBN 0-934812-01-2

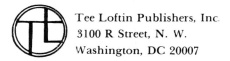

Tee Loftin Publishers, Inc.
3100 R Street, N. W.
Washington, DC 20007

"My pictures, including the wolf I caught howling,
are in this wilderness book to provide atmosphere,
enlightenment, and sometimes backup for what I say.
I left in some not-too-well focused ones, especially
of bears, that show an interesting scene. About these
fuzzy pictures I'll say that even an expert photographer
who takes off his gloves to snap a hostile, dangerous
animal close up is apt to fumble and make the camera
nervous, same as I."

Andy Nault

Staying Alive in Alaska's Wild

Table of Contents

1
Into the Wilderness For Life

*"It's the tracking and the packing and the poling
in the sun;
It's the sleeping in the open, it's the rugged,
unfaked food . . ."*   Robert Service

One day after hearing I was half-dead, I began doing
full-time what I'd always wanted to do but didn't have
time. I moved to the wilderness and trapped for a living.
Open tundras, brushy hills and river flats, forests, bays, and
beaches became my home on Kodiak Island and the brood
of islands around it.

Before I began living in Alaska's big, breezy spaces, I
lived mostly in dark rooms of a Montana nightclub. I did
my breathing in a thick cloud of second-hand tobacco
smoke, and smoked four packs of cigarettes a day besides.
My exercise was walking across the room to tote a tray of
drinks or food, and shuffling my feet back and forth in a
two-by-ten space behind the bar.

For entertainment I worried. Every night for 20 years I
slept sitting in a chair. When I lay down I couldn't breathe.

The nightclub belonged to me. I had to make it pay. If

Living outdoors on rainy, cold, windy Tugidak Island, and working hard, Andy began to regain his health. "After one week of fresh air and exercise, I slept lying down for the first time in 20 years," he says.

I didn't, the wife and younguns would shiver through those awful Montana winters without enough wool underwear and coats.

During the early years, I got outdoors a little, say half a day in the first part of the week and half a day late in the week. I'd run my motorboat from Sidney up the Yellowstone River some 40 miles, or up the Missouri from Great Falls when I lived there, to set traps or check them out. Most of the catch was beavers.

Sometimes, when my work shifts left me no other time, I'd run the river by night. By the shape of the tree line against the sky, I could tell where I was well enough to stay in the channel and miss all the sandbars. I knew my rivers as well as Mark Twain knew the Mississippi, and even in pitch dark I could find my way down the channel at 20 miles an hour.

I had learned from my father the basics of setting traps and luring the animals into them. My father's hunting and trapping were done to put meat on the table. By the time I was six years old and had in my first winter of trapping caught nine ermine—nine little weasels—I was as hooked on trapping as a gambler to the roulette wheel.

When I reached my mid-40's, I didn't have time for half-days off from work. So I just worked. One day after about ten years, I took count while looking in the mirror. I looked, and felt, like a worn out Volkswagen, such as the one I drive today and call my "Skunk Wagon."

I tell people I left Montana because it was too blasting cold, and headed north up the highway to Alaska. Of course, it was more complicated than that, and included the fact that I was well on my way to being dead.

Some time after arriving at my brother Norm's den in

Anchorage, I tried to get out of my sleeping chair one morning and knew for sure I was on the brink. I could hardly breathe. My joints didn't bend without forcing, so I didn't walk, I just slid my feet along the floor while I held on to chairs and tables.

Guys dead two weeks felt better than me.

I got to a doctor.

"Yes," he said, "you've got about six months before your emphysema, diabetes, angina, sick liver, and high blood pressure do you in. Your arthritis will finish freezing up your hands and neck and joints and you'll look more like a skeleton than you do now at 115 pounds. You're eating nitro pills like they were popcorn. How many aspirin you eating a day? Thirty-four? Plays the devil with your stomach. You're going to keep on getting littler, shorter, and smaller so there won't be much left when you're finished. Six months. No, you're an ornery son-of-a-gun so you'll probably last a year."

"A year? That's all?" I said. "So what are you going to do about it, Doc?"

"I'M going to do absolutely nothing."

That shook me up. Silence while he twiddled with the blood pressure winding cloths and while I turned what he'd said over in my head. After a while, I said, "O.K. Doc. What am I going to do about it? My body may be dying but my soul is still young."

He began to talk. "First thing you've got to do is throw the cigarettes you've got in your pocket into the gutter where they belong and don't buy any more ever. Your lungs are worse off than a junk-clogged car radiator.

"To get your circulation pump working, you need fresh air and exercise. Get outside, and I don't mean walk the city streets. Start looking at the bright lights as your worst enemy. Get to the woods, or the beach, or the water. Next thing, you've got to learn how to shoot insulin for that diabetes. You should be in a coma right now. Cut out sugar except when you're fainting from low blood sugar. And cut out alcohol forever.

"You do all that and you've probably got yourself another 20 years."

It sounded like a no-fun package but it was way above dying. Outside the doctor's office, I dropped my cigarettes into the gutter. I've not bought a pack nor bummed a smoke since and it's going on 20 years. I learned to handle a hypodermic needle to shoot insulin. I sharpened my hunting knives, bought hip boots and rain gear, began collecting traps, and headed out of the concrete maze.

Kodiak Island and town sounded good. When I first arrived in Alaska I'd tried some trapping along the highways in Kenai. I knew that was mostly automobile riding, almost like a city street, only colder in winter. In a few places, those highways have some of the coldest temperatures in Alaska—it's nothing to see minus-60.

Around Kodiak Island, the sealing season was going full blast. I knew it was hard work, but in total wilderness by the sea. There on Alaska's "Banana Coast" warmed by the Japanese Current circling the Gulf of Alaska east to west, the sea level temperature seldom gets to zero. If I could survive the next two weeks out of the doctor's office, I might live to be a summer sealer.

On the beach at Tugidak Island off the south tip of Kodiak, I could hardly walk from cabin to the water's edge, about 100 yards. But day after day I did it, gritting my teeth, pushing those joints, breathing hard, and swearing. "That doctor said I could live one year or twenty, depending on which I wanted the most. I want TWENTY!"

The first two seals I got, I had to lie down on the beach to skin them I was in such bad shape. But I finally got their hides off. It was like turning on a light in a dark tunnel—I had accomplished something.

Keep after it, I told myself. Get lazy and die. Keep after it and live. It's the pushing that pays off.

After one week of sealing, pushing myself and breathing fresh air and nothing else, I slept lying down. When I woke up breathing quiet and easy, relaxed and rested, I wondered how I had survived 20 years of neck kinks from sleeping in a chair.

That fall and winter, I went trapping in the Kodiak wilderness. By the next sealing season, the emphysema had taken off, my joints bent as limber as a goose's neck, and the ulcerated liver—well, I guess your liver works back to normal if you don't torment it too much.

Now I've had most of the promised 20 years and I've moved my dateline farther ahead. I need at least 20 more years to get caught up on all the things I'd still like to do.

2

Trapper on the Roof

*". . . I have been beaten to a jelly, torn almost
limb from limb, and nearly chewed up and spit
out by these treacherous grizzly bears."*
John C. "Grizzly" Adams, 1860

These tales of staying alive in Alaska's wilderness
begin with a picture of me in a miserable fix with a bear.
There I am, gray-bearded trapper in an old sealskin beret
sitting on a sod roof, motionless in tall grass. Beside me,
also motionless, sits a giant Native. We are hiding on top of
an eight-foot-high cabin from a 12-foot-tall bear. Any
direction we look through the cottonwoods, it's a hundred
miles from everybody else in the world.

But we are looking down. In our front yard, the bear is
looking up, around, trying to figure out where we are.
She's been very interested in us since before breakfasttime,
right on through lunchtime, and far into the afternoon.

The trapper-on-the-roof scene took place on the
flatlands of the Kamishak River about a mile upstream
from Kamishak Bay. The bay curves into the east shore of
the upper Alaska Peninsula, just where Cook Inlet

*A thousand or so "Curses horribles" as Andy
calls the brown bear clan, live around
Kamishak Bay's salmon-rich rivers. "There
you don't have to hunt the bear," Andy says.
"He's more likely to look you up as a
curious and interesting event in his kingdom."*

becomes Shelikof Strait.

Six fair-size rivers drain into Kamishak Bay—the Kamishak on the south, then the Strike joining the Little Kamishak, then the McNeil, and finally the Dunuletak joining the Paint. Their flatlands lie one beside the other in a stretch of 35 miles alongside the bay, and 5 to 10 miles inland to the mountains. The wide valley of each river wedges deep between ridges of the Aleutian Range.

On these flatlands, coastal brown bears—called "grizzlies" when they live inland or down in California and Yellowstone National Park—eat well and grow into the biggest bears in the world. Standing up, some are 12 feet tall and weigh up to 1400 pounds.

With long fangs and claws, big bears and little bears grab salmon out of the rivers of the Kamishak, especially the McNeil. An out-sized package of appetite, a bear will gulp down a dozen or so large fish daily.

Spring, summer, and early fall, salmon arrive every day, sometimes by the thousands, from far-away ocean pastures. Females are swollen with uncountable tiny orange eggs. Along the river banks, the bears are staring into the water. They jump in, wade in, slap their paws into the water, haul in their catch, stand up and hang onto the fish with both arms. They might eat right there chomping furiously, or sit down on a handy rock to tear into the flesh. Mamas throw fish to cubs on shore.

Kamishak Bay's flatland is the kingdom of the brown bears. Government bear counters estimate there're about three to every square mile, or a thousand or so in that strip of land. Some go so far as to say that's the greatest concentration of brown bears in the world. Greater Yellowstone has about 350 grizzlies, about one for every 40 square miles.

A man living in the Kamishak can hardly avoid near run-ins with at least one bear every day in warm weather. On the McNeil, you can bump into bunches of them, up to 40, 60, or 80. Even in winter when cold and snow relent for a few days in a row, I've seen as many as five in a few hours.

During the year I spent in the Kamishak in the mid-70's, I never became accustomed to these daily near-meetings. Always on first sight of the dark, shaggy body, I abruptly lost track of any thought except the name of the bear clan. *Ursus horribilis!* Except I said it "Curses horrible!" which exactly expresses my feelings about bears.

I worked at keeping all my bear contacts so uneventful I would forget to mention them at the supper table. I've never hunted bears for sport or hides nor taken anybody else to hunt them. Deliberately confronting a bear and wondering every second if I'd live to describe how scary it was never impressed me as fun. Hunting trouble on the off-chance that I might take home a bearskin rug seems a dangerous way to furnish a living room.

But in the Kamishak you don't have to hunt the bear. He's more likely to look you up as a curious and interesting new event in his kingdom.

This fine September day in 1976 the daily bear sighting went way beyond the usual.

My giant partner Chief and I had been flown in from Homer and dropped off near my Kamishak cabin to gather up equipment left behind in the spring. The plane would return in about a week to take us back, what day depending on the weather.

After drudging through equipment-sorting a couple of days, I and my partner, whose 265-pound size deserved the name "Chief," were planning to take the day off. We were going duck and goose hunting. Great spearhead formations of wildfowl had been flying south for days.

I was up with daylight. I went outside our log cabin into the nearby brush, and stood there taking care of morning routine. I was enjoying the warm air, the quiet, the isolation when out of the corner of my eye, I saw a movement in the tall grass.

"Curses horrible!" I had turned my head just enough to see rising from the grass a big black nose, its holes looking like the business end of a double-barrel shotgun. Just behind, dark eyes with very white eyeballs rolled from side to side, searching for the maker of my noise. Stiff, straining ears pointed forward, listening.

Curses curses! I had no gun! I never go out without taking my gun. But this warm, now sunny morning, with ducks on my mind, all thoughts of bears had dropped out of my head and I had sauntered outside unarmed. Careless fool. Now what do I do?

In the ten seconds that I considered this miserable question, the bear had begun pushing himself up, pushing up and up 12 full feet. Six feet and more above my head.

When a bear is towering over you almost within HIS arm's reach, it's hard to keep in mind that he can't see you if you just keep still as a tree. Or that your entire future depends not only on *how* still you can hold yourself, but on how *long*. I kept telling myself that bears, like most mammals, don't see color, so my red shirt wouldn't catch his eye. My nerves don't really believe that, but I have observed that his eyes don't seem to focus very well. I ought to look to him like part of the blurry brush.

I could smell the bear's rotten breath. It sent sick waves to my stomach but I knew the odor was a godsend. It meant the breeze wasn't blowing my scent to him.

Turning his head from side to side slowly, the towering beast looked the picture of power and doom. I could see the shaggy coarse dark hair on his belly, background for yellowish-brown claws as long as my fingers hanging from limp wrists.

Probably the next few hours were only three or four minutes long. Abruptly the bear dropped down to all fours, stretched out in the grass, head turned away. That was my cue and I ran 50 feet in the next two seconds.

I bounded into the cabin saying in a loud whisper, "Chief! Hand me my gun!"

"You see big moose?" Chief rumbled, jumping to grab my rifle. Chief had come with me to Kamishak to hunt moose and they were always in his thoughts. "Shhh! Talk low! It's a bear. The biggest, meanest bear in the world, right outside our door! I think he saw me running. He was lying in the grass, but he may be moving now, looking for me. He can push this door down in no time. We can't risk running to the tree lookout—he's too close to it. I've got to scare him off if I can."

"Maybe he so big he get stuck in little door, so no problem," Chief said in a booming whisper, and handed me the rifle. Chief was six inches beyond six feet tall. Our short homemade door frame cracked his head nearly every time he went in or out.

I snapped the rifle bolt, checking to make certain the gun was loaded to the brim the way it's supposed to be, always. Then I pushed the half-closed cabin door wide open with the gun barrel. Curses Horrible was now standing tall and awful where I'd left him, peering our way intently. Quickly I fired in his direction. Bang! Bang!

Bang! Not to hit him, just to scare him away. I didn't want three-quarters of a ton of unmovable, undraggable dead bear in our yard.

It worked. The last we saw of Curses was an enormous brown furry bottom disappearing into the brush. I watched the moving of the brush right on down the slight slope towards the river as Curses loped through, heading for a quieter and less confusing spot to nap.

"He wasn't hungry, so we were lucky," I said. "He probably worked all night killing and eating things," Chief said. "The way his breath smelled, he killed his breakfast last week," I said.

Some way to start a day, I was thinking while I fed cartridges into the rifle magazine. "Cough, cough," I heard and looked up toward the noise. In Cottonwood Lane, which ended at our door just where I was standing, a second Curses Horrible was looking at me. Its shaggy brown fur was tipped in faded orange.

"There's another Curses coming up the lane," I said in a loud whisper over my shoulder to Chief. The bear must have heard me or I must have moved a little, for it started up in a burst of speed. I froze, hoping to dissolve once more into a fuzzy blur. The bear stopped. It tilted its head a little, the way an old dog will do when he's not sure what to make of a situation. Not peeved, not startled, not even thinking of its appetite. Just puzzling out what's going on.

This bear looked as big as the one we had just scared away on the other side of the yard. On all fours, each was as high as my shoulder, and each was eight feet long nose-tip to rump bottom. With jaw power able to break an arm-size sapling with ease, they were neighbors I'd hoped would never knock at my door.

This one couldn't make up its mind what to do. It stepped forward.

It stopped, stood up. I could see that it was a female.

And poised in front of her chest were two frightful paws with five-inch claws.

Probably you've never had occasion to take a close look at such claws. I've seen them in live action and stone dead. Even on a bearskin rug ten years old they make me shudder. They're shaped like long, narrow scoops, slightly curving downward. Both edges are razor sharp for cutting apart animal flesh.

The claws, strong as steel, are great for digging, too— all those scoops cutting out dirt, and back paws kicking it away. In half an hour, he can dig a six-by-six-by-six-foot hole to curl up in and go to sleep. But the job his claw-knives do best is strike down and tear to pieces the bodies of other animals.

One swipe and rriiiipppp! a head falls off. Or an arm is hanging by a tendon. Or guts are tumbling out.

After that, the bear dines.

Some people can't believe that bears eat people. And some visitors to Alaska think stories about hunters, trappers, fishermen, or cameramen maimed or killed by bears are invented to give them a thrill. They should see my collection of news clippings. Here's one story:

A fellow went out to hunt with just a camera. When he was found, he was a scattering of blood-caked bones, a skull, and two shoes containing feet gnawed off at the ankles. The last picture on the roll showed the blurred head of a bear.

I had my rifle as I faced Mama Bear on Cottonwood Lane. While she was trying to make up her mind whether I was a tree or a live, edible animal, I made up my mind to fire the gun and try scaring her off. The bang of the gun didn't trouble her at all. She acted as if she didn't even hear it. She began loping forward. She didn't look offended, and maybe she was thinking good neighbor thoughts. But you can't waste time tuning into a bear's mind. Either I must shoot to kill or get a move on.

"Come on, Chief!" I yelled. "Let's get out of sight, she's coming too close. Climb the lookout tree to the roof!" If it had been freezing weather and I was going to be staying for the season, I could have killed and eaten her before she killed and ate me. But the weather was warm and we'd be leaving in a few days. Who wants a half-ton of meat rotting by the front door?

The year before, I had nailed an old ladder onto the trunk of a tree that had a branch hanging over our cabin. I always figure that some unlikely need is likely to arise, and prepare an escape route or a refuge. The ladder led to a tiny lookout platform 40 feet above the ground but, I thought, even if Chief managed to squeeze in beside me, the bough might break and the refuge fall. Better to walk the limb hanging over our cabin roof.

Chief's head didn't come close to the door frame as all 265 pounds of him dove out of the cabin. "Move! Move! Move!" he rumbled about a half-step behind me—except that it sounded like, "Moo-moo-moo!"

As I scrambled from tree limb to grass-covered roof, I saw Mama Bear below rocking along the path she'd seen us take alongside the cabin.

Our roof, flat except for a bit of a slant on each side, held us only eight feet above the ground. If the bear stood on her hind legs, she could lay her chin and her front paws right up there with us. I motioned to Chief to keep quiet, move to the center of the roof, and crouch 'way down behind the tall weeds.

Without those weeds to hide us, I might not have gotten to tell this story. The cabin was about the size of a one-car garage, its split-log roof waterproofed with "visqueen," the plastic tarpaulin as necessary as bread in Alaska. To keep the plastic sheeting from blowing away, my last year's partner, Bruce, and I had cut strips of moss and sod from damp, shady spots, hauled them to the roof, and rolled them out edge to edge. Through the all-daylight summer months, crowded weeds and grass had grown shoulder-high.

We sat there, Chief and I, trying to smother the noise of our heavy breathing, and peering through the weeds toward the ground where we expected to see the bear. She wasn't there. No sounds from her, either. I heard only the twittering of birds in the cottonwoods and the far-away honking of the geese we weren't hunting. Would her face soon appear over the roof's edge?

Had she gone in the open door of the cabin? The thought almost made me jump off the roof. The silence calmed me down. I've seen cabins and tents that bears have torn into. Such a shamble of upset tables and chairs, canned food, dishes, pots, pans couldn't have been made without a din of crashes, clatters, and bangs. Like the burglars they are, bears throw everything upside down. They're looking for edibles. Sometimes it looks as if they read the labels on the cans and bite open only the sugared fruits. Their fangs can put a half-inch-wide hole in any sheetmetal—except a steel gasoline drum. Once I saw a bear's tooth-scratches all around the top rim of a drum where he had tried using his teeth like a can opener.

After a few minutes of anxious waiting on the roof, we saw Mama Bear ambling across the grassy area in front of the cabin. She stopped and sniffed and sniffed at the bent grass where the male bear had sunbathed earlier. She made little whines that slid into a rumble.

"You think he and she belong together and have a family?" Chief whispered. No, I whispered back. If she had a cub it would be following in her tracks. And contrary to the Goldilocks story, Mama Bear, Papa Bear, and Baby Bear don't live together as a nice little family that eats oatmeal porridge.

Papa Bear eats *baby bear* unless Mama beats him off. Born weighing one pound, hairless and tender, a cub would disappear down daddy's gullet the first day if Mama didn't bellow, growl, snap her teeth, and wave her claws. In early spring when daddys are very hungry after their long sleep-fast, I've heard the parents roaring and fighting from a mile away. Usually Mother Love wins and Daddy grumps off to stay.

"If it were spring now, and she didn't have a new cub to look after, we might have a big problem," I whispered to Chief. "The bear that left this morning might smell her and come back. But since it's September, she may just take off into the brush the way he did."

But she didn't. She went on a sightsmelling tour of our yard and came upon my gear under some cottonwood trees.

She sniffed at a tangle of steel traps in an open wooden crate, growled disapprovingly, pushed the crate over and pitched traps right and left.

She sniffed all around my three-wheel Honda until she came to the front tire. It offended her. "WOOUF!" She clamped her teeth into it, jerked her head to one side. The machine rose as if it were a turkey and she was breaking its neck. Just then, the tire went POW! Mama Bear jumped five feet backwards. My Honda crashed to the ground, settled upright, front tire flat.

Swearing and cussing, I raised and lowered my rifle. "Shoot, shoot!" Chief boomed, forgetting the bear would hear. "She tear up your machine! Now we gotta *tote* all the gear to the river when the plane comes." That prospect hit him in a sore spot. He'd hurt his back a few days before and couldn't lift a thing.

I got hold of myself and started talking about why we'd better not kill the bear. "Listen, Chief," I whispered, "I'm mad at her about my Honda, but having a dead bear in our yard and she ten times heavier than we can move—that's big trouble. We can't bury her, so she'll rot. The stench will make us sick and draw a crowd of bears from everywhere in the Kamishak to eat her. They'll hang around for days. We'd have to stay up here hungry, thirsty, and scared."

Chief answered, "You shoot, we cut her up, we bury a hundred pounds at a time."

I answered, "Take all day long to do that, counting digging a big-enough hole. Right in the middle of the funeral, we'd have another bear who'd smelled the fresh blood and meat. They're cannibals, you know. Besides that, when you cut up a monster this big, you get blood and guts all over the ground. It's hard to cover every little bit so nothing's left to rot and stink. Remember this is Bearburg, like no other place in the world. The bear population is THE population, and we don't want a general assembly in our yard.

"I'll try shooting into the air again, Chief, if she won't

get a move on. This time, maybe two or three shots will scare her, or at least help her decide this is too spooky a place for her."

Chief grunted ummm, and we waited.

She didn't go anywhere. She snuffled, snuffled, snuffled at our gear, making me tighten up minute by minute. If she had started clawing my stuff apart, my trigger finger would have turned loose some highly emotional bangs.

But in the end, she turned her back on all the gear and went rocking across the yard. I actually said, "GOOD bear," for the first time in my life. I expected her to keep going and disappear forever into the brush.

Following her habit of doing the opposite of my predictions, she sat down at the edge of the yard and stared our way.

"She's looking this way," rumbled Chief. "We're still on her mind," I mumbled back. Did she plan to stick around and see what would happen? "With the wind favoring us, if we sit tight and keep quiet, she'll get bored and leave," I predicted.

Nothing of the sort happened. In a half-hour, she yawned "Auuooooff," lay down, and went to sleep.

"When you goin fire the gun and scare her off?" Chief rumbled at me. "Well," I said, "I was just thinking that the nap might make her forget why she's hanging around here. When she wakes up, I'll bet you a beer in Kodiak you'll see her stretch, shake herself, and go for the river. I won't need to waste a bullet."

A couple of hours later when a rain cloud huffed in, we'd hit a new level of misery. We'd sat, stretched out, propped on elbows—and now we were getting wet in a slow rain. I had to concede that we were unforgettable characters to Mama Bear, and that I owed Chief a beer. Miz Bear's routine was a 20-minute nap, a sudden sitting-up, a 10-minute stare our way, and another nap.

"When you goin fire the gun and scare her off?" Chief rumbled again, an edge in his tone.

I was ready when Mama Bear next raised her head. Bang! She got to her feet. Bang! She began running—TOWARD the noise, the way a foolish householder will do when he hears a burglar smash his window.

We lay as low as we could in the roof weeds. Mama Bear was so close to the cabin now, we couldn't see her any more. "The cabin door is wide open," I whispered to Chief. He nodded and rolled his eyes.

I'll never know why Mrs. Curses didn't find the cabin door, nor why she didn't think to look high for the source of the strange noise. But she didn't. I felt mighty grateful for her slow wits when I saw her lumbering back to her napping place.

Now it was our turn to play slow-witted.

"I'm hungry," rumbled Chief. "I'm going to sneak inside the cabin while she's asleep and grab some grub." He began getting to his feet.

"Wait a minute," I said. Getting 265 pounds of Chief down our cottonwood tree, into and out of our little cabin door, and back up to the roof again looked like beckoning to disaster. "Tell you what. I can move faster than you can, so it's better for me to go," I said. "You take the rifle and cover for me. While I'm down there, I'll get some sticks, rags, and gasoline to make torches to throw at her. That's a sure way to scare off bears." Chief grunted ummm.

It was no trouble to ease down the tree and slip into the

cabin. I threw bread and cheese inside my shirt.

I was looking around for rags to add to an armful of thick sticks and a jug of gasoline when I heard Chief hollering. "Andy! Come back! She ain't asleep!!"

Where were those rags? Oh confound. Chief kept hollering. "She's getting up, Andy!" I grabbed a handful of dirty laundry and rushed out the door yelling, "Shut up, Chief!" That door really ought to be closed. I went back and closed it. Then I had to pass the sticks up to Chief so I could have a free hand to climb the ladder. I also had to hand him the heavy jug and the rags, which were dribbling out from under my arm. All the time, Chief was swearing and saying "She's coming! She's coming!"

I dropped the last piece of dirty laundry and ran. It was like the kind of dream where you're trying hard to move but you can manage only feeble motions that don't get you anywhere. All the time my mind was picturing me climbing the tree with a bear's claws reaching out to pull me down.

My hands somehow touched the ladder steps. I stood there it seemed a minute, pumping my foot into the air, not finding the step. I heard, "Climb Andy! Climb!" I heard a gentle "Rouf."

I must have run up the trunk ladder like a squirrel, for the next thing I remember, I was hurrying along the tree branch and jumping off into the wet roof grass.

"Freeze!" Chief whispered in a face-distorting, unvoiced scream. I froze stretched out face down.

"Rouf!" Mrs. Curses' massive head rose like some Halloween monster above the roof edge. But sideview to us. She was looking at the tree. She was so close I could hear her teeth clicking, ticky, ticky, ticky, very fast. I could even see her eyelids, complete with long eyelashes, blinking. The head disappeared. It seemed like a miracle. Chief's eyes and mouth were still open with amazement. He was breathing fast, so I knew his heart was speeding as fast as mine. What a wonderful thing that bears are shortsighted and can't wear glasses, and the wind wasn't blowing her way.

We stayed immobile and silent, watching the yard beyond the line of our roof edge. At last we saw her big brown rump waddling back to her napping place and settling down. Both Chief and I exhaled as if we'd held our breath an hour.

Within seconds, Chief whispered, "I smell cheese. Since I'm done with thinking I'd had my last meal, bring out the lunch."

For dessert after this lunch I'd almost given my life for, we brought out our big question and began to chew on that: What do we do now?

We chewed the question louder and louder without noticing the noise. Chief wanted to shoot her dead NOW. I argued for scaring her away. When we happened to glance toward the yard, there was Mama Bear standing 12 feet tall and staring our way.

"We can't afford this argument." I was whispering again. "Where's the torch stuff? Let's try throwing some fire at her. Some bears are scared to death of fire."

We tied some dirty laundry to the end of a stick and wet it with gasoline. I brought out a match from a waterproof match-can hanging around my neck. I carry it all the time when I go into the wild. Chief stood up to hold the torch high above the tall grass—even though wet, our hiding place, and then the cabin, could catch fire.

One touch of the match and the tee shirt was engulfed in flames. Chief took his aim and slung the torch.

It landed a few feet from Mrs. Bear. To our surprise, she showed no surprise. She looked at the torch as if burning objects fell at her feet from nowhere every day. "Fire doesn't mean a thing to her," I grumbled. Chief silently and doggedly made another torch, aimed and tossed it. It landed at her toes.

But the landing in the wet grass smothered most of the flames, which made a lot of smoke. She began to cough. She shook her head as if the smoke had stung her eyes. Instead of backing away from the torch, she moved closer to the treacherous thing, growled at it—and bit it! "Waughhh!" she cried, and spat. Around and around she turned, her red ribbon tongue hanging out. Blistered probably. Suddenly she bounded away.

"We did it! She's gone!" Chief and I were shouting to each other—when we saw her coming back. She was mad at us and on the fight, for her ears were lying down and the hair on her back was standing. She was snapping her teeth. Deep angry noises rolled in her throat. She looked strong and mean enough to snap our lookout tree in two and bash our cabin to splinters.

"Got to get her before she gets us," I thought, grabbed the rifle, aimed, fired.

We had 1200 pounds of dead bear almost at our feet.

Since you never know for sure that a dead bear isn't a pretend-dead bear, you always wait awhile to see if it so much as bats an eyelid. Wet and shivering in the chilly air, we discussed what to do with the body.

Close up, Mrs. Curses Horrible was even bigger than she'd seemed at a distance. We couldn't budge her. She had to stay where she fell. I think she was very old, beyond cub-bearing. Bears can live to be 30 years old.

We covered her with large sheets of visqueen, letting a yard or so extend on the ground all around her. On that we piled dirt. We shoveled and shoveled, throwing up as much earthy weight as we could. Chief grunted with back misery, but he dug and threw as much as I. "With luck, the plane will pick us up inside of a week. That's about the time the stink will begin filtering through the plastic and floating over Kamishak," I told Chief.

"Ummm," answered Chief but this time it was a rumble of satisfaction.

It was dark with a cold wind that had cleared the sky before we finished, one of us digging while the other stood guard. With no moon, we were cutting our dirt and throwing it by the light of glittering stars.

All at once, the northern sky lit up.

Pale greenish-white crescents of fluttering streamers lighted the Kamishak wilderness. The Aurora Borealis, luminous curtains dangling earthward, swayed, rippled, dimming and brightening.

Leaning on my shovel, I gazed upward, then outward. I became conscious of the world I hadn't seen all day, or even remembered was there. On the west and the south I could see the dark silhouette of the high mountains. To the east, there was the sea, and sitting in it 20 miles away was a lone volcanic cone, St. Augustine. On all sides of us, I could see the cottonwoods sheltering the spot where I'd lived one of the most adventurous years of my life.

I inhaled the sweet wilderness air and held it a long moment. As I let it out again, I felt the exhileration of a man just released from prison, free, and glad to be alive.

3
Kamishak Dream

"Kamishak became the Mt. McKinley of my winters in the Alaskan wilderness. It began as a dream. It will forever thrill my memory with the singing of wolves, the roufing of bears, the swissh of whales blowing."   Andy Nault

How did I come to be standing on the roof of a Kamishak cabin swearing at a Curses Horrible?

Kamishak . . . When I first heard the name, the sound kept repeating itself in my ears. I knew it was a place I would some day be going.

I heard the name soon after I arrived in Alaska in 1958 from cold, cold Montana. I was a cheechako, a brand new Alaskan who didn't know a tundra from a williwaw.

My brother, Norm, who was putting me up, was almost a native Alaskan. He'd been in Anchorage two whole years. One thing he'd been doing was collecting success stories about Alaskans—the line trappers, the sealers, the salmon fishermen, the crab fishermen, the gold prospectors.

One night he began telling me a story about Alaskan hunting guides. Two of them advertised in Europe and got

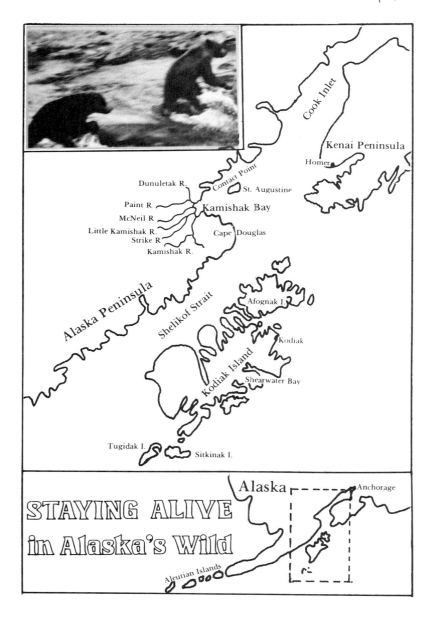

Cook Inlet

Kenai Peninsula

Homer

Dunuletak R.

Contact Point

St. Augustine

Paint R

Kamishak Bay

McNeil R

Little Kamishak R.

Strike R

Cape Douglas

Kamishak R.

Alaska Peninsula

Shelikof Strait

Afognak I.

Kodiak

Kodiak Island

Shearwater Bay

Tugidak I.

Sitkinak I.

STAYING ALIVE
in Alaska's Wild

Alaska

Anchorage

Aleutian Islands

two Germans to pay $5,000 apiece to fly half-way around
the world and hunt bears.

"Where'd they take the Germans?" I wanted to know.
At the same time, I was wondering what level of confusion
I'd have to reach to think of putting out $5,000 for a week of
bear trouble.

"Oh, they went to the best bear-hunting spot in the
world, of course," Norm said. "Kamishak! That's a bay
area on the Alaska peninsula where Cook Inlet and
Shelikof Strait meet. Not a soul living there or anywhere
nearby. Just wild animals. Man, if you want wilderness,
that's total plus. Even the natives won't live there. Too
many brown bears, too many wolves, wolverines. An Al-e-ut
or two might take a notion to come down every few years
from Iliamna Lake a hundred miles north. They know
there're lots of smaller animals along the rivers—
Kamishak, McNeil, Paint and others."

"Beavers, foxes, weasels, otters?" I asked.

"Running loose by the thousands," Norm said.

Kamishak! Pure wilderness. Untouched generations
of fur-bearing animals. One day in the future . . . The
future? With me in such bad shape, how could I think of
going anywhere in the future? My future might be just six
feeble months long. "Shut up," I told myself, "Kamishak is
my place and I'm toughening up and going some day."

"Kamishak" turned on a colorful picture in my mind.
Shaggy hundred-foot spruce towering dark green. Alder
brush and big-leafed cottonwood trees on the banks of a fast
running stream. Flashes of silver from salmon jumping
over rocky rapids.

I saw myself living in a log cabin I'd built near the
river. I'd be going out in the first snow to set a line of traps.

I'd be bringing back on a snowmachine seven-foot wolves, four-foot foxes, a dozen of the biggest beavers the world had ever seen. Six months of trapping in Kamishak and I'd have enough furs to pay for grub and gear for a year, and to cover all the expense of boats and planes to get me to the Kamishak and back.

My longing for Kamishak began.

"Of course," I heard Norm saying, "you can meet a bear every ten feet on the McNeil River. And all of them except the cubs are at least ten feet tall. Don't laugh! A bush pilot told me he saw *fifty* in a bunch one day when he flew over the McNeil. Several were at least fifteen, maybe twenty, feet tall, he said. The whole bunch rared up on their hind legs to stare at the plane, rolled back their top lips, and clicked their teeth. Some shook their fists—that's what the man said."

"You don't think I'll do more than laugh at a bush pilot's joke, do you," I said. "In the first place, whoever heard of bears going around in bunches. They're loners except when a pair is courting or when a mama has cubs."

"But on the McNeil there are so *many* bears, they can't help but bunch up," Norm told me. Then Norm started laughing.

He knew I hated bears. We'd both had dealings with them in Montana. Every once in a while, a bear would come down from the mountains, hide among the big rocks, and grab one of our cows as she walked past.

The bear's attack strategy worked perfectly and gruesomely. He waited until the cow had reached the crest and started downhill just past his hiding place. Then, galloping as fast as a horse, the bear rushed towards the cow's long tail. He grabbed it in his teeth with a hard jerk and kept going. The cow crashed to the ground. In a flash, the bear turned and was on her, sinking his sharp teeth and fangs into her neck, slashing open her belly with his claws, tearing out her udder. It happened so fast, the cow died without making a sound.

Seeing the mangled cow carcass sent me to the barn to drag out the biggest bear trap I could find. We had one four feet long of heavy iron. Once I heard of a bear trap seven feet long. A blacksmith shop had specially made it for an angry rancher who'd lost a cow a week for a month.

Well, in Kamishak, I thought, I won't have any cows for a bear to ambush, and besides, when I'm there in winter to trap, the bears will be sleeping. So I dreamed on about Kamishak. I went sealing on Tugidak Island, trapping on Kodiak, Afognak and nearby islands, and the tundra north of Fairbanks. Every trip toughened me a little more and I kept making my plans for the biggest adventure of all, a winter in the Kamishak.

For a long time I never met a soul who had been to Kamishak. I kept asking around but even the bush pilots shook their heads. The maps I found showed no names on rivers except Kamishak and McNeil. Instead they showed a village name, Chinik, by a dot on Kamishak Bay—a village I later learned hadn't existed for decades. Finally I saw an aeronautical map with the Kamishak flatlands, ridges, and mountains in relief. I tried to picture them, dreaming of being in the picture. I dreamed 15 years before I got even a look at Kamishak. Then it was just a few minutes and from a thousand feet in the air.

Having stayed alive, even come alive and well from all those years in the wilderness, I knew I was up to the "total plus" wild of Kamishak. "Up to" included physical fitness and survival skill. In 1973, the dream of going to that untouched animal kingdom was bothering me so much, I had to take the first step toward converting the dream into something more solid.

Suddenly cautious, I decided to fly over there and see if the place looked anything like my imaginings.

On a bright, cloudless, windless summer day, a bush pilot and I took off for Kamishak. North of Kodiak we looked down on an array of wilderness islands in the dark blue waters. Evergreen forests, logging camps, bright green hills of alder brush and salmonberry, sea lion rookeries at the foot of towering cliffs, barren rocks white with thousands of birds—and then the turn westward to cross the Shelikof Strait.

So clear was the air we could see the high mountains of the Aleutian Range some 70 miles away. Soon our first Kamishak landmark, Mt. Douglas, snow-capped and striped with glaciers, loomed ahead. It all but covers the south arm enclosing Kamishak Bay. Two 10-mile-long glaciers calve icebergs into the sea. It took long minutes to fly past the massive mountain.

We followed the coast line of the Bay, watching for the large cove at the mouth of the Kamishak River. For the next half-hour, I stayed in that can-it-be-true state of mind when a long-standing wish is materializing before your eyes.

There is the cove! There are river banks green with sea weeds, kelp, and salt grass at low tide. The plane quickly reaches them, passes over.

The sights, the seconds, the sensations go too fast. The scene I had long imagined unrolls below me . . . the wide strip of flatlands green with brush and grass stretching all the way up the coast and between rocky ridges . . . the wide, sparkling river . . . mountains dark green with spruce below rough stone peaks.

A mile or so up the river, I saw my grove of cottonwoods. "That's my homesite!" I shouted to the pilot above the engine noise. Down there I'd one day live a winter's adventure.

"Look!" the pilot shouted back. "There!"

Bears—a gathering of half a dozen, standing in the water and out.

More bears. "Looks like a convention!" The pilot was laughing with excitement. So was I. Brown bears might be loners at heart but here were about 40 to prove they'd stand each other's company for a picnic of salmon. Norm's bush pilot friend hadn't been joking.

Silver salmon glinted near the surface of the water. Bears stood in the water and on the banks grabbing at them. Seagulls fluttered about, waiting to pick up driblets when the bears ate.

The river, some 150 feet wide, twisted across the flatlands. When it reached a long finger escarpment, it narrowed, straightened alongside the wall, became more rocky. Bears were everywhere like lunchtime at a cafeteria. Before the pilot dipped a wing and turned back, we must have seen at least 100 bears.

"You sure you want to come here?" the pilot shouted. "I mean, to walk around on the ground with those big furry fellows?"

"They'll be sleeping while I'm here," I shouted back.

If a Kamishak bear had heard me, he'd have looked up and laughed.

I could see a bear trail—two rows of grassless footprints about two feet apart. There are two rows of bear tracks for the same reason a car makes two ruts—there's a lot of body space between each side's corner supports.

Bears wear down these footprints over many years, even for generations. Each bear steps in the old tracks. I've seen trails where the tracks, shaped like a giant human foot, were worn six inches deep in sandstone.

Along the streams below the plane, I saw the homes of a favorite bear food: beavers. To bears, the tender, sweet, flavorsome flesh of the beaver makes a five-star gourmet dinner. Catching a beaver doesn't happen often, though. They know every meateater wants to swallow them, so they mostly stay out of sight under the water.

As I looked down at the Kamishak and its creeks, my trapper's heart thrilled. Beaver dams and ponds and lodges—the most I ever saw along any streams. Plenty of beavers for me, the bears, and future beaver generations.

I heard the pilot say, "Over there! St. Augustine! It's smoking!" I looked up just long enough to spot the volcanic cone sitting by itself 25 miles away,off the northeast corner of Kamishak Bay. Smoke drifted out the top. "It does all the time. I've hunted seals on the beaches over there," I shouted back at the pilot.

Now we were close to the sea, leaving Kamishak. I fastened my eyes on my cottonwood grove and the Kamishak scene around it, more alluring than my most colorful dreams.

"There's a year of my future waiting for me down there!" I shouted to the pilot. He grinned back, nodded,and dipped a wing to the Kamishak.

4

Frozen Out Then Blown to Hell

"Andy, I got in a tight spot not long ago and I came out all right because I remembered what you told us on Contact Point about surviving in comfort and waiting for the tide to change."

Skipper Glenn, 1980

If I had a year of my future waiting for me in Kamishak, the question soon became, "Which year?"

Year One: Ice. "Look at *that!*" my brother Norm called to me when our charter boat came into Kamishak Bay. Tumbled and tossed into rough piles, the frozen sea spread like an Arctic icepack five miles to land. No way to get through it to the Kamishak River mouth. My heart sank to the bottom of Kamishak Bay.

I kicked myself for starting so late—November. That's late for starting any trapping trip in Alaska. But I couldn't find a partner that suited me and who was also dying to go spend the winter in far away Kamishak with just me. It took Norm until nearly November to get worked up over the idea of trapping foxes to make a fox-pelt bedspread. Besides, by November, the Kamishak bears would be sound asleep, I thought.

Contact Point's stone finger,
nearly a mile long, points
to the volcano St. Augustine,
14 miles from the north
end of Kamishak Bay.
"Twice I tried for the Kamishak
River," Andy says, "and both
times I was shunted off
to stony Contact Point."

Now I was finally in sight of the shore, and the door was closed. Twenty-below freezing, fresh river-water ice, ocean tides, and chilling winds had gotten together and manufactured an unbreakable lock.

CRack! CRunch! GRoan. The sea surging beneath the ice broke it, shoved up great blocks, ground them against each other, tossed them into piles of white wreckage.

My face was as long as Norm's as I looked from ice pack to a boat deck piled with snowmobiles, traps, guns, snowshoes, stacks of canned fruits and vegetables, bags of rice and flour.

"Let's go on north a-ways," Norm said. "Why waste the hundred miles we've come. We're bound to find one little place where we can land."

We didn't. When we rounded Contact Point, 25 miles north, the next day, we saw our last hope once more turned to ice. The Point is a long, sheer wall of gray stone at least 100 feet high. It brings the far northern corner of Kamishak Bay to a dramatic and sinister conclusion. Behind this massive stone finger lies a long, slender bay, Bruins Bay. When we saw it, blocks of ice as big as apartment houses covered the bay from shore to shore. In places the ice was stacked half way up the height of the rough, gray cliff.

It was spectacular, and a terror.

Not even Norm could find a word to say. We turned around and started home.

Year Two: Wind. I had begun a lot earlier looking for a partner. Norm couldn't go. But there arrived in Kodiak a young man named Bruce, fresh from the university and the concrete and plastic world in Washington state. He heard about me and the Kamishak trip, wanted to go, and searched me out to apply for the privilege.

He wanted to be a "mountain man" like the fur trappers in the pioneer days of the Old West, Bruce told me. He'd had bad luck with houses that burned down, parents he didn't get along with, routines he hated, money he had to ask for. He wanted to spend a few weeks in the wilderness and become self-reliant. He wanted to learn how to live off the land, trapping for a living like me—and like Jim Bridger, Kit Carson, and all such mountain men of history.

"A few weeks?" I said. "If I take you a whole season, all winter, like nine months, that's a short time though it will do you a lot of good. But if you're going to learn how to stay alive, and learn about the wiles of the animals you're after, it'll take two seasons. And that's with you doing what I tell you and no arguments."

"That's all right," he said. I looked him up and down. Good strong fellow. Looked sensible. Likable enough. So I gave him my spiel about Wilderness Partners, which goes something like this:

"Somebody green as you are, young, and knowing just a little about how to stay alive in the woods where there ain't no stores, where if you need something you've got to make it yourself—why, I've got to take care that you don't endanger my life while I'm trying to teach you. I ain't going to baby you and do everything for you. Couldn't if I wanted to. You'll be going out there among the wild animals all by yourself, finding your way back, feeding yourself, facing the vicious teeth and claws, the snow storms and the williwaws.

"When I agree to take somebody with me, it has to be understood that one person makes the final decision on any matter that concerns safety. That one person is me. I once had a partner who nicknamed me 'Ole Shut-Your-Mouth-

and-Listen.'

"Furthermore, there'll come happenings when I'll find out whether I can rely on you or not. If I can't, if I find out you won't stand up and protect me just like you would yourself, that's the end of the game as soon as I can get you on a plane or boat.

"That's the way it has to be to survive. Your partner's life and safety must be as important as your own—you must really *feel* that, and act that. In the wilderness, your partner IS as important as all that. If something happens to him and you're left to do everything alone, you'll quick find out that having that other person often means the difference between living and dying.

"Now this ain't no 50-50 partnership. It's 60-60. Each one has to bend over more than half. The overlap is the safety factor. Fifty-fifty leaves room for argument. We've got to get along. We can't get to hate each other in the wilderness and fight and argue. Another thing: I don't want drugs going with us. I've tried people who took such, and I'm surprised I'm alive to tell it. So that's it. Things get tough in the wilderness and the true colors of a man or woman come out in big glaring headlights. It's hard to predict, but the ones that come through true-blue will be close friends for life."

"I'm with you," Bruce answered, and we shook hands.

In early October, I with Bruce and my ailing dog, named Mr. Larson after a talkative fellow I once knew, started for Kamishak on the *Pauline B*. Skipper Glenn and crewmen Mark and Einer were to drop us and our gear at the mouth of the river and turn back to Kodiak. All went well—until we came near the Kamishak's mouth.

For the second time I was pushed away.

All in a minute from nowhere, a gale struck. Waves 20 feet high rolled toward the boat. We grabbed the handiest thing and held on for dear life. Crash! We roller-coasted for the next hour in wind and waves and pelting rain. At least I found out that Bruce wouldn't crawl in his bunk and cry like some people do when a bad storm knocked the boat around. I've had to cuss and haul out a few fellows that hid and covered their heads. It might be your time to go, I tell them, but it might not either, so get up and work until you find out.

Just as suddenly as the storm started, it disappeared. We looked around. Instead of the sandbars and seagrass in the Kamishak river cove, we saw the high rock wall of Contact Point, 25 miles north! Why did the sea keep bringing me to this grim place?

It was near dark when we turned the corner around the massive finger of stone and anchored in the mouth of Bruins Bay.

Some hours later when we were sound asleep, the storm, meaner than ever, hit us on its way back from the north. Winds blowing at 100 miles an hour yanked and jerked us at anchor. The boat leaped and fell like a wild horse at a rodeo. CRACK! the anchor cable broke. The boat spun this way and that, threatening one second to smash into shore, the next second to sweep out to sea.

Slamming about as we were, we should all have had broken heads and bones and washed overboard. Instead, in the darkness we managed through all that thrashing and bucking to attach chains to a metal door weighing more than a half-ton, drag it to the edge of the boat and push it over. Not satisfied, we chained and dragged a second steel door to push over the other side of the boat. Through the storm we rocked between those two anchors holding us away from the cliffs and a smash-up. Usually these doors were used to keep a big shrimp net open and stable on the sea floor, and were moved by a power winch.

In the morning calm and light, I saw the wind had been driving us out into the ocean! We'd been on our way into the open sea, not the cliffs, before we dropped over the steel doors.

I made my announcement. "I'm for leaving here. This place has me spooked. Every time I try for the Kamishak, I end up at Contact Point. I don't like the looks of the place or the weather it has."

But Bruce had seen the abandoned weather station on top of the Point. And the skipper and crew had gotten moose hunting on the brain. "This is as good as Kamishak," they said. "Plenty of wilderness. A place to live, all ready to move into. Looks like good moose country. Besides, with the storms coming in thick and fast, we might pass right by the Kamishak again. Then you'd end up in Afognak Island, which is pretty dull."

"Yes," I answered, "nice, quiet Afognak where there ain't no wind. I doubt a coyote would consent to stay on top of windy Contact Point where the old Army weather station is perched."

But in the end, I maximized the house, the moose, and the 25 miles around the shore to the Kamishak River. I minimized the storms, and the ice I saw in Bruins Bay the year before. We began skiffing our gear and supplies from ocean to bay beach at the foot of the towering wall of stone.

Skipper Glenn and his two crewmen borrowed a skiff and motored off for an afternoon of moose hunting at the far end of the bay. Bruce and I began driving loads of gear up a steep gravel trail that GI's had built from beach to top. The Honda wasn't big enough for the bulky stuff. We tried the short cut—steps the Army men had cut into the rock face. We nearly wore ourselves out the first trip. Finally we rigged up a come-along to hoist the heavy boxes, and even Bruce's skiff.

It was strenuous and dangerous work. If I hadn't been so interested in the engineering of it, and in the rock marmots we spotted running straight up and down the rocks, I would have sworn steadily. I felt from sealskin cap to boot sole that we had staggered into one of the worst spots in the wide world to spend the winter.

Watching the marmots kept us from thinking too grimly about our own discomforts as we worked. I first realized marmots were nearby when I heard a high-pitched whistle, one note several times. Bruce stopped to listen, too. "Whistlers—rock marmots," I called to him. "They're like big, gray gophers, except they have hair instead of fur."

We watched quietly for some minutes, not for shape or color since marmots look like rocks, but for movement. Pretty soon several appeared, running up and down the steep rock sides as if they had glue on their feet. Neither man nor dog could climb around where a marmot runs on sheer heights. In winter they sleep in holes in the rocks. But they can be caught. I once saw an Eskimo parka lined with the gray and black hair pelts of a half-dozen or so whistlers. Probably they were ambushed when they came to the tundra to graze on grass.

When the tide was going out in the afternoon, Bruce and I noticed a curious change in the Bruins Bay landscape. At its far end where Skipper Glenn and crew had gone, the land was coming closer and closer to us.

Hours later, most of the bay was land except for little ponds here and there. The exposed bottom was a litter of boulders taller than a man, and in the middle of the bay, a sprawling rock made a sizable island.

"What luck the wind was blowing us out to sea last night," Bruce said. "That must be a good sign."

No sooner said than a slap of cold wind hit us. Racing behind it in the sky was a black frothy cloud. "That must be a bad sign," I said. "Grab your rain gear."

An icy rain joined the slashing wind. "No sense running to shelter," I said. "There's no telling when a storm like this will quit. If we don't get these boxes under cover, it's quits for us. Maybe the storm is last night's howler turned around again, and it's telling us we have no business staying here."

Bruce thought I was superstitious. If the U.S. Army picked this spot for building a weather station during the war, it couldn't be all bad, now could it? "You notice they abandoned it never to return," I said. "By the way, in this weather, I'll bet Skipper Glenn and crew ain't faring too well, wherever they are."

Three hours later, at dusk, we found out just how bad they'd had it. Wind and rain had died down and we were finally on the last load of boxes. "Look who's coming up the beach," Bruce said. He cupped his hands and hollered, "Hey, you guys! Hurry up! Give us a hand with this stuff!"

They didn't answer. "They're staggering," I said.

"You mean they're drunk?"

I saw Einer drop to the ground. "Something's bad wrong!" I said.

Skipper Glenn and Mark swayed and lurched along, dragging their feet. Bruce and I ran to help them. Their legs were caked with black sticky mud. They were glassy-eyed, nearly unconscious. Einer, lying on the sand, was like a zombie. He had to be carried.

Somehow we got the three of them up the cliff. Inside the weather station, there was a stove in working order and I got going a roaring fire of left-over Army firewood. Bruce pulled wet muddy clothes off the three men and helped them into sleeping bags.

The two big strapping fishermen went off to sleep. But Einer lay stiff and barely breathing.

All night I aggravated him into living. I slapped him a little, talked to him a lot, rubbed him to stir up his circulation, heated blankets to wrap around him. He was stiff as a board, no bending his knees or elbows. It was just like he'd been frozen for the winter the way New Englanders once claimed they "froze up the old folks" and stored them away until spring.

Outside, the wind screamed madly and beat on our windows. Once I heard a bumpity-bumpity racket as if something was bouncing down the cliffside. It was. The next day, all we could find of Bruce's skiff, so laboriously hauled to the clifftop to protect it, were pieces of styrofoam floating in the bay.

About daybreak, Einer opened his eyes. I poured some hot coffee into him. He relaxed, went to sleep, and began to snore. Very beautiful.

What had happened to our moose hunters?

"It was like this," Skipper Glenn told us. "We went to the other side of the bay near the bay's end. When we tied up, there was plenty of water. A couple of hours later when we came back with the hind quarters of a moose, the boat was lying in mud and the bay was empty. What to do?

"We pulled the skiff across the mud and up to a big pile of driftwood to tie it to. Then we took off walking along the beach, heading toward where you were. We came to another mudflat, a small one. Rather than go around it, we decided to short-cut right across. It turned out to be a whole lot softer than we thought.

"Sometimes we sank in mud to our knees. Once we had to pull Einer out of a hole where he was stuck up to his waist. Pretty soon this stiff, cold wind hit us all of a sudden. Rain so cold and beating so hard it felt like sleet. Then it really was sleet. I've never been so cold and tired. I was numb in the feet, legs, even my brain was numb. The mud felt like soft ice cream. For a while I just said to myself, 'One more step.' Then, the most I could think was 'One . . .' We finally got out of the mud and back on sand. Altogether, we must have walked three hours. I barely remember getting to you and climbing the cliff."

Probably they'll never again run into a place as curious as Bruins Bay and Contact Point. But just in case they do, I've given them a safe game plan to follow.

Next time, I told them, stay out of the mud. It's dangerous stuff. It wets your clothes. It uses up lots of energy pulling against every step. Sometimes you step in a hole and can't pull out. I've heard of men drowning when they couldn't pull out, or couldn't even be hauled by a line from a mudhole. The tide comes in and covers them where they stand.

If you do manage to get out like Einer did, you're wet, and your clothes freeze on you. You chill all the way through, including your inside working parts. If it had been a few degrees colder on you fellows today, we'd have buried Einer on the beach at Contact Point.

What could they have done to keep safe and even comfortable? How could they have come to the station warm, dry, and with moose steaks for all of us?

"Next time, when you drag your skiff up on the bank, stay with it," I told them. "If the weather turns bad—or the tide drains away the water—just turn the skiff over and prop up one side against the wind. Then get under it and wait until the weather changes or the tide comes back in.

"Under your shelter, you can build a small fire if you're careful, and if you've had the foresight to take matches. I never go into the wilderness without this water-proof matchcan around my neck. One of the most important things to do when you're faced with surviving out-of-doors is keep dry.

"With a little fire, you could have roasted moose on the ends of sticks and kept warm at the same time," I said. "A few hours of comfortable, well-fed waiting, and you could have floated home."

Another big disastrous surprise awaited us that morning in Bruins Bay. When I ventured out and looked down the hundred feet to the sea, *Pauline B.* was gone! The high winds that took Bruce's skiff had also grabbed the big boat. Now all five of us were stuck here with no way to escape this hateful place. How would our food hold out? Can anybody anywhere hear our radio calls and send a boat? Will our radio even work?

I spread the alarm and all of us except Einer, still asleep, searched the watery horizon and the edges of the bay for the *Pauline B.*

"Does anybody else see a mast sticking up over there on the bank near the bay head?" I asked. "Look past this side of the rock island and just beyond the pile of driftwood on the bank.''

"Seems impossible," said Skipper Glenn, "but that's it, that's the *Pauline B.* How could it be blown miles up-bay without running into at least one of the whale-size rocks out there?"

"Maybe it did," I suggested. "Maybe you'll find it's smashed a little."

"Not that old steel hull!" said Skipper Glenn. "It was used on the Yukon River for ice-breaking for years. She may be old but *Pauline* could ram the Rock of Gibraltar and never know the difference. Hey, let's get going! Incoming tide will be reaching its high point pretty soon!"

Everybody except me jumped into my skiff and roared off at top speed, bounding on top of the waves.

Good glory be, they're pointing straight into a rock pile by the island! I shouted to the winds. Breathless, I watched. The little skiff resisted fate. It left the water and sailed over the rock pile. I saw the driver lift the outboard to clear. Somebody waved and I breathed again.

I watched them scramble ashore, haul up the skiff, and run across the rocky slope to the boat. It had plowed ashore and climbed maybe 10 feet or so.

In a few minutes, Skipper Glenn appeared on *Pauline's* deck and raised his arms to wave, "All o.k."

Now it was up to the ocean. We needed a very, very high tide to float down today a big boat lifted into place yesterday. It seemed so unlikely that I began a mental sorting and counting of our food and gear, dividing it by five instead of two.

We had a lot to learn about Contact Point and Bruins Bay. Already we'd seen storms drop down, wham, without five minutes of warning. Soon we'd see a miracle tide.

As it flooded in wave after wave, I felt the wind rise and saw it push the water forward, harder and harder. Inches at a time, water swirled up toward the *Pauline B*. Within an hour it was foaming at the propeller.

Skipper Glenn and Mark had climbed a big rock fretting toward the boat deck, and jumped over. Bruce waited and watched from the skiff hauled high up on the bank. Now were the critical moments.

From my beach across the bay, I urged the tide on, fisting the air as the waves rolled forward in their regular rhythm. "Go get 'em!" I yelled.

Splashing and rising, the sea strained to climb the slope one more foot. All at once I saw the *Pauline* move. "Roarrr!" the motor bellowed. Floating and bounding on the rocks as the gears took hold, she slid and crawled to deeper water, then to a channel deeper than her nine-foot draft. Skipper Glenn slowly made his way along the channel winding among the boulders, and anchored at the mouth of the bay.

I enjoy every second of little miracles like that, from the awfulness of the discovery, through the agonizing uncertainty, to the moment the impossible is taking place. Since it happens in the wilderness far more often than it does in townlife, it may account for my choosing to stay even in the world's worst wintering place rather than risk getting stuck in the bright lights for the next six months. It pleased me no end later when I dug out my tide book to read that the tide in Bruins Bay that one day and hour was scheduled by Nature to be one foot higher than the preceding high tide. . .

Bruce came back in the skiff and we ran up to the weather station to fetch Einer. He seemed to be fine, and we motored him to the *Pauline B.*

"We'll wait for you if you want to leave this place," Skipper Glenn called down at me. "This may be your last chance for months. We've had a blast of the weather here, and it's pretty certain that in winter it'll be meaner'n hell. Say the word and we'll wait."

I shook my head. "No, thanks. I'd just as soon stay and take a chance here as I would lug all that stuff down from the cliff and end up stuck in Homer."

"Yeah," added Bruce. "I kinda like this crazy place. It's about the wildest wilderness anywhere. I bet it's even more far-out than the Kamishak."

And so my spunky partner Bruce and I started our winter on Contact Point. He had the excitement of the inexperienced. I had the wariness of one who has seen Bruins Bay in winter piled high with mountains of ice.

"Ptarmigans by the hundreds fluttered about Contact Point sometimes. A few moose roamed the other side of the bay. Otherwise not even mosquitoes came."

5
World's Worst Wintering Place

"In Rory Borealis Land the winter's long and black.
The silence seems a solid thing, shot through with
* wolfish woe. . .*
And man seems but a little mite on that weird-lit
* plateau."*   Robert Service

In the clear sky our first night after waving goodbye
to the *Pauline B.*, we saw the Aurora Borealis waving in
vast fluttering curtains of filmy red across the sky. That
would be the last clear sky and the only Aurora we'd see
for many a month.

Next morning, I looked out the weather station
window at the desolate scene of flat stony clifftop and
endless gray clouds. There was no horizon. Clouds just
dropped off the edge of the high, narrow plateau. Wind
bedeviled the tufts of dry grass and ran in sullen and
contrary noises around our new home. I shivered in the
cold and muttered disagreeable thoughts.

I had talked myself into staying on top of this Contact
Point for the winter, but it still didn't feel right. "Look out
there. This rock sticks far into the ocean and high up in the
winds with hardly a blade of grass to shield us. Winter's

"We had Contact Point all to ourselves—the beach below the cliffs, the ocean, the winds. A sunny day was a big event," says Andy.

breathing down our chimney and we have just enough stovewood to cook a batch of biscuits."

I grabbed my ax and gasoline chainsaw and headed for the rocky path down the cliffside to the beach. "What are you going to do?" Bruce wanted to know.

"This is going to be one miserable place for keeping warm through the winter. We'll need a pile of firewood as big as a mountain." I hoped I looked grim.

Down on the beach, I tackled a tangled mass of driftwood. I sawed and chopped, Bruce toted and stacked. With the Honda and trailer, he pulled loads of stovewood to fill a shed near the weather station.

We worked nearly two weeks, until I was calm and the beach woodpile was 300 feet long and nearly tall as I was. Each day the winds had blown stronger, colder. Rain fell, snow flurried, mountain tops rising behind the bay's end turned white. Tides loped in, tides drained out. I cut on, hour after hour. Bruce stacked and stacked. I'd catch Bruce glancing at me as if he thought the wind had affected my mind, but he kept on piling firewood.

There was plenty to cut on all the beaches. The tidal wave of 1964 had swept into the bay hundreds of trees, logs, and pieces of wrecked buildings that fell here and there into the Gulf of Alaska. I was for chopping up everything.

"If we run out of wood even for a few hours in midwinter, we're dead," I told Bruce. "We'll leave the big stack down here and haul from it to refill the shed up there. Oh you might find the big stack glued together with ice pretty soon, but with all this wind whirling around, I doubt it'll be buried in snow. We'll just have to watch out that we don't get blown off the cliff into the sea."

I wondered what bureaucrat or Army colonel in

Washington looked at a map, put his finger on Contact Point and said, "That's the ideal place for a weather station. Build one there." I then pitied the men who were sent by the Army in the early 1940's to haul materials up the cliff, build the station, the workshops and sheds, the water cistern in solid rock, and then had to stay and use them.

What reports must have come back to Washington from the Contact Point weather station: "Winds high to extremely high, as usual. Warning: Keep clear of Bruins Bay. It has everything wrong with it. Sudden storms. High tide 32 feet. Low tide zero feet. Winds today made a wall of the weather station bulge inward six inches. However, the bolted wood held firm." And so on, getting worse as winter's grip tightened.

Before I learned better, I went out one ordinary windy morning to see if the tide was in. To get a good look at the bay, and to stare at the lonely volcanic cone, St. Augustine, not far away, I came close to the cliff's edge. POOF! a gust of wind hit me suddenly. It pushed me staggering closer to the edge. I had a glimpse all too vivid of the sea far below boiling and churning, beating itself to foam on the rocks. I dropped to my knees and began crawling on all fours, head into the wind, toward the station.

Sudden storms of rain and wind were bad enough. Sudden storms with sleet propelled by hurricane winds were a torture. The ice struck our faces like ten thousand needles to pain, pinch, burn, and freeze the flesh.

Snow at least was softer. But the wind never let our snow collect on the ground. We lost all its advantages for our trapping—travel by snowmobile, a tell-tale surface for tracking animals, a blanket concealing animal food supply. For weeks it snowed and snowed while the winds blew and blew, sometimes from every direction at the same instant. Left alone, the snow probably would have covered over the weather station. But swept, swirled, and whipped by wind, every flake flew off our stone flats to fall into the sea far below.

Occasionally when snow fell in a sensible, untormented fashion, we ran out and stomped it down into a snowmobile track before the wind rose. But for the most part, when we went out on the trapline, we walked, toting on our backs our traps, baits, food and shelter.

But do you think weather was our only opponent? Listen to this. At the joint of the stone finger with the mainland, terrain terrors began. The farther we walked into this foot-of-the-mountain area, the taller and deeper and more wearing the terrors. Rock-strewn fields with mere patches of low alder, then fields of massive boulders led to rows of gullies and rows of barren canyons, rocky walls and heights. Wind beat them all mercilessly. No sensible animal would live there with so little shelter. We saw marmots and Arctic hares but no sign of foxes, wolves, or wolverines. A few moose passed through the bush on the side of Bruins Bay opposite us, but terrain and ice blocked Bruce and me out.

Each storm brought the thermometer down another notch. Ten above. Zero. Ten below. Twenty below. Forty below. Add the chill factor of the violent wind. We spent a lot of time keeping the fire burning high. "Thank God for the woodpile," Bruce muttered one day. "And don't forget thanking us," I added.

Bruins Bay came alive as an ice maker, breaker, and mover. First, the fresh water from the small river at the end of the bay had frozen. Then the tidal saltwater surged beneath that ice sheet, tore it up, shook it mightily, dragged it out, and dropped it at the mouth of the bay. Twice a day the collection grew. Cold gripped harder and the saltwater froze, too. Break, toss, restack went on day and night. Crack, smack, boom! The ice talked as much and loud as the shrieking wind. By Thanksgiving, Bruins Bay looked the way I'd seen it the year before—a huge bathtub piled high with blocks of ice.

It was a violent place anywhere we looked, up at the cliff, down at the bay, across to the mountain, or over the whitecaps to the smoking volcano.

Spasmodically we worked up the gumption to go set short traplines during a few hours' lull. On the worst days, which was about half the time or more, we stayed inside around the clock—so to speak, since we deliberately didn't bring a clock with us.

Our catch all winter was scant: one straggler moose, a fox that showed up expecting to settle again in the weather station, a handful of beavers we chopped through river ice to trap, four giant Arctic hares we shot for food. A number of these big white fellows came down from the high hills above the bay's head, hopped out to the milky saltwater ice and bounded and skipped. Maybe they were nibbling for salt in between their winter Olympic games.

These few skins gave Bruce and me something absorbing and productive to do during our shut-in days. We tanned the hides with salt, water, and sulfuric acid I had brought, then turned them into coat and boot linings, hats with ear covers, and gloves.

Storms merged into one ever-present storm. Going outside for firewood or a bucket of water under two feet of ice in the cistern was an adventure of high danger.

Continuous adventure loses its appeal. Our idea of a great day was not to go out at all. We'd throw another piece of wood into the stove, watch Mr. Larson and a magpie play their game, reread for the eleventh time *The Thousand Mile War* in which somebody else has desperate adventures in the Aleutians.

And listen or talk to our shortwave radio.

We picked up shortwave operators from the native village of Iliamna, from Homer across Cook Inlet, from an occasional bush pilot in his plane. Our first exchange with each of them went like this:

Me: Hello! Hello! Hello you lucky people out there! This is Andy Nault and Bruce, wintering on Contact Point. Answer please! We'd just like to hear another human voice.

Voice: You're WHERE? Nobody but a raving madman would stay on Contact Point through the winter! It's absolutely rotten in summer and everybody hates it even if the fishing's good. But WINTER! You must of been stranded there!

Me: Well, uh, not exactly. We're carrying out a research project to see if anybody can survive without a generator on Contact Point. The answer is I'm alive enough to ask for a plane. We'd like a ride the first decent day that shows up. . .

The rest of our conversations covered wind and snow details, and news about planes that had started out to get us and were turned back by storms.

To me, the most important thing we did that winter was lend a hand to Mr. Larson and watch him make himself well.

I'd first noticed he had something wrong with him a

couple of weeks before we left Kodiak. In the yard one day, another dog dared put his foot over the line, and Mr. Larson got up to go after him.

But he didn't jump up quick as usual. He was slow and awkward and as he tried to run, I saw his hind legs weren't tracking. They were just flopping around. What had happened?

As the days went on, he became much more out of control. Finally he couldn't stand without falling over. Then he just stayed lying down, not able to lift his head. It looked like the end when he began having convulsions, shivering and shaking.

"No, it's not rabies," the vet said. "Don't know what it is. Maybe poisoning from eating dead shellfish. If it is, there's no cure I know of. Leave him here in the kennel. I'll watch after him."

I said, no, I'd rather not leave him. I thought to myself he'd get better maybe if I looked after him, spoon feeding him with mush and milk. I'd heard about how eating dead shellfish would paralyze, then kill a body, but I'd never seen a case.

Mr. Larson lay on a blanket and I tended him like a child who was a member of my family. Well, he *was* my family. We'd lived together, just the two of us, nearly six years. I'd had him and trained him since he was six weeks old. He was half Malamute, and with his wolf-face, he looked right out of a Jack London novel.

For a week, I cooked oatmeal with milk to feed him. I'd hold up his head and pour in a tablespoonful, rubbing his throat to make it go down. He stayed alive. But he didn't seem to hear me or notice me and he was still not able even to lift his head.

Then it was time to leave for Kamishak. I couldn't leave Mr. Larson alone to die. We carried him to the hold of the boat. I hate to think how he fared in the awesome storm that drove us to Contact Point.

I took him in a blanket up the cliff trail to the weather station. I left him under a small shed which stood on short pilings nearby. I kept feeding him, watering him, and cleaning him.

He just lay there. The only encouragement I got was a feeble "Rouf" a couple of times when I stroked him. He was as skinny as a hatrack.

"How long you going to keep this up?" Bruce asked after a month. "As long as Mr. Larson is still breathing when I walk over to feed him," I said. I clenched my teeth each time I came close to the shed, half-expecting to find Mr. Larson cold and stiff.

Soon afterwards, we had our hardest cold snap. High winds with gusts to 90 knots blew in cold of ten degrees. Far into the night when the wind had passed but left with us the worst of its piercing cold, I was awakened by a weak "Rouf, rouf" outside the door.

Mr. Larson? Can't be. He's paralyzed. Can't lift his head, much less drag across 100 yards from his shed to here.

"Rouf." I turned up the lantern and opened the door. Mr. Larson was lying against it. I have never understood how he dragged himself inch by inch so far. But it was do that or freeze to death.

"You've got one helluva will to live," I said to him. I remembered the days when I was so weak I had to lie on the beach to skin the seal, and how I made myself keep at it, knowing that was the only way to succeed in staying alive. I made it, maybe Larson could, too. "Mr. Larson," I said, "you're tougher than I was. There's a good chance you'll come through. Keep working."

I picked him up and brought him close to the stove. I fed him some warm milk, wrapped him in an old sack, and covered him with a blanket.

In daylight, I cleaned and examined him carefully. The fact that he had managed to move when he was faced with freezing meant the nerves and muscles were not impaired. Better still, he was looking at me, watching with some interest.

I picked him up with my arms around his belly and stood him on his feet. He toppled over when I took my arms away. His legs couldn't hold him up.

How could he regain use of his legs? All day I thought about every ailing animal I had ever known, and how they got back on their feet. I was brought up around horses and cattle and dogs, and had seen just about everything that could go wrong with them.

What Mr. Larson needed, it seemed to me, was to use his muscles. Lying down so long was bound to cut off his blood circulation. He might be more stiff and weak than paralyzed now.

"If I could just get him up and moving. . ." How?

In Montana 50 years ago, we put our horses out on the prairie all winter to pasture. In those days, anybody's horses could roam far and wide to eat whatever grass they could find. The idea of stabling and feeding them hay, fodder, or grain all winter was out of the question. We could hardly pay for food for ourselves. Whatever meat we had we hunted or trapped.

Come spring, the horses were rounded up and brought home. Once in a while, we'd find one that couldn't walk.

He'd gotten too weak from the harsh winter and lack of food. For him, we'd rig up a large tripod of long heavy poles, fix a rope to hang down in the center, and improvise a rope sling at the lower end of it. The sling went loosely around the horse's middle. That way, he could stand up with support and have enough rope slack to move a few steps in all directions.

A week of eating hay and grain and exercising his weak legs while safe in the sling did the job. The horse was strong enough to go free.

I made a rope and blanket sling for Mr. Larson. I threw the rope end over one of the exposed horizontal rafters in our main room, ran the blanket under Mr. Larson's belly, secured it to the rope ends, and stepped back.

"Now Mr. Larson," I said to him, "you've got to make those legs move. They're all right. They just need some walking and running. So you walk and run. Pretty soon you'll be chasing bears and rabbits again." He answered, "Rouf," and I knew he understood every word.

He tried to walk but his front paws turned under while his back end dragged along motionless. "Hey Larson!" He keeps his eyes on me when I talk to him. It's amazing that he can't talk he's so good at understanding. "Larson, straighten out your toes. They're curling under. Straighten them before you try to take a step."

He tried. He lifted a paw and began wiggling his toes, pushing them to straighten, placing them flat on the floor. Then the other paw. With every step he first had to get his toes set just right.

Mr. Larson in the sling took ten days to learn to walk again with his front paws. Now he was mobile even if his back end still dragged. Now he could stand in the sling to eat and was strong enough to chew meat and swallow it. Almost daily his returning strength was visible.

One day I picked up a half-frozen, starving magpie by the cistern and brought it home. In our warm room, the bird quickly came to, squawked, drank and ate, flapped his wings and flew up to a rafter. Mr. Larson perked up. He began dancing back and forth on his front legs, dragging his back legs. He's a hunting dog and he wanted to catch that magpie. He wanted to run after the bird but the rope slack didn't let him go far and his numb back legs made him much too slow.

The magpie taunted him, fluttering closer to him, and flapping away. He perched on a box well out of reach and cackled at Larson. From then on, Mr. Larson was eager to get up in the morning and get into the sling. A new light came into his eyes. He began to talk more and louder, "Rouf, rouf!"

Six weeks of the magpie game and I saw Mr. Larson's back legs taking hold and moving.

Another six weeks and the magpie fluttered past and laughed at him for the last time. Larson leaped, all four legs in action. Bird in his mouth, his head shaking vigorously, Mr. Larson looked at me in triumph.

In summer a few months later, he was chasing bear cubs across the cliff top and running down the hillside from their angry Mama. He was almost his old self again.

We two survivors were close before, but now he liked to nuzzle me, lie down close to my feet. He wanted to be with me whether I was cooking or going out to set traps or riding a Honda. What he was saying to me didn't need words.

Looking out our window, we saw the same sky of

roiling gray clouds day after day, varied only by blowing snow and flocks of ptarmigans. One calm sunny day appeared between November and April. It would have been memorable for that alone. It became more memorable as the day the bear knocked at our door.

Mr. Larson and I went out at 9 o'clock into a sky world that having thrown off most of its cover of clouds seemed vastly expanded. Better yet, even without the sun, it was all in color, pale blue between puffs of clouds. The wind was dancing rather than battering and was barely freezing. A miracle January day.

Mr. Larson ran close to the drop-off, looking down at the ice in the bay, the white-capped waves rolling off the rim of the sea. The light intensified in the east. The sun's blazing edge cut through the horizon. "Rouf, rouf, rouf!" Larson, excited, called to me. He ran a few steps toward me, barked, ran back toward the sun, barked, his tail standing in a high curl. "Rouf, rouf!" I answered. Seeing the sun after a long time stirs dogs as well as men.

"Do we dare go hunting for some fresh meat?" Bruce asked at breakfast.

"Maybe we might even dare to lug a few traps across the canyons and over the way," I said. "If we could just know that tomorrow would be half as decent as today. . ."

We never had to make a decision about that. Just then, "Look Andy! A bear!" Bruce shouted, pointing out the front window.

Sure enough, about 150 feet from the station strolled a medium-size brown bear. Sniffing the breeze, he was heading for our fortress.

"This warm sunny day waked him up. He probably thought spring had come. He's pretty hungry after a three-month fast," I said. Bruce was already getting the rifles.

If Mr. Larson doesn't first smell a bear nearby, when he hears the word "bear," he goes stiff with anger and lets loose gutteral growls and barks. They roll out loud and violent, full of throat-tearing profanity.

The bear must have heard. He stopped and listened for a moment, then came on. "He probably thinks it's foxes barking," I said. "A pair of foxes would make him a real nice breakfast."

Bruce raised one window sash a couple of inches and I raised another. We put our rifle barrels through the openings and kneeled to sight. Mr. Larson stood behind me barking and growling, talking about grabbing his life-long enemy by the rump, by the back leg, by the tail.

We waited until the bear put a foot on the doorstep, one move short of knocking at our door. Bruce and I pulled our triggers at the same second. Mr. Larson barked approval and satisfaction.

"Since our fresh meat walked itself right up to our door, we don't need to go hunting," I said. "And since it's a lot better to skin the bear out today instead of tomorrow, we won't have time to go lugging traps across the canyons. Probably something is letting us know we've got no business leaving our shelter today or tomorrow. So sharpen our long-blade knives, Bruce, and we'll start cutting."

Bruce had never skinned a bear before. Step by step he did what I told him and you would have thought at the end that he'd skinned as many as Davy Crockett. When I work on bears, beavers, and badgers, I cut the skin down the stomach and take off the hide so it lies open and flat. All other animals I "case skin" —cut from hind leg footpads to vent, then pull the skin back over the animal's head.

My instructions to Bruce started out with "Make a straightline cut from the bear's chin clear down to the vent. From that cut, make a cut straight out along each leg to the footpads." That takes a beginner about a half-hour, for bearskin is a good quarter-inch thick.

"Since we won't be taking much else home when we go, let's take this bear skin," I said to Bruce. "In that case, we'll keep the paws and footpads." I showed him how to cut around the edge of the footpad, except for the few inches attached to the toes, then how to slice under the leathery sole.

"Now we start cutting loose the skin from the legs and body," I said, and began demonstrating how to do it. "You start at the paw. Slip the knife blade under the skin, then slide the cutting edge through the fat layer. It's practically bloodless. Go all the full length—from paw to belly to chin, running your knife underneath. Lift up the skin, slide the knife under the whole length again."

By the time we had done that several times, the legs and belly skin had been freed. Then the back was easy.

The head is not so easy. I worked smaller knives under the skin around the eyes and muzzle and ears. Now with the face loose, the whole skin is apart from the carcass. "We'll have to take the head off and clean it inside and out—a nasty job the State people require so we can take it, with the fur, into an office for tagging," I reminded Bruce.

A fresh bear skin with the fat still on it will weigh about 150 pounds. Bruce and I dragged this one inside the building and laid it fur side down for the next big job. "Getting every bit of the fat and flesh off right away is an absolute must," I told Bruce. "Any scrap we miss will keep the skin underneath it from taking the salt. It will just rot, a miserable situation to have in your house."

I invented my own skin scraper having never seen a readymade one to suit me. I take a piece of iron or steel a quarter-inch thick, an inch wide, and 18 inches long. With the help of a vise, I bend up the ends of the strip, bring those ends together and bind them round and round with cord. That gives me a handle on a metal circle about as big around as a teacup.

I grind down the outer bottom edge of the circle until it's sharp. Most people draw the blade toward them when they scrape. I push it away from me. Using my tool this way, I seldom cut the skin or dig holes in it. I can scrape a fox skin in about 15 minutes.

It took two hours to scrape the bear skin. But we went over it three times. We made a collection of 60 pounds of bear fat. The skin was smooth and clean. We salted it heavily, rolled it up, and put it in our natural deep freeze, the back room.

That night at dinner, Bruce, Mr. Larson, and I settled down to eating bear meat, with about 500 pounds of it left to feed us during the next few months. Roasts, steaks, stew meat, bear and beans, stuffed bear heart, barbequed ribs. . .

Bear meat tastes much like fresh pork and except for old bear it's surprisingly tender. Some of the best fat we fed to Mr. Larson. The rest we cooked to render the grease. There's none better. "In Davy Crockett's day, people paid a good price for 'bar grease,' and not just for making delicious biscuits," I told Bruce. He already knew that folks back then used it to rub on their joints for rheumatism and lumbago, on their skin for cuts, boils, anything. It was good for whatever ails you so they swallowed it like medicine too.

From the bear's intestines we stripped pound after pound of fat. To have so much fat left in January, this bear must have had a six-inch layer when he crawled into his sleeping hole in early November.

A bear's large intestine is a curiosity and a wonder. Like all his other inside machinery, the heart particularly, a bear has a gut bigger in proportion to his body than other animals have to theirs. That's saying a lot since bears are so monstrous in size. I wanted to clean up this bear's bigger gut, cut it open and sew the strips into a waterproof slipover jacket like an Al-e-ut one I'd seen in Kodiak's Baranov Museum. Gut is Nature's best waterproof material. It looks like clear plastic and it's tougher.

But I didn't know how to preserve and sew them, so Bruce missed the spectacle of watching me wrestle with several feet of huge intestines. The Al-e-uts were wearing bear gut pullovers when the Russians came to the Aleutian Islands for sea otter furs back in the 1700's. When an Al-e-ut slipped into the seat-hole of his kayak, he draped the bear gut jacket bottom over the outside rim of the hole and tied it down. No matter how rough the sea or wet the weather, the man would stay dry and his kayak would take in no water.

The day the bear walked up our steps was the last sun and calm we saw for a spell. We went back to looking out the windows at the wind, visible as white sheets of feathery flakes that flapped and flew wildly across the stone top of barren Contact Point.

Six weeks later, we saw the first signs of spring's melting warmth. Sometimes it rained instead of snowing or sleeting. We heard great booms and rumbles and cracks in the bay as the ice jumble broke up. Piece by piece the ice floated out on the tides like baby icebergs.

One calm day marked by sudden, brief stabs of sunlight through billowy clouds, I looked out over the sea from a cliffside height and saw whitecaps. How could there be whitecaps, I wondered, when the wind is so calm? I looked again, and saw that the whitecaps were like a wide streak of turbulence in an otherwise smooth dark ocean. More curious, the streak was coming slowly toward me, coming into our bay!

Then I saw bulky white shapes bobbing in the water. "Belugas!" I shouted to Bruce. He came running.

Bruce and I and Mr. Larson found a cliffside crevice to settle into and spent an hour counting white whales. I stopped at 200. Bruce went on to 300 before he lost track. We guessed the pack was moving into the bay behind a school of fish. The whales soon left on the turning tide. I still have a sharp picture in my mind of that amazing streak of whitecaps, and I expect my own memory is as close as I'll come to seeing such a sight again.

Arrowhead formations of geese, honking steadily and pointing north, began to fly over the landmark wall of stone we lived on. And one day, peregrine falcons zoomed in. They swoop and dive and glide—and screech. It's not exactly a pretty voice, but it added flashes of drama to the solitude. So did a sort of dive bomber sound they make when they power dive a thousand feet at 90 miles an hour. I wouldn't mind living that kind of exciting daily life, springing off into space, soaring and diving, the whole scene spread out beneath my eyes.

The change of season brought us wings to fly away.

Pilot Bill DeCreeft in Homer had been talking to us for two weeks about how bad weather jumped up each time he started out to get us. On the fifteenth day he at last set down on the flats behind our station. "Come on!" I shouted to Bruce and Mr. Larson. "Leave everything! There's a storm about to hit!"

Bill barely got the plane in the sky when WHOOSH! the wind began mauling us. Downdrafts nearly broke us in two when the plane hit bottom, BAM! Shudders and groans made me think the wings were tearing off. Mr. Larson couldn't bear to watch, got out of my lap and crawled under the seat.

It was the roughest plane ride of my life, but I never stopped smiling. We were leaving far behind the worst place in the world to spend a winter. When I crawled out of the plane in Homer, my knees wanted to bend all the time, my calves were trembling. We made it to the hangar. The first man to greet us said, "Are you the crazies who've been all winter on Contact Point?"

"Well now," I answered, "it ain't polite to leave a place before finishing off the woodpile."

Mr. Larson, Malamute-Norwegian Elkhound, insisted on living despite being paralyzed by usually fatal marine poisoning. He probably ate a dead crab that washed up on the beach. In a sling that Andy rigged at Contact Point, Mr. Larson practiced walking, and in three months regained the use of his legs. "He was a fighter in every way," says Andy. "A dog fight and an otter fight gave him that split ear."

6

Beachcomber Bears

> "*The (brown) bear was verry large and a turrible looking animal, which we found verry hard to kill. . . a furious and formidable animal, and will frequently pursue the hunter. . ."*   Lewis and Clark, 1805

> "*(Grizzlies in pursuit) were flashing firey passion, their pearly teeth glittering with eagerness to mangle (my) flesh.*"   Kit Carson, 1835

Should I, must I give up on the Kamishak?

"No," I said to Bruce in June after our escape from Contact Point. "I can't give up. All my gear—snowmachine, skiff, everything—is still at Contact Point. Once we're there to get it, we might as well go on to the Kamishak. It's only 25 miles farther down Kamishak Bay."

What would try to stop me this time?

For a while, it looked as if it would be lack of a barge.

Expecting to radio the barges fishing in waters off Contact Point and hitch a cheap ride with one going down the bay past the Kamishak River mouth, we flew to our miserable clifftop. Bruce and I were relieved to find our gear exactly as we'd left it in the weather station. Mr. Larson and Jake, Bruce's big black Labrador retriever, were happy to run wild.

Contact Point behaved like its usual fun-loving self,

*Bears by the dozen dug clams, fished, and
fought within 100 yards of Andy's camp on
a beach of Kamishak Bay. "They tended
their business, we tended ours," Andy says.
But one day, Andy bumped into a bear—
and came within five seconds of leaving the
story for the bear to tell.*

blowing, blowing, rain flying, clouds roiling. But it wasn't stabbing cold with snow and sleet in the gale.

We called out to everybody on the radio dial, begging for our short ride to the Kamishak. Nobody was even thinking about going that way.

Bill DeCreeft finally called us and said he'd found a barge in Homer that would be going—in a month!

Well, what'll we do for entertainment while we wait, Bruce and I asked each other. It wasn't the season for us to do anything but comb the Bruins Bay beaches.

We ambled up and down miles of beach, poking into piles of driftwood and debris. "Hey look, Andy!" Bruce called one day. "Here's a big bundle of plywood that looks pretty good. I think it's a pre-fab cabin."

Now that's the kind of luck we need, I said. I'd been wondering how we'd fare in a tent in bear country while we spent a month or so building a log cabin. Thanks, Old Neptune, for anticipating and solving our big problem.

"Hey Bruce!" I called another day. "Here's a dory, a big Cook Inlet dory! It looks pretty good!"

That was beyond luck, I thought. That was a sign from heaven. The dory was old, it was battered, but it floated and it was big. "If that bargeman forgets all about us, we can pile our machines and skiff and the whole nine yards into this hefty old tub and ferry them to the Kamishak ourselves," I told Bruce. It would be a hard job crossing open sea, but we'd pick our day and we'd do it. Barge or dory, we get to Kamishak this year.

There were other things on the beaches, too—an overstuffed chair and broken lawnmower, for example. Where had all this stuff come from? We found out from the radio. A barge had turned over in Cook Inlet some time before. Currents and tides sweep the sea's debris to the nearest shore in their path—our beaches in this case.

"And maybe other beaches nearby," I suggested. "Let's take a little trip."

With that decision, I almost cancelled my getting to the Kamishak or anywhere else, ever.

We set out in the skiff along the coast of Kamishak Bay. Before long, we spotted a mile of beach strewn with large pieces of junk and big tangles of lumber. Here was the rest of the unlucky barge's load—battered furniture, bedsprings, refrigerators, bathtubs, and the like, and a jumble of boards.

Elated, we began pulling out boards we could use. "A stack of luck here!" I said. "We won't need to spend a month building a little log cabin on the Kamishak. We can put up a house. Let's bring a tent and grub and do the rest of our waiting for the barge down here."

In a few days we were all set up on the beach by the big junk pile, busy untangling boards and two-by-fours, and stacking them neatly.

Then we started seeing the bears.

First it was a bear walking at sunset along the crest of a hill above the 100-foot cliffs that lined the beach. Since he was way up there and I was way down on the beach, it was a pretty picture and I brought out my camera.

Next it was a Mama Bear and her three tiny cubs walking along another hill crest. Mr. Larson saw them before we did.

Barking and growling, he tore up a shaleslide in the cliff near the Mama Bear and rushed toward her. She jumped up and, bellowing and hissing, galloped to meet him. From our distance, it looked like a locomotive charging a mouse.

Larson had sense enough to wheel quickly and run down the shaleslide.

That was that, Mama Bear figured and hurried back to her cubs.

Before she had time to give each one a nuzzle, a silent Larson was snapping at her heels and biting at a cub. In one big arm sweep, Mama Bear gathered the three cubs to her, sat down to hold them in her lap, and reached out with teeth and claws to Larson.

I and Bruce, hanging on to Jake's collar, watched this dangerous drama. "She's going to break Larson in two if he won't get out of there and leave those cubs alone," I said. "I doubt he will—he loves to go after little bears—and I doubt I'll have a whole dog many more minutes."

I saw the bear make a big roaring lunge at Larson. I heard Larson shriek. "It's all over," I thought with a clench of my teeth and a vacant feeling in my stomach.

Seconds later, Larson appeared, almost tumbling down the shaleslide, then running to our camp.

When I got ahold of him, he was shaking with excitement. I gave him a short lecture. "Stay away from little bears! A mama bear will tear you to pieces to protect her babies. Stay away from a bear's feed. Any bear will tear you to pieces to protect his feed. For babies and feed, bears will fight you to the death. Remember that!" Then I tied Larson to some junk near me.

As days went past, we saw that this beach was the bears' Coney Island. But since they didn't seem interested in us or what we were doing, we kept our dogs tied, kept watch from the corners of our eyes, and went on stacking boards.

Even when we saw as many as a dozen bears as close to

us as a hundred yards, we didn't stop our work. They seemed absorbed in digging the wet sand for clams and bidarkas—their shells are curved like Al-e-ut boats—rooting seaweed, grabbing fish. They hardly looked our way. Many days we saw them playing, romping very friendly with each other. Some days, they switched in seconds from romping or lazy lolling about to vicious battling. Their bellowing and screaming echoed in the hills.

Still, they didn't bother us and after a while they were just part of the scenery. Bugs worried us worse than bears.

One calm sunny day after two weeks or more, Bruce and I decided to take a walk along the top of the cliff towering over the beach. We had the idea that we could look down at the long junk mound and see better what was inside the jumble. We might even see something useful or valuable, we thought. We climbed an easy gully to the top of the barren ridge.

We left Mr. Larson tied up, not daring to let such an over-ambitious dog run loose in bear country. Bruce's Jake trotted along with us, snuffling in holes and digging.

After a mile or so of walking and looking hard at the junk pile, we concluded there was nothing worth struggling to haul out. "If we can get our load of lumber to the Kamishak," I said, "the bears are welcome to keep the rest of this mess."

When we came to a gully and shaleslide leading to the beach, we decided to go down and make our walk back by the ocean edge. Bruce went first, half-sliding on the shale, balancing himself with his rifle. The gully was steeper and had more loose shale than we'd thought.

I started but lingered, looking over the beautiful seascape. A deep blue sea behaving calmly and sensibly has such a regular, rhythmic movement, it's almost hypnotic. I stood there letting the waves one by one erase all thought. In my seaswept daze, I heard Bruce's voice. What was he saying?

"HEY ANDY! BEAR TRACKS ON THE BEACH! FRESH ONES! HEY ANDY!"

Almost in the same moment I heard Jake somewhere on the cliff barking, growling, very excited. I looked back to see exactly where he was. What could he be barking at— the bear tracks were on the beach, not the ridge.

I glimpsed him running on a nearby slope. Close behind him was a galloping bear. Jake disappeared. The bear kept on—and turned sharply toward me and the gully.

"The bear's up here!" I hollered to Bruce and ran as hard as I could slip and slide toward the bottom of the gully. I knew it ended on a ledge and that from the ledge it was an 8-foot drop to the rocky beach.

Right behind me I heard the bear breaking down the side of the shaleslide as he clambered over, skidding along the 75 feet of gully. I was about 15 feet ahead of him when I reached the ledge. Sharp inhaled hisses—thoooo-oop— sounded at my heels. Five seconds to live unless I could jump off and vanish from the bear's sight. I jumped.

"Shoot, Bruce, shoot!" I yelled. "He's gonna jump!"

I looked up and saw the bear's face leaning over the side of the ledge, his eyes peering around for me. I saw Bruce on the same ledge just 30 feet from the bear.

"BRUCE! SHOOT!"

His rifle cracked. I straightened, whirled around, aimed, fired. The bear, in a crouch ready to jump off the ledge, slumped, looking very surprised.

Then he began to get up! I shot. Bruce shot. We both

shot again. When you're trying to kill a bear, you'd better keep on shooting until he's not even twitching.

The bear lay still, his head and paws hanging over the edge of the ledge. I could have reached up and shaken his long sharp claws.

Suddenly feeling very shaky, I sat down on a log to get myself together. Bruce jumped down. "Oh my lord that was close," he said.

When we walked along the beach toward our camp, we discovered the reason for the bear's attack. He thought we were on our way to take his feed, a cache of bear meat. It didn't take any looking to find it. The stink only a bear can appreciate was rolling out of a mound of sand, rocks, logs, and sticks.

Jake was waiting for us at the tent. He'd run home along the ridge. No doubt he'd told Mr. Larson all about what happened.

Next morning, I said, "I'd like to leave here, quick, before something else happens. I'd hate for it to be on my tombstone that I never got to the Kamishak because of ice, wind, and a bear."

By the glimmer of dawn, three in the morning, we were in the skiff with the dogs and folded tent, pushing off for Contact Point. There I would be content to stay alive and wait without any thrills until the bargeman came. At least no gnat or no-see'um, or Alaskan mosquito big as an eagle will tolerate the blowy frigid weather at the Point.

The first week of August, we chugged on the barge out of Bruins Bay. In passing, I cast a glance and shrug at the salvage beach and at the lumber we'd stacked so nicely.

Shrug turned into my fiercest growl for the tribe of bears digging and playing by the surf.

7

Kamishak Welcome: Bugs and Bears

"Well, stranger, mosquitoes are Nature, and I never find fault with Nature. If they are large, (the state) is large, her varmints are large, her trees are large, her rivers are large, and a small mosquito would be of no use."   Davy Crockett, 1835

Kamishak River at last!

Only fish got in our way as the barge motored on the back of the salty tide upstream. Wide, dark blue river, brush-covered flatlands, mountains ahead and on both sides—and there on the left, the south bank, my long strip of cottonwoods stretching to the foothills. I was clapping my hands and rubbing my palms together, laughing and telling anybody who'd listen about the beaver lodges I'd seen when I looked at the Kamishak from the plane.

For a mile, we rode with salmon swimming right and left out of our way. I was humming to myself and pushing boxes close to the barge edge when we nosed up toward the riverbank.

Pretty country, pretty country, I hummed. The bugs must have heard me. The instant we touched land, the Kamishak reception committee of ten million flying,

*Big and little bears jump in, wade in, slap
their paws into the water to catch salmon
in the rivers of Kamishak Bay. Well-
fed and unmolested, 1000 or so grow into
the world's largest brown bear, called
grizzlies when they live inland. Some are
12 feet tall when standing, and weigh 1400
pounds. Probably no other place has such
a concentration of brown bears, about
three to every square mile.*

biting bugs circled each one of us. Half of the swarm were no-see'ums. They seem to know where every hole in the human head is and to have an intense urge to get inside and look around. Another quarter of the flock were white socks, vicious white-footed gnats with teeth like sharks. They kamikaze into the skin at the edge of your cap and fight to the death to crawl underneath it, chewing as they go. The rest of the mob, except for a few hundred thumb-sized deerflies equipped with dagger-snouts, was a fleet of Alaska's infamous mosquitoes. They're the bombers that come with sirens, push through the fighter gnats, and do the big-welt job.

We were pulling up to a low and sandy spot in the river bank where no breeze swept in. Scratching, slapping, swatting, spitting out no-see'ums, we carried all our boxes ashore. But I was still smiling behind my bug-shooing arms when the barge pulled away from our long-sought wilderness shore. We'd succeeded after three put-downs! We were standing under the cottonwood trees on the Kamishak! As soon as the barge went out of sight, we'd be alone in the wilderness a hundred miles or more from our nearest neighbor.

"Hey Andy!" One of the bargemen was shouting from down the river. "Radio says a big blow and rainstorm is coming in here tonight!"

So our first night in Kamishak would be spent wide awake guarding our gear from running water, blowing water, water splashing like a waterfall on our flimsy roof.

Our shelter was the plywood pre-fab cabin we beachcombed at Contact Point. Fighting bugs for the first hour, Bruce and I began putting the pieces together around our riverside heap of gear and grub. We had no time to find a permanent spot, move the stuff, and put up the pre-fab before the storm struck.

The rising wind, blowing in a curtain of black clouds across the sky, shooed away the bugs during the second hour we worked. We fastened on the plywood roof and visqueen mere minutes before sheets of rain beat it like sticks on a drumhead.

We sat and sprawled on our boxes for 18 hours, listening to the carrying on of the wind, rain, and heavens. The storm jabbed the earth with crackling electrical prods, smashed the black clouds together with cabin-shaking booms, slapped the trees and tore their leaves, hosed the mountains, riverbanks, and our cabin full blast. A tumultuous, exciting welcome, if overdone.

When the storm moved on, we were groggy and stiff but dry, and happy to come out into the wide open air, washed clean of bugs.

About 300 feet into the cottonwoods, we found a spot higher by maybe three inches than the rest of the terrain. We picked a space between two trees and cut down the alder brush. There we toted the knocked apart pieces of our instant cabin and put them together again. All the next day we moved our pile of gear and grub into this pre-fab.

On the second day after the monster rain had drowned our bug welcoming committee, the billion eggs they left behind hatched. Gnats, no-see'ums, and mosquitoes seem to enter the world fully grown, at least in the Kamishak. They rose in clouds humming with hunger. Their taste buds had already developed a preference for furless tender skin, just like ours.

"I thought you said that this place had the greatest concentration of *bears* in the world," Bruce said early that morning. He'd gone out five minutes and run back with arms waving, hands beating his face and neck. His cheeks, forehead, and neck were welted and red. I lifted drowned no-see'ums out of his eyes while he squirmed with desire to scratch his pinching itches.

"They went after the bug repellent on my face like bees to sugar water," he mumbled. "Never saw anything like it. Are we going to be stuck until cold weather in this cluttered little cabin because of *bugs?*"

"No," I said, "we're going to dig out our portable cages and put them on."

Beekeepers are about the only folks who wear head and neck covers like the ones we wore. We put on a hat fitted with a wire frame already draped with a waist-long vest of fine-mesh mosquito netting. Strings and drawstrings closed it tight at the sides and bottom.

Before leaving the well-sprayed air of the cabin, we drew on gloves and tied cords around our pants legs at the ankles. Every inch of skin had to be completely covered and every opening shut tight.

"This netting is so thick, Andy, I can hardly see out," Bruce said. "Everything looks like a ghost of itself."

"Let me tell you a story," I answered. "Some years ago, I bought netting easy to see through but too coarse to keep out the no-see'ums and white socks. Those little devils worked themselves through the weave holes after a bit. The no-see'ums crawled into my eyes, nose, ears, and mouth. The white socks bit their way under my hat band, which was bad enough. Then they got ahold of my bald spot and chewed it raw.

"I couldn't snatch off the net. A million mosquitoes, gnats, no-see'ums, and deerflies—those big, singing blood suckers—would get me. People have died from bug attacks. Went mad first.

"I couldn't risk that, and I couldn't risk dropping my corner of a load and hurting somebody else in order to run to shelter. I couldn't scratch, slap, or rub my head. I could only wriggle my head skin, spit out the no-see'ums, and work my eyelids. Now you don't ever want to be caught in such a fix. I was nearly crazy with itching and swelling, tense as an anchor cable in storm by the time I could run to a safe place, throw off the net, and murder the scalpers."

After hearing this story, Bruce's vision improved so much, you'd've thought the net holes were big as dimes.

You might imagine that a rainy day of heavy downpours would have depressed us, but no, we got up laughing and joking. No bugs! No log chopping! We go hunting and fishing! Without heavy rains about two days a week, we'd have eaten poorly in buggy August and part of September. Wearing a net in the woods and brush could easily end in disaster and torture. Suppose you're two miles or so—an hour's walk—from the cabin and a wayward branch brushes your head cover or tears the netting. . . And who can sight a rifle or shotgun through a thick veil?

In the rain, our heads and hands free, we never had to hunt more than a couple of hours to bring home a bag of ducks. We cooked them in pairs in a big Dutch oven.

Thousands of ducks and geese nest in Kamishak in summer on beaver ponds, riverbanks, and backwaters. It's here that many pintails, redheads, and golden eyes organize their clans into V formations and in October begin the 5,000-mile flight south. Bruce and I would bring down a half dozen ducks and in two days or less, we'd have eaten them all. Each of us could put down a whole roasted duck and its bread stuffing at one sitting.

Even in the rain, the land was alive with the voices of birds—chirping chickadees, cawing crows, chattering magpies and raucous ravens, Morse code-tapping woodpeckers, squawking loons. Noisiest of all, the red-throated loons flew up and down the river most all day and half the night. Squawk! Squawk! Squawk!

Such coarse, vulgar voices they had, like a hundred fingernails scraping across slate, they got on our nerves and had us shouting back insult for insult. One day a couple of dozen congregated on a tiny river island upstream from our landing. They squawked so loud and so long, they had my brain rattling 400 feet away.

I took my revenge by shooting one for the pot. I was planning to make a mulligan with ptarmigan, carrots, and cabbage, but why not loon, carrots, and cabbage? I boiled my loon the same way I'd have boiled the ptarmigan, but it didn't behave the same way. Instead of stretching out and softening up, the loon rolled into a rubbery ball. Well, it just needs more cooking, I thought, and took the vegetables out of the pot.

Time in the pot made no change in the rubbery loon ball. I cooked it all day, using stick after stick of firewood. At breakfasttime next day, I lit up under it again, and kept the fire going another day. No change. In the meantime, we ate the vegetables. But surely a third day of cooking would break the flesh down into something chewable, I thought, and tried once more. It only shrank. I decided it wasn't really flesh. It looked like an outsize golf ball.

I threw it to the dogs. They sniffed, looked at each other, and walked off.

If anybody knows the secret of cooking a loon tender,

I'd like to have the recipe. Please include flavor improvements or cover-ups. The soup of my loon tasted like swamp mud.

Other noises in the wilderness made us stop dragging cottonwood logs to our cabin site for a minute to listen. Some noises we could identify easily, like a moose or a bear coming down a trail and making sticks break, leaves crackle. Roaring-bull noises were two bears fighting. "Arctic hare—something's grabbed him," I said when a drawn-out, hoarse scream startled Bruce. Squirrels chattered and weasels swore in the brush.

When we'd hear loud blowing, swissh! we'd drop our axes and saws and hurry to the riverbank to see the passing parade of white whales. They came swimming with the tide for more than two miles upstream, until the river became too shallow for them. That was a half-mile or so beyond our landing and water hole.

Belugas hump their snowwhite backs and shove forward to move through the water. Usually they swam in threes, a little one, a middle-sized one, and a big one about 14 feet long. A family? They stayed pretty much together. Each was busy swallowing fish running for their lives before them—salmon, Dolly Varden trout, bullheads, spine-headed Irish lords, cod. For about an hour, we would watch the belugas parade upstream. They'd start back again when the tide began to turn.

Once we saw a bear swimming in deep water behind the whales. Look, we said, a spectacle coming up! Who before us has seen a whale and a bear in a fight? But the bear had better sense than to attack a sea creature with 3,000 pounds of hitting power and a mouthful of sharp teeth. Bruin only wanted some of the fish escaping from the whales. I saw him grab a big salmon in his teeth and turn to land, the fish wildly slapping the water with its tail.

Some days we'd time our water-dipping trip for the hour just before the tide came in and brought the whale show. We had to fill our water cans before salt water reached our dipping place. Insulated by our nets from the bugs, escorted by Mr. Larson and Jake well rubbed in insect repellent, we drove the Honda and trailer with water cans to the river bank.

We made a two-man bucket brigade, one leaning to scoop the water and lift it to the other who poured it into the five gallon cans. Even in the warmest weather of August, the water coming from snow melting on the high mountains was cold enough to make our teeth ache.

"It's bound to be pure," I assured Bruce, "no matter how many beavers, fish, otters, and bears have jumped around in it. I don't believe a germ can live in such cold. I've drunk half-frozen water out of a moose's hoofprint and never felt the worse for it." Scientific fact or innocent faith, we never had a moment's ailment.

While we were down at the river watching the whales, Bruce and I checked far along the bank to collect anything useful that had washed up in the tides. We found driftwood and lumber mostly, including a 20-foot ladder. We nailed it to a cottonwood tree by the cabin for the first stage of a 40-foot climb to a small platform we installed. Standing on it, we could see the river mouth, ocean, and across all the flatlands.

A year or so later, I'd be running up that ladder to escape to the cabin roof from a woufing bear.

For weeks, Bruce and I were busy putting up the log cabin which in my dreams I had planned and constructed at least a dozen times. Having visualized every detail of measuring, sawing, notching, hoisting the logs with block and tackle, fitting them together, then stuffing the chinks, I could push the actual work along without taking time for calculating.

"But we've got to hurry faster," I said in early September. "This log cabin has got to be finished by the time Helen gets here or somebody will have to sleep outside with the dogs. There's no room for three people in the pre-fab."

There was not room even for two. All these weeks, Bruce and I had been scrambling over piles of gear, sidling along alleys between stacks of boxes, and laying our sleeping bags wherever we could find a spot on the floor big enough.

We now concentrated on log cabin building. We cut down on whale-watching time, worked inside the cabin on some rainy days. With a little cooler weather to keep our birds from spoiling, we killed more ducks and ptarmigans on less frequent hunting trips.

I was looking forward more each day to Helen's arrival. She would take over the cooking, which since the loon dinner failure and the speeded-up cabin work seemed more and more desirable.

About September 15, just as Bruce and I were putting the stove pipe through the split-log roof, we heard a plane. We dropped tools, jumped off the roof, and raced to the river. Bill DeCreeft's pontoons were skimming over the dark water. In minutes, a smiling, husky 27-year-old blond was scrambling onto the bank.

Our new partner Helen had convinced me in Kodiak that she wanted to learn how to trap. She was longing, she said, to live deep in the wilderness far away from civilization. She wanted to learn how to skin the trapped animals, then scrape and preserve the hides, especially those of the otter so she could have a fur coat. She claimed she was easy to get along with. And willing to cook. "My mother is Italian," she told me, "and taught me how to cook Italian style." I took her on. I'd heard how hard-working she'd been as a crew member on the toughest halibut fishing boat out of Kodiak. She looked strong, sensible, and cheerful.

"But," I said, "you'll have to wait to join Bruce and me in Kamishak because we've got to spend weeks going back to Contact Point for our stuff, then getting a barge to take us to the Kamishak. How about flying in about the middle of September?"

Beginning with Helen's first day in Kamishak, we ate like Italian princes—cakes, pies, meat in sauces, bread, something new and wonderful every day. She couldn't have been more pleasant, practical-minded, or helpful. I had to fuss at her from time to time to keep her from working herself to death.

Of course we took her, first thing, to see the whales. We watched and waited, watched and waited, and no whale suddenly went swisssh to blow or raised its body above water to breathe.

"Why can't one of you whales come up the river for Helen?" I called toward the river. Immediately, we heard "Swissh!" and saw the spray and the white hump. We made jokes about it, but for a few days afterwards we went through the same routine, and the whales always came when I called.

Then came the day when I said my line and nothing happened. I said it a few more times, but nothing white humped in the water and blew a spray. The actors had left for another theater.

"Where are the bears?" Helen asked a day or so later. We had heard some bellowing far away and seen tracks like a man's size 13EEE, but no bear had shown his face. "Let's hope they stay miles away over there on the McNeil River," I answered Helen. "They can do some good there, keeping that river famous as having the world's thickest crowd of bears fishing from its banks."

But just as belugas showed up right after I'd asked for them at the river, a bear responded only too soon to Helen's query. That same afternoon a bear came visiting. Maybe it was the smell of Helen's lasagna that drew him.

All dressed up in my anti-bug uniform, I was busy experimenting with a radio aerial in our cleared area. Hours of dial-twirling, calling, and listening had finally convinced us that our signal couldn't get out to Homer, our nearest grocery store and rescue port 100 miles across Cook Inlet. Perhaps if I lengthened the aerial wire, put it on a longer pole, and set it up where the trees were lower, we'd have better luck.

At the edge of our cleared area, I was about to drop the end of the pole into the hole I'd dug when I noticed a slight movement of the tall brush edging the yard. I looked up.

A bear face was peering over the alders. Its expression was quizzical, interested, curious about what I was and what I was doing. In my net gear, I probably looked to him like some giant insect. I had the feeling that the bear had been quietly watching me for some time.

We made blurry eye contact—at least I felt he saw my eyes even through the net—as I reached for my magnum pistol. In one second he'd decided this monster bug looked too threatening. He dropped out of sight. As quietly as he'd come, he departed, which was a big improvement over crashing through the brush at me.

He must have told his friends about the odd bug and smells he'd happened onto. After that, five different bears dropped by regularly, about one a day, to look at us a minute or two from the edge of the clearing.

When the dogs smelled them or saw them, they started a terrible fuss, their It's-a-Bear signal. Mr. Larson practically choked himself pulling on his leash, trying to get loose, wanting to rush across the yard to bite and fight. I kept him and Jake tied up tight just to stop them from doing such foolish things.

Instead, we grabbed five-gallon cans stationed handily by the cabin and began banging away with clubs. For weeks, the visitors got the message and politely left.

We saw them so many times we could identify them by size, color, scraggliness and personality. We gave them names. George had a short neck and a big shoulder hump. Solomo, a small, 300-pound young fellow, had a worried but determined expression. He always acted as if he was in a terrible hurry, had somewhere important to go, and had only a minute to look in and mumble, "What's doing today?" He always walked quickly, rocking like a ship from side to side.

I named Pierre for a man he looked like. Dirty Little Eddie had a dirty color all the time, and the dirty color was mostly clinging dirt. Old Joe was so fat he could hardly move. When he ran he looked to be rolling along.

Occasionally when we went to the ocean beach, we'd see one or two bears roaming, eating washed-up ripe seals, fish, or white whale. Once I saw a bear plunge into the water at the river mouth to chase an enormous salmon for a hundred feet. Salmon and bear swam equally fast, but the big bear lasted longer at top speed. He swims fast, but he runs on land faster—up to 30 miles an hour. That's why climbing a tree or jumping out of sight is the only way to win a foot race with him.

Upriver beyond our landing, the number of bears was startling, though not as many as I saw on a short, very short, visit to the McNeil River. It has three times the salmon run of the Kamishak. At every bend of the Kamishak—and there are many—there'd be one, two, or half a dozen bears standing in shallow water, pinning down a salmon with one paw and tearing it up with his teeth. Once when big dog salmon were running on the tide downstream so thick they'd have pushed over anything in the way, I saw a mama bear jump into a shallow pool and toss out salmon in every direction—a comical sight.

Near dusk one nice day in early October, I climbed to the crow's nest in our cottonwood tree and looked around with my binoculars. The first frosts had wiped out the bug population and turned Kamishak into a sweet and reasonable world. Dark solid mountains on three sides, rolling indigo ocean on the other. Miles of tall cottonwoods, bright yellow and browning. Broad acres of meadows in straw-like grass, trampled flat by bears.

And across the fast running river, on a low grassy bank, a moose migrating from the mountains had stopped for a drink.

A quick climb out of my tree. "Bruce! Put down your hammer. We're having moose steaks tonight." From our riverside, I fixed the crosshair sight on the moose and brought him down. Bruce and I crossed the river in the skiff to dress him out, grateful that he'd walked his 800 pounds of delicious meat almost to our door.

It was getting dark when we finished gutting the animal. Suddenly, Bruce whispered tensely, "What's that?" Brush crackled behind me. I jumped up, started for the skiff. "Come on. It's bears most likely. Can't risk waiting to find out. Too dark to see easy. Bears even kill one another over moose meat."

At daylight I was in the crow's nest looking across the river at what remained of our moose meat. Four bears were tearing it apart, growling, snapping, and clawing at each other as they ate. Two got mad at each other and rolled across the ground struggling and bellowing.

"If we get one rump roast out of that moose, we've got to kill four bears," I told Bruce. "Yeah, they're our yard-bears—Pierre, Old Joe, Solomo, and Dirty Eddie."

Bruce, long-faced, wished they'd all murder each other, and they sounded close to obliging him.

Three days we watched them. Eat, fight, lie around, growl at each other, eat some more. Now the meat would be putrid, sour, just the taste they like best, like putting mustard and ketchup on it. They ate slower and slower, fought less and less. Finally they seemed to come to an agreement about dividing up the bones and what little was left. Each bear dragged his part to a flat, sandy spot a hundred yards away, kicked out dirt for a hole to put it in, and kicked it back to cover. Another two days they hung around, dug up the leftovers from time to time, munched until nothing much was left. Each wandered off on a different trail.

A week later, Bruce brought down another moose but on our side of the river and only 40 yards from the cabin. We quickly skinned, gutted, and quartered him, then pulled the quarters by a rope high up into the cottonwood where we'd dressed him out. "At 30 feet, nothing can get at him," I assured Bruce and Helen, "not even any flies or bugs that might have survived the frosts. They don't fly that high. Bears are too big to climb trees."

I forgot to tell young Solomo that.

I know from the sound of the voices of the dogs and the violence of their behavior what kind of animal they smell or hear or see nearby. At the top of the scale is the It's-a-Bear racket. With the first whiff of scent, Jake starts jumping four feet into the air as he barks, his voice dropping deep in his throat, very gutteral. Mr. Larson seems to go slightly crazy. He hates bears with a passion.

Larson stiffens with anger and begins to howl. He rises on his hind legs like a bear, pulling and pulling on the rope or chain, walking around on his hind legs, lunging forward, screaming at the top of his voice.

The day after we left the moose meat swinging high in the tree, and while Bruce had skiffed to the salvage beach for lumber, Helen and I had dragged the box of traps outside the cabin for a trapping lesson. She was listening to me and working at opening a trap's strong jaws so as not to catch herself. Suddenly, Jake and Larson broke out in a terrible eruption of noise.

"YEOWWW!" Helen jumped up, startled. "They're saying, 'It's a bear,'" I said. I looked along Cottonwood Lane toward our moose tree, knowing its delicious smell was floating over the cottonwoods.

Solomo had come out of the brush onto the lane, and was doing his rock-roll walk toward the hanging moose. "That's Solomo. He's only a cub," I soothed Helen. She had jumped to her feet and headed for the cabin door. "Come on back and help bang on the barrel," I called to her. "That'll probably scare him away. He'll think a strange, big something is after him."

"But he's climbing the tree, Andy!"

So he was. He'd clawed his way up the trunk a few feet and was eyeing the hanging dinner with his mouth open and his long red-ribbon tongue draped over the side. I whammed a trap against the metal barrel. BOOM!

Solomo let go, dropped to the ground on all-fours, and scampered away.

"It's only a small bear," I said to Helen.

"He didn't look so little to me."

"But see how easy he was to scare? It's a strange noise to him and he thinks it's dangerous. He's young and inexperienced. He was probably scareder than you." I went on talking along about how most bears scare easy with noise, and I went on shouting at the dogs to shut up, telling them the bear was gone.

"ANDY! He's BACK!" Helen yelled. "Look!"

Moose smell had overcome fear. Solomo had edged half-way out of the brush. He was looking up at the moose meat, sniffing the air. "Grab a trap and beat the can!"

We banged and banged. Larson and Jake barked and yowled. The bear acted plumb deaf. All that racket hadn't hurt him before, why should he worry about it now?

I reached for my rifle to make it a little hotter for him. I put bullets right under his feet.

He hardly noticed.

What else could I do? Mr. Larson was straining at his chain, leaping out and jerking back, speaking unspeakable opinions of this bear and bears in general.

"Larson can take care of that small bear," I said to Helen. Her face grimaced in doubt. "And himself, too. It's not too big a bear. That's why he can climb trees. We can't have him staying practically in our yard and making a big success at getting our moose. If he does it once, we'll have him all the time. Watch this."

Larson was tickled as could be when I spoke to him about what I wanted him to do, and then untied him. He jumped away, racing toward the bear like a shot. Solomo had just embraced the tree when Larson ran up and bit him in the rump. Solomo, surprised, flip-flopped to the ground, off balance. Bears are so large and powerful, they seldom have a lone, smaller animal rush into them and bite. I've only seen a wolverine, more fierce and swift than Larson, run a bear off a carcass by biting him over and over on the haunches. I've seen a pack of wolves surround a mama bear sitting with her small cub in her lap, slapping at the attacker. They kept grabbing at her back until she let go the cub to turn and swat a wolf. In less than a wink, four wolves had the cub. While they tore into him and dragged him away, two wolves kept after mama bear's backside in a delaying action.

Mr. Larson, part wolf, also knew to stay on the bear's backside away from the claws. He took a mouthful of fur and skin and clamped down hard. He finally bit his way to pain. All Solomo could do was show his teeth, bellow, flatten his ears back, bristle his hair—and turn around in a circle. Larson always stayed just out of reach.

Unable to shake off this fierce small monster, the bear headed into the brush, pulling Larson along in a hind leg walk, his teeth gripping the bear's behind.

Out of sight, they made noises that had me and Helen

gritting our teeth and shuddering to imagine what they were doing to each other. For a few minutes I thought I had made a terrible mistake. Too proud of Larson, I had underestimated the bear. It sounded as if those two were logging off the whole country behind the thick alders.

I looked around to say as much to Helen—and she was nowhere in sight.

Just then the growling and scuffling and wrestling racket stopped. What in the devil was going on anyway? "Helen! Where are you?!"

Larson ran out of the brush. His tongue was hanging out, his tail was hanging sober. He was panting heavily. Although tired, he was alive and uninjured.

In a minute, here came the bear. He was panting heavily, his tongue hanging long. Bear and dog sat down to rest, eyeing each other over several yards while they caught their breath.

"HELEN! WHERE ARE YOU?!" I shouted.

"I'm here!" I heard her say, and moved around to see her running toward the cabin door.

"Keep going!" I called, "Climb up the tree to the lookout! We'll be safer up high!"

"I'm scared of heights, Andy. I can't climb up there."

"You want a mad bear or one of his friends springing at you? I see Larse is circling around behind Solomo, going back to chew him again.

"Now you get up that ladder! I'm coming too!" I growled like a bear.

She got. "Faster!" She speeded up. We scrambled into our small platform 40 feet above the ground.

From there, I could see that Larson and the bear had moved to a clearing behind the moose tree. The bear was

lunging at Larson and Larson was still grabbing at the
bear's rump. When Larse got a hold, he braced his hind legs
on the ground, clamped teeth onto hide, and pulled.
Solomo began to whirl around and around, trying to rid
himself of this ferocious little creature. Larson held on
until the fur came out. When he had to run, he ran in a wide
circle, just out of Solomo's reach. The bear gave up chasing
him. Larson bit the bear's bottom and ran, over and over.
Neither dog nor bear was making much noise now. They
had to save all their strength, each determined to outlast the
other. They would both sit down and rest a minute from
time to time, jump up and go at it again.

The noise of battle was now coming only from big,
black Jake still tied up by the cabin. He'd hardly seen a bear
before he met the beachcomber bear that nearly got me. He
wouldn't know any better than to try for the bear's throat,
right where the bear with one lift of his front paw and claws
could slice him open end-to-end.

Solomo heard Jake. Solomo stood and looked over the
brush through the trees at him. Larson tore into his back
end. The bear whipped about and came down right on top
of the place where Larson was—but wasn't any longer.
Solomo began crashing through the brush toward Jake.
Larson's energy peaked and shot him off like a steel spring.
He ripped out a mouthful of fur from the now ragged
rump. The bear whirled, struck at him—and missed.
Hissing and growling, he began backing into the brush
toward Jake, still bounding and straining against his
chain, wearing his throat out with insults and profanity.
To get at Solomo's bottom now, Larson had to break
through the thick brush behind the bear.

"Look at that—Solomo's got a new strategy," I said to

Helen. "He's just 20 feet of brush and a swift lunge from killing Jake. Larson can't get through the brush fast enough. I've got to help."

I aimed and fired.

As Solomo fell, a bullet in his brain, Larson jumped to grab his ear in a sharp-toothed clamp. The bear's head moved violently back and forth.

"He's not dead, Andy!" Helen cried out. "Shoot, shoot again!"

The bullet knocked off a streak of hair as it broke the bear's back. Still the head kept flopping. "He's still not dead," said Helen. "Oh the bear's dead enough, Helen. That shaking is Larson, yanking at the ear. He's of a mind to aggravate Solomo all the way to bear heaven."

Larson couldn't seem to let go. He acted as if he still had a job to do, that the bear was going to jump up and go after him once more. It took all my strength to hold him, squeeze his jaws to release the bear's ear. I grabbed his collar and hauled him bucking and wild-eyed to the cabin.

He finally heard me and calmed down.

"Good work, Larson. The bear is dead. You saved old Jake. You saved me. You saved Helen. You saved the moose meat. You're all in one piece, unharmed. And I'm sure glad, my friend. You're a great dog, Mr. Larson, a great dog."

Mr. Larson, the bear hater, dared to
throw his 50 pounds of muscle against
those mighty beasts. Forefeet on the bear's
rump, Mr. Larson sank his teeth into the
grizzled fur and hung on—always out of
reach. For his fighting skill and audacity,
Andy rewarded Mr. Larson with rides
on the back of the Honda.

8

The Wolverine War

"Eskimos. . . called (the wolverine) Kee-wa-har-kess, Evil One, because he plundered traplines with almost mystical cunning. . . His body (they said) housed the soul of a great hunter, whose only pleasure was to plague other hunters. . ."
National Geographic Wild Animals of North America

Snow changed the Kamishak world into a silhouette of itself. White ground . . . black mountains with white peaks and ledges against gray sky . . . black skeletons of cottonwoods, black-green spruce, each branch outlined in white.

Winter's first heavy snow lay smooth and inches thick on the Kamishak, calming my nerves and exciting my trapper's spirit.

I had waited impatiently for the first hard freeze that always precedes the first heavy snow. From the time Helen arrived, we'd kept busy making furniture and unpacking boxes in the log cabin. The room seemed spacious and luxurious to me, compared to living squeezed between boxes in the pre-fab.

Bruce and I also cut six cords of birch firewood, pieces four feet long for the steel-barrel stove, and thick enough to last through any below-zero night. We brought all three of

"Wolverines are the meanest, cleverest, fastest, strongest-biting creatures in the wild," says Andy. They spring traps without getting caught, take the bait, kill and eat trapped animals, then foul the area. Wolf-like tracks and scissors teeth probably brought the wolverine its name.

us up to grade in target shooting—a dime at 27 yards, a 4-inch circle at 250.

We relayed by radio our last list of groceries and gear to Homer, and Bill DeCreeft flew them over in a hurry, unloaded them in a hurry, and left in a hurry. Then we waited. We hunted and fished and ate ourselves tight into our clothes on Helen's wonderful cooking. But to me it was waiting all the same.

I was as restless as a caged weasel. We'd been in the Kamishak ten weeks and I had an urgent need to lay a line of traps. That required bad weather, hard weather, and hungry big animals interested in trap bait or scent.

Finally, on October 16 a cold snap bored in during late afternoon. The river froze over in three hours. By morning the ice was an inch thick. The booming, snapping music of the tides heaving ice sheets into crazy pieces, stacking and re-stacking them, began.

"This is it!" I announced. "Trapping season has started." All the tasty woodchucks, rockchucks, gophers, and mice were hiding and sleeping in their burrows. Beavers were safe under their pond ice. Ducks have flown. So what will the foxes, wolves, and wolverines eat now? Each other, of course. Moose or caribou for the wolf packs, with left overs, maybe, for the other animals. An Arctic hare or a porcupine for the quick and the brave. AND—some interesting gut piles and chunks of porcupine lying close to a log that wasn't there yesterday.

"When do we start setting traplines?" Bruce was as restless as I was.

"Soon as the first big snow hits. That'll get rid of the last bear. They'll be all curled up in crevices, holes, or brush to sleep for the next five months. Thank heavens bears don't operate year-round. When we see them again, the grass will be out and they'll be grazing like cows."

Hibernating bears often dig into the side of an earth bank. Or they get into a ready-made hole in the rocks. Or they have a pretend hole beneath a three-foot pile of brush. They're not particular. When snow covers them, their insulating underfur and the long guard hairs grow thicker and longer as fast as they need more insulation to keep warm. I never heard of a bear freezing to death even during the hardest winter.

With such heavy snows as those in Kamishak, you'd think the bear would smother under a ten-foot snow blanket. But the steam of his breath keeps a chimney hole open for air. When you see steam coming out of the snow in Kamishak, watch out.

"So how soon, exactly, what day, do we look for the snowstorm," Bruce persisted.

"Oh about a week after the freeze is my guess. Just long enough for the animals that don't sleep away the winter to get good and hungry. So let's start getting ready. Let's shave our beards off."

I've found that a heavy beard such as I usually wear is a poor outfit in below-zero weather. Even with a mask of fur or skin to cover it, the outer layer of beard collects moisture from my breath and shortly I have an ice-crusted mustache and chin beard. Off comes the mask so I can shake out the hoar frost and icicles.

Without a mask over the beard, it's worse. Snow falls into all the beard, already icing up with breath vapor. Zero minus is quick-freeze, so first thing I know, I'm toting a cake of ice on my whole face. I have to stop, crack it, and scratch it off.

It's more comfortable to shave smooth and wear a wool mask pulled over my head like a cap.

On October 21, four days after the cold snap, a two-foot snow fell. The next morning, no snow predicted, Bruce and I dressed to go. "We'll take you when the snow ain't so soft," I told my other pupil. "It's too loose today to support three riders on the snowmachine and toboggan."

Gliding over the snow for miles in just a few minutes in a motorized sled always tickles me. I think of those Montana days on the ranch when slogging 10 miles across snow, and 10 miles back was enough to ruin a whole day and most of my disposition. Since snowmobiles, which I usually call snowmachines, appeared in the 1960's, I've been a much easier trapper to get along with.

"We're looking first for wolverine tracks," I told Bruce before we set out. "This area has never been trapped and that means more than the usual headaches with thieving wolverines. Ordinarily we might expect three or four in an area, but here there's probably a half-dozen. Unless we catch them first, we could go home practically empty-handed of fox, wolf, beaver, otter, and ermine furs."

Wolverine, I had explained to Bruce and Helen, love to steal your bait or your catch, then foul the trap with stink worse than a skunk's. I should say "foul the trap *and* a 50-foot circle around it, with oily scent, urine, and feces." It smells so vile, no other animal will come near. Wolverine scent is bad enough to knock a dog off a gut wagon.

To clean the traps of the odors, you have to drag them through salt water several miles. Or boil them, and pour off water with oily secretion three or four times. Either way, it's a big job. Unless you catch the wolverines right off, you can spend the whole trapping season losing your just-caught animals to the stinkers, then cleaning the traps of their nastiness. Some trappers get so disgusted and mad at wolverines, they quit and go home.

I knew what we were up against trying to clear out these short-legged devils. The wolverine is the meanest, cleverest, fastest, strongest-biting creature in the wild, I think. The Al-e-uts call him "skunk bear," and "glutton," and "thief." He's all those. They must have thought he was like a skunk because he has two white stripes on his brown-black back, and his scent is gagging. But from the front, his face looks like a young bear's, and he's shaggy with some orange on his belly. You could mistake him for a bear cub at a distance, especially if you heard him hiss like a bear. He's about the size of a short-legged, medium-sized dog, between 25 and 50 pounds.

Then why "wolf-erine"? Where wolves live in the deep wilderness, the wolverine lives, too. Like a wolf, he has two pairs of scissors-action tusks that can slice through fair-sized bones or cut through the hide of a bear's rump. Like a wolf, the wolverine hunts at night mostly. Many trappers have never seen one, but only the gruesome evidence of where he's been. Looking at that mess and smelling it, they can only guess at what animal made it. When they see bones sliced in two, they think "wolf." Many trappers catch only one wolverine in a lifetime. He's actually a bush badger, a weasel, with neck and heavy jaw all one bone.

That first day of trapping in the Kamishak, Bruce and I glided out of the cottonwoods and skimmed across open white flatlands to hilly brush country. Even bare of leaves, the alders and shrubs were too thick for machine travel. Besides, I'd been watching tracks in the snow. I stopped the snowmachine.

"Lots of wolverine tracks here," I said, pointing to a line of footprints. They were shaped like a large dog's, or a wolf's track. "A wolverine's wide feet make good natural snow shoes. Let's get into ours, follow the tracks into the brush a ways, and set a trap."

The tracks looked sharp-edged and fresh. "See, he's a loping animal. The hind leg tracks don't follow right in line with the front ones the way other animal tracks do. The hind ones are off to the side a little, like a car's chassis when it's out of line."

During Alaska's almost nightless summers, I've watched wolverine through binoculars as they jogged in their curious manner, always getting somewhere fast. I've sat on hilltops or mountain ledges keeping sight of them loping off a mile in no time across grasslands, through brush, along beaches. Running fast looks so easy for them.

Add to routine loping a burst of speed for an attack charge. A victim will go down like a bullet has struck him. I've seen a wolverine's fast charge into a large flock of ptarmigans. Unsuspecting of danger, the birds stood deep in fluffy snow with only their white heads sticking out. Suddenly the wolverine was there, slapping off bird heads right and left. He knocked off a half-dozen before the rest of the ptarmigans could flap a wing.

Vicious and swift, wolverines are the greatest hunters in the animal world. Their clever strategy and lightning strikes have brought them credit for many a mysterious deed, mischievous and destructive. Some Native legends say that wolverines are inhabited by the spirits of wicked dead men.

"Now here's where our wolverine has picked up a fresh fox track," I called to Bruce. Foxes run over and over the same trail the way bears do. The wolverine lopes within a territory, say a mile or so wide and five miles long in this valley, but he zigs and zags and circles about, investigating, checking fox trails, ermine runs, porcupine crawls, and beaver lodges. Look at the long claw marks in that track. They're curved and powerful—like an eagle's. With those claws they can dig holes fast as bears. They can run up a tree like a monkey. They can open up birds, foxes, even porcupines so fast you think they were zippered.

But do they ever get mixed up with Porky's quills? Not much. You'll see beavers with mouth and cheeks all swollen and infected with quills still hanging in the flesh. They haven't come by them in a fight. It's simply that when Beaver and Porky, both bark eaters, meet on a trail, neither will give way. They rub past each other and the beaver's face gets the worst end of Porky's coat of nails.

A wolverine wastes no time arguing. He's hungry for meat. He just smacks Porky in the face and knocks him on his back, exposing his soft, quill-less belly. Slash go the skunk bear's claws. Then, his muzzle never touching a quill, the wolverine bores out and devours Porky's insides and flesh. All that's left is a shell of skin and needles.

"To catch an animal, you have to find out from watching how he behaves what he must be thinking," I told Bruce. "Wolverines act as if they think thieving food is more fun than killing their own. So let's make the bait of our trap look as if some fox hid it there for future reference. Wolverine will see the slight change our trap set has made in the groundscape, and he'll come over to investigate. He has a full-grown curiosity and he'll enjoy the prospect of stealing and messing up a fox's tidbits."

We chose a sturdy, thick-branched alder to chain the

trap to. Against the alder, I laid a quarter of a porcupine. A foot in front of this bait, we scooped out a shallow hole, just big enough for the open trap to fit into and be flush with the top. We picked dry grass to cover the trap, then sifted snow on top. "We can't hide the trap just under snow, as you know," I said to Bruce. I sprinkled some bottled fox urine and stuck short, pointed sticks in the snow beside bait and hidden trap.

"Now when wolverine comes to see what this is all about, he won't be able to get at the bait from the back because of the alder, nor from the sides without stepping on sticks that hurt. The best way, he thinks, is to walk on the flat snowy grass—nice and smooth. Clack! The jaws have him by the leg."

Off we went, reasonably sure we'd catch a demon wolverine by morning.

We spotted some fresh fox tracks and turned the trail they made into a trapline. Various animals will use a fox's trail. For foxes and wolves, we made "blind" sets—no bait, just fox urine, right in the trail. For smaller animals, we made a "cubby and trap" set beside the trail. The cubby, a roofed but open-front little shelter of sticks, limits the approach to the bait and scent.

"If we put the cubby on the trail itself," I explained, "the animal will see it as a big obstacle, take the course of least resistance, and detour around it. So we stop him on the trail by sticking into the snow some rows of short, pointed sticks. He thinks they'll hurt his feet if he steps there. We place them to guide him into detouring past the door of the cubby. There he smells the bait and a stick I dipped in sexy scent. He steps toward it on some nice soft grass. Clack! He's ours."

For each trap we set, I made an X on a diagram I drew in my trapline notebook or log, noting the date, landmarks, distances, trails, bait, type of set.

The next day, I took Helen to a creek to set a line of traps for otter, so it was the following day that Bruce and I returned to check out our wolverine and fox-trail sets.

Snow hole, porcupine, and trap for the wolverine looked as if a herd of drunken goats had kicked it all night. It smelled even worse. The trap was sprung and pitched behind the alder, the porcupine was gone except for the quills, the snow hole kicked out ten times as big as we'd made it. Spots of yellow urine and brown feces, dribbles of oily, foul scent decorated a large area of snow. Slick as a pickpocket, he'd stolen the bait. How did he spring the trap without getting caught?

We went on to the first trap on the line. A worse wreck and stench. In the trap a fox leg was still caught in the jaws, but the carcass had been eaten, the fur ripped to pieces and scattered with the bones as much as 20 feet away. Scraps of innards and flesh and spatters of blood desecrated the snow.

Bruce was shocked at the carnage. "He must have gone mad for a while to do all this. Why does he have to tear everything up and mess on it?" I shook my head.

I could only tell him that wolverines behave this way often. I couldn't tell him why. "It would be mighty interesting to watch one of these performances during the night," I said. "I'll bet it's the closest thing to a blood orgy in the wilderness. I wonder if he screams and hollers as he works? Books say he only hisses, and that's all I've ever heard him do. But that seems too tame for a spitfire dragon like the one that did this."

We went from one scene of fury and wreckage to

another. Most of the traps we'd set were sprung and stinking. Around a couple that had each trapped a fox, it was like a slaughterhouse with a wild stench. Little had been eaten. Had only one lone wolverine done all the damage? It looked like enough work for ten.

The smell of cooking wolverine traps polluted the cabin for a month. All that time, the three of us talked about wolverine psychology, devised variations on trap setting that might actually catch one of the devils. But we never devised anything that tricked or fooled a single one into getting caught.

We didn't marvel that an animal could be so smart, we just swore and worried about our trapping losses. Gloomily we saw ourselves taking home very little at the end of a whole winter in the wilds of Kamishak, defeated by four-legged criminals.

"We'll kill the wolverines by working them to death," I cheered Bruce and Helen finally. My plan was to set every trap we had. "There're over a hundred, so they can't work all of them every night," I predicted. Doggedly we labored until every trap, even those in the cookpot, was set in lines across the valley.

Every day we checked half the traps. Every day, we picked up a stack that had been sprung, the bait or the catch taken, the location fouled. Only a few traps caught a fox we got to keep ourselves.

"How do they know where every single trap is located?" Helen asked.

"They go up and down their territory and zigzag across it every night. They take notice of everything. That includes our snowshoe tracks leading to each trap. They follow them. Our big feet show their big feet the way."

Toward the end of the first month of the Wolverine War, Helen took my course in snare-setting and became an expert in catching rabbits. If she couldn't go home with an otter fur coat because of wolverine thievery, she'd try for a white Arctic hare coat instead.

Within days, her snares tilted the Wolverine War in our favor, besides snaring furs for Helen's coat and filling the stew pot a half-dozen times. It happened like this. . .

I had brought several new fine-steel wire snares, each with a device that pulled the circle of wire tighter and tighter about neck or leg the harder an animal jerked to pull himself out. Helen practiced how to suspend the saucer-size wire loop low to the ground in the middle of a trail. Hares had packed down a trail about a hundred feet from the cabin. On moonlit nights we'd watched them hopping back and forth in little bounces, or in leaps of six or eight feet.

Arctic hares are four times the size of ordinary jack rabbits—in fact when Helen held one up by the hind legs, he stretched out more than a yard long. Bouncing along peacefully, they get where they're going at about five or 10 miles an hour. But let a fox or dog start a chase. Even Mr. Larson couldn't catch a hare springing 40 miles an hour.

Foxes ambush them. When they're caught they let out a full-size horror movie scream. It's a scary sound if you've never heard it before or you didn't know that rabbits and hares make such blood-curdling noises. Foxes know. They do an even worse scream themselves when they're in trouble. But I think when a rabbit screech blasts just inches from a fox's ear, he must sometimes open his mouth in a gasp—and out the big hare pops.

But it's the Arctic hare's kick that counts the most. His

hips are bigger than a Thanksgiving turkey's, and his powerful back leg muscles are as strong as a kangaroo's. I've been told that a solid wallop by those legs will break a rival hare's neck, or even the neck of an attacking fox.

Helen and I found a place where the hares' trail narrowed to pass between two trees. "We can chain to one tree the long, heavy arm holding out the wire circle over the trail. On the other tree, we'll tie the thread that holds the circle of wire upright and straight.

"The center of the circle of wire has to stand exactly at the height of the hare's head when he hops along the trail," I told Helen. He follows exactly in the tracks of the trail. If the snare is at the right height, the hare's head just naturally goes through the wire circle. The force of his forward movement snaps the thread holding the wire circle in upright position, and zing, the wire pulls tight. The hare jerks against it. The circle squeezes smaller. . .

Helen added various improvements. Twigs helped to break the outline of the wire circle. Upright sticks placed by the circle helped to keep the hares from jumping over it instead of sticking their heads in.

One day she thought of another improvement. She took some fish oil to the snare and dripped some on a tree root. That might slow the hare to a crawl, and hold his head to the ground as he sniffed out the source of the odor, she thought. Helen didn't know that hares aren't interested in fishy smells since hares eat bark, not fish.

The next morning, instead of the white, soft-furred hare she expected, Helen found a black-brown shaggy creature with two white stripes down its back and a face like a little bear. She'd never seen a wolverine—not many people have—and she thought from a distance the snare had caught a bear cub.

It was a wolverine. We'd caught one at last! Snared, not trapped.

In other years I had snared a few wolverines, but they broke the wire and got away. Snares weren't very practical for the strong claws of wolverines, I decided. But this sliding wire noose Helen had used had worked well and the strong wire had held.

"Let's set up all the snares for wolverines!" I said and we went to work, sure now that the Wolverine War was coming to an end. We hung snares across every likely trail we found and sprinkled fish oil nearby.

A week later we had snared one fox. The wolverines— we were now convinced there was a band of the bandits— haunted our traplines, springing and robbing our sets worse than ever.

"Maybe we're aiming for the wrong part of the body with these devils," I said. "If they've caught on to the neck snare danger, let's try snares for the legs."

We climbed trees and nailed generous chunks of porcupine into the crotch of branches 15 feet above ground. We figured exactly where a wolverine would be stepping to get to that meat. On the tree trunk just before he'd pull into the crotch, we positioned a snare for him to step into. We used small wire circles for a tight fit.

I figured that a wolverine finding his foot caught in a tightening wire would jump, trying to pull out. So we secured the snare with extra strong wire wrapped around the branch. When the wolverine jumped, he'd find himself swinging in the air, unable to touch ground. There he'd be hanging, waiting for me in the morning.

All that was waiting was a short piece of the snare wire,

frayed at the end like a worn-out flyswatter. The devil apparently didn't jump! He must have sat on the branch and chewed and snipped until he'd bitten in two the wire circle on his leg.

"His pair of special tusks, remember, work like scissors," I grumbled when Bruce and Helen and I sat pondering our new failure. Did he free himself in minutes, or did it take hours? All I will ever know for sure is that he didn't leave that tree hungry.

So neither a snare by itself nor a trap by itself was the weapon to win the Wolverine War. I went back to thinking while the three of us went back to baiting and setting leg traps on the mass scale.

The enemy night after night sprang the traps or killed our catch. How did he keep from getting caught? Did he throw a rock at the pan—or poke it with a stick the way some beavers will do? Around our raided trap sets, I never found a stick in the jaws or a rock on the ground. Helen suggested the wolverine threatened the trap with a whole sack of scent and the trap clanged shut to protect itself. How ever they made the jaws close, the wolverines went free and ate like kings.

True they had some close calls doing their trap-springing trick. Occasionally the jaws grabbed their toes. So the wolverines bent the traps, broke them, and twisted off toes to get free. One tore off the trap pan. If I wanted to tear off a pan, I'd need a vise, hammer, chisel, and plenty of whacking. Another trap, the trigger was twisted off, roots and all. I'd need two pairs of pliers to pull it out. The wolverine used his teeth. Some traps the jaws were bent. Others the bottom bar was bent. Bruce and I tried to straighten them with sledgehammer blows, and couldn't.

The day before Thanksgiving, more than a month after the war had started, I complained bitterly to Bruce. We were laying our umpteenth piece of bait at the back of one particular cubby and resetting the empty but sprung trap. "All we're doing is toting dinner to this bandit every day. He's smarter now, too. He's making his thieving easier for himself by not fouling the trap and the place it's sitting. We don't move it and he doesn't have to find it. I'll bet he hasn't hunted a thing for himself since we put out our first bait. He's been living on our handouts, like he was in a zoo. Well, if you spring this trap tonight, Old Skunk Bear, I've got another plan for you tomorrow."

I knew he'd spring it and I had my plan with me when I came back. "If he's so smart, I'll give him three things to figure out at the same time," I told Helen. "I'm going to catch him at both ends so at least one end will stay held—maybe—until I get back here."

I'd picked a particular place to try my plan. I'd noticed two trees that stood close together, one leaning against the other. On a branch of the lower, straight tree, I hung a bait of porcupine meat. I then hung not one but two snares. Helen listened without comment to my explanation.

"If that devil comes up the leaning tree figuring to reach the bait from above, he'll have to stick his head through a snare to do it. If he comes from the ground up the straight tree he'll put his head in the other snare guarding the bait. Just as insurance, I'm adding a leg trap on the ground in a strategic spot.

"This leg trap is placed exactly where his hind foot will have to swing down if either snare catches him. Even if he wrings and twists so much that he breaks the snare and frees his head and shoulders, the leg trap chained to the tree should hold him."

I doubted myself that this rig would catch him. No wonder the Natives thought wolverines were evil spirits. Probably by some amazing maneuver he'd turn the snares around and catch me. Or he might think of springing the leg trap before going for the bait. Or he might break the anchor wire and run off. Nothing seemed improbable after so many weeks of defeat.

But the next day—aahhhhh! there he was, stretched out, head in the top snare, one hind foot in the ground trap. Three things to think about was one too many.

This skunk bear had thieved and fouled his last time. He'd been a tough and wily fighter, and I paid my last respects by saying back to him the distinctive sound he'd just said to me: "Hiissss!"

We ended up catching 23 wolverines by the finish of our Kamishak stay. I'm told that's the biggest wolverine catch on record. Eight of those Evil Ones we caught in two days—five one day, three the other. That's an even more amazing record for trapping wolverines

I'm now wearing those eight in the world's most spectacular hooded parka—black and brown and orange shaggy fur with 16 white stripes. Claws and tails dangle down the front for decoration. It's a curious fact that when I'm inside that fur, I have a much bigger appetite and feel eight times my usual devilish self.

*"Twenty-three wolverines in one season—
that's the biggest catch on record I'm told,"
says Andy. He proudly displays the skins in
the Kamishak wild where he trapped them.
Until he found a way to catch the
wolverines that were eating the fur-bearing
animals in his traps, Andy faced the gloomy
prospect of going home empty-handed.*

9

Frozen Trapline, Fiery Volcano

"And though the morn on blizzard borders,
I chuckle in me guts and say
'It's just the day the doctor orders.'"

Robert Service

Moose antlers framed the wintry world ahead of me and made me smile. I had tied an old moose head to the snowmobile handle bars to fool any wolves that crossed my path. "They'll think this moving, legless 'moose' is walking half-buried in the deep snow," I told Bruce and Helen. "When the wolves run to attack their prey, we'll have an easy shot. Once I fooled a coyote with my motorized moose head, so why not a wolf hungry enough to hunt in daylight?"

Bruce rode on the seat behind me, holding on to my parka. On the toboggan attached to the snowmobile, Helen sat among boxes of emergency food and gear. We had only a day's outing planned, but we never went anywhere without three day's rations, dry, warm clothing, sleeping bags, a small tent, our trap box, a box with bait and scent, and when Helen didn't come, a CB radio. We could call her

*Handsome foxes roaming the Kamishak in
search of rabbit, squirrel, mice, and insect
dinners, provide the wolves with a diet
staple—and the trapper with a valuable fur.
Colors of pups in a fox litter range from
rusty red to black, silver, or red with a large
dark cross on the back and shoulders.*

and say where we were, and when she might expect us.
This bright day in late January, we were going to the area around the mouth of Little Kamishak River, ten miles north. Bruce and I had gone there the day before and set about 20 traps.

Helen had begged to come along on this trip to check them. Except for the stovepipe tip, our cabin was buried in ten feet of snow. No light came in. With the view of the world the same as a hole in the ground, it was depressing to stay there inside the cabin all day long, alone except for the dogs. We didn't take the dogs in deep snow. They sink in so far and get so tired pulling their legs out, they're walking on their tongues in less than two miles.

Helen had mastered the whims of our steel-barrel stove, both as a cooker and a heater, to the point that she could shake a finger at it, tell it what to do, and it would do it. So I said, all right, Helen, boss that stove into keeping the place from freezing for the next 10 hours, get dressed for 10 below just in case, and hop on the toboggan.

It took us about 30 minutes to dress for the cold in two layers of everything, topped by fur-lined parka with a hood that fitted tight around the face. Then our fur-lined mukluks and gloves. The cold won't hurt us now—unless we get wet.

"Here, hold this and keep it safe," I said when we were loading, and gave Helen the tape recorder. "I want to try playing the mink squeals we taped and find out if they'll draw Kamishak minks from their holes."

It was such a clear, fine day with the temperature only 10 degrees ABOVE zero, with the radio weather news just as fine, we didn't bother to take face masks. Bruce and I wore our dark glasses and Helen put on soot make-up over and under her eyes to cut snow glare.

These days in winter's depths were short, no more than six hours of daylight. But if the skies stayed clear, they also had the brightest nights, lit by the Aurora Borealis and the moon shining on the snow. With a little luck, we should be back by suppertime loaded with foxes, minks, wolves, and maybe a wolverine—enough catch to make us whistle and sing in the nightlights of the wilderness.

It turned out to be a day that included a taste of every kind of winter adventure Kamishak has to offer—plus the first signs of the next big drama that Nature in the form of a volcano would bring to our log cabin in the cottonwoods.

First hazard of the day was getting across our own river's rugged ice. Piled in crazy towers 25 feet high in places, it had the added danger of surprise breakthroughs. Half-hollow salty sea ice was mixed with hard fresh-water ice. But I felt reasonably sure the three of us on the snowmobile and toboggan would make it safely across. A couple of weeks before, Bruce and I had gone out in the flesh-searing weather to string a nylon safety line from one side of the river to the other.

Before I go on with the story of our special late-January day on the trapline, let me tell you the awful story of Kamishak's most-of-January weather.

Winter had set in full-time just after a long Christmas season of rain when temperatures went up as high as 40. With January, the snows began and storms ran on the tail of storms. Going out between storms, we might have as little as two hours before thick, blinding, blowing snow began to cover us. Linger a minute too long and you might never stomp snow from your boots at the cabin door again. We stayed home indoors a lot more than I liked.

I never saw so much snow. We heard the wind roaring through the treetops at 60 to 80 miles an hour. But unlike Contact Point, the snare of high, naked branches and lower alders and willows trapped much of the gale's power before it hit our cabin.

Week by week the height of snow rose. Three feet. Five feet. Eight feet. Ten feet. We climbed steps notched in the snow to get out of the cabin. A passerby wouldn't have known our cabin was there. Wild animals thumped across our roof. One night I thought it might be a bear. Bruce slipped out into the moonlight and looked. On the roof, a wolverine was trying to drag away a 200-pound moose leg. The wolverine saw Bruce. Run or fight. The wolverine chose to run.

During the first week or so of this raging weather, we heard the groans and bone-chilling cracks and crunches of river ice twisted by relentless tides. When the river fell silent, we knew ice had won over the sea even, and we went out to look at it.

"How will we get across that jumble with a snow machine?" Bruce said. "If we don't find a way, we're cut off from half our traplines."

"So we have to get a pole to prod the ice where our next step will be, and foot by foot pick out a path," I said. "The prodding is for rotten ice. That's salt water ice the tides drag upstream. Salt water freezes at 28 degrees and expands so much it's as holey as a sponge. It's weak. Step on it and it crumbles. No pop or crackle to warn you. First thing you know, your leg is in the water. If it's a big patch of honeycomb ice, it crumbles when you grab it, trying to pull out of the water. The more you grab, the worse off you are. If you slip in waist-deep, say goodbye. Five minutes in icy water and your heart, lungs, and liver freeze up.

"So we have to figure out how to anchor and string a safety line. Let's start with those heavy logs and a thick nylon rope."

We strung the line across the river and tied the far end to a tree. Back at the cabin, we attached heavy metal rings to the snowmobile bumpers. Whenever we wanted to cross the river, we threaded the safety rope through the rings, watched in front of the snowmobile for insurgent milky sea ice and drove across as fast as rough ice allowed.

Every river crossing was five or ten minutes of tight-lipped tension.

And so it was the morning of sunny skies when the three of us started out for our traplines on the Little Kamishak. Safely across our Kamishak, we joked and laughed and zipped along at ten miles an hour over the open snowfields.

Deep snow had covered every sign of the earth below—except for a half-dozen markers a few feet high shining like red-striped barber poles. They marked strange black pools of hot water. After the first snow months ago, we'd seen their steam rising from them. Some were five feet across, others as much as 25 feet. I'd pushed long poles into them and never found bottom.

"Let's mark them," I said. "We might have to drive home in the dark sometime. Think of tumbling into one of them . . ." The thought sent a shudder through me. If we didn't drown, we'd quick-freeze when we crawled out soaking wet. We spent a whole day making 15-foot poles striped with luminous red tape, and posting them beside each sinister pool. Now we kept well away as we headed for a creek that ran into the Little Kamishak River.

From open tundra we glided through a patch of tall cottonwoods where even the tallest brush was under snow. For a few minutes we were riding though an artist's painting of a winter scene, black and white with rows of gray shadows.

I saw fox tracks . I slowed to read what story they told.

"You see marks on fresh snow and you think about them as messages written to you, telling some news about a wilderness event," I said. "Anything moving out here in the snow writes with feet or wings or tail where he was going, what happened on the way, whether he ever got there. You already know, at this time of year, the reason for the trip: food."

I stopped the machine where I saw the fox had stopped and danced around a bit. By his tracks, I saw two lines brushed like a broom across the snow.

"There's a wilderness drama. The brush lines were made by wings. An eagle or owl made a pass at the fox. It's a wide spread of wings, so it was most likely an eagle. But there's no blood on the snow. Probably the eagle swooped down to grab something the fox was carrying in its mouth—a ptarmigan or maybe a hare. There's a white feather—and another. So it was a ptarmigan. The eagle would have grasped the bird with his talons, threatened the fox's eyes with his sharp beak, made him turn loose the bird, and flown off with the fox's dinner. There are the fox's tracks, leaving. He's swearing but he's not hurt."

When we went on, I began to see tracks of a big moose and a little moose going the same way we were. A half-mile later, we saw the Mama Moose and her calf.

They saw us and stopped. Our moose head puzzled Mama Moose about ten seconds. Then she began trotting toward a thicket of trees where the tops of tall alders were barely sticking out of the snow. All at once the back legs of the calf broke through the crust and sank deep in the snow. He began grunting and pawing the snow in front of him. We stopped to watch.

Mama Moose stopped to watch. Baby heaved and pawed and gruuunted. He couldn't get out. He stopped doing anything.

His Mama walked back and studied him for a minute. Then she whacked him on the right shoulder with her front hoof. He grunted and moved a little to the left. Mama whacked him again. He moved again. She struck him over and over, hard, making the fur fly, making him move in a circle, trampling down the snow.

Then I expect she said something like, "Now jump out or I'll give you a harder hoof," for he lunged forward in the new leverage space, and scrambled up to his mother. It was worth using a quarter-hour of a short day to see.

Now we were running among the willows near a creek. "Fresh bait coming up," I called to Bruce. I'd seen a porcupine track. I guided the snowmachine alongside a foot-wide trail in the snow. Shortly we saw old Porky waddling along, his belly and quills brushing the snow. A bark eater, the porcupine was probably on his way from a den to a patch of ungnawed willow or alder.

Porky saw us and the moose head. Hair and quills stood straight up all over its body. He flipped his pincushion tail up across his back, ready to swing if we came too close. "Hunh, hunh, hunh!" The greeting was like a pig's grunt. He clicked his teeth fast and stomped his feet. A smaller animal than I would have fled, terrified.

Animals love the tender, fat, greasy, small-boned body

of the porcupine so much they'll risk getting stuck with some of his 30,000 quills to eat it. "Thirty *thousand?*" Helen once said, cutting her eyes doubtfully. "That's what the book says," I answered. I never counted them and have no plans to check out the book man's total. They're so mean, those quills, that bears back away. Once embedded in the flesh, the quill's rough surface acts like a barb, almost impossible to pull out. It hangs for weeks, swelling the flesh, festering. I've seen a beaver that died from quills covering almost the whole side of its body.

Bruce shot Porky, then nudged him over on his back. He tied a long cord to one foot. We keep porcupines at a distance, pulling them well behind the snowmobile. The track he makes in the snow has his scent—for other animals to follow straight to one of our traps.

This porcupine's a big one, nearly a yard long, counting the tail. I thought he was more than 10 years old. Underneath the bushy array of devilish needles is a long, humped body. We'll not undress him. He'll freeze and we'll quarter him with an ax to bait traps and cubbies with an irresistible appetizer. The meat smells and tastes bad to me, but then I haven't been fed porcupine since I was a baby the way many wild animals have.

On the creek bank, we began to see a lot of mink tracks, especially around small holes going down through the deep snow to the edge of the frozen creek below. Mink, like otter and beaver, live in holes on the banks of a pond or a stream. Sometimes a mink and as many as six kits will move into a vacant beaver house. They all swim in the creek to get from one place to the next, and to catch fish.

A big freeze puts a thick crust on the water. The water animals locate air holes or even stick their noses against the ice to breathe the air it holds just beneath it. Later as winter freezes all the water in the mountains, the creek loses most or all of its running water. Under the thick crust of ice is four or five feet of empty space.

In this tunnel, the mink, beaver, and otter run back and forth, digging the banks for roots, shielded from the cold winds—and wolves and foxes.

Some trappers crawl into these tunnels to set traps. Dim light comes through the ice roof unless it's covered with deep snow. A stretch of tunnel might run a half-mile.

I don't like crawling in tunnels, especially tunnels where wild animals are running loose.

I'd rather lure the animals to come outside. I got the idea of how to call them out when I was looking around a mink ranch. I noticed that whenever a mink would squeal, all the other minks would run to the top of their cages to look this way and that, trying to see what was going on. A mink squealing at the opening of a mink den might have the same effect, I thought.

The first mink we had caught in the Kamishak, the first one that the wolverines didn't steal, I tormented a little when he was still in the trap, and tape-recorded his squeals. He's a small animal, only a slim 16-inch body at best, attached to a furry tail almost as long. But, inch for inch he's as strong as a bear and every bit as vicious. I stayed well beyond his reach. I've seen a pound-and-a-half mink pushing a three-pound redbelly sucker upstream ahead of her. I've seen a mink's needle-sharp teeth hold a duck by the neck while the body of the mink rode the duck's head, pushing it into the water, trying to drown the bird. Minks are fearless hunters. They'll jump on much bigger animals and clamp deadly teeth into the neck for a kill.

So, I poked my trapped mink with a long pole to make him fight back and squeal—anger? threats? calls for help?—before hitting him to kill.

Now on this trip to the Little Kamishak, I would find out how well the taped mink-sound lure worked.

On the creek bank, where we found a lot of mink tracks around some holes in the snow, I laid the tape recorder close by and started it playing, loud. Helen, Bruce, and I knelt some yards away with our rifles aimed and ready. Several minutes passed. I had begun to think there was nobody home or these minks were low on curiosity.

Then a small dark head popped out of one hole, and a mink slipped out on the snow, looking this way and that. By agreement, he was Helen's. Her shot was good, as I expected. We waited while the tape recorder screamed on. But no other minks lived there. Or if they did, they had scampered into the ice-roofed tunnel, away from the strange crack of rifle fire.

Along this creek, which in three more miles would enter the Little Kamishak, we saw many beaver dams with frozen ponds behind them and scraggly piles of sticks and tree branches—lodges—beside them. This stretch of creek had nearly 50 lodges, the thickest beaver population in the world, probably.

But we won't see much, if anything, of beavers until spring. They stay safe and cozy inside, eating their underwater store of food—bark gnawed from birch, willow, and alder sticks.

We moved slowly along the creek. In a patch of timber, I spotted a line of doglike tracks, each as big as my spread-finger hand. "Wolf! Never saw a track so big. He's a monster size."

"Let's get him," Bruce and Helen said at practically the same moment. They began to pull dead leaves and twigs from tree branches to camouflage a trap.

Every night lately, in our house buried in snow, we've heard the wolves howling nearby and far away. The dogs would howl back, bark, jump, plead to run wild and fight Mr. Larson's cousins to the death. "Lie down," we'd say, and turned out our kerosene lamp to sleep. During the night, Larson would hear something snooping around outside and tell me. First he'd growl low. "I *think* there's a beast out there." Then louder. "Oh yes, boss. It's a wolf soft-padding around." Louder yet. "Boss!" I'm sitting up now. It doesn't take long for your head to clear when you're sleeping in the woods among wild animals. Larson again: "I'd do something about that wolf if you'd let me, boss."

"Hush, Larson. I'm listening."

None of the wolf tracks we'd seen anywhere came close in size to matching this one we'd found near the Little Kamishak River. Bruce and I cut a sizable limb from a cottonwood tree and dragged it with the snowmachine to a spot beside the wolf trail. I dug out a hole in the trail exactly where I figured one of the wolf's feet would be stepping. The open trap, chained to the tree limb, fitted down into the hole. Helen covered it with the gathered leaves and twigs. I poured on a little odorless anti-freeze solution and sprinkled snow over the leaves and chain.

With such a "blind set," I count on the wolf's coming jog-jog-jog along the trail, not paying too much mind to his feet. One foot back or front is almost bound to step on the trap. Not always, though. I've seen tracks showing how the wolf walked up to a trap, stopped, backed up 10 feet, then detoured in a wide circle before hitting the trail again.

But if he does step on the trap, I help him do it right. I make him step on the pan. The pan releases the trigger holding open the jaws. I make sure the animal doesn't step on the trigger itself. If he does, the trigger flies up, throws his foot out of the trap before the jaws slam together, and the animal gets away.

So I guide his foot away from the trigger. I make him want to avoid stepping on that particular place. I do it with a sharp-pointed stick. It needs to be hardly bigger around than a kitchen match, but long enough to push firmly in the ground or snow and stand up two or three inches above twigs and snow covering the trap. With great care, you locate it by the trigger. The animal will see the stick. He will think the sharp point will hurt his paw. He won't step there. He steps instead where the ground seems flat—which is where the pan is waiting. His foot is lingering there when the jaws clang shut.

One more detail. We need to hide the smell of man.

I poured fox urine, taken from a dead fox's bladder, around the trap. The wolf, if he stops and looks at the not-exactly normal snow camouflaging the trap, might think the fox scent means the fox buried some food in this spot. When foxes hide food, they urinate there so they can find it again. Maybe they think they're the only animals that know this, but they're wrong.

I'd brought the trapline log and map showing where we'd set traps along the Little Kamishak, frozen and piled with rough ice like the Kamishak. Everywhere I saw wolverine tracks and sure enough, the first trap was out of the hole, lying shut and empty on the other side of the log as if it had been tossed there in a fit of anger. It stinks. The whole place stinks. The bait is gone.

I was annoyed, exasperated, irritated—and puzzled. How many wolverines prowled this flatland?

"We've caught a half-dozen wolverines in our snare-trap rigs. That's more than anybody I know has ever caught. Now it looks like there're a half-dozen more," I said. If a wolverine had walked up right then and told me I'd catch almost twenty more and leave plenty of footprints behind, I probably would have said, "You like lying as well as stealing."

I was disgusted with cooking the stink off the traps, and decided not to bother taking this one home and cleaning it. "Wolverines like their stink, so we'll use it to keep other animals away and lure the wolverines. Some day one may be careless. He doesn't have to be careless but once and we win the game."

In the next few minutes, we came upon an amazing sight, one I never expect to repeat itself for me. We saw three traps 20 feet apart, each one with a catch—a red fox, a cross fox, and the careless wolverine I'd just wished for!

The red fox was lying quietly in the snow, but his tongue was hanging out in a pant from working so hard to shake off the trap. The cross fox was barking and growling. The wolverine had dug a pit three feet deep around the end of the log the trap chain was nailed to. Was he working just to pass the time? Or was the pit part of an escape plan? Another wolverine some weeks later dug the anchor log loose, then dragged it away with his trapped foot.

Our line of traps went along the river bank to the ocean. Half of them were sprung. Wolverines. We speculated yet again about how they did their dirty, clever trick. Helen thought the wolverines might have learned about hitting the trigger so it kicked the paw out while the trap was closing.

But how, I said, could these devils have learned about such when not even the Natives have trapped in the Kamishak for a long time? "Figured it out just by looking at it? Listen, I know plenty of trappers who haven't figured it out in 40 years after looking at traps every day."

No, I contended, wolverines are just what the Natives say: ghosts of evil men returning to bankrupt trappers.

On down the line, we found in four of our traps a fox, a rabbit, a mink, and a magpie.

"Magpies—they hang around the otters during the winter when they're fishing on the beach," I said to Helen. "It's no puzzle how magpies keep from starving in such hard winters: They follow the land otter and eat his feces. And fish scraps he leaves behind. And bits of crab left in shells the otter has mostly cleaned out. The puzzle about magpies is how they keep from freezing."

Otters move season by season up and down the waterways. In summer they fish in the cool highland ponds and creeks. As their swimming pools freeze, they go to the lowlands where water and fish are still running. When those streams harden, the otters move to the sea to fish under the icepack.

It isn't hard to spot their dens in the clay banks around the beaches, or in the rock ridges jutting into the ocean. Where magpies congregate nearby is the otters' toileting place. Conscientious non-polluters of the water they and their food swim in, otters run far up on the beach, their long bodies undulating, to leave their droppings.

The ocean here looked like the ocean at the mouth of our own Kamishak—ice cakes and ice jumbles as far as we could see. Underneath them, the otters would be flashing through icy water, grabbing even the fastest fish.

"Look!" I heard Helen call. "St. Augustine! It's putting out a lot of smoke."

The volcano's ghostly white cone rose high above the dark water 20 miles away. Its smoke plume was the biggest I had ever seen it. At Contact Point where we were a few miles closer to it, we'd seen no more than wisps of smoke.

"Think it's about to blow, Andy?" Helen asked.

I wished I knew. "I know it's plenty alive. I've camped on the black lava and 'gray wacky'—layered slatelike clay rock—at the foot of the cone. I've heard it rumble, like thunder far away. I never felt easy camping there beside a furnace close to a mile high that was red-hot melted rock inside. But nothing ever happened. I heard it did erupt about 1962. . ."

Seal hunting had drawn me there. On broad sandy beaches at the foot of high cliffs of volcanic ash and lava, about 20,000 spotted seals and a colony of sea lions sprawled from May until mid-August. Most were mamas and their new-born pups. A few thousand sea otters liked the boulder-strewn beaches, too. We only watched them playing games in the water. Killing one sea otter could mean a heavy fine, even prison.

We hunters—this was before hunting all kinds of sea mammals was stopped in 1972—set up camp on a lava ledge away from the sour, putrid smells and the constant crying of the babies. Above us towered the sharp cone of the dark volcano looking as rough as a pile of old candle drippings. It covered all except the ragged edges of an island 10 miles long and five miles wide. Nearly every day we could see a thin trail of smoke at the top, as if the candle had just been blown out.

The most vivid picture in my memory of the place is our tent flying through the air in a fierce wind, pots and pans and sleeping bags following, and all landing in the sea. After that, we lived in a driftwood house.

While Helen, Bruce, and I pondered the smoke of Augustine, we'd kept alert for movement on the ocean ice pack. The returning land otters would be crawling out of the water through breaks between the ice cakes. They'd likely be running on their short legs for their toilet places.

"Better get a move on setting traps before otters begin coming out of the water," I said. On the trail leading to a toileting place, Helen scooped out a shallow hole in the snow for the trap while Bruce and I dragged up a log we found in the edge of the icy surf.

"I'd use a smaller, lighter trap than the one you've picked," I advised Helen. Even if the otter is six feet long and all muscle, his short leg bones break easy. Once the trap jaws have broken the bone, the otter may get away. He'll twist and roll over and over until he's wrung his leg apart to free himself." Some people swear that animals gnaw their leg off in order to escape the trap. They don't. I once watched a beaver turn over and over to break skin, flesh, bone, finally tendon, and limp away. It took two hours.

Helen set another trap at the other end of the log, and we loaded for home.

"Tomorrow or the next day when you come back, remember to keep your distance from the otter," I reminded Helen. "We don't want him wounding the best cook and hardest working woman in this part of the world. Otters are tough customers, you know. I've seen an otter rush a dog, grab him by the nose, whirl him around and toss him high over her head."

As the snowmachine slid alongside the ice-jammed Little Kamishak, we saw that clouds we'd noticed piling up behind the near mountains were now flying high and fast. With the sun moving down behind the mountains to the west and dark clouds spreading over the sky above us, daylight quickly turned to dimlight.

Drafts of cold air dropped down on us. "I'm running for home," I called back to Bruce and Helen.

The winds propelling the clouds swirled and capered, until the darkest cloud hung directly over us. Sleet began beating like tiny gravel on the metal snowmobile.

"Bad surprise," I said. "Hang on. I'm going to run this machine as hard as I can."

Gritty sleet sandpapered my face even though the winds were at my back. I slipped on my dark glasses, and took them off in a minute when they had iced up. Grains of ice cut into my squinting eyelids. I held one gloved hand before my face and drove with the other.

Bruce partly shielded me from the gusting, angry wind slamming the hard crystals against us. Helen turned her back and leaned down on the foxes and wolverine.

The land looked level. Why was the snowmachine tilting as if we were going down a steep hill? Now the sound of the straining motor made it certain we were climbing. Snow and light were playing tricks with my eyes.

Harder and harder the wind whipped the sleet against us. What if the machine broke down? I listened for the slightest sound of rebellion. But we have a tent, sleeping bags, and rations, stop worrying. The worrying went ticking on, magnifying each second into visible ribbons of time like the tracks I was following in the snow. I knew they stretched about an hour, or nearly 5,000 seconds, ahead. At least dull daylight might stay with us that long.

At last I saw the tree where the safety line across the Kamishak was tied. My arm and elbow, aching from holding my hand before my eyes, didn't want to unbend. Bruce did the icy fumbling to untie the rope, thread it through the snowmachine rings, and retie it. Now for the slow, anxious crossing, slippery with sleet. At the anchor log, it took both Bruce and Helen to release us and resecure the safety line.

Only a quarter-mile to go. How can wind so heavy with ice move so fast? Snow and ice drove through the crack between my hood and head. Ice built up an inch thick on my eye-shielding glove.

Home. Stiff with ice and fatigue, I nearly fell off the snowmobile seat. Creaking and popping like come-alive ice statues, Bruce and I pushed machine, trailer, carcasses and all into the shed while Helen held the flashlight.

Mr. Larson and Jake had been barking since we first drove up. We could hardly get inside the door they were so eager to touch us.

The door closed on weather havoc. Helen, holding the flashlight, was putting a match to the lampwick. I poked the fire, Bruce laid on wood.

I looked around at two faces lit up with "cabin appreciation" and knew mine said the same thing. Helen laid all the words we needed on the next important event. "Now," she said, "let's get that lasagna on the table."

"Something unusual is going on out there," I was saying a couple of days later. The storm had died, but the radio static had thickened steadily. Now on this clear, sunny morning, static was scratching out everything.

"Maybe a monster storm from the top of the world is about to throw a fit," I said, "or a spectacular Aurora Borealis is about to burst upon us. Either one would make heavy static."

Bruce switched off the nerve-jangling noise. We kept hearing it—only louder and louder. "It's a plane!" we all shouted and jumped to pull on our outdoor gear. Dogs barking and bounding around us in excitement, we hurried to the river.

On the deep-snow "runway," the river bank, we saw a young fellow walking from a Piper-on-skiis.

"Hello! I'm Pete from up Iliamna way."

"Oh yes! We've been talking to you on the radio."

"I said I'd hop down one sunny day to see you, the first people we know about who ever spent a whole winter at Kamishak. The last guy here scared out when the snow got to 10 feet. He skied a hundred miles to us.

"But listen! The big news is the volcano! When I passed by Augustine, smoke was pouring out several places. I didn't see any glow of fire, but I saw lots of lightning flashes in the smoke! My radio was all static. Then just as I made the turn to land here, I saw a big, BIG plume of white smoke coming out."

"Let's get to the beach and see what's happening," I said. "We can't see much here—there's a ridge blocking our view of the volcano."

We hurried on snowmobile and toboggan to the beach. On the northeast horizon of the ocean, we could see Augustine. Out of its top puffed thick, boiling white smoke which formed a billowing mushroom cloud miles high and broad across the bright blue sky. The cloud kept expanding and expanding. Every minute I expected something bigger to happen out of that vast roiling, out of that darkening, thick cloud.

Instead, the plume began to tear and fall apart, flying into shreds with what must have been a fierce draft of hot wind from the volcano.

Tense and wondering, we watched this awesome spectacle for a quarter-hour. When the smoke lessened and turned dark, I knew the first great plume had been the big blow-off of the volcano, even if we heard no sound. Later, the radio news said that the top of the plume climbed eight miles high, and was seen in Homer, 100 miles away. But we four on the Kamishak beach were the nearest eye-witnesses to the January 23, 1976 eruption of St. Augustine. I believe I made the only picture of it.

At the time, we stood staring across the water and wondering if there'd be another blow-out, guessing how long the dark ash would keep coming out of the mountain. What did it mean for us? Cut off from the world by the screen of radio static—it was caused by the electrical charge created by dust friction in the volcanic cloud—we could only watch and wait. "But we're going to load the snowmachine and toboggan, ready to run to the mountains if we need to," I said.

Our visitor decided it was past time to leave. We saw him in his tiny plane ski off along the narrow airstrip of the river bank.

That night we could see fireworks spraying out of the volcano. Red flashing sparks showered out of the top of the cone in spasms, a shocking and dazzling display.

For six weeks we kept an eye on St. Augustine's dark smoke by day and fireworks by night. So far, the ashy cloud blew east, or north, or northwest, sometimes in perfect smoke rings. When would our turn come? Was the ash likely to cover the Kamishak the way Mt. Katmai's ash covered Kodiak in 1912? Months before I'd noticed in our river banks that under two feet of humus lay four feet of gray volcanic ash. Did it come from Katmai—or Augustine? The blow-out of Katmai had created the Valley of Ten Thousand Smokes. Was it Augustine that created Kamishak's smoking black pools of hot water, marked now by our red-striped poles? And Contact Point—I remembered seeing on the end of that granite finger a whirlpool-shaped hole 20 feet deep in an old lava bed. Melted rock had boiled—in the heat of erupting Augustine? Our Kamishak log cabin was only a few miles farther from Augustine than Contact Point. . .

Through the irritating scratchy noises on the radio we caught a word here, a word there. "Anchorage . . . fine ash . . gone. . . lava . . . tidal wave . . ."

Tidal wave! We could be washed away in a mountain of water hundreds of feet high. Was it for real—or just maybe? We got no impression of warning to evacuate.

Many nights we listened, wondering. Whenever the static increased, we ran to look to the northeast at the smoke or fireworks.

For days at least one of us stayed home, listening constantly to volcano news. The wind had shifted, we heard, blowing ash away from Anchorage and onto the McNeil River area up the bay from us. Pilots reported inches of fine gray dust covering the deep snow. "Looks like a farm that's been plowed."

The wind shifted a little more. We first knew it when we smelled sulphur inside the house. Outside the sky was dark with fine ash and clouds. Dust crept inside through tiny cracks around the door. The snow turned gray in an afternoon.

Bruce went out for firewood and came in layered with ash, coughing, eyes burning. We made wet masks to wear outside, marveled when we took them off and saw the dust we would have breathed.

"Tidal wave . . . " scientists were still speculating. The explosions might split the island, cold seawater might pour into the hot interior, steam might build up for a mighty explosion, the ocean floor might shift, and the shift would cause a tidal wave.

A couple of times we were on the verge of leaving and riding the snowmobile to the mountains. Then the talk and the volcano would quiet down. We'd quiet down with it.

By the time Augustine blew again—twice in one day—two weeks after the first explosion, the wind had shifted away from us. A foot of snow had fallen, covering the powdery gray. The landscape shone bright again.

Somehow we had become used to seeing the spectacle, to discounting the speculations, to going on about our business. It was merely interesting when we heard a pilot say one day as he flew near St. Augustine, "There's a crater a half-mile across. I'd say a couple of hundred feet of the mountain top is gone. Heat waves are rocking my plane."

In our Kamishak world, we found a remark from Helen that same day far more fascinating. "Look at this!" she said. "This otter's belly is rubbed clean of fur! And Andy, you said otter is the most durable fur in the world. But sliding on ice full of St. Augustine's ashes must be like sliding on sandpaper. The fur is worn off to the skin!"

"I probably made the only picture of St. Augustine's biggest blow January 23, 1976 (above). Heavy smoke draped the top of the volcano for months (below)."

10
Kamishak Queen of the Wolves

A wolf is a majestic animal, beautiful and intelligent. For a wolf, I'll go through more and try harder. Alongside a wolf, a bear is a mere nuisance about as interesting as a pig.

Andy Nault

Huge wolf tracks in the snow, then a story the visiting pilot from Iliamna told me, and I began to be haunted by the shadow of a great white wolf, the Kamishak Queen.

While the pilot and I had walked to the beach to see if the volcano was blowing off, he had asked me about moose hunting in the Kamishak. "Great. Always one outside the door when we get low on meat," I said. Ptarmigans? "Millions of them." The foxes? "Plenty of them, all colors." The wolves?

Well, it's an odd thing, I said. November, a cold snowy month, and December, a rainy, thaw month, we caught several wolves. Then during the awful storms of January, we didn't hear or see a sign of them.

Now they're out there howling every night. They don't sing chorus, they sing rounds and harmonize. I told the pilot that it seemed to me when the wolf voices were

Anger and hostility raise a high ruff of hair around the neck of the Kamishak Queen of the Wolves. Across a mile of soft, deep snow, she pulled a log with her trapped foot. Andy crawled, snowmachined, and tumbled into snow at her feet to get pictures, and to stare into the eyes of the huge old lone wolf.

loudest, the notes saddest, the sessions longest, there followed the worst storm imaginable the next day. When I first heard so many wolves howling so mournful, I just said, "Listen to that sad song. The wolves must be in trouble. Something must be hurting them. They sound so mournful it makes you feel right sorry for them."

"Owoooo-oooo-oooo-oh-uhhh!" running down the scale to a hollow low note, trembling lower and lower to the last "uh."

Then I noticed that within hours, the wind would rise and howl back at them, drown them out. I began to predict weather by the wolves. "The wolves are crying, complaining, and cussing," I'd say. "It's a bad storm rolling in tonight." Sure enough, it was. You should have heard them around New Year's Day.

The pilot laughed when I told him this, and said he'd have to watch and see if that was true around Iliamna. I don't think he believed me, but I was serious, and I believe it myself.

"The other interesting thing I can tell you about Kamishak wolves," I said, "is that there's a giant one roaming about. Just yesterday we saw the tracks. They were super-size."

"*How* big?" the pilot asked. I spread out my hand, wide. "If I hadn't laid my wide open hand into the track to measure, I wouldn't believe it either," I said. "Six inches by five, no less. This wolf has to be at least eight feet long, a foot or more longer than some of the biggest. The tracks went across the Little Kamishak River and we lost them. We've set a trap big enough for a bear."

The pilot stared at me quizzically. He looked far, far away. He licked his lips. He said in a half whisper, "The

White Queen."

"I'm going to tell you something," he said. "This must be the great white wolf that we at Iliamna know. We have known this wolf for many years. Ten years at least. She comes and goes. Now you say you've seen giant wolf tracks down here. So she must run this coastline for a good hundred miles.

"A few at Iliamna have seen her, and I and a lot more have seen her tracks, BIG, like you said. Some of us have almost run into her lying in the snow. She makes off, vanishes in the snow, like a big white ghost. We call her The White Queen. She's a loner. Doesn't run with a pack.

"We've talked many hours about why she's a loner. Some think it's because she's strong and smart enough to lead the pack and she knows it. But that's nearly always a male's place. Number-One wolf, he is. Wolves each have a rating in the family pack, you know, highest to lowest. Each one eats less the lower he is in rank. Maybe the pack didn't like the way this wolf looked, so white, so big. Maybe they didn't like the way she acted, so hungry, so strong, so bossy. They tried to put her at bottom rank, the scapewolf all the others could attack, keep away from the food. She couldn't stand that rank, going hungry. She tried to move up, eat more. The pack jumped on her. So she left to kill food for herself and her big hunger. That's what we think. But she has to keep moving. Since she doesn't belong to a pack she doesn't have a right to kill where any pack hunts. If they catch her, there's a big fight. She learned to be watchful. She learned how to disappear fast.

"Now what you say makes me think she's here," the pilot went on. "Well. You say you've set a trap big enough for a bear. Hm. Don't get your hopes up. Still, you never can tell. She's been around a long time, she might be getting old and foolish. If you catch her, call me right away on the radio."

And with that, the Kamishak Queen, as I fell to calling her, became a ghost haunting me.

When I heard the wolves howling that night, saying primitively pleasant things to each other (my weather prediction: fine tomorrow), I listened for a strong new voice, one sadder, more lonesome than the others. But perhaps loners don't howl with the crowd, especially love songs like these tonight—"Youououououooooo!"

Perhaps she was on her way back to the far north when she made the tracks we saw. I could hardly wait to return to the trap that we had set to catch a giant wolf.

Blowing volcano or no, we went the next day.

As we came in sight of the cottonwood log lying in the snow, I was leaning forward, straining to see. Yes! The snow was all stirred up. An animal was pulling at the trap. But it wasn't The Queen. A dark animal instead.

A wolverine. "A wolverine, Andy! That's great!" Bruce said.

"Yeah, Well, yeah, that's great. So that's our seventh. . ." But my mind was on The Kamishak Queen, wondering if she'd gone for good, if she was so trap-wise I'd never catch her even if she was still around. If the Native trappers had been trying ten years and more and she was still a ghost to them, how could I expect to catch her in one day?

Still. . . surprising things can happen in the wilderness—or anywhere—if you persist. There's that one moment when perfect circumstances meet each other and you're waiting at their crossroads.

Of course we had to move the set to get away from the

stink and wreckage the captive wolverine had made.

"Let's improve on this set, Bruce," I said. "This big lone white wolf needs a lot of food. Probably she's hungry all the time. We'll add some bait just in front of the trap and guide her right up to it."

We sawed off two more cottonwood limbs, trimmed them of branches, and laid them to border the sides of the trail. Crosswise the trail at the head of the logs we stacked a barrier of branches. Some feet back from the branches, in the space between the logs, I dug the hole for the trap.

"Now we add a nice mouthwatering gutpile," I said. "Lay it between the trap and the branches. And right with it, push in this stick I've dipped in the scent bottle. The only other thing we can do to improve the chances for a white wolf catch is to add mouth-watering bait to our other trail sets. Let's hop to it."

For weeks, we baited our traps lavishly—gut piles, an old moosehead, porcupine, Arctic hare.

Wolves and foxes and another wolverine stepped on the grass and snow hiding them, and were caught. But not The Kamishak Queen. Each time I glimpsed a trail trap from a distance, I had a feeling of high expectancy, a today-is-the-day excitement. Sometimes I could even see a large white animal lying beside the trap. Always the mirage faded into ruffled snow where a worn-out, panting fox or wolf lay, or where a wolverine had made his mess.

I didn't even see a big wolf track all that time.

Then one day in early March, I came on them again.

It was the first snow-softening day. The crust on the snow was barely strong enough to support the snowmobile with one person, so I went alone. I was checking traps on our side, the south side, of the Kamishak.

All of a sudden I came upon a large hole in the snow, red and bloody, trampled around the edges. Inside lay the bony remains, hooves, and head of a caribou.

I went looking for the story imprinted in the snow, piecing it together scene by scene, a drama that took place by moonlight. Tracks of the caribou came down from the slope and ambled across the flat snow toward the river. Then I saw wolf tracks emerge from alders the caribou passed—huge wolf tracks! The sight thrilled me. The Kamishak Queen! She followed the caribou, moving faster and faster.

Caribou hooves began kicking up snow with speed, then went springing and bounding. Suddenly the wolf sprang. Her teeth tore into the soft belly. Hide and flesh ripped. Guts spilled out under the caribou's feet before it sank to its knees.

The Queen was very hungry. She took bite after bite as fast as she could gulp. In a few minutes, her sides bulged with 20 pounds of caribou.

Perhaps the Queen then threw back her head, pursed her lips, closed her eyes and howled, "Owoooo-ooooo-ooo-uh-uhhh!" Mellow, satisfied. Then she left for a long sleep in a snowbank, her muzzle between her hind legs, her furry tail over her head. Cold wouldn't bother her. She has super-thick fur, an amazing thermostat, and footpads with anti-freeze in them.

The return of the Queen made big news at the supper table in the log cabin. "She's back! Now we really bait those traps fancy!"

Bait them we did, and waited. Ten days went by.

No Queen. No huge tracks. Nothing. I dropped from glum to glummer. I didn't even want to talk about the likelihood that the Queen had tracked northward days ago at the steady wolf speed of five miles an hour. And then—

About March 15, I went out alone on the snowmobile at sunup, even though the snow would be treacherously soft in a few hours. I had to do the rounds and get back before the bright sun made a mush of the snow crust and I was sinking into it with the machine.

Ordinarily on a day as pretty as this with snow glittering under the sun and blue sky, I'd have been happily conscious of the landscape, enjoying the fast sledding, the little dips and rises, the snowy mountains hemming in the flatlands, the companionable put-put of the motor.

But today I was at the bottom of my glum. Uptight with disappointment, critical of every detail of how we'd made the sets, I was absorbed in consoling myself with endless theories as to the Queen's whereabouts.

I came in sight of one of our sets. I lean forward, squinting. If a set looks unchanged, I stand back and don't go tramping around it. Something different about that set, though. Is it *whiter?* My heart bounded, and in a second it and the machine motor were racing at the same speed.

Then I was standing there looking at the trap scene and saying, "Well, I'll be cursed!" The place was whiter all right—because both the trap and the log it was chained to were GONE!

I looked around to see which way the animal—another wolverine?—had dragged the log across the soft snow. It would take a strong animal to pull by one trapped paw such a heavy drag. Well, a wolverine did that once, so. . .

But this log, I thought, was longer, bigger, heavier. Too much for a wolverine, too much for a wolf. But not a bear. One might have come out on a sunny day to look for a bite to eat.

There was the drag trail going off to the right. It wiped out the tracks of the animal pulling it.

What was that red spot on the snow by the big cottonwood where the trail led? Blood. . . The animal must be there, only 50 feet away. I stared intently. Something moved. Then, rising out of the snow was an enormous white wolf—The Kamishak Queen!

It was a moment I still think of often and relive that surge of pure joy.

She looked like a small pony she was so big, the kind of wolf that inhabits folk tales and legends.

What to do. Shoot her quick? I raised my rifle and looked at her through the telescopic lens. Lord, what an animal! Majestic was the only word for her. I had to have a picture of her. I slung the rifle back on my shoulder and dug into a pouch for my camera. I fumbled and fumbled getting it out, my mind on figuring how to get closer to her across the softening snow. Minutes passed while I gritted my teeth, exasperated at myself for not bringing my snowshoes. Where had my head been this morning? Too much fretting about this Queen.

I broke off two yard-long sticks from the branches at the head of the trap set. With one in each hand, they and my lower legs would take the place of weight-distributing snowshoes when I crawled.

Queen saw me crawling toward her, made a right angle turn from the tree and headed toward an open snowfield. I saw she was caught by a hind foot, and with it she was slowly dragging the heavy log behind her. If it been her front foot, she'd still be at the trap site. . .

Thinking I could crawl close enough for my pictures

before she moved very far, I kept on. How can an animal pull a heavy log like that when a paw is squeezed painfully in steel jaws? I've heard that the clamp shuts off circulation and nerves, numbing all the pain.

Queen was having a hard time going. Not only the soft snow slowed her down by giving away under a paw now and again, but tops of stiff brush sticking above the deep snow held back the log.

I was having a hard time myself. Crawling is not my strongest skill, especially with a rifle that keeps sliding off my shoulder. I saw she was going to make it to the open field in a few minutes and I tried to crawl faster. Even with her burden she outdistanced me. She reached the meadow and speeded up.

My dream of bringing home The Kamishak Queen was fading before my eyes while I was on my hands and knees, moving like a four-legged animal. "Crawl back to the snowmachine, man, get on it and catch up with her, head her off!" I told myself.

Slowly, so slowly, I crawled back. All the way I thought of the Queen pulling the log in the opposite direction across the snow. The sun beat down on everything, softening the thin crust.

At last I crawled up into the seat of the snowmachine. Panting, mumbling, angry at myself, at the Queen for being so strong, I started the motor.

The trick would be to skim over the dissolving crust so fast that the machine wouldn't sink into the snow. I gave it the gas, raced away, twisting a trail between bunches of brush tops. When I came to the smooth snowfield, the runners began to sink. More speed, pull up and out of sink-spots, stay on top by sheer momentum.

The Queen was not in sight. Her trail was, and I followed it. It led toward an area of big cottonwoods. At least the snow crust would be stronger in their shadows.

There! There she was! At least there was the log, stopped by a pair of big trees. I drove around behind, keeping my distance at 15 feet, and cut the motor. She was lying flat, her chin between outstretched front legs, her back legs drawn up under her. She appeared to be asleep.

I began fumbling again with my camera, excited fingers doing everything wrong. Finally I sighted and pressed the shutter. No, that's not good enough. I need some height. I scrambled to climb and balance myself on my knees atop the driver's seat.

Just as I pushed the shutter, I tilted the machine and went diving into the snow.

What now, I thought, feeling foolish and apprehensive. I peered over the edge of my snow hole toward the Queen, now only 10 feet away.

She was awake, staring at me, baring and clicking her teeth, slowly getting to her feet, her neck hair standing in a ruffle. She looked big as a horse.

"Supposes" ran through my thoughts: Suppose she sprang. . . suppose the trap chain broke. . . suppose the worn-out tendons of her leg broke. I grabbed the rifle off my back, laid it across the top of my pit, and pulled myself out—all faster than is really possible.

Back on the driver's seat, sitting this time, I reorganized my thoughts, my fingers, the camera, the rifle. The Queen lay back down and closed her eyes. I thought I saw dark, hostile pupils staring through slitted, upslanted eyes in her white face. Was she playing a game?

You're going to fool around one minute too long and

get yourself in a mess of trouble, I told myself. One more shutter click. One rifle shot.

When the shot finished echoing and the Queen lay still, I felt both relief and a let-down. She was an amazing creature in size, in color, in the life she'd live, loping along 20 or 30 miles a night, always alone. No pack hunts for her, no playful cubs, no friendly wolf voices answering her moonlight messages. The only animals she had any contact with at all were those she ran down, or ambushed, killed, and ate. She must have had poor hunting to want my trap's frozen gutpile so bad.

How could I get her home when she was so big, the machine so small, and the snow so soft? I wished for a minute that Bruce was there to help me tie her up and lift her across the back of the machine. But then I was glad nobody was there to watch me struggling, sweating, and cursing the next couple of hours.

I followed my old trail, figuring the runners had packed down the snow enough to hold me and Queen without sinking. It almost worked. As long as I stayed in the tracks, we stayed on top of the snow. But Queen's weight unbalanced things and I kept running off the trail, bogging down.

Stop and skin her, my better sense told me. Keep trying to get her home to show to Bruce and Helen, my pride replied. I wrestled in and out of soft snow every 20 feet for five miles. Sometimes I had to take Queen off, rev the motor to a running jerk out of a hole, fly across to a firm spot, and drag Queen to the back seat again.

By the time I saw the smoking stove pipe sticking out from the snow under our cottonwoods, I was the world's most completely tuckered out wolf trapper. Bruce and

Helen burst out of the cabin door as soon as Mr. Larson leaped to his feet, barked and whined. They were shouting and backslapping, Larson was leaping, licking, and bounding while I stood there numb and dumb—and smiling. When Bruce called the pilot at Iliamna on the radio after we ate, I was stretched out, unconscious, snoring.

The next day we took the Queen out of the pre-fab, measured and weighed her before starting the skinning. Eight feet with the tail, a little over 100 pounds. "But she's real skinny," Bruce observed. "I'll bet when she was eating well, she weighed at least 150." I'm sure she would have.

Her head and body told us about a few major events in her life. She had been in a terrible fight, I thought. With a bear? or the wolf pack? She'd been slammed into something that broke out several jaw teeth and cracked the jaw bone. She'd once attacked a moose that was too big and strong for a lone wolf to kill, so she got a hole kicked in her forehead for her boldness. Her body was lean, very lean, a reminder of hard times in winter when prospect after prospect escaped and meals were a week, or even two, apart. And her body was old, at least 15 years old.

It had been a difficult life but probably a satisfying one from a loner's point of view. The great white animal had been totally self-reliant, feeding herself, traveling the world for a hundred-mile strip, exploring its seashore, flatlands, and ridges in summer and winter. She had made a name for herself, perhaps in wolf society as well as with a few men. Like the other wolves, she'd amused herself playing with ravens, picking berries with her teeth, staring at ripples in river water, wading and herding a salmon into a shallow pool to grab it with curved fangs, running alongside a deer, slashing at the hams. And eating, eating.

As long as the great white skin hung on my wall, I felt a twinge of regret along with a thump of pride each time I saw it. And always after that day with the living queen, whenever I listened at night to the howling of the wolves across the valley of the Kamishak, a picture came to mind of a great white wolf, eyes closed, muzzle turned to the sky, singing in the wilderness. "Owooo-oooooooo-oooooo-ohhh-uh!"

Bruce and the hide of the Kamishak Queen.

11

Spring Beaver

"We just unfurled our heels and shoved."
Huckleberry Finn

"Yelp, yelp, yelp! Roouuf! YELP!" Larson leaped up, rushed to the window, partly uncovered now, and almost beat his fists against it.

"First sign of spring," I told Bruce and Helen. "That's Mr. Larson's hate-bears noise. The pests are coming out. But just a few—the hungriest, meanest. It'll be a couple of weeks before bears are out in force in mid-May. We should be gone by then."

The end-of-April bear didn't knock on our door. He was too busy pawing and kicking out a trench in the deep snow to get across our yard.

For two weeks now, spring thaws and rains lasting as little as two hours and as much as two days, had been playing hit-and-run with hard freezes and ice storms. Day began to cut off slices of night, sunlight against cold moonshine. Longer, warmer days loosened and shrank

Ten feet of snow begins cracking away and sinking below the cabin roof at the first warm touch of Spring. In a few days, rains will melt the snow and make Andy, Helen, and Bruce wade knee-deep in flood water. "But it was also melting the beavers back into my trapping world," says Andy, who took off for the lodges and met an astounding beaver.

the snow. Cold nights and rushing winds stiffened the landscape back again, then beat the naked trees until they moaned and crackled.

Twice a day, once in darkness and once in light, the ocean tide came up the river and shoved spring ahead. The incoming water pressure squeezed the river's thinning ice, split it, shook it, rattled it, just as it was doing to the ice pack in the bay.

Aside from the hatefulness of thaw-and-freeze weather, it's treacherous for travelers. Under the crusts of night-freezes, the holes of yesterday's melt are waiting. After the thick-falling feathery snow of early morning, the rain at noon will strand a snowmobile in slush.

And what have you got if you run all those risks and trap a fox, or wolf, or snare a wolverine? A spring-y fur. The thick, soft fur of winter is shedding—the animals are taking off thermal underwear and putting on tee-shirts against the coming heat.

Besides that, the animals are into the serious part of this year's sex and family life. Some are still mating. Some are pregnant. Some are tending newborn babies.

So one day we collected all our traps and settled into wilderness cabin life.

We listened to the whole show—the pouring rain and dripping snow, the cannon booms of cracking ice fortresses in the river, the crackling night-ice in the cottonwoods, the screeching male foxes chasing a female, porcupines grunting in the brush. The hollow-noted "Youuuuuuuu!" of the wolves floated seductively across the flatlands.

My restless trapper's thoughts were rambling out of the cabin confines and around the beaver ponds and lodges. Well now, it's the first of May. I know Mama Beaver is very pregnant. But the pond ice hasn't thinned yet, having still a heavy layer of snow lying on it and re-freezing every night. Mama is getting more irritable every day. She's crowded into a large pantry-size room with four big children who've been growing bigger all winter, and a male partner who's been broadening with fat and thick fur.

Mama Beaver is as impatient as I for the ice to melt and stay melted. The store of wood with bark-food on them is getting low. And she wants to kick out most of her crowd so she can rest, then do her birthing job in peace.

I'll be glad when she kicks them out where I can get at them before the beaver trapping season is over in mid-May.

In the two months since the season opened, I've taken only four beavers. Bruce and Helen have half-a-dozen. The government fellow who picks the opening date chooses mid-February when a yard of ice and three yards of snow separate beaver from trapper. Nevertheless, I gritted my teeth, tried to chop a hole down to pond water, and drop in a trap.

I quit when I found myself standing practically on my head to reach the re-frozen bottom of a nine-foot-deep hole in the snow—and almost tumble in. I was reaching to the bottom either to hack ice with an ax to break open a hole for the trap, or I was trying to lower the trap on a chain into the ice hole, or I was trying to haul up the trap and see if it had caught a beaver.

I quit for good when the deep snow hole got the better of me and I slid in head-first. With just a little bad luck, my own head could have sprung my own trap in the water down under the ice hole.

Not only did struggling head-down make me feel ridiculous, I just didn't have time for such. I had so much work looking after the traps that were bringing in foxes, wolves, wolverine, and otter, I didn't have time to spend a whole day—six hours or so of daylight—shoveling and chopping and crawling upside down for a 50-50 chance to catch one beaver.

But now the spring breakup was at hand. I kept thinking about how many beavers were in each Kamishak lodge. (Six) And how many lodges, average, on each stream. (Say 25.) Six times 25 is—150 beavers! How many streams? At least 14 creeks and three rivers. About 2,500 beavers within walking or paddling distance! That kind of figure would make any trapper jump up and dive out the door, no matter the weather.

More figuring. Rules and regulations limit each trapper to 40 beavers. Bruce, Helen, and I were entitled to 120. Sounds like a lot, but one wolverine will harvest as much in a year as I'm allowed to take.

Wolverines are the real enemies of the beaver—worse than bears. At least bears take time out to eat lots of grass, fish, berries, roots, mice, grubs, and even ants. Wolverines just eat meat.

During the winter before the snow piles too deep, the wolverine will search along the bank edge of the beaver pond for an ice crack he can get his claws into. There he digs away the ice. He makes a hole big enough to squirm into. Sometimes the space under the ice has little water and he wades to the beaver lodge. Sometimes there's enough water he must swim. He goes straight for the side that has an opening to the waterport inside the lodge. About a quarter of the floor space of the lodge is water. The rest is a platform of sticks and rocks a foot or more out of   the water. There the beavers are sleeping or nibbling on the bark of tree branches from their underwater pantry.

The wolverine clambors up the platform enough to slash his terrible claws into the nearest beaver belly, and drag the carcass off into the water.

If it's a kit and no parent home, the wolverine gets away easy. If even one adult is home, the wolverine may run into a bloody underwater fight. Maybe he wins and hauls his dinner out the ice hole. Maybe he doesn't win. A beaver's broad, chisel-sharp teeth can snap off even a wolverine's sturdy leg.

Since I have no insulated fur suit like the wolverine, I impatiently wait out the winter, planning to try for beaver when the big thaw arrives.

It came overnight in clouds spilling over with rain. Such pouring they did. All in a few hours we had snowmelt and icemelt flowing, rainwater cutting gullies down to and into the earth. Everywhere we heard the sound of running water, the sound of Spring.

In three days, the ten feet of snow became two and in places none. A foot of snow equals an inch of rain, so in a day we had the new inches from the sky releasing the old inches from the snow. Snow-water from the mountains began pouring into creeks, creeks into rivers. I was feeling happier by the hour. The beavers were melting back into my trapping world. Maybe tomorrow would be a good day to go visit them with a few traps.

About that moment, the ocean tide rushed in fast, piled high with ice cakes from both bay and river. It jammed the cakes into a ridge 30 to 40 feet thick and some 20 feet high above the land. Broken ice cakes coming downstream lodged behind it. Night's swift chill stuck it tight together.

The river now had a dam. Behind the dam, snowmelt from the creeks, running so fast and voluminous it had no time or still surface to freeze, rose through the night. It rose higher than the river banks and swirled out across the flatlands. It went coursing across the brushlands, crusting over with ice, breaking through in new surges, spreading into a thin lake for miles. With daylight and sun, it ran faster, rose inch by inch as mountain, creek, and dammed river drained themselves where they could.

Helen awakened me. "ANDY! WATER! There's water running under our door!"

I jumped down from my top bunk to look, and wet my feet in water coming up through the floor boards.

"FLOOD!" I shouted. "Water will keep rising. Quick, let's get busy! Grab all the boxes, anything that matters, put them on the beds, shelves, table, anywhere. The water may rise knee-high. And it may do it fast. I've been in floods before. Me and my kids had to sit in the trees once waiting for the flood water to go down. It was six feet deep in the house. Took all day and all night."

"Awww, Andy," Helen said skeptically.

We went to doing things hand-over-fist, running in boots through water now an inch, now two inches deep. We saved the skins in the shed, hoisted the food, dry stovewood, and clothes. Bruce and I brought wood from the woodpile to raise a platform in the shed for the snowmobile, Honda, and outboard motor. The dogs, tied on long ropes outside, were barking and carrying on, splashing in what was soon six inches of water. In an hour they climbed the woodpile to jump on the roof.

In a few hours, we were splashing in knee boots in water a foot deep—inside as well as outside the house.

Rain started again, pouring, sloshing-down rain.
Snow melted away like ice cream at a summer picnic. We
had to change to hip boots. Water was now above our
knees. Our stove, sitting on a boxed-in mound of dirt two
feet high, was in danger. We took out a section of stovepipe in order to raise it and our fire. We sat it on a tin
wash tub placed face-down on two boards laid across the
rim of the dirt box.

I slogged out to the tree line close to the river bank to
see why our world was flooding so fast and deep. Just
upriver, I saw the ice dam. It was dribbling and trickling
water. Everywhere else, the water was sprawling and
running wild.

"If the rain doesn't stop soon, or the ice dam doesn't
break and free the waterway, I'm bringing the skiff in here
for us to sleep in," I told Bruce and Helen. They didn't have
any trouble now believing anything I said.

Our bottom bunks were still three inches above the
water when the rain quit and night's freeze put a stop to the
running of water and melting of ice. "The freeze will hold
off a water rise until sunlight," I assured Helen, Bruce, and
myself. "At least we can go to sleep and not worry about
finding ourselves afloat in bed in the middle of the night."

For three days the rain stopped and the chill reduced
the water flow. We lived mostly in our bunks, reading,
talking, sleeping, mending our clothes, watching the
waterline we'd marked on the bunk post. It stayed steady.
We took turns getting into hip boots, wading through two
feet of water to carry food to the dogs, put wood on the fire,
and open tin cans of food. For drinking water, I fetched
rainwater scooped out of the skiff, floating tied to a tree and
open to the skies.

Listening to the radio and contacting our pilot in Homer was the one important pastime we couldn't enjoy. We had accidently crossed some wires when we put in a new battery. That burned out the resistors. "We'd better spend a bunch of time facing Homer and praying," I grumbled. "Bill DeCreeft is supposed to have us on his schedule for pickup the fifteenth of May. But writing a date down more than seven months ago is a lot less reliable than hollering at him on the radio the fourteenth of May."

On the fourth day, I couldn't stand being cooped up another minute. The sun was out. The water didn't seem to be rising or falling. "I'm taking the skiff to the river and see what's going on," I announced, took my rifle, and sloshed out. Bruce was tinkering gloomily with the insides of the radio. Helen, who hated wearing hip boots, would stay in bed all day re-reading old magazines.

I floated and paddled the skiff in two feet of water to the tree line just above the ice dam. One reason the flood waters hadn't risen was visible. Dribbles and trickles through the dam had enlarged to gushings and spoutings. Two days in a row like this sunny one would bring the ramparts down.

With my paddle I found the edge of the river bank, pushed the skiff into deep water, and dropped the outboard down. It roared to a start, then pulled strong against the weak bankside current. I was feeling better by the second.

I turned up the first creek, marked by faster current coming in from the side of the river.

I had beavers on my mind, and traps in my skiff.

In two minutes I saw three beavers swimming toward me, one behind another. They raised their heads high to see where the motor noise was coming from, saw me, and made startled dives out of sight.

Probably a Papa beaver and his two-year-olds, kicked out of the lodge at last, I thought. My spirits began to rise higher. There'd be at least six lodges around the pond, and from each one a Papa and two large children would be emerging. My chances for getting a trap down before all the Papas and younguns were kicked out looked good.

I use the term "kicked out" because that's what other trappers and woodsmen say. But what actually happens? I wondered. A big fight? A heart-to-heart talk? A tribal custom, so she only needs to bump him in the shins and he goes? Or is he watching for weeks to find the first possible moment to escape her ornery, nagging company?

The beaver dam, some 40 feet of carefully entangled brush and sticks six feet or so in height, is out of sight, buried beneath a roaring waterfall. Behind it, the flooding pond water is covering the lower half of six dome-shaped lodges sitting about 40 to 100 feet apart. Such high water means the inside dry ledge of the lodge isn't dry any more. So where are the beavers that usually sleep and laze on that ledge? In the pond water? Lying on top of the lodge? Don't see any. Maybe nibbling at trees and brush on two or three high spots, or humps, I could see standing above water to the left of the pond.

Before I see a single beaver, I hear two sharp noises. "SLAP! SLAP!" They'd seen me. Two had slapped the water with their leathery ping-pong paddle-tails to warn the others.

"Well," I think, "the Papas can't run and hide inside their houses, even if the Mamas would let them." No room, with water close to the lodge ceiling. No room for Mama, the one-year-olds, and the new babies, either. How were they coping with this emergency, I wonder.

Finding out what's going on inside a beaver lodge is nothing I'd ever use my hands to do. There's an air hole in the top of the dome and people have been known to stick an arm in to feel for a beaver. Those people who found a beaver at home are now going around with four fingers instead of five.

It's no use either to try to break into the lodge by pulling the sticks apart. That structure is put together so well it's like a steel wire-reinforced concrete wall. I've seen lodges that bears had broken into, but not easily either. A man could spend a half day hacking away at it and never see the inside wall. Anyway, tearing up a beaver lodge is illegal. Besides that, no beaver would be waiting there. He'd have run out the bottom into the water, or into a tunnel through the earth, and come out in a patch of alder 10 to 30 feet away.

Just short of the waterfall, I cut my motor and paddle until the skiff touches the bank hidden beneath a foot of water. I splash out and tow the skiff around the end of the dam and into the pond. Staying away from the current, I paddle slowly and quietly, close to the lodges and what ought to be the edge of the pond.

Now I can see many scattered, moving spots of air bubbles in the pond water, with the slight ripple of a wake following. Now and again a dark head breaks the surface. Good! Some are bound to be males still hanging around the home pond. I could shoot one, but all the others would run away, and the dead one would sink in the swift water. I could put down some traps, but I'd have to come back tomorrow to take the catch—if any.

Best to use the club.

I'll have to use the skiff to cut one big male out of the swimming ranks and run him toward the closest hump standing above water. Then on the hump, when I hit him I'll be sure he won't just sink to the bottom of the pond.

There's a beaver with a wide V-shaped wake. I'll try him. Looks pretty big, going in the right direction. He's not paying me any mind. Actually he appears to be on his way to the hump. Probably thinking of eating lunch over there. He bumps into the bank and crawls up.

Foot after foot of beaver slides out of the pond and onto the bank inches deep in water. I never saw so much beaver on one set of legs. He's nearly as big as I am. He's a once-in-a-lifetime catch, an XX super-size beaver blanket, one four feet long and four feet wide—or bigger! The inches added together equal the beaver's weight—96 pounds!

My heart is pounding with excitement. I feel so keyed up, I begin stepping out of the skiff before it touches the bank. I catch myself. Now I can jump and grab the line. A foot of flood water is just enough to float the skiff with the weight of its outboard.

Big Beaver is moving fast, half-swimming, half-walking. Something on that hump has got ahold of his attention completely. He doesn't show a sign that he knows he's being followed. What luck! I'm catching up fast.

He's pulling up on the hump. He's shaking himself, water flying. Off he waddles.

I'm pulling the skiff up on the hump. I'm shaking with tension. I pick up the club. I start to run.

I come up close behind Big Beaver—unbelievably BIG!—just the right spot to reach out and strike. WHACK!

He's jumping into the air, turning toward me at the same time. Angry face, mouth open, orange chisel-teeth protruding, he lunges at me.

I must have jumped ten feet to the side. And ran as hard as my hip boots would let me go. Where WAS that skiff! Where did my club fly to?

I glimpsed XX super-size beaver as I curved my path to go toward the skiff. He was waddling, moving his 96 pounds nowhere near as fast as I was moving much more weight of mine.

No skiff was ever towed so fast or launched so swiftly, even recklessly, into the creek below the dam. Big Beaver was still coming and he was still baring his teeth at me.

Only when I was turning from creek into river did I think about how this story was going to sound to Helen and Bruce—and all those people at home. Andy chased home by a BEAVER?

Well, I didn't *have* to tell anybody, did I? But I began to go back over the way it happened, explaining to myself how it happened, describing that beaver big as a bear, how he turned and grabbed at me, how far I had to jump, how fast he was running, how I was splashing and hauling the skiff and nearly falling into the icy creek—

I got so tickled I knew there'd be no stopping myself from telling it all, with unavoidable exaggerations at crucial points.

I spilled it all out the first half-hour at home, standing in the middle of the cabin in two feet of floodwater, Helen and Bruce in their bunks hanging over the sides laughing. It did us all a lot more good than a four-by-four soft fur beaver blanket.

Our laughing even got to the ice dam in the river. We suddenly heard it crack up, split its sides, fall down in a heap with a roar, swept off its feet.

In two warm days, the flood waters about the cabin had drained off or soaked into the feet-thick layer of loose volcanic ash under the humus.

We spent a day scraping the mud out and scrubbing the place, another day packing our furs and dufflebags. Come on, Bill DeCreeft, wherever you are. We're on your calendar, you can't forget us.

It took him two weeks to hear us. Bright June sunshine turned the spray into rainbows when his plane floats hit the sparkling water of the Kamishak River.

Sprawling lakes glinted in the sun when the plane circled with us and the two dogs over the Kamishak flatlands, our wilderness home. In the deep shadows of the canyon where ridges towered over the Kamishak, I saw massive snowdrifts. I knew remnants would still be there in autumn when I returned for my machines and gear.

Through the greening branches of the cottonwoods, I saw the log cabin and the plywood pre-fab sitting empty in the clearing.

Home. For a second I had a rush of "cabin appreciation." My throat tightened. I needed a bit of a joke to break the mood. I turned to tell Helen that the bears were standing on their hind legs waving goodbye. There were tears in her eyes.

12

Seal Hunting on Tugidak

*"There is a universal reality in the natural world . . .
Nature gives short shrift to the weak, the incompetent,
the disadvantaged and the unlucky . . ."*
                                    Dr. Durwood L. Allen

I will tell you about seal hunting the same as I told my pretty, young seal-hunting partner one season. Barrett Andrews came walking down the dock in Kodiak's boat harbor on a wet, cold day in March, and I had my first look at her. She was wrapped in heavy rain gear. Hardly anything showed except her neat nose and a determined set of mouth and jaw.

"She looks tough enough to be a good seal-hunting partner," I thought, and when she came closer I asked her the time of day. We got on, and within a few weeks became occasional lunchroom companions and dock walkers. Without her hat, she was a pony-tail blond. A good-looking one in a strong way, with what I call "high society" features. I began calling her Katy.

Katy had been through college, then gone adventuring in the rain forests of British Columbia for a year or so.

*"Starvers"—baby seals abandoned by their mothers—lie
listless, weak, and dying on a beach by Tugidak Island's
great lagoon. "Game officials tell us that about half the
seals born won't live to be adults," Andy says.
"Harvesting pups—the stage when the natural death
rate is highest—is the least wasteful of Nature's over-
bounty. Their soft skins make strong, warm clothing for
people enduring long, hard winters."*

She would have made a great pioneer woman, loving the woods, the scarcity of people and things, enduring the roughness, the wetness and chill, the unpretty reality of doing and making-do to feed and protect yourself.

British Columbia was on the way to Alaska, and one day she took a job on a fishing boat which brought her eventually to Kodiak. She was fishing halibut when I met her on the dock.

About the first of May when the halibut season was near closing for several weeks, I said to Katy, "I'm off in a few days to hunt seal on Tugidak Island. I think you're tough enough to make a good seal-hunting partner."

She answered as if she'd made up her mind some time back. Right away she said, "I think I'd like to find out what sealing is all about."

"This won't be like any job you ever saw before," I warned her. "It's primitive. It's killing seals and cutting their hides off. But you'll learn a lot about living, as well as about life and death in Nature. I mean, it's healthy for body and mind living on Tugidak. When I first went there I could hardly lift a bat to hit a seal. I hadn't breathed right in years. Living out-of-doors put me back in tune.

"Course, we don't live out-of-doors completely. We have a shack set back in a sandbank. Just one room. No privacy, kind of crowded. And the island is a long way from any store. You'll miss having a lot of little things. You probably won't love the weather. Fog, gray. Rainy, cold. Lots of wind. Where we live, it's sand and water. The rest of the island is rough and flat. No trees. Nobody lives there. Just a handful of seal hunters in summer. Long before we leave, you'll be praying for the fog to lift so a plane can get in to pick us up."

"I'm not expecting a rose garden," she said, and we went on a big steel crabber to Tugidak.

Katy and I, Norm and two teen-age boys to help him, made a full house in our one-room dugout.

Katy laughed at the cranberry bushes growing on the roof, and said she'd never seen such a house anywhere before. That's because there isn't anything like it in the rest of the world.

The first day, we drove the Honda and its trailer from the dugout across the sand to beaches by the big lagoon. According to high or low tide, those beaches vary in width from just a few yards to as much as four miles. On them, about 10,000 seals begin their pupping in May. About mid-August, most all the seals begin moulting and moving away from Tugidak to other bays.

The first three pups Katy and I came to were flopping around, crying, and wailing. I called a halt, jumped off the Honda, and grabbed my baseball bat. "When they're this young, you can walk right up to them. They won't run away. They look like starvers."

I started swinging the bat. Bop, bop, bop.

I'm picking up the dead seals and trying to tell Katy about hitting technique when I hear sniffing. I look around. Tears are running down Katy's cheeks.

"What's the matter?"

"I'm not used to seeing animals killed." Sniff.

"But you know that hunting, seal hunting or any other kind, means killing animals."

"I know. So I'll be all right tomorrow."

"Listen," I say, "you don't have to do the killing. We can go back to the dugout and you can stay there doing things that don't make you feel bad. I'd rather take you back. I'm here to make a living and I can't be distracted by anybody crying over dead seals."

"Well, now (sniff)," she says, "tomorrow is another day. It won't be like this one. Tomorrow I'm going to take the bat and knock those seals in the head as calm as you."

"Listen Katy, cooking for us and washing the skins are just as important as killing and skinning the seals," I say.

"I came to hunt seals. I'm going to hunt seals."

"It's true you can get used to doing the killing as a job," I say. "It's another way of thinking for most people. I look at it this way. I'm doing a difficult job to make some money by taking Nature's over-bounty. Otherwise it'll be wasted. Taking the pups is the least wasteful because that's the time when the natural death rate is highest.

"The game officials say about 50 percent of the seals born will never live to adult age. You'll see plenty of 'starvers' on the beach. They're babies abandoned by their mothers. Lots of the half-grown pups that leave in mid-August will be caught by killer whales, or sharks, or sea lions. Others will starve because they're not very good at catching fish."

Nature doesn't see dying as cruelty, I go on. All through Nature you see that the life of one animal can go on because there's another animal dying to provide the day's food.

In the ocean, you see a sea lion's big flipper wipe a seal off a rock. Sl-uh-ff! The seal is in that enormous belly with hardly a bit of chewing. In the wilderness, you see a pack of hungry wolves attack a moose and bite out big chunks of flesh before he's dead. Survival. Swallowing, filling the gnawing belly. That's the key impulse. About this Number One matter, Nature is not compassionate and gentle.

The State Wildlife people have counted seals for many years—they know about how many seals can be, ought to be, harvested. They set a quota. That limits the hunting season. Up until a few years ago they paid the hunters $3 bounty for every seal they killed.

"At least the seals that die when I strike them die without suffering," I say. "Just the way the meat packing plants know that a swift blow to the head with a power-driven steel mallet is the quickest, least painful way to kill cows, or cute little lambs, the seal hunter knows a hard, swift blow to the head is the quickest and least painful way to kill a seal."

"Tomorrow I'll be all right," Katy repeats.

The next day we go out on the beaches where about 50 mamaless pups are lying on the sand. Some wail, some lie listless and weak..

Katy gets off the Honda, picks up a bat with one hand on the bat's top end, the other hand half-way down.

"Well, now," I say, "if you hold your bat like that, all you'll do is hurt the seals. You have to hold the bat at the top with one hand so you can swing it free and hard. You have to hit hard enough to kill instantly with one strike."

She firms her lips, practices a few swings. She walks to the seals. Bop. Bop. Bop. I follow and pick up carcasses to load onto the trailer. "It's inevitable—killing to survive, kill plants, kill animals," Katy said without tears. "I have to be here on this primitive beach, far away from class-rooms, to accept survival facts. Rock bottom. It's hard."

Within a week, Katy is swinging a bat in each hand. She is crouching and crawling over the tidal flats, sneaking up on a herd like the rest of us.

In another week she was cutting a ring around the

seals' necks and flippers to make it easier for me to skin them. She had to learn how to sharpen a knife on stone and steel, and to keep it sharp. Nothing wastes energy, and messes up a skin, more than a dull knife. The third week Katy was skinning seals too. The first one she did all on her own was a beautiful job. We were amazed, she was amazed. And proud.

We started our day at 3 in the morning, walking out of the dugout when the first crack of light ended the four-hour summer night. Rain with a few flakes of snow greeted us a couple of times the first week. Katy never said a word about the miseries, she just tramped and rode right along with us, carrying her bat and knife. "It's hard to believe that somewhere it's summer," was the nearest she came to a complaint after a month of chilling winds.

Norm noticed how fast and good Katy was at scraping, washing, salting, rolling up, and placing the skins in the brine pit. He asked her if she'd do his skins, too, for pay.

She decided to try. "She can't tote enough water to do all that," I thought, "she doesn't have the muscle." But she was stronger than she looked. From fresh water spring to old Maytag washing machine she carried five-gallon cans of water, one in each hand. A handful of detergent thrown in to take the grease from the skins, a yank to the gasoline engine, and off the washer would go, sloshing water out the open top. Katy, calm and cool and determined, handled about 800 skins by the end of the season. That would be a backbreaking job for anybody.

What a different story I have to tell about my own first seal hunt on Tugidak. I flew almost straight from the doctor's office in Fairbanks to Kodiak, and on south about 150 miles to Tugidak Island. My brother Norm had persuaded me it was just the place for me to get fresh air, exercise, and distance from city life while earning a living despite being half-dead. He'd come to this island the year before, one of the first to hunt seals there. Now it was May and pupping season and he was going again. So I went.

Flat, treeless, this oval island stands about 100 feet high at one end. It slopes down to sealevel so gradually across its 15-mile length, it looks flat. At the low end spreads a great lagoon, created by curving arms of sandbars piled high with moss-covered dunes. Sandy beaches edge the lagoon and almost the whole perimeter of the uninhabited clay and rock island.

I could see herds of seals clustered on a sandy point at the lagoon entrance and on the lagoon's beaches, narrow at high tide. Later at low tide I'd see those beaches extend dark and wet and endless, while the lagoon shrank to a shallow pond with a shifting channel.

Norm's little plywood cabin was sitting on dunes near the entrance to the lagoon. The cabin was nothing special having been built single-handed out of beachcombed plywood and two-by-fours. But it looked good to me as a resting place after using up my breath helping get our gear under shelter.

Fifteen minutes later, Norm had me moving. "Come on, let's get down to the lagoon and get a few pups today," he said. Then it seemed to me we walked a hundred miles, dragging our boots through sand.

Breathing hard, putting all my strength into the swing, I struck at a wailing "starver." Then I had to skin him. I was exhausted. I lay down on the beach to do the cutting, real slow. My arms shook, but I got that seal's hide off. That cheered me so much, I felt less tired instead of more tired on the walk back to the cabin. Maybe there was 20 years of future lying out there in front of me after all.

Norm never let me rest. He fumed and badgered and swore and taunted until I got up and went out again with bat and knife. After weeks of feeling irritated and half-mad at him for all that, I felt so much better I made him promise he'd keep on being mouthy, nasty, and pushy as long as I needed it.

What a contrast this treeless, windblown wilderness was to my smoky Montana nightclub. A whole day could pass without my thinking about money. Tramping the beaches in icy rain, cold drizzle, fog, and a wind that never got tired . . . bending over to skin the seals . . . hauling, scraping, washing, salting all the hides . . . living outdoors more than half of every 24 hours—it's a rough day-after-day routine. But it's a fast way to rid your body of the effects of life on the neon strip.

Having such a curious, interesting scene around me helped too. Everywhere I looked, a birthing was taking place. I could stand in one spot and see a baby seal emerging into the world every minute. Snow white with embryonic hair, they change color during a few rolls around on the sand. The white fluff rubs loose, and the babies are flopping about in lightly spotted gray hair coats.

Like all baby creatures, their smallness and softness are very appealing. Their wailing and crying are not. "Wai-ih! Wai-ih!" Seals sound like human babies. "Wai-ih! Wai-ih!" They go on non-stop. When thousands of those little squallers are going at the same time, you can hear them a mile away. When I'd wake up in the middle of the night, I'd hear them still wailing as hard as they had been at noon.

The first hour of every day on the seal-herd beach nearly knocked me out. The smell was like a ripe pig pen. I barely drew my breath until my nose became unconscious. Only then could I pay interested attention to the curious scene of seals—mamas birthing, babies yelling, bull-faced males occasionally fighting. Almost as soon as this season's babies emerge, the males start their females on next year's crop.

I've watched many a baby come out crying into the world, heave on its flippers across anything in the way to a teat. It would suckle, then hurry after mama across the sand, and into the lagoon for a swim. Sometimes a baby would ride piggyback on its mama into the water, tumble off, and paddle frantically back to shore. They have the busiest, most exciting birthday of any animal I know.

A few days later in the baby seal's life, the drama I enjoy watching the most is what I call "the firedrill."

One mama seal seems to be left with 50 or 60 pups to look after while the other mamas swim out to eat some fish. Babysitter lies snoozing in the midst of the squalling brats, raising her head to growl occasionally at them. She's probably telling them to shut up. That's what I'd be growling.

All of a sudden, the babysitter begins a rush for the water, making loud gutteral, huffing sounds. She moves by lifting herself on her front flippers, heaving forward, falling flat on her belly, lifting herself again. I've imagined myself doing that and it seems the least likely way to go anywhere fast. But the hair seal can make those flippers work like windmills. I have to run hard to keep up.

On the way to the water, babysitter will swat two or three babies to hurry them along. I stop whatever I'm doing to watch the mottled gray mama and her six dozen pups heaving and hurrying into the water. She leads the mob up and down and around in the lagoon for about 20 minutes. Abruptly she leaves for the beach. Sooner or later the little ones flop back too.

Most sprawl, some roll on their backs, for a nap.

A half-hour later, the babysitter's squawk goes off again. She throws the same kitti-kwatti, heaving to the water, babies flippering after her. All day she "firedrills" them. Quicker and quicker they can race from beach to water, practicing escape from predators. In the water they can dive and hide, get stronger, swim better. On the few sunny, warm days, the water cools them. Baby seals sleeping in the sun too long can overheat. Then the fur will fall from the skin.

A month after they're born, the pups weigh 35 to 50 pounds, which is twice their birth weight. All of a sudden, mama won't let them suckle. They've got to chase fish or die. Maybe a quarter of the pups have already died before they're a month old. They're "the starvers."

Many mama seals take off soon after birthing the pup and never come back. No other mama seal will, or can, suckle orphans. They're pitiful. They crawl about crying and wailing, pushed away by the adults. Often they get together in a bunch to wail, flop weakly along, and die.

Hunters kill many of them. Eagles kill some—and some well-fed ones besides.

When I saw an eagle circling around, then lighting on the beach, I knew a drama was about to start. The eagle had spotted a pup to tear apart and eat.

The eagle walks close to the pup. In one swift movement, the eagle picks out one of the seal's eyes, then the other. The pup flops about, dying. The eagle begins eating while his dinner is still alive.

He pulls the brains out through the eye sockets. He peels back the skin and tears off the flesh around the head and neck. He peels back more skin, gorging himself on the tender flesh. Full, he flaps his great wings and flies off to his nest—except that I've seen eagles so heavy with food they couldn't get off the ground. In the nest, baby eagles are screaming their hunger. Daddy upchucks a bite at a time, and drops the seal meat into little eagle throats and around the nest. It makes for a messy, smelly dining table.

Mama and Papa Eagle make several trips from dead seal to hungry babies. They tear off bites, eating their way down the body. They pull back the skin until it's like a sleeve turned wrongside out. When the carcass is light enough for Papa Eagle to pick it up with his talons, he airlifts it to the nest. On the wide walls of the huge nest, the eagle family finishes the job, swallowing everything except skull, backbone, and ribs.

Tugidak eagles build their nests on the ground since the island has no trees. I've watched them hover in the air a hundred feet above the nest site and drop large sticks near the nest, pick them up later and put them in place.

The most spectacular nest I ever saw sat like a tower of driftwood on the tundra by the big lagoon. It was 12 feet tall! At the bottom, it was 14 feet in diameter. It tapered to about four feet across at the top.

When I first saw it, I couldn't imagine what it was. I was thinking about climbing up to find out when I saw an eagle zooming in from a distance. A whistling noise started up in the top of the tower. I recognized baby eagle sounds and got out of the way, fast.

One of the Natives who came to hunt seals on Tugidak later told me that the eagle nest had been there since the days of his great-great grandfathers. As the years and generations of birds passed, the nest mound grew taller. It was as if, having no tree, the eagles built one, layer after layer to live in, a family tree.

After I saw the eagles' method of killing seal pups, I had no doubt that the hunter's single blow to the head was far more humane. We usually killed a few at a time, then stopped to take the skins off, scrape and wash them, lay them in the brine pit.

Often we worked a 16-hour day. Bad weather—the cold, wet, windy, foggy days the seals loved—we took as the normal state of life and worked on. Once it snowed and rained and blew for eight days running. We bent to the wind and kept warm by working harder. With continuous effort, I and a partner might have 400 or so skins between us in about six weeks. We never knew how much the market would pay for them until we sold them. Most years it was around $10 a skin.

Biggest payoff for me was a working pair of lungs, a heart trying to behave the way it ought to, unfrozen joints, and diabetes on the wane. Besides that, the island for all its blustery, wet weather, had its lovable side. In spring, it turned a fresh, almost glowing green with grasses, moss, and low brush covering its thick top layer of peat. Acres of wild flowers colored large areas yellow, white, purple.

So many ptarmigans nested and lived in the grass, we could have "chicken" every day for the price of a short hike with a gun. The beaches always had the latest washup of firewood, lumber, buoys, and interesting if useless junk. Sometimes we found on the beach a no-good motorcycle, or even a jeep, that some hunter couldn't take with him when he finally got a ride off the island. Getting into, or away from, Tugidak can take weeks. Often fog and bad weather seem tossed back and forth between the north end and south end of Kodiak Island.

Tugidak is so out of the way, difficult and expensive to go to, only a half-dozen or so hunters were there at one time. We didn't see much of them, and I could enjoy the feeling of uncluttered space. In this isolated and primitive place, the rest of the world was remembered as a snarl of people-complications in which a million "necessary" possessions were entangled. On Tugidak, thought and action, time and energy all went to deal with the natural, physical world. Rock bottom, as Katy said.

Nature threw some big excitement at us from time to time. One day it was Dungeness crabs—millions of them it looked to me. They had filled a long, 30-foot-wide inlet near our dugout, and stayed there in heaving layers squirming and crawling over each other, until the tide dragged them out.

Another day, a williwaw spun down from the mountains on Sitkinak Island just across a narrow strait, grabbed Norm's cabin on the lagoon sandbar, and slung it round and round. Norm was inside. He slung around, too, along with pots, pans, dishes, and gear. The whirlwind carried the cabin 40 feet, then dropped it—and Norm— tilted on the side of a sand hill. When I got there from a protected beach where I'd waited out the sudden storm, I had to walk uphill from front door to bunk. That night I tied myself in bed to keep from tumbling off.

"Now listen here," I said the next morning to Norm, who had bruises but no breaks. "I'd rather live like a gopher than fly through the air in a williwaw. The Natives tell me their ancestors used to live in caves—'barrabaras'— and now we know why. Let's dig a cave in a sandbank and line it with planks. We've got plenty of lumber in that old shipwreck down the beach.''

Norm thought the planks were rotten. "That wreck must be 50 years old. Maybe 150.''

"I've looked it over and the top section is solid. It's the bottom part that's rotten, the part that high tides have hit twice a day,'' I said. "There're lots of good planks at the top, and they're three inches thick. Plenty of lumber—the ship's 90 feet long.''

We got busy. We knew exactly which sandbank we'd build our house into—one next to the only fresh water on the lagoon end of the island. We'd happened on it one day by noticing a covey of ptarmigans flutter into some tall, very green grass.

Looking down at them from the higher sand dunes, we saw their heads bobbing. "They're drinking!'' It seemed impossible. But when we walked over, there was the little pool of fresh water bubbling up out of the ground. A spring only 50 feet from the salty sea! To a man on an isolated, uninhabited island, that's a treasure as valuable as furs.

We shoveled it out and set into the hole a steel barrel with both ends out. No more water cans to transport across five miles by Honda. No more stinting. Fresh water to wash our seal skins. Fresh water to wash our own skins.

At the shipwreck, we pried off planks, stacked and tied them up near the edge of the surf at low tide. A long line attached them to the skiff. When high tide lifted them afloat, the skiff towed the heavy wood a few miles to our building site.

A few steps from our bubbling well, we dug out a notch 12 by 14 feet in the sandbank, and pounded corner posts into the ground. With the antique, hammered, square spike-nails saved from the ship, we attached the planks. Devilish jigsaw puzzle when you have no saw and all your planks are different widths and lengths. But we got four walls, more or less neat, a floor and a roof out of them.

We wrapped the outside of the whole thing in sheets of visqueen to hold out water and sand dribbles. On the roof, we rolled out strips of moss and weeds. When we pushed the sand in place against the back and sides of our dugout home, it slumped forward about three inches. Just enough to give it architectural distinction.

Where else could you find a house with low bush cranberry, mooseberry, and grass holding down the roof? Or a picture window of plastic overlooking the dunes, lagoon, and ocean? And everything for comfort—six built-in bunk beds, a steel drum cooking and heating set-up complete with stove pipe, a table by the picture window, and shelves to make it possible to put order to things.

But raise your level of comfort on ten sides, and you become acutely aware of the remaining discomforts. How can you crawl into a new bunk bed, or sit down to dinner in front of your picture window when you're stinking with seal grease and sweat and grouchy with fatigue?

At the end of one sunny day when we'd skinned 40-pound juveniles from four in the morning until nearly midnght, Norm said as we fell into our bunks, "I'm going to make us a bathhouse. I've heard that a hot bath rests you as much as three hours of sleep. Besides, I'm so greasy, the stink could even keep me awake."

"What's this about a bathhouse?" I said at breakfast.

I'd been wondering what he'd do for pipes and fittings and water pump in this far-out place. "How about a sauna?" Norm grinned.

He did most of the work, taking time off from sealing one day. The bathhouse had a bench to lie on, a steel drum stove topped by a metal box of rocks. Build a fire, heat the rocks, throw on a dipper of water to make steam. Relax and let the seal grease melt away.

Seal skinning is a greasy greasy job. Oil oozes out of the thick fat layer underneath the hide and soaks your clothes. It runs down your hip boots. Your hands are slippery with it. The bigger the seal, the harder and closer you have to grasp him to move him, and the worse the grease problem.

The seal's size and the strength and speed that go with it also change the way you hunt. By July, you can't walk up to them any more. You have to kill them from a distance. Telescopic rifle replaces baseball bat.

Two-month-old seals as well as the adults are wise to hunters now. One sees a man approaching and begins running. Every seal head pops up. Flop, flop, flop, they heave themselves quickly across the sand toward the water. The babysitter's "fire-drills" are paying off. They outrun a hunter with a club.

The hunter comes back the next day with his rifle and telescopic sight.

He aims and fires. But within days the seals leave the lagoon's tidal flats and the sharp crack of the rifle. They take to the sandbars a mile offshore. The hunter follows in a skiff. But one firing of the gun and the seals in two seconds have flopped into the sea. They dive deep. Only when they stick their heads out of water for a breath of air does the hunter have a target.

The hunter has practiced target shooting. He must be able to hit a swimming seal's head at 100 to 200 yards. The telescopic sight makes it possible.

Through the telescopic sight, the hunter sees a pool of blood reddening the water and knows the seal has been hit. Skiff throttle open, the hunter hurries toward his kill, hoping the seal is floating. Usually it is. With a long-handled hook, the hunter pulls in the seal and hauls it into the skiff. He's lucky if the sea is calm. Even if it's smooth as glass, a hunter hauling a 200-pound seal into a little skiff gets as wet as the seal.

A week is about as long as seals will stay on a beach after hunters find them and begin shooting. You have to go looking for them. If a head surfaces, you shoot from the skiff, if you have time. Perhaps you find a herd on the other side of a big sandbar, or five miles away on a Tugidak beach. But when they're killed after scurrying into the water, you've got to retrieve them in a skiff.

For some seasons, I looked at my dog Cisco and wished he could do the retrieving for me. He was a red Labrador-Weimaraner, a good retriever and swimmer. But I was afraid swimming in ocean waves was asking too much of him. Suppose he drowned. Suppose a huge wounded seal attacked him. Suppose his 50 pounds couldn't push or drag a seal several times his size, but he wore himself out trying.

One day, I happened to see a dog no bigger than Cisco pushing a huge seal through the waves and onto the beach. He didn't have a bit of trouble. He was a Chesapeake, a "water dog," and belonged to a young fellow hunting just for a week. "My dog's a trained retriever and all I have to do is tell him 'go get 'im,'" the young fellow said. "No seal has ever attacked my dog. They're afraid of dogs, I think."

"Go get 'im!" I hollered at Cisco his first day of seal retrieving. He rushed into the water, following the smell of blood to the seal. He knew to grab a mouthful of seal skin and push toward the beach. Cisco was so pleased with his new job, he danced in front of me, looked me in the eye, and barked to hurry me on with the shooting. With a dog to haul in the seals, hunting became for me much easier, more interesting—and much drier.

That winter, Cisco was stolen. I had to start all over.

I looked for a hunting dog with speed and daring, strength and stamina. A Norwegian elkhound, I thought. I knew an elkhound would bay a grizzly—no other dog will do that. I knew the elkhound was a great hunting dog, rather small but husky.

One day I heard of a litter of half-elkhound pups for sale in Kodiak. The other half was Malamute. That combination sounded even better than pure elkhound.

I picked out of the six pups the most troublesome, bothersome, alert male. He was six weeks old. He had the wolf face and long legs of the Malamute, the husky body and spirited personality of the elkhound. He would turn out to be the best dog I ever had.

I was a tough teacher. I demanded absolute obedience. If I didn't get it, I was angry with him and showed it in word and deed. Cruel to strike a dog? Not really. He liked to learn and do exactly right, I could tell that. The best way to let him know he wasn't doing what I wanted was to treat him rough. Before long, he was so familiar with my actions and words, I didn't have to say anything twice, and words were the only toughness needed to straighten him out. "Get in the hole!" was bad punishment. He'd rush to go under the table and stay there until I told him he could come out. His English-tuned ear learned the difference between similar sounding words. "Rat!" made him bound to his feet, run about looking at the ground, growling. "Hat!" didn't even rate a muzzle-twitch.

When he arrived for the first time at Tugidak, all I needed to teach him about retrieving seals was not to be too eager. Barking and bounding with energy, he wanted to go back for another seal as soon as he dragged one on shore. He was a powerful swimmer with far more stamina and grit than Cisco. He had the urge to DO, to GO, this very minute. I could hardly hold back Mr. Larson—I'd named him for a Norwegian character I once knew. Sometimes I had to tie him to the skiff to keep him from working himself to death.

He constantly amazed me. If Mr. Larson had gone to college he'd have come out a top rank engineer. Here's how Larson, weighing 60 pounds, beached a seal more than three times his weight.

About ten yards from shore, he disappeared with the seal under the breakers for a minute. I have the idea that he was looking at where bottom was and how soon the seal would be stalled on it. When he reappeared, Mr. Larson had a hard tooth-grip on the seal's side. As each wave lifted the seal and swept forward, Mr. Larson pushed the seal hard to take every advantage of the buoyancy. In between waves, he held on and waited. At the waterline, he let go long enough to turn around. With every wave, Larson added a big yank to a little buoyancy. Three waves and the seal was beached.

Mr. Larson helped me in other ways. After skinning a seal, I would scoop out a hole in the sand, roll the carcass in, tell Mr. Larson to cover it. He'd go at it with all four feet, literally working like a dog. Hole filled, he'd pat and smooth the sand down.

His reward was a ride on the back of the Honda with me. When he took a notion to run, he'd jump off and race the machine. I'd slow down when he glanced around as if to tell me he wanted to ride again. "Get on the back!" I'd holler. At exactly the right instant he'd jump on the seat behind me. He would have made a great circus dog as well as a good engineer.

The 1972 season was the last sealing season before the Federal moratorium shut down the killing of any sea mammal, except by Natives. There's talk in 1980 that one year in the future, hunting may be allowed again under a seasonal quota system like the one we used to have. But that may just be talk.

Still, I've heard State Wildlife people say that the number of Alaska's seals stayed the same during the no-hunting 1970's as it was in the 1960's when I helped take a quota harvest. So the quota figures they set to control seal hunting look square on the conservation nailhead, with no threat of wiping out seals or even diminishing them.

Knowing that, I'd pack my gear in a minute and hitch a ride to Tugidak if a quota and season were announced.

Mr. Larson would jump and bark, wildly happy—if he were still around. But he disappeared one summer day in 1980 from a Kodiak beach where he loved to run free. Maybe he smelled a seal five miles away and took out after him. Maybe he'll show up one day, hauling that seal onto Kodiak's waterfront, proud of chasing it half-way around the world, and bringing it home to me.

"From our dugout in the sandbank we went every day in Summer to Tugidak's beaches to kill and skin seals."

13

Williwaw Shipwreck

"Poor naked wretches, wheresoe'er you are, that bide the pelting of this pitiless storm. . ."

Shakespeare

"Storm warning!"

"Storm warning!" the voice from the radio repeated. "Eighty to 100 knot winds!"

Coast Guard talking. I had just noticed a strong wind had come up. I looked at the sky. A swirling roof of black clouds was swinging toward me, my partner, and my boat in Kodiak Island's Shearwater Bay.

Mazie L., my floating home, was equipped with everything a trapper and hunter might need. I'd lived on it like a wilderness king for nearly a year, motoring where I pleased along Kodiak's coast. But I'd never been caught in it when there was a hundred-mile-an-hour blow. Coming off the mountains, that strong a wind would make one williwaw after another.

Williwaws! Wicked winds. The awful word filled me with dread.

Andy sits in the unsinkable skiff he rode during the storm from his wrecked floating home to the beach at the old cannery site on Shearwater Bay. With his own ingenuity and with the astonishing gifts of the tides, he and his partner survived an incredible week on a rocking wooden island. "And all the time," says Andy, "I was wearing only the clothes I had on when I leaped from shipwreck to skiff—my long underwear."

My young partner, Dock, was a curly headed, bearded fellow I'd picked up on the wharf as I was pulling out of Kodiak boat harbor. He'd begged to go. I'd needed a helper for a short Thanksgiving season trapping trip. Dock didn't know anything about trapping and only slightly more about boats. He made good talk and he had big muscles. But how would he do in a bad storm?

"Hear that radio?" I said to Dock. "We gotta move fast. Bad storm coming over the mountains. Before you know it, the williwaws will be coming one after another, gusting and spinning, roaring like freight trains down long funneling canyons from the mountain tops. What's a williwaw? It's a hundred-knot bear of a wind that's climbed a mountain and jumped down bellowing on the other side. It tumbles and twirls and twists and whirls all the way down. It's a hurricane, then a whirlwind, then a tornado, and when it hits the sea and grabs up water it's a waterspout. I've seen them 200 feet high in this very bay."

I once saw williwaw waterspouts coming from three directions at one time. They crashed into each other. My boat swung violently round and round on its anchor line, while I sat braced for hours to save me from a skull cracking. I could see Dock and me doing that same kind of swinging in Shearwater Bay for the next unpredictable number of hours. I couldn't bear to think about the ordeal and I didn't dare mention it to Dock.

The black clouds hid all the sky. Lashing winds and rain struck us. It was useless to think of getting out of the bay—Kiliuda Bay that Shearwater opens into would be having lots of its own williwaws.

As I struggled to guide the boat toward what I hoped was a more sheltered part of the bay, the boat began to turn as if it had entered a wind tunnel of spiraling air. My arms began to ache from bracing the wheel, trying to hold the boat steady.

"Tie a safety rope on yourself and go pitch out the anchor!" I shouted at Dock. He surely threw it over, for the boat began to lean, and rock, pitch, jerk in the heaving sea. The needle of the compass went slowly all the way round the dial—again and again.

I saw water running on the tilted floor and heard an ominous gushing sound. Crawling to its source, I found that the tilt of the boat let water fill the drain of the galley sink. I took off one of my socks and crammed it into the drain to slow the overflow.

Dock and I sat at the galley table and braced ourselves. Through the roar of the wind, I heard sheets of rain and saw them out the window beating the air.

JERK! It felt as if the boat flew a ways and fell SLAM! into the water. A williwaw had jostled us with a hundred-foot-a-second push. Then it whirled us fast, like a carnival ride. Everything in the boat flew, fell, rolled back and forth, back and forth. Even the stove was dancing.

How many hours, how many jolts, swings, and yanks must our bodies endure? "I can't stand it any more, I've got to get out of this," I thought. "But there's no way out. I have to stand it."

We braced ourselves, put our arms around our heads to ward off the blows. If we'd been in a revolving cement mixer tumbling end over end downhill, it couldn't have been worse.

After a long while, in the darkness I felt a change in the rhythm of the swings and jolts. Swings less violent, falls more severe. O lord what if we were blowing out to the big bay where williwaws would be coming from every which way! Crawling, Dock and I went down to the bilge, brought a 200-pound chunk of iron anchor up the ladders, pushed and dragged it across the floor, the deck, tied it on, and rolled it overboard. It pulled the boat level and I thought would keep us from moving very far.

The awful crashing waves, the bucking, and twisting kept on all night without a let-up for one second.

Fifteen hours we endured the torture.

About six in the morning, still pitch dark, through all the tumult I began hearing a bumping and clunking against the side of the boat. Scary—until I'd figured it had to be our lifeboat, a whaler, bumping against the *Mazie L.* instead of trailing on its line.

But then I began to hear bumpings and scrapings on the other side of the boat. What could that be?

Suddenly, with a horrible scrunching sound, the boat's prow rose into the air on a wave's crest, fell with a spine-jamming jolt and another loud scrunch. I untied myself from my bunk bed, fell out, and began to crawl to the cabin door. "Dock! Get to the deck! We're in trouble!" I had to see what kind.

On deck, I flashed my light in time to see a monster wave hovering over the boat. A monster wind blasted the top from the wave. It fell backwards with a crash.

Hanging on to the railing, I beamed the light down to the water, looking for the source of the scrunch and the scraping noises.

I saw old log pilings standing upright under the heaving water. They told me exactly where we were and what had happened.

Our anchors hadn't held. We'd dragged them and

moved about a mile around the bay.

We were just offshore from the ruins of a fish cannery in Shearwater Bay. I'd often seen the pilings, once supports for a dock, running 200 feet out from the shore. Two rows of dragon teeth, those pilings were, waiting to punch holes in the *Mazie L.* when she rose and fell in the waves. We've got to get away from here!

I crawled inside the cabin and wheelhouse, pressed the starter. The engine ran easily. I put the gear in forward. Nothing happened. Reverse. Nothing happened. The propeller won't turn! An anchor line has wrapped around the propeller shaft as the boat swung in circles.

Once more I heard the pilings rake the side of the boat. The bow was going up—and falling. PUNCH! CRACK!

Dock yelled from the hold. "Andy! Something's come up through the floor! Water's coming in!"

"Come out of there!" I yelled back. "We'll be broken up in minutes! Get to the whaler on starboard side! We'll try for the beach!"

"We can't leave the boat!" Dock shouted. I heard wood breaking around the piling as waves twisted the *Mazie L.* We were hung up like a shrimp on a toothpick.

"What do you mean we CAN'T! WE'VE GOT TO!"

"But what do we do about this boat?" Dock said, presumably standing in water to his knees.

"Wake up, man! We ain't got a boat!" O lord help us. A problem partner.

On deck in the whirling storm, I shined my flashlight on the whaler. Its tow line had miraculously wound around the *Mazie L.* and brought it snugly against the hull, ready to save us. All we had to do was jump into it in the dark as both boat and lifeboat surged wildly up and down in giant waves.

Dock jumped first while I held the flashlight. I had to cut the whaler loose and jump before it took off. I jumped at exactly the right split-second. Lucky. My chest hit the seatboard. Not so lucky. The breath knocked out of me, I gasped and gasped to bring it back—and felt a stab of pain with each movement.

The whaler was riding the waves well, and I knew we had an onshore wind that would blow us to the beach. Just then the bottom hit the sand. And before we could scramble out, a powerful comber wave rolled under us, and sucked us back to sea.

"Grab an oar, Dock!" I yelled over the noise of wind, rain, and tossing waves. "ROW! Back to the beach! Jump fast when we get there!"

Once more the whaler scraped sand. I jumped out, holding the bow line. I hit water. A wave knocked me flat and washed over me. I crawled out of the seawater into pouring rain.

I was freezing. In getting out of my bunk and out of the *Mazie* so fast, I never even pulled on my trousers. All I had on was my wool socks, my long johns, and a belt with the flashlight hooked to it.

Waterproof, it still made a light. With the lift of the waves and my yanks on the bowline, the whaler slid out of the reach of the sea. I spotted a log higher up on the beach and tied the bowline to it. Perhaps I should turn the whaler over, prop up one of its sides, and use it for shelter. Too dark to find props strong enough. Wind would blow it over anyway. And we're wet and cold and need a big fire.

But where is Dock? What happened to him?

I looked around with the flashlight. Just a few feet up

from the surf, I saw all that remained of the cannery, destroyed in the tidal wave of 1964. There wasn't much. Only a wooden floor, the beach side supported by short pilings. And one corner of wall no higher than my shoulder.

"DOCK!" From somewhere in the ruin, I heard his voice. "Yeah!"

I climbed onto the wooden floor and headed for the corner of wall. My foot kicked something soft. Visqueen! At last one tiny piece of good luck. My feet in near-freezing wet wool were numb. I wrapped them in visqueen boots.

What was Dock up to? "DOCK!" Again from the darkness, "Yeah!" Well, he must be all right. I was shaking with cold, standing in the rain and gusting wind. "Gotta get a fire going, gotta get a fire going," I thought and began looking for something to build it with and something to build it in or on. The light picked out a sizable broken section of a thin concrete slab lying in the middle of the wood floor. A hearth!

Just then, Dock showed up out of the darkness.

"What're you doing?" he asked. "Gotta get a fire going," I answered. "Look for some firewood." I noticed that Dock had on heavy pants, shirt, and boots.

In a few minutes I was thinking, "This wood will never burn without a lot of help." Besides being soaked through, it had to burn on a hearth open to pouring rain and howling gale.

"There's a can of gasoline in the whaler," I remembered, and half crawled, half walked to get it. Slosh, slosh, slosh I poured gasoline on the wood and stood back. WHHOOSH! it went when I took a match from the waterproof can around my neck, lit and threw it.

Fire shot up. Heat! Light!

I was laughing. Dock had run in from somewhere and he was laughing. For about two minutes it was a great and wonderful event.

Then before I knew it, Dock had the can in his hands and was sloshing, sloshing gasoline on the fire! WHOOSH WHOOSH!

"Drop that can!" I yelled. He dropped it and I snatched it away from the fire. When I looked up from capping the can, I saw Dock's shirt, beard, and hair in flames. He didn't say anything, he just began running. As he went past me, I tripped him into a sprawl.

He screamed and swore at me, trying to get away as I held him down and rolled him around on the wet floor to put out the flames. I swore back at him and shoved him harder about the floor.

When I let him get up, his clothes were smoking and scorched, one side of his bushy beard was gone as well as all the hair on the same side of his head. Skin on the ear and cheek bulged with one continuous blister. His eyes were bloodshot from the smoke and heat of fire that had burned off eyelashes and brows.

Among the scattered junk on the floor, I found two big rusty oil cans for us to sit on. Four or five hours I stayed as close to the fire as I dared get, trying to dry a few inches of my long johns despite the pouring rain. I resoaked them in the rain with each trip to bring firewood.

The only help that showed up was another piece of visqueen, which I made into a rain cape. And daylight helped, letting me see the whole appalling scene. The scariest sight was Dock with his burned head, sitting, staring, mumbling to himself. What a way to spend Thanksgiving.

All this time, the tide had been coming in, and now it surged far beneath the floor section resting on short pilings. Each wave lifted the sagging, rotting floor six inches, then let it down creaking and groaning. It seemed to me the floor had come alive and I was standing on a breathing, wheezing, sometimes snoring giant.

About noon, I saw the waves slosh above the sagging edge and begin a relentless crawl toward us and our fire. The concrete hearth was very low, and too heavy to move. Floor stains looked as if the high tide mark was just beyond our hearth. What to do?

Long and far I searched for a container to put our fire into and save it. I didn't have enough matches and gasoline to rebuild the fire every day for an unknown number of days. When at last I returned, cold, wet, dragging my feet in wrecked wrap-around boots, I had an open-end steel drum.

I was too late. Waves were washing over the concrete, and scorched firewood floated in the surf. No fire!

Dock, not appearing to understand what was going on, had moved to the dry, slightly raised back side of our platform. He sat on the oil can, rocking gently back and forth, eyes to the floor.

Could things get any worse? Oh yes, I thought. This wooden island acts as if it might float away in the high tide any minute. Well, we'll jump off and get in the little whaler, still safe on high land. And Dock. No predicting what he'll do. And food. When did we eat last, when again? At least we have plenty of water, what with the whole sky a wide-open faucet.

Listen you, I said to myself, this drama has to be dealt with minute by minute. Do what you have to, do it when you have to do it, and don't waste your energy on problems that haven't happened. Go get some firewood instead.

When I returned with a big armful, the tide had begun its retreat. I rested an hour until there was a spot on the hearth big enough to build a fire. I used the last of the gasoline. If we lost our fire again. . .

More firewood, always more firewood. I searched for sticks near the wooden island, keeping an eye on the fire and Dock—and I stepped on one of the most thrilling surprises of my life. A tin can, unopened! Close by, another, and another. And my medical box with my insulin! And a waterproof sack with blanket and sleeping bag inside!

I laughed, I talked to myself, I hugged those cans close to my belly, so happy I could have cried. What a Thanksgiving I felt.

We'd been saved by the high tide, by wave power sweeping like a broom through *Mazie L.'s* broken hulk, moving food from boat pantry to our beach shelf. Everything suddenly looked fine. Even the wind and rain had slacked off some.

"Breakfast is served," I said to Dock when I came back to our hearth. "What is it?" he answered.

"Let's find out." I jabbed a hole in the can with a piece of broken pipe I'd picked up. "Peas! Good old green peas!"

"Eat peas for breakfast? You think I'm crazy? What's in that other can?" Dock said.

"Corn."

"That makes more sense." He gulped corn, I dined on the world's best canned peas.

I brought out the sleeping bag. "It's your sleeping bag," I said. "You could go to sleep."

"It's daylight. I'm not sleepy." He went back to rocking. I draped him with the bag.

An hour later, when it was dark, Dock woke up and said, "Hey Andy. Where'd all this stuff come from?"

"From the *Mazie L.*," I said. "Did you go get it?" Dock said. "No, didn't have to. The tide brought it. Groceries will be coming in twice a day now and dropped off right at our doorstep."

"Well ain't that the beat'n'est." He tried to smile. After that he worried me with "I'm hungry!" every half-hour.

A couple of hours before high tide would reach our hearth at midnight, I was ready with the steel drum and anchor wires. Dock watched with silent puzzlement as I swept the burning wood and glowing coals into the drum, set it upright on the hearth, and ran wire to anchor it to some heavy pipes lying by the hearth. "Don't want the fire can to float away on the tide," I explained.

"We need some more firewood," I said a little later, and went off with the flashlight to get some. In just minutes, I heard, "Help, Andy, help!" coming from the sea-side edge of the floor now two feet under water. I ran. Then I was wading in tidal water on the platform, throwing the beam of light all about to find him.

I couldn't believe my eyes. Dock's head was barely sticking out above the same surf that was flowing past my knees. "I'm in a hole and can't get out," he looked up and said calmly.

"What in the devil were you doing over here?" I said.

"Looking for wood."

I pulled him out. He'd stepped through a rotten spot and dropped into the three-foot-high space made by the pilings under the floor.

"Listen, this part of the floor is rotten. You walk on it, you'll fall through. Stay away from here. Come back with me to the fire," I said.

Once more I went off to pick up firewood. In five minutes Dock hollered again. Back I went. He was in the same fix in a hole only a few steps from the first. He looked dazed, his burned face, ear, and scalp were raw, his clothes trailed kelp.

I led him to the fire, smoking badly in a wet can with no draft, but still burning. Sopping wet, he sat near it and I draped him with the sleeping bag. "This is crazy, this is crazy, this is crazy," and "I'm hungry!" and "We're gonna die here!" repeated 500 times were all Dock had to say the rest of the night.

In the darkness, the winds rose and roared then quieted, the rain poured then slackened. The cold grew harder to bear, even after the tide pulled back and I had the open fire roaring once more. "Just a little colder and we'll freeze instead of shiver," I said to myself. "What can I do to make a shelter so we can get dry and stay dry?"

Daylight finally. The day after Thanksgiving. The tide was a few yards from our platform. I searched the beach, under the floor by the pilings, and found a treasure. Could I be so lucky? Here was a tarpaulin of heavy plastic that had washed up from the sea! It looked like the one I had used in *Mazie L.*

With it, I could roof over the shoulder-high corner boards of the platform, and curtain off a triangular space. Inside that, we'd be out of the rain—and some of the cold. No struggle with high tides, either. They never reached that corner, the highest place on the slightly tilted floor!

While I made this wicki-up, the tide was inching

forward once again. Soon I'd have to transfer the fire to the steel drum again. Except, if the drum had a draft hole in one end, I'd have a stove! A stove would turn my wicki-up into a warm, happy home! I fairly ran—in new plastic poncho and boots—to find a substitute chisel and sledge hammer. They were the broken-pipe "can opener" and a massive pipe to beat it with.

"What's all the racket?" Dock asked irritably.

"I'm making a stove for the wicki-up."

"You can't make a stove out-of-doors in a place like this," Dock said. He watched and I banged. I banged until the steel drum had a hole in one side near the closed end, proving once more that you can do anything if you absolutely have to.

Beginning at a rotten edge touching the floor, I broke out a hole in the corner wall big enough to push through the closed end of the steel drum with its new smoke hole. A piece of scrap tin and some rocks stacked against it made a door for the open end. I built a fire in the drum and in a few minutes the wicki-up was nice and warm. The smoke curling out of the hole outside looked very homey.

"That's real nice, Andy." Dock had walked over to look, and to get out of the water on the low side of our flooding island.

"You gonna let me come in?"

We stayed in the wicki-up from that Friday noon, and got dry and warm all the way through. I used the rest of the plastic tarp to make Dock a rain poncho and head covers for both of us.

It wasn't a bad life. Food washed up every day, water fell from the sky, woods and brush provided plenty of firewood, the weather was bound to get better. The big problems were, first, Dock's burns, then not knowing how long our stay would last, and then wondering if Dock would drive me crazy.

He was getting more irritable and gloomy every day. Still, he didn't complain about the pain of his burns. He just repeated over and over "We're gonna die here. We're gonna die here." Or, "We'll never get out of here, we'll never get out of here." All day long, a spree of it every hour.

Finally I couldn't stand to hear it another time.

"SHUT UP YOU FOOL!" I shouted.

He looked up at me, surprised, silent.

"Listen, you," I went on, deciding a hard line might be having a good effect. "What have you got to gripe about? You're warm and dry, you've got a sleeping bag, you're eating regular, and the heavens are giving us plenty of pure drinking water. Stop complaining!"

"Yeah, uhhh, but we never know what we're gonna eat. It's a helluva thing not to have a label on the can."

"You ain't gonna eat the label!" I shouted. "It's a crazy miracle we get the cans and they're full of good stuff. Now shut up!"

He slunk back into his sleeping bag. We quietly went back to watching but not suffering from tide-in, tide-out, heaving wood island, wind, rain. I gathered firewood, picked up the groceries, and listened to the williwaws hit other parts of the bay. I didn't even mind having nothing to wear but my long drawers, blanket, and plastic poncho with matching boots.

Monday. In the distance, tatta-tatta-tatta-tatta! "Helicopter, Dock!" Very excited, Dock scrambled out of the wicki-up and ran with me to the beach. We grabbed pieces of wood, trying to lay them into a giant SOS. Before we got the first S made, the chopper clattered past, tatta-tatta-tatta.

Dock was yelling at it to come back, come back, you so-and-so's. "We're gonna die! You're leaving us to die!"

Tuesday. The winds have calmed, the skies have faired, the sun's popping through the clouds now and again. Maybe I should try to get us out of here in the whaler, I thought. Dock's burns are looking like wet raw hamburger. Weather like this, though, can I trust it? Are the williwaws really finished? Besides, if I get out on the water and Dock does something foolish. . .

"Let's take the whaler out to the *Mazie L.*," I said to Dock to see how he'd act. "She's not gone under. Her deck looks to be a few inches above water. Probably her styrofoam insulation is acting like a lifebelt. Maybe we can salvage the motor and some clothes."

"Let's go," Dock said and crawled out of the wicki-up.

"Funny lad," I thought. "He complains about can labels but not a word about pain."

We cut out the nice engine of *Mazie L.* I grieved to myself at seeing her wrecked and ruined. My pride and joy, my biggest investment, my house and home—gone.

I found my dufflebag, full of sopping wet clothes, but offering the prospect of trousers, shirt, and jacket. I thought I was lucky the sea took my old boots and left me the never-worn new ones—until I put them on and found they were both right footers. I wore them anyhow. Sore toes are better than naked feet.

That afternoon while I was drying my clothes in the wicki-up, Dock disappeared. I called off and on—"DOCK!"—for an hour. No answer. Then I saw him walking out of the brush carrying a long stick. He looked expressionless, his eyes glazed. His burns were drippy red flesh. "Where've you been?" I asked.

His answer was a slurred jabber. Finally it sounded as if he said he'd been trying to catch a rabbit.

By early afternoon the next day, Dock was incoherent.

The tide was going out and I decided we had to go with it, come what may. I tugged and pulled the whaler, dragging it toward the water's edge, when—

Could it be?—a boat engine! I ran to the shoreline. Around the bend came a boat, one I recognized as an Old Harbor fishing boat, one I had lived on with the Christianson brothers during a trapping trip.

I jumped in the whaler and rowed out to meet them. "Andy! It's you! What happened? That's the *Mazie* sunk over there?"

"Yeah. But quick, let's call Kodiak on your radio and ask for a plane. Got a man here who needs to get to a hospital fast. Bad burns."

Within an hour, a Kodiak Airways plane landed in the bay. In minutes, the pilot had taxied it up to the beach, and I was walking with Dock to the door. He looked gruesome, unsteady, but he was able to climb in by himself.

"You going too, aren't you?" the pilot asked. "No. You just get him to the hospital," I answered.

When I saw the door slam shut and the plane begin to roll, I got so lighthearted I felt giddy. No more Dock worries, trials, and irritations.

As for me, I'd already talked to the Christianson brothers and made some plans.

"You want to get on the plane?" they'd said.

"No, I just want to see Dock get on that plane."

"You want to go to Old Harbor? We'll take you."

"Well now, what were you fellows planning to do today?" I answered.

"Go hunting for ducks and deer. You o.k.? Come along with us!"

"I'm dry, my belly is full, and I've even got new boots for both my right feet—why shouldn't I go with you?"

They laughed and laughed while I pulled a towel from my dufflebag to tie tight around my sore, cracked ribs. Then I was ready to go hunting, because, hell, there wasn't anything wrong with me.

Andy in the wolverine coat made by Violet Mack of Kenai.

Andy Nault, formerly of Montana, lives in Kodiak on Kodiak Island. "If you're ever here and want to find me," he says, "just stop anybody on the street and ask him where I am. Chances are he'll know, or he'll know somebody who knows. In a town of 5,000 or so people, a man can hardly help from being known—especially a man as full of stories as I am."